THAT BLOODY WOMAN

The Turbulent Life of
Emily Hobhouse

John Hall

ISBN **978 185022 217 0**

Published by Truran, Croft Prince, Mount Hawke,
Truro, Cornwall TR4 8EE
www.truranbooks.co.uk

Truran is an imprint of Truran Books Ltd

Cover image: Emily aged 34 (Jennifer Hobhouse Balme)

Printed and bound in Cornwall by R. Booth Ltd,
The Praze, Penryn, TR10 9AA

CONTENTS

Prologue — 1

1 Monday's Child — 5

2 "A Foolish Virgin" — 17

3 God and the Mauser — 26

4 "The Last Time of Feeling Young" — 35

5 K of K — 41

6 "A Storm of Abuse" — 50

7 "The Walls of Jericho Would Fall" — 56

8 "Woman-hater" — 64

9 "Crass Male Ignorance" — 71

10 "The Whole Talk was of Death" — 80

11 "Methods of Barbarism" — 90

12 "Traitor to her Country" — 101

13 "Unyielding as a Rock" — 109

14 "A Little Bluff Now Would Finish the War" — 118

15 "An Hysterical Spinster of Mature Age" — 123

16 "They Will Carry You Away Like a Lunatic" — 131

17 "Carrion Crows Will Tear and Rend Me" — 140

18 "We Are Good Friends Now" — 148

19 "They Will Never Forget Her" — 156

20 "Can These Dry Bones Live?" — 162

21 High-souled, High-thinking Friends   175

22 Miss Hobhouse's Unpardonable Indiscretion   181

23 "A Blank Nothing Could Fill"   188

24 "A Little Worm of Doubt"   196

25 "Holding on Till Death"   201

26 "Bury Unforgiveness and Bitterness"   209

27 "The Germans, Poor Dears"   220

28 "Just the Man to Boss the Politicians"   231

29 A Private Invasion of Germany   244

30 "I Never Tell a Lie"   254

31 "Sweet But a Little Mad"   261

32 "That Den of Thieves"   268

33 "Undaunted by All Opposition"   272

34 "Too Brave"   282

35 "She Gave to Us All She Had"   293

Epilogue   297

Key Figures in the Story   301

Notes   309

Original Sources   313

Further Reading   313

Bibliography   315

Acknowledgements   320

Index   322

Emily Hobhouse at the end of the Boer War.

SIMPLIFIED PEDIGREE OF HOBHOUSE OF HADSPEN

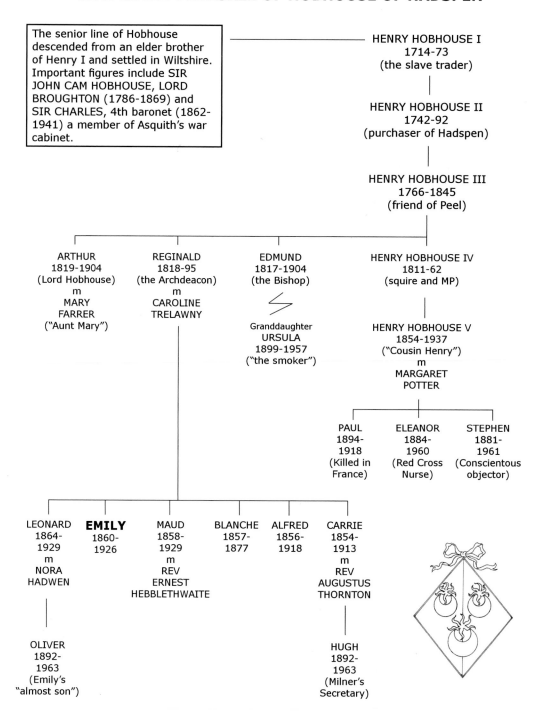

The senior line of Hobhouse descended from an elder brother of Henry I and settled in Wiltshire. Important figures include SIR JOHN CAM HOBHOUSE, LORD BROUGHTON (1786-1869) and SIR CHARLES, 4th baronet (1862-1941) a member of Asquith's war cabinet.

HENRY HOBHOUSE I
1714-73
(the slave trader)

HENRY HOBHOUSE II
1742-92
(purchaser of Hadspen)

HENRY HOBHOUSE III
1766-1845
(friend of Peel)

ARTHUR
1819-1904
(Lord Hobhouse)
m
MARY
FARRER
("Aunt Mary")

REGINALD
1818-95
(the Archdeacon)
m
CAROLINE
TRELAWNY

EDMUND
1817-1904
(the Bishop)

Granddaughter
URSULA
1899-1957
("the smoker")

HENRY HOBHOUSE IV
1811-62
(squire and MP)

HENRY HOBHOUSE V
1854-1937
("Cousin Henry")
m
MARGARET
POTTER

PAUL
1894-
1918
(Killed in
France)

ELEANOR
1884-
1960
(Red Cross
Nurse)

STEPHEN
1881-
1961
(Conscientous
objector)

LEONARD
1864-
1929
m
NORA
HADWEN

EMILY
1860-
1926

MAUD
1858-
1929
m
REV
ERNEST
HEBBLETHWAITE

BLANCHE
1857-
1877

ALFRED
1856-
1918

CARRIE
1854-
1913
m
REV
AUGUSTUS
THORNTON

OLIVER
1892-
1963
(Emily's
"almost son")

HUGH
1892-
1963
(Milner's
Secretary)

PROLOGUE

This is the story of a mislaid heroine. Today almost entirely forgotten, Emily Hobhouse was in her time one of the most controversial figures in the world. In the year Queen Victoria died, the mention of her name would bring an audience to its feet cheering or booing, and an appearance in the flesh guaranteed bouquets and missiles. No Englishwoman was more loved and more loathed – Kipling dubbed her "The Unspeakable", while Mahatma Gandhi was a great admirer, hailing her as "one of the noblest of women".

She was a whirlwind of contradictions – a bluestocking without formal education, a peace campaigner with a weakness for generals, a humanitarian with a cutting and combative manner, an evangelist who shrank from talk of God. As a feminist, she combined a sweeping contempt for the male sex with a craving for wedded bliss and babies. There is a weird justice in the fact that she is the only pacifist to have had a submarine named after her.

Emily Hobhouse spent the first half of her existence becalmed in a Cornish country rectory, the duty-bound daughter of a cantankerous invalid. His death in 1895 freed her, at the age of thirty-four, to transform a life of furious discontent into a romance. From that day on she devoted herself to a string of unpopular causes leading from one high adventure to another. Single-handedly, she set about the reform of a lawless frontier town in the American west. During the Boer War she was forcibly deported from South Africa after exposing the concentration camps run by the British Army; she returned to aid the destitute and starving, to found a network of industries for workless women, and to protest at the plight of the black majority. Appalled by the slaughter of the First World War, she risked arrest as a spy on an impetuous one-woman mission to stop the fighting, and was denounced as a traitor in the House of Commons. The law of England had to be changed solely on her account. After the Armistice she organised the mass feeding of children throughout war-shattered Europe; there, as in South Africa, she saved thousands of lives.

Her achievements came at great personal cost. Over the years she fell out with practically every friend and relation. Most of her fortune disappeared in the course of a disastrous romance with an American adventurer. In bringing succour to others, she wrecked her own health. Reviled, ridiculed and ostracised, she ended her days in poverty, a lonely and desperately unhappy woman. Yet after a hole-and-corner cremation at Golders Green, the final twist in her story was the redemptive triumph of a state funeral on the other side of the world, with thousands gathered to "bury her like a princess". One of the finest funeral orations in history was spoken over her ashes.

So here then is a genuine heroine, and all the more fascinating for her feet of clay; for the flaws in her character ran deep. As admirers ruefully observed, it was easier to love Emily Hobhouse from a distance. Praised as a second Florence Nightingale, an "angel of love", she was also branded overbearing, calculating and manipulative. She never flinched from exploiting her femininity or her high connections. She could be embarrassingly gushing to those of whom she approved, and grandly condescending or dismissive to others – especially to social inferiors. A hundred years on, her put-downs of hapless clerks and junior officers can still curl the toes. Predictably, this was a woman who experienced lifelong "difficulties with servants".

That enemies should call her a hysteric, implying sexual frustration, was perhaps inevitable, but close friends too could be highly unflattering. Many believed her debilitating illnesses to be a sham. The Quaker philanthropist Ruth Fry, her first biographer, wrote sternly of her lack of humour, caustic tongue, self-dramatisation, and proneness to hasty judgment. She was "one of those masterful women who quietly crushes everyone who comes near her," according to the novelist Olive Schreiner. Her long-suffering confidant Jan Christian Smuts, statesman, philosopher and field-marshal, conceded that she was maddening, perhaps even mad, while even a devotee like the historian Sir Keith Hancock called her "that wild woman". Tellingly, she managed to make enemies of the leaders of both wings of the women's suffrage movement, the militant Mrs Pankhurst and the constitutionalist Mrs Fawcett. At least four prime ministers came to dread a scolding from Miss Hobhouse. There is no denying she could be an extremely difficult woman.

At times then it is tempting to settle for a caricature of Emily Hobhouse – part Joan of Arc, part Florence Nightingale, part Vanessa Redgrave. Like St Joan, she heard voices telling her to save an oppressed people from brutal invaders. Like the Lady with the Lamp, she battled against an incompetent wartime officialdom that was killing more people than the war itself. And only an actress of outstanding power could do justice to the scenes of Emily's career, for hers was a life defined in images of great drama and pathos.

As in the harrowing spectacle when she forces a lax official to watch the dying moments of a child. As in the riot when she stands alone between a future prime minister of Britain and a gang baying for his blood. As in the episode during her tempestuous campaigning tour of England when, faced with another howling mob, she remains on the platform in complete silence for exactly the time it would take to deliver her speech. Or in her verbal duel with Britain's chief spy-catcher, who knows she is secretly in contact with the enemy; or the excruciating moment when she is reduced to uncontrollable weeping by the gruff kindness of a soldier, but only after retiring from sight with ladylike composure. There is unexpected comedy too, as during her first mission of mercy to a concentration camp in her ostrich-feathered hat, when she attacks an adder with her parasol.

There was more than a touch of Lady Bracknell in Emily's make-up. Rarely could she bear anyone else to have the last word. Time and again she would charm or browbeat cabinet ministers, generals, archbishops, pro-consuls – for, at least in her younger days, men tended to be putty in her hands. As she aged, a growing isolation and sense of failure made her pronouncements more dogmatic, her acts more bizarre. Who else could have dreamt of stopping a world war single-handed? Certainly she was capable of moments of staggering naivety and caprice.

Yet whenever the picture of Emily Hobhouse threatens to tip into parody, a more complex figure comes suddenly into focus. Her failings cannot obscure her towering moral courage. Her *prima donna* outbursts are outnumbered by the agonies borne in silence. The snubs and insults offered from every side count as nothing compared to the tortures inflicted by her relentless self-examination. Intense, defiant, vulnerable, accident-prone, Emily was often her own worst enemy, and she knew it.

So why is this extraordinary woman almost unknown, even in her native Cornwall? Why did so many eminent contemporaries strike her name from their memoirs? How she fell from grace, a casualty of the prejudices of both Left and Right, is a curious tale in itself. How the heroine of the Boers became a victim of apartheid is just one of the many paradoxes that littered her life.

And told here for the first time is perhaps the strangest aspect of Emily Hobhouse's story – the links with her great adversary, Lord Kitchener. To all appearances Kitchener and Emily were polar opposites, and as such they polarised public opinion. He was the Empire's most idolised soldier, the favourite of Queen Victoria, though widely reputed to be a woman-hater. The lofty figure of Kitchener, first as commander-in-chief in South Africa and then as secretary for war in 1914, is inseparable from that of Emily, with the two incompatibles bonded by intriguing affinities and symmetries.

Emily's campaign against the concentration camps brought the pair into conflict for the first time, and a tremendous battle of wills ensued. He called her "that bloody woman", while she denounced him as a brute and a disgrace to his country. It was on Kitchener's personal orders that she was carried onto the first troopship out of Cape Town trussed like a lunatic – according to the officer in charge, Emily looked like a Madonna but fought like a devil – and her response was to try to have Kitchener gaoled on his return to England. After South Africa, their destinies crossed again during the First World War, which he intended to win at all costs and which she intended to halt. Yet they would have been horrified to learn how much they had in common.

Had she championed any people but the Boers, Emily Hobhouse would be listed among the most famous Englishwomen of the past century. Had she not persisted in her quixotic efforts to make peace with Germany, she might have been showered with honours in her own lifetime. As it is, her name is far better known abroad than in her own country, where she is scarcely remembered beyond a paragraph or two, usually riddled with factual errors, in the histories of a distant colonial war.

This amazing woman deserves much more.

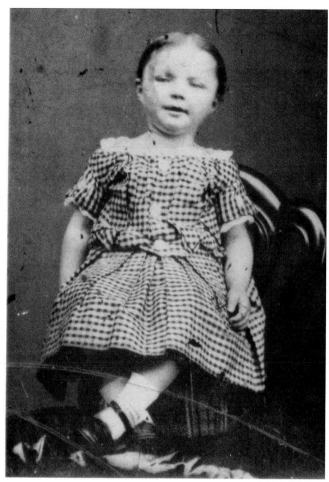

The earliest photograph of "the Missis".
At the age of two Emily felt "part of everything round me".

1 MONDAY'S CHILD

Emily Hobhouse was born in 1860 at the Rectory of St Ive, pronounced Eve by the locals, a small and unremarkable village near Liskeard in East Cornwall. The birthplace is often mistakenly given as the artists' colony St Ives in the far west of the county, an error compounded by Emily's unhappy choice of St Ives as a refuge for her twilight years. St Ive is not far from the river Tamar which separates Cornwall from the rest of England; it is a separation is more ways than one, and Emily's fierce identification with the Cornish helps to explain the sense of "otherness" she felt all her life.

She was somebody from the day of her birth, and she never forgot it. The Hobhouses were affluent, respected, and well-connected – her father Reginald was Rector of St Ive and neighbouring Pensilva, and her mother Caroline, a daughter of Sir William Salusbury Trelawny, eighth baronet, head of one of Cornwall's oldest families. The baronetcy was conferred by Charles I, but the Trelawnys claimed a prominent role in Cornish affairs predating the Norman Conquest; certainly they had produced knights, sheriffs and members of parliament from early medieval times. Among her ancestors Emily's favourite was that independent-minded Bishop Trelawny imprisoned in the Tower of London by James II, of whom Cornishmen still sing "And shall Trelawny die?" It is a song with anthem status in Cornwall. At the stormiest moments of her career Emily would console herself by linking the bishop's sufferings with her own.

Her birth date of April 9 fell that year on Easter Monday, and Emily fulfilled the nursery rhyme that makes Monday's child fair of face. An Emily Trelawny occurs in the family tree as an aunt of her mother, suggesting a likely reason for the choice; the name itself derives from ancient Rome and is said to carry the meaning *to strive* or *to excel*. She was christened in her father's church on May Day.

Reginald Hobhouse owed the crown living of St Ive with Pensilva to his father's influence with the prime minister of the day, Sir Robert Peel. The fact is not without its irony as Peel is nowadays regarded as a reformer who curbed the historical abuses of preferment to church appointments, but happily for Reginald a modest form of prime ministerial patronage survived for services rendered personally to Peel. In the family tradition, Emily herself would never fail to exploit her connections in a good cause.

Certainly she retained a sense of self-consequence throughout her life. Time and again, in letters and reported speech, the authority derived from high social status would ring out unmistakably in her tone. She never forgot that Uncle Arthur was a peer and privy councillor; or that other close relations included two members of parliament, a bishop, and baronets on both sides of the family; close kinsmen included John Cam Hobhouse, Lord Broughton, the intimate of Byron. The origins of the Hobhouses might not have been ancient, but marriages contracted by the fast-rising family during the Georgian era linked the clan with the higher reaches of Britain's landed classes and aristocracy; as a kind of seal of gentility, a Hobhouse had fought and died at Waterloo.

But there was a skeleton in the Hobhouse cupboard, a painful matter for the ultra-respectable and high-minded generation of Emily's time. The family fortune was founded on the slave trade.

*

Emily's great-great-grandfather, Henry Hobhouse, came of humble Devon farming stock, and set himself up as a merchant in Bristol when that city was one of the great world centres of commerce. As England's second port it grew wealthy on the transportation of shackled slaves and slave-produced commodities, overtaking London itself in importance by the 1730s. As Bristol grew rich, so did Henry Hobhouse. He amassed wealth enough to establish his son, also Henry, among the ranks of the gentry by the acquisition of a fine family seat, Hadspen House, set within two and a half thousand acres near Castle Cary in Somerset. His son Henry III, the follower of Peel, was a lawyer who rose to the rank of privy councillor, and enjoyed the means to send four sons to Eton and Oxford. The motto adopted by the family – *meliora spero*, or *I hope for better things* – was an apt one, and not only in the pious sense.

Of course the Hobhouses were not the only prominent family of their day to benefit from the fruits of slavery. William Ewart Gladstone himself owed his comfortable circumstances in life, likewise begun at Eton and Oxford, to the West Indian slave plantations acquired by his father, a fierce opponent of abolition. In the same fashion as the Liberal leader, the Hobhouses embarked on a moral migration that severed them from the sentiments, if not the material gains, of their ancestor, and it is not difficult to believe that the almost morbid sensibility of many of Emily's close relations was rooted in an abiding sense of profiting from sin. The story of her eccentric cousin Stephen Hobhouse, who went to extreme lengths to distance himself from ancestral wickedness, will be told in a later chapter.

Reginald Hobhouse was a silent, forbidding man. As a younger son destined for the church, he left Balliol College with an undistinguished record, arriving at St Ive in 1844. There he stayed for the rest of his life. Blessed with private means – as well as his stipend of £362 a year he received a portion of over £10,000 from his father's will – Reginald was able to marry seven years later and built a new home for his bride next to the 14th Century church. Though the material was the intractable local granite, he insisted on touches of the gothic style then virtually mandatory for a clerical residence.[i] The new rectory was not the only call on Reginald's pocket as he also carried out a major restoration of the chancel at his own expense.

Emily was the fifth of six surviving children and the youngest daughter. The first daughter, named Caroline after her mother but always known as Carrie, was born in 1854; the first son, Alfred, in 1856. Two more girls arrived before Emily – Blanche in 1857, Maud in 1858 – and Emily was followed by another boy, Leonard, in 1864. Yet despite this quiverful the parents' marriage was overshadowed by the loss of two earlier children in infancy, and Emily came to believe that the shock of these deaths so afflicted her father that he could never summon proper affection for the living children.

But if the father was gloomy and remote, the mother was by general consent a delightful and witty woman who, despite a tendency to extravagance, made an excellent wife and mother. Caroline Hobhouse's child-bearing continued to an unusually late age for the times. She was thirty-nine when Emily was born and nearly forty-four when she had Leonard. Emily told her Quaker friend Ruth Fry that while her mother could not be called handsome she had fine eyes and "the rich golden brown Trelawny hair", adding feelingly that her sense of humour was "the salvation of our home". The children always identified with the more glamorous Trelawny side of the family, Leonard and Emily especially taking pride in a mercurial Cornish temperament. A school friend of Leonard's would remember him as "very frank and open with a quick placable Cornish temper; he was emotional and un-British".

Emily's mother Caroline was no beauty but inherited the much-admired Trelawny hair.

In later years Emily could recall her first flash of self-awareness at the age of three or four, when she was staring up at the big nursery clock as it struck the hour: "Before, I had seemed part of everything round me, and now I found out that I stood alone, outside and different from my environment. It was a curious revelation; it had been very nice being part of everything, with no separate sense of individuality. Yet I felt suddenly very proud and puffed up with a quite new sense of dignity."

Emily's childhood nickname was "The Missis". The name originated in an obscure family joke over a Valentine card, and the fact it stuck to her all her days testifies to her lifelong bossiness. Leonard, destined to be a distinguished academic, was the sibling who remained closest to her throughout life. The departure of this golden-haired paragon to school at the age of eight or nine was a dreadful blow to Emily, and Leonard's subsequent returns on holiday "lit up the home and evoked an emotional response" not only from mother and sisters but from the taciturn father.

The other great favourite of young Emily was her father's curate, Kenneth St Aubyn Rogers, a poor, solitary old bachelor who became her devoted slave. Rogers, who would be regarded with deep suspicion by many parents of today, established a kind of secret fellowship with the children. He loved playing hide-and-seek, battledore and shuttlecock, and would relieve the awful tedium of dinner at the Rectory by expertly flicking bread pellets, undetected by the other grown-ups. Emily joked that "Old Rodge"

Emily, left, with elder sister Maud,
"so coaxing and so arch".
Probably taken in 1864.

was her first love, despite his glassy blue eyes and huge red nose; alas, the Rector failed to appreciate Mr Rogers's merits and he departed to become a missionary in Africa, "leaving one little broken heart behind him".[ii]

In contrast to the hypochondria that would plague her later years, the six-year-old Emily bore illness with notable stoicism. An aunt who saw the Rectory children struck down with some childish malady wrote: "Emily has been much the least poorly, and has taken her illness, as she does other events of life, with more calmness and resolution than the others. She is a remarkable child, and seems to me to have quite a manly character in her girlish frame."

The children would remember their father as a devoted clergyman and dutiful family man, though in their forthright Hobhouse way also labelled him as inflexible and inhibited, "remorseless in exacting duty and the repair of neglect". Leonard was to say that he seemed to them all "an incarnation of justice and iron rectitude", oblivious to the psychological effects of his regime on his offspring. And in a family of markedly liberal leanings, Reginald was a deep-dyed conservative.

He seems always to have been a troubled man. Though taking enormous pains over each sermon, he felt a compulsion to suppress any emotional content for fear that his pent-up feelings would unman him. In latter years it was not unknown for Reginald to sob in the pulpit, and Emily would retain all her life the aching memory of one particular sermon on All Saints' Day during which her father struggled repeatedly and in vain to prevent his voice from breaking. Certainly he never achieved a true rapport with his congregation of Cornish farmers and miners; it is telling that, shortly after his death, the average number of communicants at St Ive Church was recorded as seven and at Pensilva as nine, out of a parish population of around nine hundred.

Reginald's ministry saw years of turmoil and controversy in the Church of England. The future Cardinal Newman preached his last sermon as an Anglican at Oxford during Reginald's final term there, and Darwin's *On the Origin of Species*, regarded by many contemporaries as a direct assault on Christian belief itself, had been published just six months before Emily was born. Yet the Rector seems to have flinched from the great theological debates of the day, confining himself narrowly to parochial affairs.

The one great enthusiasm of Reginald's early years at St Ive was a gathering campaign to re-establish the see of Cornwall. Since the Norman Conquest the spiritual needs of the Cornish had been in the hands of the bishops of Exeter, who invariably found more pressing concerns than the poor, far-off people beyond the Tamar. Neglect by the established church notoriously left the Cornish with a superstitious attachment to piskies and buccaboos, along with a susceptibility to the stark glory-or-hellfire message of John Wesley. Reginald's ministry coincided with the zenith of Methodist expansion in Cornwall, with chapel people outnumbering Anglican churchgoers almost three to one; that superstition was still alive and well was amply demonstrated during Emily's childhood when, following the last public hanging at Bodmin, women in the crowd pressed forward to be touched by the dead man's hand as a cure of ailments of the neck.

Reginald Hobhouse was among the more prominent figures working to secure a revival of the ancient diocese, not least as a means of mobilising resistance to Methodism. In the year of Emily's birth he published a curious sixpenny pamphlet dedicated to the local grandee, the Earl of St Germans, which sought to draw a parallel between the sorry state of affairs in Cornwall and the fact there were no bishops in the American colonies on the eve of revolution. The long campaign was rewarded in 1876 when Edward White Benson, one of the outstanding clergymen of the day, was named first Bishop of Truro. Yet even the official history of the bishopric struggles to find very much positive to say about Emily's father beyond noting him as one of the "earnest labourers in the vineyard" and praising his "steadfast immoveableness".

And indeed, all his life Reginald must have felt overshadowed by others, not least by his brothers. The eldest was the destined squire and head of the family, while the other two brothers took first class degrees at Oxford, as compared to Reginald's fourth; and in this fiercely competitive family, a third was considered a disgrace. Edmund, one year older than Reginald, became a bishop; Arthur, younger by a year, was raised to the peerage after a distinguished career as judge and legislator.

The part Reginald played in the revival of the Truro diocese was acknowledged by elevation to the rank of archdeacon, but by the time of this modest high point of his ministry, tragedy was again stalking his family. In 1877 Emily's sister Blanche died of consumption at the age of nineteen; in 1879, when Emily reached the same age, her beloved Mamma died of a brain tumour. Life at St Ive would never be the same.

Shattered by the loss of his wife, the Archdeacon himself became dangerously ill and, though nursed through the crisis by his daughters, had clearly lost what little gaiety of spirit he ever possessed. In the meantime Emily's siblings were flying the nest. Carrie, the eldest daughter, escaped the claustrophobic atmosphere of the Rectory by marrying a well-heeled evangelical parson called Augustus Thornton, and moved to his handsome rectory in the nearby parish of St Mellion.[iii] Worse was to follow. The elder son Alfred, previously accounted an indecisive youth, suddenly rebelled against Reginald's ambition for him to follow into holy orders and left St Ive to make a life for himself in the colonies. Crushing disappointments were piling on the Archdeacon's head.

Photographs of Reginald Hobhouse in old age, with his striking deep-seamed face and snowy side-whiskers, seem to conjure an affluent gentleman-parson from the Barchester chronicles. On closer acquaintance the reader of Trollope's novels is likely to be reminded not of that *ne plus ultra* of archdeacons, the worldly Dr Grantly, but of the Reverend Josiah Crawley, that unhappy mixture of "pride, humility, manliness, weakness, conscientious rectitude, and bitter prejudices". Every defeat in life is etched on Archdeacon Hobhouse's brow, and it is easy to understand why Leonard would remember any reproving remark from his father as "falling with the weight of tons".

*

With Leonard away at Oxford, only two girls remained at home. Since the death of their mother, the role of Lady of the Rectory was shared by Emily and her sister Maud, and it was now she began to visit the poor and sick of the parish. Maud – "so coaxing and so arch," according to their aunt Lady Hobhouse – seems to have been rather less devoted to good works than the youngest sister, and confined herself to visits close to home. Emily meanwhile strode out alone across the windswept landscape to distant farmhouses and miners' cottages, the basket on her arm brimming with titbits, cast-off clothing and improving texts.

Here among these scattered inbred communities she first experienced the kind of hardships – overcrowding, lack of sanitation, disease – she was to see writ large in South Africa many years later; here, as in South Africa, she grew accustomed to the tearful gratitude of the sick and dying. With the nearest doctor miles away, Emily would treat ailments with the help of a book of herbal cures inherited from her Trelawny grandmother, and earned herself a name as a white witch. Roaming the parish, she remembered, gave her a taste "to embrace wide tracts of country and large masses of people", while dreaming of their universal conversion to goodness – a state the teenaged Emily fondly imagined as the exclusive preserve of the Church of England.

Emily's Cornwall was not the picturesque unspoilt land sought by Victorian tourists. The parson-diarist Francis Kilvert visited the county in 1870 when Emily was

A high achiever at Oxford, Leonard Hobhouse dismayed his father by mixing with radicals and freethinkers.

ten years old, and contrasted the anticipated beauties with the grim reality of the mining districts where he found "the bowels of the earth ripped open, turned inside out in the search for metal ore, the land defiled and cumbered with heaps and wastes of slag and rubbish, and the waters poisoned with tin and copper washings". Outside the favoured sightseeing spots, Kilvert reported Cornish villages as characteristically bleak, barren and ugly, unsheltered by a single tree, and surrounded by monotonous wastes.

Emily bitterly resented her lack of formal education. The prevailing middle-class view of the day was typified by a hugely popular tract called *Daughters of England*, published during Reginald Hobhouse's time at Oxford, which ordained that the first requisite for a young woman was to be inferior to a man, "inferior in mental power in the same proportion that you are inferior in

St Ive Rectory. The "pleasant little abode" remembered by her siblings was a scene of secret torture for Emily.

bodily strength". So what the Hobhouse girls received from their mother and a string of governesses were the ornamental accomplishments of a Victorian lady – tuition in piano, violin and singing, and some acquaintance with the sketchbook and watercolour box. The governesses proved an indifferent lot, unequipped to draw out one of Emily's intellectual potential. "They never told me the thing I wanted to know," she was to say. "If you asked, you were told 'Little girls should not ask questions'."

One of her sister Maud's school exercise books, a chance survival from the early months of 1873, provides an insight into the home life of Emily as a girl of twelve. An English composition entitled "Our Rectory" gives a detailed description of a house that is neither large nor pretty, but accommodates the family conveniently. Besides the schoolroom there are three sitting rooms, Maud's favourite being the bow-windowed drawing room with its little sofa, piano, writing table, and piles of books: "In summer white curtains lined with green gauze are put up, which gives the room a pleasant and cool air. In winter the warm crimson ones appear again, and very comfortable the room is when the curtains are drawn and a bright fire glows in the grate."

The girls' schoolroom, painted green with a quaint beamed ceiling, commands a view over meadows and the busy stable-yard. The household's second piano is stationed here next to shelves filled with their lesson-books and many other interesting volumes. Along the passage on the next floor is the governess's room, which boasts the best view from its window. On the same landing are the servants' rooms and on the first floor is the White Room, "so-called because it used to have a great deal of white dimity" – cotton fabric with raised stripes or fancy figures. Maud and Emily sleep here, and "next come the bedroom and dressing room for our visitors, Mamma's room and Papa's dressing-room". There is a pleasant shady garden around the house: "It is a very good size, plenty of flowers and vegetables in their season; there are four fields and we have two cows, two pigs, and hosts of pets. In this pleasant little abode, which I have tried to describe, I have spent fourteen happy years!!"

Another of Maud's compositions, an account of the excesses of the Roman Empire taken from Gibbon, dwells on scenes of slaughter and rapine – "defective spelling and indifferent writing," reproves the governess in the margin – while other pieces draw on direct observation from family holidays abroad. In the French countryside, for instance, "many a poor woman may be seen leading her cow to feed on the grass by the roadside", while in Switzerland "the men live in little wooden chalets and make cheeses". These regular trips abroad, a great childhood pleasure for Emily and the source of her later wanderlust, were dictated by the Archdeacon's recurring bouts of ill health.

The longest and most significant essay in the schoolbook tells the story of Joan of Arc, which Maud considers "one of the most extraordinary things that history ever related". The young heroine, much moved by the suffering of the people, pits herself against an invading English army, and inspires the people to believe she has been sent by God to help them. Joan could not get their miseries out of her thoughts, "and they so worked on her mind and her imagination that at last she really believed herself called by God to be the saviour of her people" – an appropriately careful wording for an Anglican clergyman's daughter to apply to a future Catholic saint.

Even so, Maud is clearly entranced by the tragedy of a brave and pious woman who, after triumphantly crowning the Dauphin Charles, is brought down by the cruelty and stupidity of men. "Poor Joan! She was thrown into prison, only being taken out to be burnt alive, while in all her trouble that ungrateful man Charles never lifted a hand to help her," Maud lugubriously concludes. "Thus ended the life of this poor enthusiast, the Maid of Orleans." At the foot of the page the governess comments: "Written very hastily and untidily, otherwise the composition shows care to have been taken."

The lesson must have worked powerfully on Emily at twelve, the age at which Joan of Arc first heard her voices; and indeed, the saint's story will echo down Emily's years. In old age she would remember how her young mind had turned in upon itself, giving unhealthy stimulation to a natural bent towards mysticism and romance. "I lived," she wrote, "with heroes in this imaginary world and fell ardently in love with these fabulous beings." Towards the end of her life she would come across a sketch done from the window of the White Room and find herself moved to tears by a re-awakening of girlhood aspirations: "Yet as I look at it, knowing the dreams are gone forever, I am sensible of the same aspirations, the same stirring desires and lofty aims."

By 1875, when she reached fifteen, Emily's feeling of isolation deepened with a sense of dawning womanhood which she "could not in the least understand". Packed off to a finishing school in London, she found the standard of teaching so poor that her stay lasted a mere two terms; besides, at the time there was little money for low priorities such as Emily's schooling, what with the expensive travels for the sake of the Archdeacon's health and Mrs Hobhouse's inability to resist persuasive shopkeepers. Craving the kind of education that clever brother Leonard was receiving as of right at Marlborough and Oxford, Emily found herself palmed off with religious books, sermons and "goody-goody stories".

Most galling of all, out in the wider world women were claiming their place. In the year of Emily's birth Elizabeth Garrett began the medical training which after epic struggles would lead to her qualifying as England's first woman doctor. The first women's college at Cambridge, Girton, opened in 1869, and by 1876 an act of parliament had banned universities from refusing a qualification on the ground of sex. Even in Cornwall the voices for women's suffrage were heard. The pioneer suffragist Jeanette Wilkinson addressed meetings in the county as early as 1871, the Liskeard Liberal Association being the first political organisation to invite her to speak. A missionary active in

Cornwall during Emily's teens was the eccentric Jessie Craigen, actress-turned-temperance worker, who travelled around with her dog Tiny, haranguing miners at packed outdoor meetings reminiscent of Wesley's Cornish tours the century before.

But these momentous events passed Emily by. For one of her background the only permitted opening was through church work, and even here the Archdeacon instantly put his foot down if he considered the nature of the proposed activity inappropriate for a daughter of his. What he considered appropriate – apart from looking after himself – was limited to leading the singing at church, playing the organ, and helping out at Sunday school.

Sister Maud, on the other hand, braved fatherly opposition to marry another of the St Ive curates, Ernest Hebblethwaite. Unlike Augustus Thornton, Maud's suitor was poor, and Reginald took great exception to the match, forbidding any communication between the lovers for a year. In the end Maud prevailed – at this period

Emily at fifteen, living with heroes in a world of imagination but troubled by "dawning womanhood".

one Englishwoman in three remained a spinster, and at thirty-one she must have seen the unexciting Ernest as her last chance. Shortly before the marriage Hebblethwaite secured the living of Poundstock, a tiny gale-swept parish near Bude on the Atlantic coast. As the Archdeacon would have been quick to point out, it was a church with a sinister history for its incumbents. In the 14th Century a priest had been murdered at the altar and another gaoled for life for complicity in a killing; in Tudor times a third was hanged for his part in the Cornish revolt against the Book of Common Prayer.

No sensational tragedy awaited the Hebblethwaites, but the marriage proved an unhappy one. Ernest's strength was sapped by the constant struggle to maintain a ruinous church in a poverty-stricken district possessing, as he was soon complaining, "no resident gentry". For years he poured out a stream of fund-raising letters containing the pathetic line, "a postal order for one shilling will greatly oblige". Maud would struggle to bring up three children at the remote vicarage, never free of money troubles, and often forced to borrow from her sister. But her departure from St Ive in 1889 left Emily to cope alone with an increasingly sick, morose and demanding parent.

*

Early portraits show Emily's features as handsome rather than beautiful. She was over medium height and slender of waist; her hair was fair and fine with a natural wave; her eyes were a noticeably pale grey-blue. Photographs in profile show the nose as rather beaky. It must be said that none of the Hobhouse girls was a great beauty, though Emily was certainly the pick of the bunch. The years alone with her father were to give her face a settled look of melancholy remarked on throughout later life, though there was general agreement that her sudden smile was vivid and disarming. There is also ample evidence that she retained the power to charm long after the flush of youth had faded.

So what of her own romantic aspirations during these St Ive years? According to Ruth Fry, suitors of the girls "seem to have broken the monotony of life fairly frequently", but those with an eye on the youngest must soon have retired discouraged; in any case, few unattached males of suitable status could have visited so remote a corner. And though comfortably off, Archdeacon Hobhouse did not command the means to launch his daughters into London society, a matter of course for the girls of the opulent Hadspen branch. As to Emily, he appears never to have looked beyond his own need for a carer.

Unconfirmed by family records, a story has come down from servants at the Rectory that in her early adulthood Emily formed an attachment to a young man, John Barrett by name, who sang in the church choir. Barrett came from a poor local farming family, and for Emily's father the merest suggestion of a breach in the class barrier was intolerable. A stormy two-hour interview ensued behind the locked door of the Archdeacon's study; Emily emerged in tears; the young man packed his bags and left for America.

It was not only in matters of the heart that Reginald played the heavy-handed father. Benson's successor as bishop, Howard Wilkinson, was impressed by Emily's drive and ability, but when he suggested that she head a women's committee to raise funds for the proposed new cathedral at Truro, the Archdeacon refused to hear of it.

Emily would break the tedium of the breakfast table by reading aloud to Reginald from *The Times*, the paper that was to lead savage campaigns against her in later years. These readings fed her growing interest in the great events and political issues of the day. It would have been in the breakfast room at St Ive in 1884, when all Britain was anxiously devouring news of the expeditionary force sent to relieve General Gordon in Khartoum, that she first encountered the name of a soldier who was beginning to take a hold on the public imagination, and who would one day play a key role in her own life story – Herbert Kitchener.

Nowadays we wonder at the overwhelming sense of duty and self-discipline that could tie a spirited, intelligent woman to a difficult invalid, yet countless Victorian daughters saw their best years drain away in this fashion. Florence Nightingale, a figure with whom Emily would often be compared, drew from bitter experience when she wrote: "I know nothing like the petty grinding tyranny of a good English family." As a child of her age and class, Emily had been brought up to think of her father as all-wise and all-powerful, only to see the belief languish and expire during these long years, especially with the enforced intimacy of the last six. It is unlikely that Emily was familiar at this time with the observation of John Stuart Mill, later a great hero of hers, that the self-sacrifice of women only confirmed their menfolk in selfishness and arrogance. What is certain is that the depressive melancholy Emily suffered for the rest of her life took firm root when she was twenty-nine, with Maud's departure. Those crushing years alone, Emily wrote later, "are recorded only on my spirit, and fortunately will die with me. It was in a word a period of torture". Rebellion was unthinkable; no escape was possible except by her father's death or hers.

A connection of Emily's by marriage had found herself in the same situation a few years previously. The sister-in-law of Henry Hobhouse of Hadspen, later famous as Mrs Beatrice Webb, shouldered the nursing role expected of her when her widowed father suffered a massive stroke. For seven years, until released by his death in 1892, the dutiful Beatrice ran a huge household in which existed, as she noted in her acerbic way, "ten persons living on the fat of the land in order to minister to the supposed comfort of one imbecile old man". At least Beatrice had already met Sidney Webb and quietly determined to marry once her father died.

For Emily the misery endured a further three years after Beatrice's liberation, with unrelieved gloom as her home life, varied only by the stifling boredom of countless hours in an almost empty church. No faithful lover was waiting to make her his bride. Emily confessed that the strain of the situation left "scorching marks" upon her, and the experience led to what Ruth Fry would call

"An incarnation of justice and iron rectitude": Archdeacon Hobhouse's interminable demands on Emily left "scorching marks".

"morbid introspection and hysteria". That terrible epoch alone with her father cast such a shadow over Emily's life that in later times she tended to overlook the "pleasant little abode" recorded by the fourteen-year-old Maud and the times of happy games and jokes recalled by her brother Leonard.

After Emily's death Leonard was to have a rude awakening when leafing though private papers which revealed the true extent of her emotional legacy from St Ive. At least in her younger days, he had fondly imagined, his favourite sister enjoyed "a period of such tranquil happiness as one would wish as a background to the storms and stresses of later years", a kind of unquestioned security and confidence lost to later generations of children. The only cloud upon the picture, or so he had thought, came from "the doctrine of eternal punishment with which the air of a Cornish parish of that period was overcharged". Only after she was gone did Leonard grasp that what had obsessed Emily was not eternity, but her vanishing youth.

*

Reginald's death in the bitterly cold January of 1895 brought to an end a reign of fifty-

In deep mourning for her father, Emily at thirty-four is on the threshold of her great adventures.

one years as Rector of St Ive.[iv] At the age of thirty-four Emily was finally free. A century ago, far more than today, this was seen as prohibitively old for striking out in a completely new direction; indeed, had she known it, Emily's allotted span of years was more than half over. She was sorely conscious of lacking a structured education, and her first thoughts, of either studying at university or training as a nurse, were met with rebuffs from every side.

But thanks to the fortune handed down from the long-ago slaver she was a woman not only with stirring desires and lofty aims, but with considerable means. Her share of her father's will alone was around £6,000 – over £300,000 in today's money – and she had earlier received a substantial legacy from an aunt. To her startled siblings she declared her resolve to carry out good works abroad, and with the assistance of the wife of Edward Benson – by this time Archbishop of Canterbury – conceived a plan to travel four thousand miles and become a missionary among the Cornish miners in the American west. Within a fortnight of the Archdeacon's funeral she had left the village of her birth, never to return.

Those who knew Emily only as the quiet, dutiful daughter of an invalid clergyman would have been incredulous if told that she was about to embark on a career that would make her loved and loathed like no other woman of her generation. Yet this was still some time in the future, for the first stage of her new life would take Emily among the prostitutes and drunkards of the American wilderness.

2 "A FOOLISH VIRGIN"

The history of mining in Cornwall goes back nearly four thousand years and only in recent years has it come to an end. The Cornish were known as skilled tinners to the Romans, and from Norman times provided a legendary source of revenue for the English crown. At the industry's peak during the Napoleonic wars and the Industrial Revolution at least fifty thousand worked in tin and copper mines throughout the county, with one site alone – the Caradon copper mine near Liskeard – employing no fewer than four thousand. Then came an almighty crash. By the mid-19th Century tin and copper had been discovered in distant lands where labour and production costs were far lower, and Cornwall's tin trade faced extinction.

For the displaced miners there was little choice except to starve or emigrate, and emigrate they did in their tens of thousands, to Australia, South Africa and America. During Emily Hobhouse's thirty-four years at St Ive, a third of all Cornish miners left their native land. And their skills were eagerly sought, not only for the mining of tin and copper, but of iron and lead, silver and gold. The diaspora led to the saying that wherever in the world you find a hole in the ground, a Cornishman will be at the bottom. Perhaps it was after being shown a letter sent home by one of these Cornish Jacks, as they were called, that Emily first dreamt of being a missionary in America.

*

After leaving St Ive, Emily stayed with Leonard at Oxford while she laid her plans. A letter setting out her credentials was posted off to the bishop of the Episcopalian diocese of Minnesota, who eagerly accepted the offered assistance as "the wonderful Providence of God". Six months after her father's death Emily sailed from England on the first stage of a long and arduous journey to a remote settlement called Virginia City, built to serve the iron ore mines scattered amid the dense pine forests of the Mesaba range. Here she confidently expected to find Cornishmen in need of her ministrations.

Landing in New York in late July 1895 Emily was entranced by the cable cars, electric trolleys and elevated railroads – "I feel as if I were in fairyland or the Arabian Nights," she wrote excitedly to Maud. On New York, as on practically every subject under the sun, her view was diametrically opposed to that of Rudyard Kipling, who on a visit around this time dismissed the city as "the shiftless outcome of squalid barbarism and reckless extravagance".

Within days she was off again. She arrived in Virginia on August 14, according to a report in the *Minnesota Missionary and Church Record*, after a lengthy delay caused by the railway line near Duluth, the nearest major city, sinking into a bog. The journal noted that Emily would begin "her noble and self-denying work among the miners" from a small rented cottage in Maple Street. Whatever vicissitudes fate had in store for Emily during her life, the lack of a personal servant was rarely among them, and a young girl called Mary Scourey travelled with her as her lady's maid.

Emily knew every ounce of her reforming zeal was needed for the task ahead, and at first sight of the place confessed to an impulse to turn and flee. Formerly Dakota Indian territory, Virginia was unquestionably the back of beyond. Set in a small clearing in a seemingly never-ending wilderness of forest – "thick, black, impenetrable" – the little settlement of cramped clapboard houses had been founded as recently as 1892 and had already burnt down once.

The earliest settlers had been lured by false rumours of gold but instead uncovered great deposits of iron. Conflict with local tribes led to terrible massacres and reprisals, and by the time Emily was a little girl most of the remaining Dakota of Minnesota had been forced onto reservations. Two years previously Virginia's prospects had been vastly improved by the coming of the railway, the self-styled city having previously been avoided by stagecoaches because of the surrounding swamps. Despite being razed to the ground by brushfire that same year, the population was now three thousand and rising. There were forty-two saloons and four "houses of ill fame", as Emily primly termed them, the largest offering twenty girls and non-stop gambling. "Ugliness obtrudes itself upon you at every turn," she wrote home to England in her bold, clear hand. As to the people, "all the riff-raff, the tag-rag and bob-tail of society, the dregs of population who cannot get in anywhere else flock to a place like Virginia".

The weather presented a serious challenge to one who had lived all her life in Cornwall's wet but mild climate. Although Virginia's summers were searingly hot and plagued by mosquitoes, near-arctic winters meant that the average temperature over the year was scarcely above freezing point, and it was not unusual for fifteen inches of snow to fall in twenty-four hours. The one advantage of the bitter cold was that it froze over the filthy quagmires that passed as Virginia's streets.

But things there were not as Emily had been led to expect. To start with, only a handful of Cornishmen could be found among the miners – the opencast workings of the locality required little of their deep-mining expertise, and miners of Scandinavian origin, Swedes and Finns, made up the majority. Emily's rented cottage turned out to be bug-infested and had to be abandoned for a room in a boarding house – *not* clean and *not* well-run, she recorded grimly – until a more suitable home was identified on Central Avenue.

Worst of all, Emily was immediately at loggerheads with her sponsoring church. The newly-appointed Episcopalian minister, one James McGonicle, had no intention of letting the grand lady from England steal his thunder, and at their first meeting scolded her for an hour. He strenuously objected to Emily's plan to target the city's sinners regardless of religious denomination – as in Cornwall, nonconformists greatly outnumbered the Anglicans – and said St Paul would have disapproved of her holding mission services at the logging camps. Emily retorted she would carry on all the same. It was only the first of many acrimonious disputes with the Rev Mr McGonicle. This backwoods minister must have cut a poor figure in the eyes of one used to the company of clerics of Archbishop Benson's calibre, or indeed of Emily's own uncle Edmund, formerly Bishop of Nelson in New Zealand and Suffragan Bishop of Lichfield.

Emily threw herself into the labours she felt were most needed. She visited the sick in their miserable shanties and in the vile little hospital where no doctor or nurse could ever be found; she visited poor drunken wretches in the prison; she organised a Sunday school and took charge of the church choir; she founded a lending library which, in defiance of McGonicle, she opened on Sundays. Funds for these good works were raised by staging entertainments at which she sang and played the piano. Early in 1896 she wrote home to Maud – who would have known every item on Emily's programme from sing-songs round the Rectory piano – joking of a memorable evening's performance when she was almost struck down by a flying champagne bottle.

Most of her energies were consumed by a campaign against drink. The weekly newspaper, the *Virginia Enterprise*, was soon carrying regular announcements of meetings of Emily's Virginia Temperance Union, and she began to haunt the swing-doors of saloons with a stack of temperance pledge cards at the ready, pouncing as each drunk came reeling out. The unmistakable ring of Emily's voice can be caught in an advertisement in the *Enterprise* calling on all who hated drink to "come boldly forward and show your colours, joining hands together against the mighty curse".

Come boldly forward and show your colours! It would be the clarion-call of Emily Hobhouse for the rest of her life.

"Daily more drunkards sign," she reported gaily to Maud in November. "I never go out without a bundle of pledge cards and a pencil." And it was wonderful, she thought, walking down Main Street, to see "all the hard icy faces melt before me" and to be told of the respect that the vilest wretch in town held for her: "Why, I cannot explain. Only I know, I need no revolver, I bear a sort of hallowed life among them."

Emily's pity had always been powerfully aroused by those who "fall down and worship before the drink idol" and she acknowledged that no mother, wife or sweetheart far away in a sheltered Cornish home could judge the temptations facing a lonely miner. Even so, she was proud to say that amid this mass of corruption the Cornishmen stood out. Of course a few would always be terrible drunkards – during her childhood the stocks at Liskeard were still in regular use to discourage such individuals – but in general the Cornish rose to the top of the heap by their sobriety, energy, skill and hard work. One disappointment, however, was her own Cornish servant girl, who parted company with Emily in circumstances which remain unexplained, except for a passing reference in a letter saying Mary had "proved fickle".

The missionary work continued in flagrant opposition to McGonicle, who had taken to thundering against Emily from the pulpit, branding her "one of the Foolish Virgins". It was an early demonstration of Emily's lifelong knack of making powerful enemies. And not content with flouting the authority of her minister, she now became loudly critical of the corrupt civic authorities. There was a lot wrong with Virginia, and Emily was never backward in pointing out fault.

She saw the police bend the rules to suck up to the powerful. She saw fraud and graft on every side. Indeed, among Virginians the providers of booze and prostitutes were reckoned as prominent citizens. With mounting exasperation Emily wrote to Maud: "The little timid group of churches all huddled together in one corner are absolutely powerless and do not attempt to touch or reduce the crying evils of the place. The Ministers *dare* not speak out, they *dare not* give offence… I verily believe I am the only person in the place not afraid to say and do what I think right." These confrontations between the English crusader and Virginia's clique of get-rich-quick merchants provided an enthralling spectacle for the rest of the townsfolk.

As well as finding enemies Emily found friends, and many touching little offerings were left on her doorstep. There would be a sack of potatoes from an anonymous admirer, or a rabbit prepared for the pot – this was some years before she became a vegetarian – or a bundle of firewood from "a grateful drunkard". Many lively, amusing incidents filled the letters that flew home, free of the rhetoric and hectoring style that would mar much of Emily's later writing.

Yet it was in these unlikely conditions she found her first love – or at least, the first since the unthinkable Cornish suitor was shown the Rectory door. Emily let her guard down, and for the first time in her life, at the age of thirty-six, formed a serious attachment, and in circumstances far removed from the constraints of the English class system, family pride, or clerical decorum.

*

The full details of this strange and blighted romance will never be known but it appears that Emily was first taken in, and then jilted, by a swindler who relieved her of most of her money. But the truth is rarely so simple. There are intriguing gaps in the story; there are inconsistencies, contradictions.

John Carr Jackson was unlike anyone in Emily's experience. The two first met at her seedy boarding house, where Jackson's New World drive and ambition immediately impressed her. Here was a young man indisputably on the make. He had arrived out of nowhere in the spring of 1893 and within months had risen from a lowly clerk's job to a partnership in a substantial store. On his partner's retirement in 1895 he became sole proprietor of Jackson and Co, purveyors of general merchandise and camp supplies. Under Jackson the store's range was rapidly extended beyond the staples of feed, hay, grain and flour; by the time he encountered Emily, he was also Virginia's foremost supplier of silverware, glass, crockery, hats, shoes, raincoats, and much besides.

Jackson's rise appeared unstoppable. Early in 1896 the *Virginia Enterprise* reported approvingly on rumours that Jackson was to be the next mayor. As well as being "a resident of long standing" – that is, having lived in Virginia for very nearly three years – he was "a competent energetic young man known for honourable dealing". Jackson's next move was to boost his status in the community by involving himself in politics and by accepting the vice-presidency of Emily's lending library.

By the summer of 1896 she is in love. In a letter dated July 24 to her Aunt Mary – wife of the judge Lord Hobhouse – Emily confesses coyly that Mr Jackson is consuming a good deal of her time and goes on: "I respect and admire him more every time I see him. He did not seem at all raw after Englishmen, quite the contrary… We are sort of half engaged and expect to be wholly so in a short while." Within days it was all settled: "I wanted to lose no time in writing to tell you that I promised Mr Jackson on Sunday night that I would marry him so now we are really engaged and I feel very happy over it and quite at home with him." She adds touchingly, if a little smugly: "As he has never known home or comfort or happiness, he is quite dazed with joy."

But Emily never found it easy to confide in Aunt Mary and to her sister Maud she offered more intimate details about Jackson, now referred to by the pet name of Caro. In August she writes dotingly that the "poor old stupid" had feared losing her affections during her absence from Virginia that spring, when she returned to England for a three-month holiday, to add to his worries over "business matters going wrong". The lover's anguish had turned his hair grey, but even so he was very handsome. In a clumsy but telling passage she says: "He puts himself into my hands for training as regards all that part of himself which from the circumstances of his life is necessarily only slightly developed." When her relations' response to the romance turns out decidedly cool, Emily is hurt but undeterred.

Curiously, the engagement between two of Virginia's best-known citizens was not announced in the *Virginia Enterprise*, though its owner was a close associate of Jackson. And from now on the twists in the story become even odder. In September Emily resigned from the library committee and the *Enterprise* carried an item stating that Miss Hobhouse was leaving Virginia City for Cleveland, Ohio, where she

Man on the make. John Carr Jackson's American drive and ambition captivated the wellborn lady from England.

expected to remain for some time. On September 30 Emily was escorted by a crowd of well-wishers led by the city temperance band, all the way from her house on Central Avenue to the railway station. Imagine twenty-five Finns playing brass instruments, she wrote to Maud, *all* out of tune.

What the well-wishers did not know was that Cleveland was only a staging post on an extraordinary secret journey. Jackson had cooked up a scheme to make his fortune in far-off Mexico and the venture was to be funded by his fiancée's money. Perhaps the exhilaration of the adventure blinded Emily to the dubiety of allowing people to assume that the move was connected with her missionary work, but if she felt a pang of guilt she left no record of it. Earlier in her life such conduct would have been unthinkable, yet – presumably at Jackson's urging – not a word of Mexico was breathed before Emily's departure. And there were to be other occasions in her career when Emily wished to hide the reason for a significant journey, leaving herself vulnerable to accusations of subterfuge.

Jackson was certainly in big trouble, and must have been pondering a fast exit from Virginia for some time. The city was entering one of its periodic economic crises and, with mines and lumber mills closing all around, Jackson's Store was losing customers hand over fist. However, as newly-elected mayor he had a front to keep up, and Emily – whether by her own wish or Jackson's – set off for Mexico alone. The plan was to set up her future husband as a rancher. The first step was to buy up land cheap, then plant coffee, pineapples and bananas. It was a remarkable venture for a woman of Emily's sheltered background.

*

The Mexico of the 1890s had emerged from a convulsive period of its history under French rule and was now enjoying relative prosperity and peace under the strong-arm presidency of Porfirio Diaz. Even so, it was still regarded as a fairly wild, unstable country unsafe for women, and in a letter home Emily mentioned that it would be necessary to carry a gun "like everyone else". Fortunately her social standing was recognised in Mexico City, and she was soon attracting admiring glances as she whisked about in a private carriage drawn by magnificent cream-coloured horses. She was invited to grand receptions and feted at the Presidential Palace, where she reported being "entertained with almost royal splendour" by the President and Mrs Diaz.

Over the winter of 1896/7, while buying up land and supervising the building of a house suitable for married life, she occupied her spare time with sketching and learning Spanish. Above all, she found herself revelling in the heat and vivid colours of the country. She would never again willingly live in a cold climate.

Meanwhile back in Minnesota Jackson's affairs were attracting ugly rumours, and the tone of the *Virginia Enterprise* became noticeably less friendly. On April 9, 1897 – Emily's birthday – the paper announced the sale of the entire stock of Jackson and Co to coincide with the sudden departure of the mayor for Mexico, where he was said to have been offered a lucrative position. Jackson was reported to have obtained power of attorney for "Miss E. Hobhouse, formerly of this city", by whose influence the Mexican position had been secured.

Nor was this the only story to set the city agog. A rival paper, *The Virginia*, weighed in with an account of Mayor Jackson leaving the city without a handshake or parting word, his hasty departure being attributed to a telegram from Miss Hobhouse asking Jackson to meet her in Chicago for the purpose of marriage. Further sensational disclosures followed. Within days the new owner of Jackson's Store was forced to close "pending the settlement of threatened legal complications". The *Virginia Enterprise* announced the appointment of a receiver for "John C. Jackson, allegedly insolvent", while the city council hurriedly chose a stand-in mayor for the remainder of the fugitive's year of office.

Jackson left Virginia's finances in complete disarray. Shortly before his disappearance, a former mayor had protested over the city debt climbing to fifteen thousand dollars, a figure which was coincidentally the year's revenue from the sale of liquor licences. However, no proof was forthcoming that Jackson had personally misappropriated civic funds, and his behaviour immediately prior to departure demonstrated what would be a sublime degree of nerve in a guilty man. Certainly he indulged in rather large talk about his prospects as a Mexican estate-owner, and airily promised jobs to a number of cronies.

How much of this reached Emily's ears can only be guesswork. Jackson must have sent a letter to Mexico giving some version of his troubles since Emily wrote to Aunt Mary that it was "a great sorrow to him to have had such bad times in money matters". What is known is that after an absence of nearly six months she returned to the United States in order to marry Jackson in Chicago, but though the couple were together for a few hours the marriage failed to take place.

Emily was shocked by the alteration in poor Caro's appearance. He looked very ill and "all threshed out" after a bout of influenza, she wrote to Maud, but she hoped a complete change and the glorious climate of Mexico would restore him to health and spirits. It is unclear whether she knew about the bankruptcy proceedings, but it seems to have been Jackson's idea that the wedding be put off for a few months on the grounds that he needed to familiarise himself with his new way of life in Mexico.

An appalling accident occurred on Emily's train journey out of Chicago, hours after saying goodbye to Jackson. The engine of the locomotive exploded and the carriages came to a sudden standstill with a mighty crash. Emily watched in horror as the body of the engine driver was hurled aloft, cutting through a thicket of telegraph wires and falling mutilated to the ground, while the charred corpse of the stoker landed at the door of her carriage. Luckily she was uninjured, though profoundly shocked by what she had witnessed.

This was a period of acute unhappiness for Emily. She had agreed to postpone marriage, but felt it proper to return to England until Jackson decided he was ready. So it was that she happened to be in London as an observer – no doubt a censorious one – of the exuberant public celebrations to mark that apogee of the Victorian age, the Diamond Jubilee of June 19, 1897. She would have endorsed Beatrice Webb's description of the crowds thronging the capital as "drunk with sight-seeing and hysterical loyalty".

*

The stay in England was an unsettling experience, and brought on severe depression. Her betrothal to an uneducated American of obscure origins and rocky finances did not go down well with the family – the parsons' wives, the Oxford academic, the bishop, the judge – and it is easy to picture Emily on the receiving end of many wounding remarks and much unwelcome advice. Even worse, while in Mexico City she had paid out between £1,000 and £1,200 of her diminishing funds in an effort to obtain a government concession on Jackson's behalf, and Uncle Arthur sharply censured the speculation. The criticisms stung, but in the face of united opposition all her stubbornness came out. Emily was determined to stick by her man.

For a time she tried to lose herself in social work, making a special study of the effects of factory legislation on children, but early in 1898 she decided to return to Mexico and find out whether life as Mrs Jackson was still on the cards. She must have remained hopeful since she packed a wedding dress. On leaving London, she just missed a letter from Jackson urging her to delay her departure.

On February 10, with a poor relation called Annie Batchelor as a companion, Emily sailed from Liverpool on a passenger-tramp, the *William Cliff*, bound for Vera Cruz by way of various ports in the Caribbean. As the daughter of an impecunious Cornish

We are not amused. Leonard and Nora Hobhouse, right, pose grimly with Emily and the unsuitable fiancé Jackson.

clergyman, Annie had been a regular childhood visitor to St Ive Rectory and shared many of Emily's interests including watercolour painting. She must have jumped at the prospect of being her cousin's bridesmaid, and seeing something of the world in the process.

The journey proved ill-starred for both women, beginning with the ominous discovery of thirteen names on the passenger list. Then, when the boat put in at Colon, they heard alarming reports of an impending war between Mexico and the United States. Emily was later to record her disgust at the demonstrations of war-fever she observed in the New World, citing "wearing flags and such puerilities". The phenomenon she put down to American excitability, never expecting to see the English similarly aroused.

The *William Cliff* arrived at Vera Cruz after a month and a day at sea. Poor Annie Batchelor found the Mexican heat too much for her and had to be packed off home to England, while Emily journeyed on to Mexico City alone. Once there she found Jackson still busily familiarising himself with the country, with little time to spare for his betrothed. There is the merest hint in one of Emily's letters home that "dark-eyed Spanish belles" might be proving a greater attraction to Jackson than an English spinster approaching her thirty-eighth summer. Whatever the reason, within a few weeks Emily too was heading home, the much-travelled wedding dress unpacked. Yet even now the engagement was not formally ended and later that year Jackson surfaced in England.

A photograph of Jackson at the time of his ascendancy in Virginia City shows a lean, clean-shaven man in his thirties with carefully brushed short dark hair. Emily's opinion as to his good looks might not be universally shared, and he must have appeared overdressed to English eyes, with his sharply-cut check jacket, large tie-pin, and heavy watch-chain, fob and seal. By the time of the visit to England, when he was photographed with a decidedly glum-looking Hobhouse family group, he had also acquired a Kitchener-sized moustache. Unsurprisingly, the man found no admirers among Emily's clan, and after this there was no more talk of marriage.

So what went wrong? Which one broke off the engagement, or did it end through mutual agreement? At thirty-eight Emily must have feared this was her last chance of love, yet as a member of the high-minded Hobhouse circle she could not have shut her eyes indefinitely to Jackson's failings. That he was her social and intellectual inferior might be overlooked, but what happened once it became clear he could never measure up to her moral standards? Perhaps she felt soiled by the kind of dealings in which Jackson had embroiled her; perhaps the latest postponement of marriage proved a humiliation too far.

As to Jackson, the novelty of landing a grand English lady might simply have worn off. It may be suspected that Emily's allure was not unconnected with her money, and by this time most of the money was gone – for Uncle Arthur's prediction about the Mexican speculation had proved only too true, and for the rest of her life Emily would know financial worry.

But the fact is that a veil descends. No one knows if there were high words and furious tears, or a gradual deterioration of mutual esteem measured by silences which finally proved intolerable. For whatever reason, the engagement came to an end. Among the family the whole episode was considered an aberration, an incomprehensible lapse of taste on Emily's part, "a something not to be spoken of" – to the point where a later generation of Hobhouses would pick up a vague idea that the fugitive lover had been "a butcher or something like that". And so John Carr Jackson fades from the story.

*

The great affair had ended in shame and disappointment. Against her nature, Emily had tried to act the submissive, dutiful fiancée, and her older and wiser self, alone in London, must have squirmed at the memory of those coy and simpering paeans to Caro in her old letters home. The time of self-deception was over. Never again would Emily willingly submit to the authority of a male, and her disdain for the common run of men would become entrenched. From now on her only heroes would be very old, or dead, or at least safely married.

Yet there is a telling passage in an article Emily contributed to *The Cornish Magazine* in 1899, a year after the engagement ended. The people of the far western states of America, she wrote, might be raw, ignorant, and hot-headed, but they were also full of life, hope and energy. And she went on: "One would be insensible, indeed, to live in such an atmosphere and not be conscious of the throb of youthful heart-beat, and this it is which charms and attracts." Jackson was not yet wholly out of her system.

3 GOD AND THE MAUSER

In the meantime she was landing herself with unnecessary troubles. During the stressful months spent in London while Jackson was supposedly finding his feet in Mexico, Emily had taken a flat near the British Museum. Though a far cry from the home of her own she craved, it seemed a suitable stop-gap considering her straitened circumstances.

Chenies Street Chambers was a very up-to-date kind of development, a block of purpose-built flats for "ladies who earn their own living" which had been erected on the initiative of the famous Garrett sisters. Most revered of these was Elizabeth Garrett Anderson, Britain's first qualified woman doctor, whose younger sister was Millicent Garrett Fawcett, the leader of the burgeoning women's suffrage movement; an unmarried third sister, Agnes Garrett, was a pioneering spirit in the field of architectural decoration, and had assumed the chief role in running the Chenies Street enterprise. But it was the formidable Mrs Fawcett who had performed the official opening ceremony of the building in 1889, and whose name would soon loom large and ominously in Emily's story.

At first sight the Chenies Street building, of handsome redbrick and stone facings, appeared to be ideal for Emily's purposes, though she would have disliked its location directly opposite the drill hall of the local volunteer unit, the Bloomsbury Rifles. To Mrs Fawcett, on the other hand, the crackle of gunfire sounded like music, since she was fond of declaring that the British were a very great people with a mission to rule over others.

Each set of rooms at Chenies Street had its own front door for privacy, though the tenant enjoyed access to a kitchen and communal dining room. Emily's flat was on the top floor up interminable flights of stairs, but the sitting room was light and airy. Above all, it was cheap, the rent for one of the smaller two-roomed flats being just ten shillings a week. However, Emily was a different woman since her sojourn in the New World, and she burst disturbingly into the calm and tidy milieu created by the Garrett ladies. From the start she fell foul of the management, not only because of her sudden and prolonged absences but because of her persistent challenges to the rules, in particular the liability of each tenant to a standing club room charge of ten shillings a month. Before long, the newcomer was a focus of discontent.

Returning from her final stay in Mexico, Emily became embroiled in fresh disputes. Possibly the outcome of the Jackson affair had made her more fractious, as the minutes of committee meetings during 1899 carried with increasing frequency a section headed simply "Miss Hobhouse", each tersely itemising the latest grievances of the occupant of Flat 22.

On the surface they were trivial squabbles. On April 27, for instance, in response to several letters from Emily complaining about draughts in her room, committee secretary Miss Anne Townshend was instructed to suggest that Miss Hobhouse provide herself with a draught excluder. Characteristically, Emily declined to take no for an answer, and pressed the attack on another front. Going over people's heads was becoming an engrained habit, and whatever her complaint – the inadequacies of the bathroom and the cisterns were favourites – she would typically draw a blank with the committee secretary and then follow up with a personal letter to the chairman, a clergyman friend of the Garrett sisters, or to Miss Agnes Garrett herself. Either to underline her disapproval or because of financial embarrassment, she also stopped paying the rent.

It was not one of Emily's more glorious moments. After surviving the rigours of the Minnesota backwoods uncomplainingly, making a drama about drains and draughts was something of a comedown, as she must have sensed in her calmer moments. Perhaps at this time her nerves were simply shredded.

Meeting on July 4 to consider the latest batch of complaints, the management committee instructed the secretary to write back pointing out how much rent Emily owed. They may have felt their harassed employee was out of her depth as the letter was to be sent "as dictated to Miss Townshend". By this time the Chambers were reverberating with grievances over the rule book, and it is not difficult to discern Emily's hand in the sudden appearance of a petition signed by a number of previously compliant tenants. The committee dealt with the unprecedented upsurge of discontent by formally rebutting the objections and ordering that public notices be pasted up around Chenies Street denying that tenants had ever been refused a hearing – one of the claims in the petition. Matters came to a head on July 17. A line in the minutes notes baldly that a letter from Miss Hobhouse to Miss Garrett had been read out and referred to the board of directors. The directors convened an emergency meeting the same afternoon and ordered that notice to quit be served on Miss Hobhouse.

Emily did not move out until October 31, still owing four months. Even then she did not go without a parting shot – the next committee minutes noting without comment that "Miss Hobhouse's letter upon leaving her flat was read" and resolving to take no further action over the outstanding debt. Neither Emily's letter nor a note of its contents was preserved, though the decision to turf out a tenant seems to have been without parallel in the history of the Chambers.

With her departure an almost audible sigh of relief rises from Chenies Street. The name Miss Hobhouse was not to reappear in the minutes for fifteen years. Yet in the weeks immediately following Emily's departure, amendments to rules she had fought for in vain were quietly granted to all remaining tenants – and a complaint from a Miss Fell-Smith over draughts in her flat was sympathetically received, the management taking the momentous decision to pay half the cost of a draught excluder.

*

Emily found a new flat in Rossetti Mansions, Chelsea, and tried to distract herself with the familiar round of social work. For a short time she assisted Octavia Hill, the celebrated campaigner for the London poor. Octavia Hill, who took up philanthropy after a blighted love affair of her own, had spent nearly forty years improving East End slums with the financial backing of John Ruskin. Also around this time Emily made a concerted effort to improve her finances by exploiting her talent for writing. During an earlier stay in London she had drafted a novel centred on the effects of the Factory Acts on children, but she now dusted off the manuscript only to burn it. This act of destruction was blamed by friends on depression over the failed romance, but in old age Emily would say that writing the book was part of an unconscious preparation for the great tasks ahead – "it was not for others to read but for my own education".[v]

Freelance journalism promised a crucial supplement to her income, and examples of her work began to appear in some of the leading highbrow publications of the day. Among her first published articles were a striking piece describing how poor women sorted rubbish by hand in London's Docklands and her well-informed account of the temptations besetting Cornish migrants in America. Emily's writing style was fresh and lively by the standards of the time. Upper class usage combined with occasional Americanisms, and she exhibited an American fondness for making verbs out of nouns. Like most contemporary writers she inclined to moral instruction, with repeated appeals to such capitalised concepts as Honour, Truth and Virtue; yet the best of her work possessed a down-to-earth quality absent from much social commentary of the time.

A commission to write about working women for the magazine *Nineteenth Century* offered Emily an opportunity to strike back at her old landlords, the Garrett ladies. In a thinly-veiled description of life at Chenies Street, she attacked the management committee over high charges, bad food, and vexatious rules. This small act of revenge, no doubt highly satisfying at the time, would one day rebound on Emily in a completely unforeseeable fashion.

Emily's journalism was encouraged by her brother Leonard. Still in his early thirties, Leonard Hobhouse had been a dazzling high-achiever at Oxford. As an undergraduate he had mixed, to the dismay of the Archdeacon, with known radicals, freethinkers, suffragists and the like. But after taking a double first at Corpus Christi he had matched his Uncle Edmund in being awarded a fellowship at Merton and was now on the threshold of a remarkable academic career.

Alas, Leonard was no longer the golden-haired boy who had captured all hearts at the Rectory. Now thirty-five, a shaggy bulky figure with a droopy moustache, he gave the impression of being perpetually in nervous movement, his spectacles perched on his puckered forehead, his massive balding cranium wreathed in smoke from a pipe crammed with pungent Player's Navy Cut – a source of much annoyance and discomfort to Emily on her visits. Like his sister, Leonard prided himself on his Cornish impetuosity; like her he was becoming a helpless prey to hypochondria and bouts of deep depression. Some colleagues found him "self-centred and somewhat arrogant", in the words of a future biographer, while his greatest admirers conceded that he was often inconsiderate, difficult and irritable.

Whatever his faults, Leonard was a devoted husband. He and his wife Nora, the daughter of a Yorkshire mill-owner, first met while "stirring up village workers" near Oxford, and their courtship had proceeded on the lines of that of their friends the Sidney Webbs, blossoming while on "agitations" together on behalf of the downtrodden working class, as they tossed back and forth quotations from Aristotle. They were to remain happily married for thirty-four years.

Leonard Hobhouse came to be regarded as one of the pioneers of sociology, and to the present day rates lengthy entries in the kind of biographical dictionaries that ignore his sister's existence. Already by 1899 he was a respected author, his preoccupations showing in titles such as *The Labour Movement*, *Mind in Evolution*, and *Democracy and Reaction*. As a regular columnist for the leading radical newspaper, *The Manchester Guardian*, he helped Emily place a number of articles on her American travels. For some she was paid as much as fourteen guineas. Yet readable as her pieces were, Emily was always conscious of lacking not only the trained mind and self-discipline, but the feather-light touches of humour that made her brother one of the outstanding journalists of the day.

A key influence on Emily all her life, Leonard was gripped by a new obsession as the century drew to its close. Far off in South Africa a long history of conflict between Boer and Briton was coming to a head, and the looming war was to prove the bloodiest and costliest struggle that Britain had engaged in since Waterloo. Leonard Hobhouse, like many of the family's friends and relations, was instinctively drawn to the side that critics would label "pro-Boer", and there was never any doubt where his sister's sympathies lay.

*

Few in 1899 had the slightest inkling how the coming war would unfold, but its course strikes a familiar note in the present day. It was a conflict which ranged the world's greatest power against a small distant country. It was fought by a coalition of Anglophone nations in the face of international condemnation led by France, Germany and Russia. Supporters of the war talked of the need to protect national security, to overthrow a dangerous and corrupt regime, and to bestow democratic values on a benighted people; opponents insisted that the war was really about control of the invaded country's greatest natural asset.

At the outset, protesters at home were vilified by government and most of the press, were accused of giving comfort to the enemy, and even branded as traitors. Following an invasion by an overwhelming force, the war was prematurely declared to be won, only for a deadly protracted guerrilla phrase to ensue. A generally supportive mood at home was soon tempered by unexpected casualties among the occupying troops and succeeded by deep concern once the death toll of civilians – above all, of children – began to exceed the combatant fatalities on both sides by a huge margin. And controversy spread throughout the world over persistent stories of abuse in prison camps.

*

The land now called South Africa had been contested from earliest times. The first known humans at the temperate Cape of Good Hope were ancestors of the Bushmen presently fighting to survive in the Kalahari Desert, and appear to have been driven out by more warlike tribes. But exactly who did what to whom and when is a cloudy issue coloured by faction and fashion, and scarcely any statement formerly accepted as historical fact would not be challenged nowadays by some political or racial interest.

To Emily Hobhouse's contemporaries, the general outline of South African history was quite clear. A small population of Dutch Calvinists, descendants of the first white settlers of 1652, had crushed the dominant native race, then known as Hottentots, and later mixed with incoming groups of French Huguenots and German Protestants. The result was a people known as Boers, the Dutch word for farmers, or Afrikaners. Later immigrants tended to be British, mostly Scots and Irish. For a century the Boers expanded inland, colliding with migrating Bantus who had been expelled from their homelands by rival tribes. Beaten in battle, these blacks stayed on under the white man's rule.

During the Napoleonic Wars, control of the Cape passed to and fro between Holland and Britain, becoming British for good in 1814. Notoriously resistant to government from outside, the Boers were unwilling subjects of the Crown from the outset, and further antagonised by the Empire-wide abolition of slavery in 1834 – for no one disputes that from the earliest days of white South Africa the economy depended on black labour.

To escape British rule, first hundreds, then thousands of Boers moved further inland by ox-wagon in what became known as the Great Trek. In response the British wavered between desire to bring the Boers to heel and acceptance of the near-impossibility of exercising control over the vast new territories they occupied. From the mass migration sprang several embryo republics that in time were either annexed by Britain or absorbed into two surviving Boer republics, the Transvaal and the Orange Free State. The coastal territory of Natal, a battleground between Boers and Zulus, was declared a British colony in order to protect the trade route to India. Then in 1852 a vaguely worded treaty was signed whereby Britain gave up any claim to Boer strongholds between the Vaal and Limpopo rivers on condition that the Boers accepted the end of slavery.

Neither side lived up to the terms of the treaty. In 1877 Britain annexed the Transvaal and was soon afterwards embroiled in war with the Zulus. Shock waves reverberated throughout the world when nine hundred British troops were massacred at Isandhlwana, while the Boers marked with interest the destruction of a vaunted British army by a tribe which had suffered devastating defeats at their own hands. But the Boers played a waiting game, hoping for a change of heart in Britain – after all, the Transvaal annexation had been denounced as a hideous crime by Gladstone, the Liberal leader then in opposition. Gladstone's portrait had pride of place in many a Transvaal home, though he privately called his Boer admirers "a dirty lot".

News of the Zulu War of 1879 would have been followed avidly at St Ive Rectory. For the Hobhouses, a special interest of the conflict was the role played by the Bishop of Natal, a fiery Cornishman named John Colenso, who was branded a heretic by Church of England superiors because of his controversial views on the Old Testament. A strong partisan of the Zulus, Bishop Colenso had long outraged propriety by baptising polygamous converts without insisting that supernumerary wives be cast aside. After the defeat of the Zulu army, the maverick bishop led a campaign for the release of the captive king, Cetshwayo.

Boer hopes rose when the Liberals came to power in 1880 but, once ensconced in Downing Street, Gladstone underwent a change of mind. The stage was set for armed conflict and the first Boer War broke out in December 1880 when Emily was a girl of twenty. Was she ever tempted, during the breakfast table readings of *The Times*, to voice sympathy for the tiny nation at war with her own? Or did the words wither on her lips under the gaze of the ultra-conservative Archdeacon?

For months, from Britain's viewpoint, the war news was bad. The fighting exposed the hopeless inadequacy of an outmoded military system pitted against committed guerrillas, and the British suffered successive defeats. The Battle of Majuba Hill on February 27, 1881, was a humiliating rout of elite regulars by a smaller force of Boer farmer-militias, and the debacle decided Gladstone on a course of appeasement that outraged the Conservatives, half his own party, and Queen Victoria herself. The Tory leader Disraeli accused the government of "trailing the standard of England in the dust". A speedy armistice was sealed by a treaty that gave the Boers almost everything they wanted, including formal recognition of a republic of South Africa under its first president, Paul Kruger – a gift to the cartoonists with his piggy eyes, untidy fringe of beard, and battered top hat.

A bitter legacy remained. A shamed British military thirsted for revenge; among the Boers, success against the mighty foe only strengthened the belief that God fought on their side. Yet the first Boer war would probably have been the last but for the fateful discovery of gold in 1887 near the Transvaal capital, Pretoria. "Instead of rejoicing you would do better to weep," President Kruger told his people, "for this gold will cause our country to be soaked in blood."

As he foresaw, the gold rush brought into their midst wave upon wave of adventurers, mostly from Britain. Many were Cornishmen, and it was one of these known as "Cyanide Jones" who discovered how to use the eponymous poison to facilitate the deep-level mining of Rand gold. The Boers saw their fundamentalist way of life under threat as the newcomers they called Uitlanders – outsiders – quickly became a majority. The immigrants for their part made no effort to rub along with their Bible-thumping hosts and fiercely resented the heavy taxation and voting restrictions forced upon them.

The Boers' belief in a destiny under a republican flag was not shared by Cecil Rhodes, the most remarkable empire-builder of the Victorian era. Like Emily Hobhouse, Rhodes was the child of a Church of England parson, but there any comparison ends. Others like Emily might live to see towns or lakes named after them, but only Rhodes would give his own name to a territory covering a million square miles. Dreaming of a map of Africa coloured red from the Cape to Cairo, he saw no reason why a petty nuisance like the Boer republics should spoil the grand design. Only seven years older than Emily, he was already one of the richest men in the world through his control of the Kimberley diamond mines, but the Boers' gold was as much a lure to Rhodes as to the poorest prospector. By 1897 he reasoned that the Boers' harsh treatment of Uitlanders presented sufficient excuse for Britain to resume control in the Transvaal, and secretly financed an armed revolt led by his close friend, Dr Leander Starr Jameson.

It was a serious miscalculation. The so-called Jameson Raiders found no support among the Uitlanders and all five hundred mounted troopers were ignominiously captured. For the British, now with a Conservative government under Lord Salisbury, the Jameson Raid was a dreadful embarrassment, and the German Kaiser rubbed salt into the wound by congratulating Kruger on crushing the rebellion. For the Boers, the attempted coup seemed a warning of things to come, and the Orange Free State, previously less hostile to Britain than the Transvaal, moved closer to the hard-line Kruger. And from that time on the Boers would spend much of their newfound wealth on equipping themselves with the best rifle in the world, the rapid-fire German-made Mauser.

*

Two figures who now step centre-stage were to be major players in Emily Hobhouse's story. Britain's colonial secretary, Joseph Chamberlain – a disillusioned Liberal calling himself Imperialist Unionist – made the critical choice as high commissioner for South Africa of Sir Alfred Milner, a career diplomat who was said to have gained his dry and impervious arrogance from his time at Oxford. Between them Chamberlain and Milner planned to reverse the years of fudge and failure.

Each in his own way strove to keep Britain as the supreme world power. But the shrewd, self-made Birmingham businessman Chamberlain, famous for his monocle and orchid buttonhole, favoured the long game; the bachelor Milner, lean and pale with strikingly close-set eyes, was obsessed with the idea of English "race patriotism" and schemed to goad the Boers into war. In this he was aided by a burgeoning spirit of jingoism at home that hailed the bungler Jameson as a hero and decried Kruger as corrupt, hypocritical and full of peasant cunning – "sloven(ly), sullen, savage, secret, uncontrolled," as Rudyard Kipling saw him; "a maddened baboon," according to the writer Frank Harris; "a frock-coated Neanderthal," in the words of Milner himself.

On the Boer side also appeared a man who would play a pivotal role in Emily's life, and become South Africa's only world-class statesman before Nelson Mandela. Jan Christian Smuts had unexpectedly emerged as President Kruger's right-hand man. Though of small-farmer Boer stock, Smuts was a Cambridge-educated intellectual and, as South Africa's new state attorney, stood out as a conciliatory liberal among nationalist bigots; his was the only shaven face amid the massed ranks of patriarchal beards. This pale, intense young lawyer would one day hail Emily as one of the great women of the age. But in 1898 this was in the unknowable future, and over Christmas of that year Smuts was faced with a dangerous new dispute between Boer and Briton.

The match that threatened to light the powder-keg was the shooting of a Uitlander, a Lancashire-born boilermaker called Tom Edgar. What began as a drunken brawl between Edgar and another immigrant escalated into an international incident when, during a confused scene inside Edgar's house, he was killed by a trigger-happy Boer policeman. The Uitlander community rose in uproar over what they saw as a clear case of murder. The policeman was arrested but quickly released on bail facing a reduced charge of manslaughter. Smuts ordered his re-arrest, but the damage was done. A mass demonstration followed, with the Uitlanders petitioning Queen Victoria to protect her loyal subjects in the goldfields.

Events were playing into Milner's hands. The Transvaal authorities arrested the leaders of the demonstration while a Boer judge and jury acquitted Edgar's killer. Milner ignored conciliatory Boer offers channelled through Smuts and urged Chamberlain to

A fateful choice as high commissioner for South Africa, the career diplomat Sir Alfred Milner schemed to goad the Boers into war.

take a strong line. Still cautious, Chamberlain persuaded the cabinet to intervene – but only after entrusting to Milner one last attempt to force a climb-down by Kruger. Milner cannily made his sticking point the franchise for Uitlanders. The Boers regarded it as fantastical that Britain would risk war to uphold the rights of a disreputable lot who wished to become citizens of a foreign state – after all, Milner's own deputy had called the newcomer population "probably the most corrupt, immoral and untruthful assemblage of beings in the world".

Milner's detestation of the Boers went unconcealed in letters to his close friends, most of them adoring females. Long before hostilities broke out, he was speaking of the republics as "the enemy", and characterising the Boer notion of government as "the most disgusting system of espionage, subornation, bribery and humbug". That Kruger's state was corrupt there could be no doubt. Between 1886 and 1899, for example, government officials in the Transvaal bumped up their own salaries from £50,000 to £1,200,000. And Milner was genuinely shocked by the Boers' treatment of the non-white majority. One of the first official protests he made as high commissioner was against a Boer court that had heavily fined two "slightly coloured" men for walking on a pavement reserved for whites. And he was astonished by the Boer uproar when, at a celebration for Queen Victoria's jubilee, the wife of a British official kissed a black girl who had handed her a bouquet.

A so-called peace conference held in the Orange Free State capital of Bloemfontein in May 1899 brought Kruger and Milner face to face. Negotiations broke off after six days of fruitless haggling with the seventy-four-year old Kruger famously letting out the choked bellow: "It is our country that you want." Milner and Smuts, two clever, arrogant men, had taken an instant dislike to each other, but while Smuts pressed Kruger to make further concessions to avert war, Milner urged London to assemble an overwhelming force.

Chamberlain persuaded a reluctant cabinet that Kruger would "bluff up to the cannon's mouth", and an ill-prepared force was patched together from various corners of the Empire to reinforce the small body of soldiers on the ground. In response came an ultimatum from Kruger on October 9 calling for the withdrawal of all British troops, failing which the Transvaalers, supported by the more reluctant Free Staters, would regard themselves as at war with Britain. The Boers had placed their trust in God and the Mauser.

For Emily, the great moment had almost come. A stage stood empty, waiting for a heroine to sweep in from the wings.

*A clean-shaven face amid massed patriarchal
beards, Jan Christian Smuts would be a key
figure in Emily's life.*

4 "THE LAST TIME OF FEELING YOUNG"

I n the spring of 1899 Emily had taken a break from the quarrels at Chenies Street to join her Uncle Arthur and Aunt Mary. The childless elderly couple, who had been lent an idyllic riverside country house in Oxfordshire, invited their favourite niece to stay, and to a sympathetic observer like Ruth Fry she seemed to be slipping into the role of the daughter they never had. "But much as I loved them I never found it easy to talk to them very confidentially," Emily admitted long afterwards. "The conversation at their table was always on a lofty plane."

Like Gladstone before him, Lord Hobhouse had an unhappy knack of turning every conversation into a debate. Emily was recovering from a bout of influenza, and the combined demands of his intellectual rigour and encroaching deafness were hardly calculated to lighten her mood. And then, perhaps Emily had heard once too often the worthy peer's favourite story, how on a visit to the United States in 1883 he had shaken hands with Sitting Bull, "whose impenetrable smile reminded him of Disraeli". The ponderous humour of his anecdotes of his time as a judge in Simla, as when he would declaim from *Lycidas* with great gusto while out walking, to the admiration of Indian bystanders who believed him to be observing some solemn religious rite, must have palled with repetition.

Yet as the lull before the storm, these weeks would remain in Emily's mind as "full of peace and loveliness". The newspapers at the breakfast table were crammed with South Africa stories, and Lord Hobhouse startled her with his prophecy of war.

Eighty that year, Lord Hobhouse refused to label himself a pacifist but, according to Emily, "certainly was one in the best possible sense", never shrinking from exposing what he saw as the underlying causes of war – greed, desire for territory, and commercial advantage. Even among judges he was noted as particularly conscientious and painstaking, and to the end of his days espoused liberal reforms and

Emily's Uncle Arthur, an early champion of women's rights. The worthy peer had a tiresome knack of turning every conversation into a debate.

women's rights. He had been the moving force behind a landmark law of 1869 that protected the property rights of wives for the first time. Yet photographs taken throughout Arthur Hobhouse's life show the dejected, careworn face of one who lives in constant expectation of the human race disappointing his high ideals.

In August 1899 the Hobhouse clan gathered to celebrate the golden wedding of Arthur and Mary at their country retreat, Charlton House near Bristol. It was another welcome respite for Emily, then under notice to quit Chenies Street, and during the visit she revived an old friendship with a Quaker neighbour called Ruth Fry, her future biographer. Daughter of the millionaire Sir Edward Fry, Ruth was a teenager at the time of her first meeting with Emily and already a committed peace campaigner. Her siblings were a formidable lot, among them the educationalist Isobel, the penal reformer Margery and the artist-critic Roger.

Emily later recalled: "We were hardly back in London before the storm broke. There had been days of growing tension. I well remember the crucial moment when coming through Trafalgar Square we saw the Ultimatum placarded and knew the last hope was gone." War was formally declared on October 11 and, in Emily's words, "it sounded the death knell of tens of thousands of people completely innocent of its cause and it bore within it seeds of things worse than death for England."

These sombre reflections were not shared by another observer of events in London that day. The fledgling war correspondent of *The Morning Post*, twenty-five-year-old Winston Churchill, thought it very sporting of the Boers to take on the whole British Empire, later recording that "everyone was in that mood of gaiety and heartiness which so often salutes an outbreak of war". Churchill's chum Lord Gerard, a member of staff of the new army commander, was presented with many cases of the very best champagne and the very oldest brandy which the cellars of London boasted to carry off to South Africa. Alas, Gerard's ruse of labelling the cases "castor oil" proved too clever by half, as on arrival at Durban docks all were promptly seized and shared out among the military hospitals.

A South African Conciliation Committee was set up within three weeks of the declaration of war with the stated aim of ending the conflict, and it was through this committee that Emily came into contact with a wider circle of likeminded people soon to be reviled as "the pro-Boers". Emily gave herself wholeheartedly to the cause, dropping earlier pet schemes such as the study of factory children, and her new flat in Chelsea quickly became the nerve-centre from which anti-war pamphlets flooded the country. Reports were received from "the best and most reliable South African sources" – that is, anti-imperialist sources – and disseminated by Emily and a small group of women she called her "ardent workers". But the pro-Boer label would rankle to the end of her life. As Emily later declared: "From the first I, and indeed all whom I knew, had been concerned primarily about our own country and whether or not she was acting upon the highest principles of justice and humanity." To critics that claim would always appear disingenuous or worse.

Emily joined the committee at the invitation of its president, and old family friend, Leonard Courtney. If men in general now excited Emily's disdain, a shining exception was Mr Courtney. Though almost blind and in his sixties, this bald Penzance-born intellectual was MP for East Cornwall, and a leading figure of the so-called "Little

Reviled as pro-Boers, the blind MP Leonard Courtney and his heiress wife Kate were Emily's steadfast supporters.

Englander" faction of the Liberal Party opposed to the war. His stand turned his own constituents against him – he was hissed when speaking at Liskeard after the outbreak of hostilities – and brought an avalanche of hate-mail to the House of Commons.

All this only added lustre to Leonard Courtney in Emily's eyes, as did his vocal support for women's rights. Then too his wife Kate was one of the celebrated Potter girls, the bluestocking daughters of a wealthy railway magnate. Kate's clever younger sister was already earning renown under her married name of Beatrice Webb; a second sister was the mother of Stafford Cripps; a third was married to Emily's MP cousin, Henry Hobhouse V of Hadspen.

Always on hand with helpful guidance, always willing to help the politically ignorant, Mr Courtney was "so wonderfully easy of approach, so lenient towards inexperience, so wise in pointing out the best way", that Emily never came away from his delightful mansion on Cheyne Walk without feeling mentally enlightened and morally strengthened. Yet contemplation of the Courtneys' famously happy marriage must have caused Emily a pang or two; the couple had fallen in love when Kate, till then resigned to spinsterhood, was thirty-six, the same age as Emily when she met Jackson. The Potter girls tended to marry late; Beatrice was thirty-four before she became Mrs Webb.

Many years before Emily, Kate Courtney had helped Octavia Hill in London's poorest parish, Whitechapel, using her own money to buy and renovate houses to rent out to rescued slum-dwellers. After her marriage to Courtney in 1883, Kate had noted in her journal, the wedding breakfast was attended by forty family and friends and "a hundred of my poor people". Ruminating on the ceremony afterwards, the officiating vicar had rejected a passing thought that there was something "bizarre, forced and fanciful" in the spectacle of overworked paupers being handed to their seats by "the quality" and firmly reminded himself that all the guests, "however far apart in mental and social degree", were united in love and respect for the bride.

Alarmed by public support for the war in South Africa, Emily realised that her own people were no less prone to the excesses of patriotism than the Americans. As she wrote much later, "since those far-off days we have all had too much opportunity for studying war-fever in all its stages and degrees, from mere puerilities and credulities down to the extremest exhibitions of inhumanity and cruelties". Only a few like the Courtney circle could be trusted to keep cool heads while the populace at large, "fanned by the Press and the Pulpit", gave itself up to mad exultation over each supposed British victory in the field.

It had been an exhausting year. Emily jumped at an invitation to join the Courtneys for Christmas in Switzerland, following them to Caux, near Lausanne, with her brother Leonard. Though now permanently short of money, she had kept back a spare £20 note "in a kind of mental stocking" to finance the break, though it meant the rigours of second-class travel. Emily was always to look back on this as one of the few real holidays of her life: "The exhilarating air, the beauty of the Swiss mountains, the companionship of interesting and sympathetic friends combined with the real if childish enjoyment of the winter sports in the snow, formed material for a few weeks of what would have been perfect mental rest had not the war cast its shadow over all." There was the spectacle of the staid and dignified Mr Courtney on his toboggan to chuckle at, and the simple, healthy exercise of sliding over the snow like lightning from morning till dusk. In Emily's poignant phrase, "it was memorable as the last time of feeling young".

In mid-January the party returned to London and the grim realities of the new century. In the year ahead, Emily would forge herself a role that carried her name around the world. At the outset, busying herself with repetitive paperwork and leaflet-mailings, she had no idea that the year 1900 would be the last of comfortable obscurity. Though she had recently been elected honorary secretary of the women's branch of the Conciliation Committee, as yet she was only one of a number of society ladies and intellectuals who had adopted the anti-war cause. Pro-Boer politicians were the target of public anger, chief among them Mr Courtney, whose standing in Cornwall sank to a new low with the gallant death of a Cornish-born general, Sir William Penn-Symons, in the first major action of the war.

There were new troubles too on the domestic front. Both her uncle and aunt were ill and in need of regular visits, and a young Indian medical student who Emily had invited to share her rooms in Chelsea was suddenly laid up with a painful disease of the eyes requiring tender care from her flatmate. But one occasion for rejoicing was the appearance that January of the first London edition of the *Manchester Guardian* – a great support for all on the side of sanity, in Emily's view – with a pioneering form of distribution by "early bicycle". And support was sorely needed, with most of the British press firmly in the jingo camp.

The divided Liberal Party held a conference on February 14 in the hope of kissing and making up. Emily, an impatient observer of this all-male affair – she was one of a handful of women to gain admission to the hall by offering to make tea – fired off a seething letter to her brother. "I have one thing against that Liberal conference," she wrote, "in that they were so far lukewarm, so far *bad* Liberals, that *they did not invite a single woman* to share their deliberations. Is not this to cut off their best arm, their most ardent support, their most enthusiastic workers, and relegate them to a lower place?" She was anxious too over the prospect of Sir Edward Grey, a leading Imperialist, becoming Liberal leader. "If I were a man I'd stir Heaven and Earth rather than let it be him," she told Leonard, ending the letter with her now-familiar cry against the male sex – "*You are all so hopeless*".

As committee work snowballed, Uncle Arthur made an unwelcome demand on Emily's time. Her sick flatmate, Alice Sorabji, belonged to an old Indian family befriended by the Hobhouses, and Arthur, believing she would benefit from a holiday, offered to pay for the two women to go abroad. For the first and last time in her life Emily was reluctant to leave England but could not deprive Alice of a much-desired treat. The pair toured Italy until late in April, taking in the sights of Rome and Venice. On their return Emily threw herself into the committee work with renewed vigour, but much had happened in South Africa in the meantime.

The new commander-in-chief, the bluff, crimson-faced Devonshire squire Sir Redvers Buller, VC, had sailed from England on the day the Boer ultimatum expired. On board to hear the cheers from the quayside were Winston Churchill and his drinking pal Lord Gerard. Yet before the troopship reached Cape Town the Boers had invaded Natal and laid siege to the strategic towns of Kimberley, Ladysmith and Mafeking, and brave Penn-Symons was dead.

"Black Week" in December 1899 had witnessed a stunning run of Boer victories, and what little success Britain could claim was at a terrible cost in lives. To the unconcealed delight of rival powers like Germany and France, the British Empire once again saw its army outmanoeuvred and humiliated. As so often in the nation's history, disaster stiffened resolve at home, with news of Black Week bringing from the Queen herself the famous response: "We are not interested in the possibilities of defeat; they do not exist." This time there was to be no acceptable outcome but the Boers' surrender.

Though a brave soldier revered by his men, General Buller failed to measure up to the job. His replacement was another holder of the Victoria Cross, the diminutive but highly pugnacious Lord Roberts of Kandahar, otherwise Kipling's "Bobs". A great hero with the public since his Afghan campaigns twenty years before, Roberts accepted the South African command in London on the same day his only son was killed at the Battle of Colenso while valiantly rescuing captured guns.[vi] The new commander-in-chief landed at Cape Town on January 10 as Emily was savouring the last few days of her holiday with the Courtneys.

Towering a foot above Bobs on the dockside was the impressive figure of his second-in-command, a soldier whose exploits against the Dervishes of Sudan had made him Britain's latest military idol. Like those other great generals, Wellington and Wolseley, he was Irish-born, though he would have thanked no one for calling him an Irishman. In honour of his victories he had recently been raised to the peerage, taking the title of Baron Kitchener of Khartoum.

5 K of K

Horatio Herbert Kitchener, soon to figure as the *bête noire* of Emily's story, was the second son of a half-pay army officer who retired from the Indian service in order to purchase a bankrupt estate in Ireland. Ballygoghlan, near Listowel, was one of many such properties available to a shrewd speculator in the aftermath of the Potato Famine. Like the Hobhouses, the Kitcheners came from modest English farming stock and achieved the status of gentry through prospering in trade – in the case of the future field marshal's great-grandfather, by importing tea into Georgian London. If there was anything in Kitchener's pedigree Emily might have envied, it was that one of his direct forebears – the tea-merchant's wife – traced descent from Thomas Clarkson the early abolitionist, a more desirable ancestor than a slave-trader.[vii] Kitchener on his part might have preferred descent from John Cam Hobhouse, secretary for war in the previous reign.

Ten years older than Emily, Kitchener was brought up in a corner of Ireland as damp and misty as Cornwall. The name Horatio was a family one, marking his father's birth within days of Nelson's victory at Trafalgar, but the boy was always known as Herbert. As with Emily, the choice of name was prophetic. Herbert commemorates the powerful Welsh military clan that rose to prominence in the Wars of the Roses and derives from a Teutonic word meaning *bright warrior*. One of a close family of five siblings ruled by a rigid disciplinarian of a father, Herbert Kitchener watched his adored mother die of consumption when he was just fourteen.

So the briefest outline of Kitchener's family history throws up a number of close similarities with the household at St Ive – the privileged middle class home set amidst the poverty of a Celtic land, the authoritarian father, the saintly lost mother. In the heyday of Empire such a background was far from unusual; nor was it out of the way that Emily Hobhouse and Herbert Kitchener were destined to spend almost their entire careers abroad, shunning the English climate. Least of all was it remarkable that both grew up as committed Christians. Yet as the story progresses, uncanny symmetries appear in their lives and their deaths.

Both Emily and Kitchener hid a shy nature under an outward display of fearlessness, battled against physical handicap and bouts of severe depression, lavished an unusual degree of affection on animals, and repeatedly talked of longing for death. Earnest and dedicated, both were strangers to false modesty, self-deprecation and self-mockery, yet possessed a genius for cultivating influential contacts. Both formed a view of the opposite sex that was extreme even by the standards of their time. Both remained unmarried but underwent one great blighted romance, exposing in the process a capacity for recklessness that threatened career and reputation. Both became outstanding fundraisers for pet charitable projects. Both suffered financial hardship because of unwise speculations abroad, and endured vitriolic press campaigns. Both would be able to buy a retirement home thanks to the public purse – for Kitchener, a sprawling country seat in Kent financed by grants of parliament, for Emily a modest seaside villa in her beloved Cornwall, its price met by a half-crown subscription appeal.

Both had hospitals and schools named in their honour, and streets without number. Kitchener had a city, a mountain and an island named after him, along with a peony and a class of locomotive, while Emily gave her name to a town, a dahlia, and – of all things – a submarine, coincidentally the instrument of Kitchener's death. Yet both hated the surnames they made famous. Emily lamented "my very ugly name"; Kitchener, on elevation to the peerage, protested that his was "too horrible a name to put Lord in front of."

They shared almost exactly the same lifespan, one decade apart – Kitchener would die in June 1916, just short of his sixty-sixth birthday, Emily in June 1926, shortly after hers. Each death sparked an outpouring of public grief and unprecedented posthumous honours. Neither was destined to rest in a grave in the common sense of the word, each being commemorated in a cenotaph erected by a grateful nation, though in Emily's case that nation was not her own.

Both, in all probability, died as virgins – the likelihood being slightly stronger in the case of Kitchener, whose strait-laced views on sex were the stuff of legend. Emily was in many respects a conforming woman of her time and class; but she was passionate by nature and, due to the circumstances of her early life, susceptible to male dominance. During her romance in America, she was for practical purposes unfettered by convention and in open defiance of her minister of religion; in her thirst for knowledge she enjoyed the advanced, even free-thinking views heard in academic and bohemian circles; in later years she knew Henry Havelock Ellis, author of banned books on the psychology of sex, and counted as a close friend that flamboyant free spirit, Olive Schreiner. Yet on balance it is most likely that Emily's strict upbringing, not to mention self-respect, acted as a shield against temptation, and she is entitled to the presumption that she died a maid.

Both Emily and Kitchener were strongly attached to material possessions, though their fortunes differed greatly; for just as Emily was coming to terms with the relative poverty to which the Jackson episode condemned her, Kitchener was being heaped with the first rewards of his glittering career, the parliamentary grants, the presentations of jewel-encrusted swords and caskets, the groaning tables of gold plate.

As there are striking similarities between Kitchener and Emily, so in other respects they were absolute opposites. While he would have been mortally offended to be called an Irishman, she gladly embraced and even exaggerated her Cornishness.

*

Legends grew of Herbert's childhood stoicism. The Kitchener boys played endless games of soldiers and, encouraged by their father, imposed mock field punishments on one another. Herbert was once discovered by his mother uncomplainingly spreadeagled on the lawn under a hot sun, his arms and legs secured to croquet hoops.[viii] Besides three brothers Herbert had one sister, by coincidence christened Emily but always known as Millie. Two years older than Herbert, she was notorious for her bossy nature. Kitchener is generally agreed to have been a shy, lonely, repressed adolescent whose feelings for his dead mother may well have arrested his sexual development. From the start his mother was his model of the ideal woman, and her proper place was on a pedestal. All his life he remained incapable of coping with a woman who descended from that station.

Herbert's father, who retired with the rank of lieutenant-colonel without ever seeing action, was an eccentric martinet, running his household on strict military lines. His habits were said to include sleeping between sheets of newspaper. But whatever the Colonel's oddities he dearly loved his wife, and on being advised in 1863 of her worsening condition of health he immediately sold up the thriving Irish estate and moved his family to the beneficial mountain air of Switzerland. It was at Montreux that Kitchener received his rudimentary education, thus avoiding the English public school experience common to his class and acquiring a perfect command of French into the bargain.

"Aloof and alone, a molten mass of devouring energy and burning ambition": Kitchener with the medals and decorations of his service in Egypt.

There was never any doubt as to his career and at seventeen he was sent to the Royal Military Academy at Woolwich. Though six foot three and ramrod-straight, he was handicapped by indifferent health and bad eyesight – curiously enough this was what gave him the cold, penetrating stare that contemporaries found so unnerving. A thoroughly unpromising cadet in the early days, Herbert performed poorly at exams and, because of the slight cast in his left eye, never learned to shoot straight.

As it happened his first summer vacation was spent not far from the Hobhouse rectory, walking the famous Cornwall beauty spots from the Lizard to Land's End – very fine in their way, he reported to his sister Millie, "but nothing so awfully grand as the Alps". Back at Woolwich, he set about overcoming his disabilities through sheer perseverance, and as a nineteen-year-old cadet-sergeant, during the academy sports day, briefly met the man who would remain the great hero of his life – Charles Gordon, a fellow sapper officer, was already famous as "Chinese Gordon" after masterminding the brilliant campaign that ended the Taiping Rebellion. Nobody dreamt that, twenty-five years on, the names Gordon and Kitchener would be bound together in the annals of Empire by the title "of Khartoum". Like General Gordon, Kitchener was a devout Christian, and strongly drawn to the High Church practices of the Oxford Movement. These would have been distasteful excesses in the eyes of Emily Hobhouse, with her powerful evangelical leanings and lifelong sympathy for Quakerism.

One uncharacteristically rash act nearly finished Kitchener's career. At the outbreak of the Franco-Prussian War in 1870, while on leave in France to visit his father

– Colonel Kitchener had moved there after losing most of the family money in a property speculation in New Zealand – the twenty-year-old Herbert, though a serving British officer, volunteered to fight under the French colours. However, he saw no action before catching pleurisy and pneumonia, and on being invalided home to England was lucky to escape with a reprimand.

A reform of the British Army that came into effect that year was of enormous significance to Kitchener. The purchase system, under which every would-be officer had to buy his commission and pay for each subsequent promotion in rank, was effectively abolished, opening up paths of opportunity for the gifted which had previously been the preserve of wealthy aristocrats. Nor was it to be so great a disadvantage in future to belong to a less fashionable corps like the Royal Engineers.

His first career break came when, as a twenty-three year-old lieutenant, he was appointed aide-de-camp to a general sent to Austria-Hungary as official observer of that year's army manoeuvres. The general falling ill, Kitchener found himself the official representative of Queen Victoria with a seat next to the Emperor Franz Josef himself. Soon after he was in Palestine, mapping the sites of the Holy Land and honing an unexpected talent for dealing with the wily agents of the decaying Ottoman Empire. He became fluent in Arabic and Turkish and, long before the birth of Lawrence of Arabia, habitually wore native robes and passed himself off as an Arab.

The exacting conditions of the Middle East hardened Kitchener physically, as shown by contemporary descriptions of him as "lean as a gutted herring", "active as a panther", and "tanned to the blackness of an Arab complexion". As well as rooting out cruelty and corruption, he earned high praise as a negotiator with local leaders of all faiths. In this he was reacting against what he saw as the wrong-headedness of his fellow countrymen, damning them for coming out "with English ideas in everything and a scorn for native habits or knowledge of the country". The result, he told his sister Millie, was fatal; however good his intentions, the average empire-builder created nothing but chaos.

Between 1878 and 1883 Kitchener was engaged on a trigonometric survey of Cyprus, which had recently come under the British flag.[ix] This was a period of frustration as the job kept him from opportunities to see action and rapid promotion, such as the Zulu War and the Arabi revolt in Egypt. But the posting led to an abiding passion for collecting antiquities and directing archaeological digs– among the lesser known achievements of his life, he founded the Cyprus Museum – and even gave him the leisure to try his hand at journalism. A piece written for *Blackwood's Magazine* in 1879 was uncharacteristic of Kitchener in its lack of gallantry towards the island's women, both Greek and Turkish. "It is rare to see a face even tolerably good looking," he wrote, "and their figures and voices are very objectionable. The Turkish women veil their faces, which is an advantage."

An interesting episode at this time was the presentation by Greek admirers of a dancing bear. Kitchener used to loll in a chair and clap his hands while the animal performed, but one hot evening the bear decided to join its master in the bathtub, then jumped out and dried itself by rolling in his bedclothes. After that the creature was seen no more. Another curious fact is that Kitchener's survey work coincided with the residence in Cyprus of Rimbaud, the French poet – also soldier, explorer, and gunrunner

– who during one of the less colourful spells of his short life found employment in the island's construction trade. After labouring as a quarryman, Arthur Rimbaud was made foreman of the team building the British governor's summer residence in the Troodos mountains, and though no record of a meeting survives the two men's paths must have crossed on numerous occasions. The mind shies from imagining conversations between Kitchener and Rimbaud.

Kitchener was thirty-four, a major in the Egyptian Army, when confronted by the pivotal event of his life. His hero Gordon, then governor-general of Sudan, was besieged in Khartoum by the fanatical Dervish followers of a mystic calling himself el-Mahdi, or the Expected One. The prime minister, Gladstone – who had won the election of 1880 calling for "righteousness" in foreign policy – delayed sanctioning a rescue until cowed by public outcry, with the result that a relieving force, with Kitchener as chief intelligence officer, arrived outside Khartoum the day after Gordon had been speared to death. True to form, Gladstone called off the campaign, leaving most of Sudan to the nightmare rule of the Mahdi.

Returning to England, Kitchener was presented to his sovereign for the first time, and enlisted her as a lifelong ally. Promotions followed with remarkable speed, for though he was commonly credited with greater skill and patience in dealing with Orientals than with his own race, Kitchener learned how to cultivate the most important personages of all, among them the Queen and the Conservative leader Lord Salisbury. By 1886 he was governor-general of Eastern Sudan, consolidating his reputation for skilful handling of local chiefs by encouraging an anti-Mahdist league. For though the Mahdi himself survived General Gordon by only a few months, his sway had been extended by a successor known as the Khalifa.

Attacking a Dervish force the following year, Kitchener was badly wounded – a bullet lodged near his windpipe and threatened to choke him until he swallowed it – and his hugely enhanced status was underlined when Queen Victoria telegraphed to ask about his condition. In another striking move, the sovereign personally insisted on his appointment as one of her aides-de-camp. By the age of forty-one he was a brigadier-general with the title of Sirdar – commander-in-chief – and in the year that Maud Hobhouse's marriage left Emily alone at St Ive Rectory, his cavalry inflicted huge losses on a Dervish army, thereby foiling an invasion of Egypt.

The path of Kitchener's career would have been familiar to Emily from her breakfast-table readings of *The Times*. England had taken Kitchener to her heart, though the great man remained ambivalent regarding the press that made him famous. His private view of newspapermen was probably best summed up by an outburst to a group clustering outside his tent – "Get out of my way, you drunken swabs" – but he was by no means insensitive to their usefulness to a career soldier, and would write home suggesting the leaking of tit-bits of information about his doings.

Six years passed before the Sirdar was allowed to initiate a campaign to avenge Gordon, and his preparations encompassed the same time-span as Emily's American adventure. While the novice missionary was experiencing the depths of winter in Minnesota, Kitchener – now Sir Herbert – began his famous advance along the Nile, and Emily was on the point of her fateful departure for Mexico by the time he crushed a vast Dervish force at the Battle of Dongola. Back in Chelsea, fiancé and fortune lost,

Emily would have heard the newsboys crying Kitchener's victory at Omdurman that broke the Dervish power for good. Omdurman was a vaulting success. An overjoyed Queen Victoria decided not only to reward her favourite general with a peerage, but as an exceptional honour to tell him so by personal telegram. A grateful parliament voted him £30,000.

A telling foible is revealed by the hero's reaction when told of the peerage. His wish was to assume the title Lord Khartoum, he earnestly confided to a friend, thus ridding himself of his horrible surname. And indeed, shorn of associations with the man himself, a less aristocratic handle would be hard to imagine. But it was firmly explained to him that the public would refuse to be robbed of a name that had become the pride of the Empire – Kitchener he must remain, with the Khartoum tagged on. And the public's instinct was right. As pointed out by one admirer, the title Kitchener of Khartoum "rolls like a whole corps of drums".[x]

Praise for the Omdurman campaign was not universal. Kitchener was condemned by several influential figures including Winston Churchill for dynamiting the Mahdi's tomb to prevent it becoming a shrine, and to the end of his days he was dogged by a story that he had made the Mahdi's skull into an inkpot. Radicals at home, among them the circle to which Emily would gravitate, decried the slaughter of spear-throwing tribesmen by machinegun and artillery, and some even believed claims that Kitchener had ordered the killing of wounded prisoners. But while the *Manchester Guardian* kept up vigorous attacks on the Sirdar, the bulk of the press and an overwhelming majority of Britons offered "K of K" nothing short of veneration.

Kitchener entered Khartoum on September 2, 1898, and the following day attended a memorial service for Gordon at the place he had fallen. Those present witnessed what was touted as the unprecedented spectacle of Kitchener in tears, though he had also been seen to weep at the burial of British dead after an earlier battle – "he was very human for at least a quarter of an hour," as one of his officers put it. In fact, Kitchener-in-tears sightings were to be noted regularly through the years.

Within days of the victory Kitchener left Khartoum under secret orders from Lord Salisbury to confront a small French expeditionary force that had raised the *tricolore* over a fort overlooking the White Nile – a deliberate act of provocation in what Britain saw as a vital sphere of influence. Kitchener's cool defusing of what became known as the Fashoda Crisis earned warm gratitude from the prime minister, who had feared war with France over the issue.

*

All who knew Kitchener recognised him as an extraordinary phenomenon, but some of those close to him figured amongst his bitterest critics. Kitchener's second-in-command on the march to Khartoum, Major-General Archie Hunter, wrote to his brother: "He is inhuman, heartless, with eccentric and freakish bursts of generosity specially when he is defeated: he is a vain egotistical and self-confident mass of pride and ambition, expecting and usurping all and giving nothing: he is a mixture of the fox, Jew and snake and like all bullies is a dove when tackled." Yet the writer of this diatribe became a devoted admirer, serving Kitchener with distinction in the Boer War and choosing him as best man when he married.

A man who famously regarded himself as a most superior person, Lord Curzon, later recorded in similar terms that Kitchener stood "aloof and alone, a molten mass of devouring energy and burning ambition". Another memorable observation comes down from Lord Edward Cecil, a son of Lord Salisbury, who acted as Kitchener's aide-de-camp in the Sudan: "His cynicism was in a large measure a part of the curious shyness which declined to show any inside portion of his life or mind. He loathed any form of moral or mental undressing. He was even morbidly afraid of showing any feeling or enthusiasm, and he preferred to be misunderstood rather than be suspected of human feeling."

Kitchener endeared himself to politicians by his gift – a rare one in a general – for achieving results while exercising extreme economy. The bill for his great Nile campaign came in at a bargain £800,000. His great effectiveness as a soldier lay in taking infinite pains over detail and in his determination not simply to defeat an irreconcilable enemy, but to annihilate him. It was no surprise that on elevation to the peerage he chose as his motto the single word *Thorough*. One of the century's leading military thinkers, Helmuth von Moltke, called Kitchener's Nile expedition the best-organised army operation of its time. Such plaudits were at odds with the forecast of Kitchener's own father that he would never scale the peak of his profession, since great generals were always short men like Napoleon and Roberts.

Like Emily, Kitchener led an intensely lonely life but the notion that he was homosexual is a posthumous invention, supported by no contemporary evidence and believed by no one who knew him in his lifetime, even amongst the host of enemies in government and military circles.[xi] Even so, the idea struck a chord with later generations that had no conception how a soldier of Kitchener's time could see himself as married to his profession, or how anyone professing to live his life "sober, upright and chaste" could be anything but a canting hypocrite. So today the "fact" of his homosexuality is routinely peddled, the key points of evidence being his bachelor status, his habit of surrounding himself with young men as staff officers – though a choice of elderly staff officers would have been more remarkable – and his liking for flowers and porcelain.

A matter of record is his horrified incomprehension when a fellow officer in India was accused of sodomy with native boys – "What a horrible thing this has been about Macdonald," he exclaimed. "I expect he went quite mad." If the charges against the man were proved, he told the Viceroy, he would like to see the brute shot. Kitchener's latest biographer has painstakingly sifted all available material and found no case to answer, pointing out that any hint of homosexuality would have been impossible to suppress in the oriental countries where Kitchener served.

The idea is further contradicted by his dealings with women. The memory of his mother was an inescapable influence, with a fellow officer in Egypt, quoted in one of the earliest biographies, remarking that his taste in womankind tended to the "motherly and unsmart". His older sister Millie, a very severe-looking lady, appears to have discouraged dalliances on his part, so may well have inspired Kitchener's known aversion to "a managing woman".

Though army officers of the period were strongly discouraged from marrying early, he was known to enjoy flirtations from his cadet days and there is a body of evidence that at the age of thirty-four, in Cairo, he fell in love with and proposed to an eighteen-year-old beauty called Hermione Baker. The problem was her father, a disgraced former British officer then serving in the Egyptian Army. Valentine Baker had been cashiered from the British service and jailed for a sexual assault on a young woman in a railway carriage. This hardly made him ideal father-in-law material for an ambitious soldier – if there is unanimity among contemporaries about any aspect of Kitchener's character, it is that his ambition was unbridled – and only a man in the grip of an intense passion would have pursued the suit.

It came to be accepted that the couple would marry as soon as circumstances permitted but only months later Hermione was dead of typhoid fever. Her sister, later Lady Carden, said long afterwards that Kitchener always wore a locket containing a miniature of Hermione under his shirt, but was to leave it behind for safekeeping with her family before embarking on the sea journey that claimed his life in 1916.

Among other claims of romantic attachments is one that the newly ennobled Kitchener, hopeful of founding a dynasty, made a spurned proposal of marriage to Lady Helen Vane-Tempest-Stewart, daughter of the hugely rich Marquis of Londonderry. Indeed it was not until Kitchener was raised in the peerage to a viscountcy, at the age of fifty-two, that it occurred to him to ask if the title could pass through the line of one of his brothers – two were distinguished soldiers in their own right – in the event he himself remained unmarried and childless.

His friend Lord Cranborne, Salisbury's heir, characterised his attitude to women as "a chivalry of mind belonging to a bygone age which placed them on a pedestal" and recalled Kitchener's resentment at "some note of coarse disrespect where he considered there should only be reverence". Lord Edward Cecil acted on the same thought when, at the peak of public adulation for the victor of Omdurman, he secretly burnt a cascade of love-letters from female admirers which he felt the chief, with his exalted ideas of women, would find deeply offensive. Alfred Milner, with whom Kitchener was to struggle for mastery in South Africa, never lost personal respect for his rival, and singled out his "appreciation of good women" as one of his most interesting characteristics. Curzon, later his rival for supreme power in India, believed that Kitchener was half in love with Lady Curzon, while others were convinced Lady Curzon was in love with him, and she herself wanted him to marry her sister.

Nothing speaks more eloquently of Kitchener's moral scruples than the printed letter he was later to have distributed to every man in his command in India. Warning of the dangers of contracting venereal disease, he wrote: "Remember the better influences of life. What would your mothers, your sisters, and your friends at home think of you if they saw you in hospital, degraded by this cause?" And many years on, when the British Expeditionary Force set out for France, every soldier would carry a personal message from the field marshal pasted into his pay book: "In this new experience you may find temptations both in wine and women. You must entirely resist both temptations, and while treating all women with perfect courtesy, you should avoid any intimacy."

*

Throughout his life Kitchener suffered fits of depression as severe as Emily's. Despite a long habit of concealment, his inner turmoil burst out on occasion, as when he wrote to a friend in Cairo soon after the Diamond Jubilee celebrations of 1897 to complain of constant anxiety, worry and strain, adding: "I do not think I can stand much more, and I feel so completely done up that I can hardly go on and wish I were dead." Few of the worshipping public of his heyday could have dreamt of their hero's recurring attacks of nerves. Yet even in 1914, on the eve of the supreme challenge of his life, he would totter on the brink of a complete nervous collapse known only to a handful of intimates like Lord Edward Cecil. That hidden anguish was the price exacted for preferring to be misunderstood rather than show human feeling.

This then was the extraordinarily complex man destined to become Emily Hobhouse's great adversary. On the outside utterly confident, inwardly racked by self-doubt, Herbert Kitchener landed in Cape Town on January 10, 1900, as the British Army was reeling from the disasters of Black Week.

6 "A STORM OF ABUSE"

By the time they landed in South Africa, Kitchener had helped Roberts to devise a strategy that would almost immediately turn the course of the war in Britain's favour. Yet before General Buller could be released from overall command, he blundered into yet another trap during an unsuccessful attempt to relieve Ladysmith. After the Battle of Spion Kop on January 24, 1900, the British counted nearly eighteen hundred casualties compared with enemy losses of three hundred – "a sickening fiasco," admitted Joseph Chamberlain – leading to fears of armed rebellion in the Cape itself. But the days of great Boer victories were nearly over.

In early February Roberts and Kitchener secretly massed a great force some six hundred miles north of Cape Town, catching the Boer leader General Cronje off guard on the banks of the Modder River. Even as the trapped Boers waited for the British onslaught, Cecil Rhodes's Kimberley was relieved on February 15. With Roberts ill, Kitchener took overall command and launched a furious attack that caused massive loss of life on both sides but ended in Cronje's surrender with four thousand men. The battle of Paardeberg, the first British victory of the war, was the more welcome for being won on the anniversary of the disaster of Majuba.[xii] Within a fortnight the siege of Ladysmith was lifted and Roberts marched into the Orange Free State capital of Bloemfontein on March 13. The Boers appeared on the verge of total defeat.

After enduring the humiliations of Black Week and Spion Kop, England went wild with relief. Crowds erupted dancing onto the pavements at the news of each Boer reverse. The celebrations which so disgusted Emily Hobhouse reached their climax on May 18 with the relief of Mafeking, where a resolute defence had made a national hero of the commander, Colonel Robert Baden-Powell. "The populace poured into the streets of London and in mad exultation over the taking and relief of that tiny village indulged in all kinds of licence and buffoonery," wrote Emily. "A leading feature of the proceedings was the tickling with feathers; numbers armed themselves with peacock feathers for that purpose, insolently tickling the faces of passers-by, and obliging self-respecting citizens to remain within doors."

Divisions within the Liberal Party cut deeper than ever, while the new leader Sir Henry Campbell-Bannerman sat on the fence. In this fraught atmosphere Emily came up with the idea of a women's protest meeting against the war. Many Liberals longed to protest, she believed, and women should take the lead. The brainwave came at a London dinner-party hosted by Leonard Courtney's sister, at which Britain's proposed annexation of the Boer republics was roundly deplored. To Emily's delight she won the support of Mr Courtney: "Thus backed, I carried the idea to our next women's committee and urged it there with success."

*

The date fixed was June 13. Emily resolved to do things on a grand scale and booked one of London's best-known public venues, the Queen's Hall. From then on the flat in Rossetti Mansions was the nerve-centre of the campaign. With the help of a friend, Emily laboured daily for six weeks to rally support, starting at eight in the morning and working through till eleven at night. The result was "a magnificent assemblage of women" from across England, with a strong contingent from the Women's Liberal Foundation – by luck, this body was holding a London conference around the same time. As Emily later told Isabella Steyn, wife of the Orange Free State's wartime president, the protest was only partly to express sympathy over the threat to Boer independence. It was, she explained in the high-flown language now becoming second nature, "more largely due to our proud desire for England's Honour and our horror lest her Rectitude be marred by an unjust act".

The women's meeting provoked immense opposition with a jingoist press excelling itself in "virulence and inaccuracy", as Emily saw it. Chalked graffiti appeared below the windows of her flat – "there are folk in all populations," she remarked, "idle enough for such stupidities and foolish enough to imagine they could have any deterrent effect" – and a letter arrived from the landlord's lawyer demanding that she stop issuing campaign material as it constituted an infringement of the terms of her lease. Emily retorted that the relevant clause prohibited business circulars as distinct from those of a charitable intent, and carried on as before. The incident was just one more instance of "the pinpricks to which pacifists were continually subjected".

Held in the immediate aftermath of the fall of Pretoria, her ticket-only meeting drew between three and four thousand women and two men. These were the Queen's Hall organist and Mr Courtney, the latter lurking excitedly behind the curtain. This precaution Emily felt to be necessary: "There was the strict prohibition of men and, besides, Mrs Courtney was nervous and did not wish him to be present fearing lest there should be disturbances." Always nervous of platform appearances, Emily was further distracted on catching sight of her mentor's bald head poking out of the red curtain just as she launched into her speech.

The meeting blamed the war on government policy, protested against attempts to silence critics, and passed a resolution condemning "any settlement which involves the extinction by force of the two republics". It fell to Emily as organiser to propose the final resolution, "that this meeting desires to express its sympathy with the women of the Transvaal and Orange Free State, and begs them to remember that thousands of Englishwomen are filled with profound sorrow at the thought of their sufferings, and with deep regret for the action of their own government". The wording chimed exactly with Emily's personal feelings and was to form the keynote of her thoughts and actions for years to come.

Predictably, the reaction of hostile newspapers "made it almost impossible to give Truth even a bare chance" and instilled in Emily a lifelong contempt for press opinion. And though stung by criticism that the meeting was useless in practical terms, Emily took comfort from Mr Courtney's view that even when nothing concrete could be achieved, it was always worth registering a protest against injustice. Writing to her brother Leonard, she suggested hopefully that many sympathisers were silent for fear of having their windows broken and "we shall sweep them in with the turn of the tide".

Her next step was to speak against the war all over England.

*

There was now no turning back from a course that would cost Emily dear. The life-changing moment came soon after the Queen's Hall meeting when she travelled back to Cornwall with the radical young Welsh MP David Lloyd George, who vied with Mr Courtney as the Liberals' most outspoken critic of the war.

The Conservative government had sought to capitalise on public euphoria over the Kitchener-Roberts successes in South Africa by calling what would become known as the Khaki Election, and Emily hoped to strengthen Courtney's chances of retaining his seat by promoting the anti-war cause. But if she was counting on the reputation of the Cornish for independent thinking, she made a serious miscalculation. The tone of the national debate had been set by Chamberlain's slogan "To vote for a Liberal is to vote for the Boer", and Emily's open meeting in the Public Hall at Liskeard was to show all too plainly how few in the East Cornwall constituency were ready for her message.

The headlines in the *Cornish Times* of July 7 sum up the disastrous outcome: *Uproarious Proceedings... Speakers Refused a Hearing... Platform Stormed... Meeting Broken up in Disorder.*

The evening began with a noisy reception for the chairman, the distinguished Cornish writer Arthur Quiller-Couch, with the *Cornish Times* reporter managing to catch only the odd sentence from the platform between prolonged bouts of booing and stamping. And it has to be said that Emily's lecturing manner – very much *de haut, en bas* – can only have infuriated the hostile elements of the audience, and perhaps antagonised the undecided. Having begun by remarking that if the Queen were present, she would be heartily ashamed of her Cornish subjects, Emily declared over the resulting uproar that it was a strange thing that Cornishmen would not listen to a Cornish woman. The report goes on:

> I have addressed meetings lately," she continued after two or three minutes' interval, "all over England – in Leicester, Leeds, Bradford, Liverpool and Manchester – but it has remained for me to come to Cornwall to see the worst behaviour of all. I am quite sure that is not the best of the Cornish people –" (hear, hear from the platform). "It is only a few thoughtless and foolish spirits –" (derisive laughter and hoots, and a deep voice from the back of the hall shouted "How do you find 'em in London?". Stamping of feet again ensued, and "Trelawny" was hoarsely voiced. Miss Hobhouse, when she was permitted, thanked the audience for having sung to her the old ballad of her family, but she had heard quite enough of it.

Emily struggled bravely on, but ineffectually:

> "Trelawny" and "Soldiers of the Queen" were again shouted and when this was done, Miss Hobhouse indignantly exclaimed, making her voice heard above the din, "It seems strange that the people of Liskeard should allow a few thoughtless and ill-mannered boys to spoil a meeting –" (disorder). "But this kind of behaviour," she

continued under great difficulty, "will do more to advance our cause than the most eloquent speeches we could deliver. The account of this meeting will be printed far and wide through England, and Cornish people will be held up to shame because they would not give a fair hearing, especially to a lady, on this most complicated question –" (uproar).

Matters went from bad to worse. "Round about the platform," Emily remembered later, "were thronging friends from my childhood, people who had walked in from St Ive to see and hear me once more. Their tears fell as the mob of roughs howled us down." Emily's prim reproof to the audience that "manners maketh man" met with derisive laughter, and further efforts to speak were drowned out by cheers for the generals at the front, for Mr Chamberlain and Tommy Atkins, while raucous singing of *God Save the Queen* and *Rule Britannia* continued. Four burly policemen took up positions near the main entrance and order was temporarily restored. But the reception for Emily was mild compared to that for Lloyd George. As he rose to speak, the meeting erupted into a riot:

The Hon. Member, as he came forward, was greeted with hoots, cheers, catcalls, shrill whistles, and booing, followed by "Soldiers of the Queen". The crowd was evidently getting dangerously excited, and many more ladies left the hall... while Mr Lloyd George stood smiling at the table, but did not attempt to utter a syllable. It was perfectly evident that the crowd would not hear the Welsh MP at any price. Then came the culmination of the disorder.

About fifty young men, many bearing Union Jacks, stormed the platform singing *Britons Never Shall be Slaves* and set up a barricade of chairs. A khaki-clad local in the audience, a private of the Duke of Cornwall's Light Infantry, was hoisted shoulder-high and carried around the hall in triumph to blasts from a bicycle horn and a tin trumpet.

The proceedings might still have passed off without violence, according to the *Cornish Times*, had not Mr Lloyd George and a clerical member of the platform party attempted to remove the barricade of chairs. In a moment they were surrounded and rudely hustled till they retreated again. This further inflamed the crowd, and when some of the other pro-Boers on the platform made a further attempt to pull away the barrier, an ugly rush was made at them. On both sides the chairs were thrown in all directions and as the two parties got within arm's-reach several blows were struck.

At this point the police intervened. Emily, Quiller-Couch and Lloyd George were persuaded to leave the hall, and the crowd formed a lane and allowed them to leave unmolested, with cheers for Lord Roberts ringing in their ears. The mob remained in possession of the platform and for a quarter of an hour longer continued to amuse itself with shouting, singing and horseplay.

Quiller-Couch said later he had been passed a note on the platform saying someone had a gun and intended to shoot Lloyd George. One of the young rowdies – a local solicitor's son, later to become Major-General Sir Wyndham Childs – remembered a less drastic but botched plan to seize the Welsh MP and duck him in a cattle-trough. As soon as the mob made its rush, according to Childs's version, "Mr Lloyd George disappeared through the door leading to the platform, but Miss Hobhouse stood guard over the door, so naturally there was nothing more to be done".

An older and wiser Emily lamented: "How little they dreamed, those passion-blinded people of Liskeard, that the man they would not hear would one day lead the country." But the intensity of feeling against the future prime minister and war leader was not confined to Cornwall. Not long after this, rashly accepting an invitation to speak in Chamberlain's Birmingham, Lloyd George sparked a major riot in which a youth was killed while he himself had to be smuggled out of the building disguised as a policeman.

Figures like Lloyd George and Leonard Courtney were in Lord Salisbury's mind when he complained: "England is, I believe, the only country in which, during a great war, eminent men write and speak publicly as if they belonged to the enemy." He might have added eminent women too, for Emily wrote later that the Liskeard meeting, together with others at which she spoke that summer, "were followed by a storm of abuse from relatives and acquaintances, some of whom even attacked me in the press. I lost the majority of the friends of my girlhood and it was a great loss."

It came as a tremendous shock to Emily to be on the receiving end of such treatment in the county of her birth, not only from those of her own class but from the kind of people who could normally be expected to doff their caps. The withdrawal of that automatic respect she had enjoyed all her life – as a lady, as daughter of the rectory, as a Trelawny – was perhaps the most painful sacrifice ever demanded of Emily. She learned to live without that respect, but it was a loss that always hurt. Though compensation was to come in new friendships with those of like mind, she would reflect in old age, "yet these later ones lack some precious qualities that seem to belong only to the ties made in youth".

*

Emily's efforts on behalf of another leading pro-Boer politician met with greater success. John Burns, a firebrand radical, fought Battersea at the Khaki Election with Emily as one of his electioneering helpers, and topped the poll despite loudly proclaiming the Boers to be morally the superior side.

The connection with Burns was a gift to future critics, and went a long way toward explaining why Emily's protests that she had no political axe to grind would be treated with derision by any Conservative administration. Burns had been goaled for sedition in the Golden Jubilee year of 1887 for leading a violent disturbance in Trafalgar Square. This, the original "Bloody Sunday", was a march of radicals and socialists broken up by mounted police and soldiers at a cost of two demonstrators dead and seventy-seven police injured. Once an MP, John Burns went on to distinguish himself as the first working-class cabinet minister, though his vehement denunciations of South Africa's Jewish capitalists make uneasy reading today, and serve as a reminder that in the febrile atmosphere of the times the pro-Boer stance was repeatedly linked with anti-Semitism.

For Mr Courtney, however, the days in his beloved House of Commons were over. The writing had been on the wall since Kruger's ultimatum, when the unbending Cornishman had harangued his local Liberal party – "for an hour and a half," as a sorrowful Kate Courtney wrote in her diary, "without recourse to a note, full of argument, reason, passion, and pathos" – on why it was wrong to fight the Boers. The response of the constituency committee was formally to withdraw support for Courtney, and days before the dissolution of parliament a Liverpool alderman was chosen to stand as "a *bona fide* Liberal".

7 "THE WALLS OF JERICHO WOULD FALL"

The Khaki Election of October 1900 saw the Conservative Unionists returned with their majority increased, though by a mere six seats. Chamberlain, taking his cue from Lord Roberts, declared the Boers beaten. With the fall of his capital Kruger had fled into exile, never to return, taking with him to Holland a war-chest of Boer gold – the so-called "Kruger Millions" which remain untraced to the present day – and the demoralised Boer leaders sounded out Roberts about terms of surrender. Then an unexpected success stiffened the doubters. A small force under Christian de Wet, the most charismatic of the Boer generals, severed communications between Bloemfontein and Pretoria, and the revival of Boer fortunes fed Liberal claims that the Tories had won the election under false pretences.

Kitchener knew the Boers were far from finished. He knew their well-armed bands of commandos could still strike where and when they chose, and melt away into the veld; as he cried out in frustration, they would not *stand and fight*. The new Boer leadership pinned hopes on an intervention from one of Britain's rival powers, especially the Kaiser's Germany, or on a change of heart in Britain brought about by the pro-Boer agitators – Milner, writing secretly to Chamberlain, said the only thing he really feared was a "wobble" in public opinion at home.

This was never a real danger. The Liberal Party itself remained so hopelessly divided that a debate on the war in July saw thirty-one Liberals voting with the government, forty against, while the thirty-five abstainers included the leader Campbell-Bannerman. Even the Fabian Society was split down the middle, with George Bernard Shaw remarking that when he thought about Kruger, "to my great embarrassment I found myself on the side of the mob". As he observed ruefully, it was astonishing what bad company advanced views may get one into.

Beatrice Webb dismissed the entire war as "an underbred business" waged by the "flashy" Milner and the "vulgarly provocative" Chamberlain against a remnant of 17th Century Puritanism, and pointed out that neither Boer nor Briton seemed to remember that the whites struggling for power in South Africa were a tiny number "amid a vast majority of Kaffirs". Privately she noted in her diary that "the Boers are, man for man, our superiors in dignity, devotion and capacity" – a sentiment that Emily might well have blurted out in an unguarded moment.

*

Kitchener assumed overall military command in November. As Roberts arrived home to tumultuous applause and magnificent rewards – an earldom and garter bestowed by the Queen, £100,000 voted by parliament – the new chief set about prosecuting the war with ruthless efficiency. In his dealings with enemy leaders Kitchener was always more inclined to conciliation than his popular reputation might suggest, and it was Milner who, spurning the general's advice, urged the government to insist on unconditional surrender. There was a particular reason why Kitchener was in a hurry to make terms. He now had hopes of the Indian command, one of the greatest plums that could fall to a British soldier – but only if he could finish the war in South Africa in time to succeed the outgoing commander-in-chief.

There lay the rub. It was "a horrid war", mused Kitchener, with no straight fighting, and he did not see how it could be ended except by utter exhaustion on the part of the Boers. Thousands of determined commandos remained on the veld, ambushing British troops and wrecking communication lines – among them the former state attorney Jan Smuts, now a seasoned general with a price of £1,000 on his head, who carried a Greek Testament and Kant's *Critique of Pure Reason* in his saddlebag.

Kitchener's considered response to the enemy's hit-and-run tactics was to cover the country with a network of blockhouses – mini-forts made of corrugated iron – linked by lines of barbed wire. The first blockhouse appeared early in 1901 and by the end of the war over eight thousand would be erected. Once having penned the Boer commandos into definable areas, Kitchener planned to give his cavalry the role of beaters on a grouse shoot. The comparison was an apt one since thousands of the reinforcements now pouring into South Africa were volunteers from the hunting and shooting fraternity in England, men who matched the enemy in riding skills and marksmanship. At the same time he decided to continue the policy introduced by Roberts – and initially opposed by Kitchener himself – of torching any farm on which commandos depended for shelter and supplies. With their crops destroyed and livestock driven off or killed, he reasoned, the Boers would finally be starved into submission.

As the numbers of refugees from the burnt farms increased, so did the camps to house them. Under Roberts's command around ten had been set up; within four months of the Kitchener takeover there were twenty-seven and by the end of the war forty-six.

*

The farm-burnings are central to Emily's story and must be examined in some detail as they led directly to the concentration camp horrors. Though isolated cases occurred as early as November 1899, the burnings did not become a settled policy until some months later. The first farms to be deliberately targeted were in the Orange Free State – after the annexation of the smaller Boer republic the following May, it was the British view that any Free Stater in arms against the Crown counted as a rebel, so between June and November over six hundred farmhouses were destroyed on Roberts's orders. One of the first farms to go up in flames was that of Christian de Wet, whose exploits had scotched an early British victory. The fugitive general remarked that his house had cost him a few hundreds to build but its destruction would cost the British taxpayer millions, and his words were prophetic.

It is an irony that the genesis of the concentration camps can be traced to an incident during the summer offensive of 1900 when Roberts packed off several thousand Boer women and children refugees towards the enemy lines, an action which drew an indignant protest from the opposing general, Louis Botha. The truth was that neither

The farm-burnings were initiated by Lord Roberts to starve the Boers into submission. More than thirty thousand went up in flames.

side wanted responsibility for feeding extra mouths, and the Boers saw no contradiction in demanding that their families be well fed and sheltered by an enemy whose supplies were constantly disrupted by Boer attack. Yet more than any direct act of war, the camps would leave the losing side with bitter memories of the conflict, while among the British public would be a large minority who remained unconvinced by the official line that internment was a misunderstood act of humanity or even chivalry.

The first refugee camps or "government laagers" set up were not meant for those made homeless by the farm-burnings, but for displaced loyalists and disillusioned Boers who had answered Roberts's call to lay down their arms. These so-called "hands-uppers" now stood in danger of reprisals from the "bitter-enders", since the outlawed Free State president, Marthinus Steyn, had ordered the shooting of all who took the "oath of neutrality". In August, Roberts countered with a proclamation containing a specific threat to raze any farm found to be harbouring the enemy, and at this time Kitchener seems to have been a lone voice among the generals in opposing the policy. Others, like Lord Methuen, agreed that the best way to deal with the Boer was not to rush about the country in his wake but to destroy the farms that succoured him – in effect, to lay waste to the country.

The war diary of the improbably named Major John Pine-Coffin, an Old Etonian squire who went off to fight the Boers in 1900, offers a remarkable insight into the mentality of one officer involved in the burnings and the subsequent rounding-up of homeless families. Laconic entries in the journal such as "very hot", "very cold" or "had some niggers flogged" are interspersed with jottings on cures for equine ailments, records of Pine-Coffin's consumption of whisky and cigars, and the tally of shooting expeditions on the veld, in which familiar names like partridge and widgeon alternate with wildebeest and ostrich. His bag of Boers is also carefully noted.

On October 31 Pine-Coffin wrote: "Any amount of women and children came in late at night, they had to sleep in open cattle trucks"; then on November 1: "Ventersburg Town was burnt today. All refugees sent off". The entry for November 7 reads "Nothing much happened. Still sending the Dutch off", but adds that General Botha had sent in a letter under a flag of truce: "It said he did not wish to feed his own women and children. I said I did not intend to do so." Yet Pine-Coffin is clearly uneasy in his mind, and on November 28 wrote of rowing with his superior officer over the feeding of refugees. "Suppose he wishes them to die of starvation," notes the major disapprovingly.[xiii]

The Boers claimed the scorched earth policy contravened the Hague Convention recently signed by Britain, and were in turn accused by the British of ignoring the conventions of war. Roberts protested at the wholesale

The Free State's fugitive President Steyn was hailed as "the soul of the war" after the flight of Kruger.

expulsion of loyalists from their homes during the invasion of Cape Colony, and there were repeated recriminations over the Boer use of expanding "dum-dum" bullets and alleged abuses of the white flag.

*

Emily Hobhouse made the acquaintance of her first real live Boers that July. A small deputation of Cape Colony elders had travelled out to England to explain the cause of their republican kinfolk to any sympathetic hearers, and something about these grave old men appealed to Emily's romantic streak. Most deeply impressive was the deputation leader, one Professor de Vos of the Dutch Reformed Church, who with his "saintly bearing and old-world dignity" resembled some prophet of old. Emily immediately bundled De Vos into a cab and rushed him over to Aunt Mary's in Mayfair to meet the Hobhouse circle. Speaking with eyes closed and hands folded as if in prayer, the professor "seemed to have stepped out of the Old Testament into our garish modern life". Alas, though Emily booked halls throughout the country in order that the Boers might state their case to the British public, the British public did not wish to hear it. Emily could only shake her head in disbelief over her countrymen's "lack of desire even to listen to facts".

An account of farm-burning appeared in the *Manchester Guardian* as early as May 1900 but not until September did detailed descriptions of harrowing scenes – many written to local papers by ordinary soldiers involved in the destruction – begin to cause widespread concern. Lord Roberts had something of a reputation for incinerating civilian homes, as Emily tartly pointed out, and she thought it a great irony that Chamberlain, the very man who was now colonial secretary, had signed a petition against the burnings carried out during Roberts's Afghan campaign; though of course that had been long ago "in Mr Chamberlain's radical days". Chamberlain in turn claimed that the South African war was now being prolonged because the enemy's hopes were kept alive by pro-Boers like Emily.

As the months dragged on Kitchener's sweeps brought in ever-increasing numbers of homeless Boer women and children who were concentrated in facilities modelled on Roberts's laagers – at that time the term concentration camp, freely used by Kitchener and others, carried none of the connotations it would acquire during the Nazi era, when Hitler's henchmen gleefully parried protests over the death-camps by declaring that the concentration camp was a British invention.[xiv] Overcrowding in the camps led to epidemic diseases – dysentery, typhoid and child-killers like diphtheria – which swiftly overwhelmed the few available doctors and nurses from the Royal Army Medical Corps. Supplies of food, medicine, and fuel were hopelessly short and the army bell-tents unsuited to families used to life on the open veld. The death toll in the camps began to mount.

New arrivals at a concentration camp guard their few possessions in the long queue for a tent.

The refugees were a source of great irritation to the new commander-in-chief. Kitchener complained repeatedly that it was the Boer women who were dragging out the war, and harboured far greater bitterness against the British than their menfolk. As early as December he formulated a plan to deport the worst of the "female irreconcilables" abroad along with the captive fighting men – now dispersed in prison camps as far away as the West Indies – though the move was blocked by a jittery cabinet. In Kitchener's eyes the wretched state of affairs developing in the camps was the women's own fault. As he wrote home to his friend Lady Cranborne, "the doctor's reports of the dirt and filth that these boer ladies revel in are very unpleasant reading". In any case, he added, they would be far worse off in their own homes, or subjected to the kind of conditions suffered by the British refugees in Boer hands.

To Emily's mind, only a minority who followed the events in South Africa had any conception of the plight of the women and children. The burnings described by the soldiers' letters in the press – "which, to their honour, they for the most part evidently found distressing" – was turning into an obsession: "Thus the constantly renewed picture of women and children homeless, desperate and distressed, formed and fixed itself in my mind and never once left me," she would write many years later. "The thought deepened to torture and by a kind of second-sight such as had often visited me in my life the whole became a vision of vivid reality wherein I saw myself amongst the sufferers bearing relief. I never doubted then that I should go."

Second sight, a vivid vision, a mission to relieve sufferers – Emily's words summon the image of Joan of Arc whose story had enthralled the little Hobhouse sisters in the Cornish rectory schoolroom. To recall the words of Maud's essay: "She could not get their miseries out of her thoughts, and they so worked on her mind and her imagination that at last she really believed herself called by God to be the saviour of her people".

*

Back in London after a visit to Lord and Lady Hobhouse's country house, Emily was seized by "a curious and most solemn feeling" that resolved itself into a plan of action. But first the idea must be subjected to that infallible litmus test, Mr Courtney. Hurrying round to Cheyne Walk early next morning, allowing the sage no time to finish his breakfast, Emily opened up her heart: "He let me expound my ideas to him and my desire to open a public fund for the burnt-out women and children. He demurred at first… he rose from his chair and paced the room as he so often did when considering a matter; then went and stood before the window looking out into their charming little garden where the autumn tints were already glowing in the sunshine."

One by one he marshalled the objections. Who would distribute the fund and how? Would the military allow it? Emily answered point by point and at last Mr Courtney, "if somewhat constrained and dubious", consented to the launch of a public fund. For the moment that was all Emily wanted, and she went off buoyed with the feeling "that in like manner all the walls of Jericho would fall".

Lord and Lady Hobhouse in Mayfair were next, and at first they seemed wholly in sympathy. Aunt Mary, a string-puller *par excellence*, volunteered to join the committee. Personal letters were fired off to dozens of leading figures, among them Lord Lansdowne, secretary of state for war, and even Mr Chamberlain himself. So thanks to her aunt's foresight Emily was later able to claim backing from the heart of government – indeed from the very men whom she was cheerfully blackguarding behind their backs as the architects of the war.

Both Chamberlain and Lansdowne grudgingly promised to write to Milner in Cape Town in support of Emily's scheme, but since the fund was presented to them as "purely benevolent, non-political, non-sectarian, national", and having as its object "to feed, clothe, shelter and rescue women and children, Boer, British or others", it would have been difficult to do otherwise. Others were made of sterner stuff, and Emily never lost a sense of outrage over the refusal of peers and even a bishop to subscribe to her charity, now officially named the South African Women and Children Distress Fund.

"It was quite an education," she remarked of her fund-raising efforts among the pillars of society, and the experience "modified adversely my too idealistic view of human nature". Indeed, "the chilling attitude of some accounted most saintly, the lack of imagination in others whose known gifts presupposed imagination, the fear of those with big reputations lest those should be marred" – all left an indelible impression on her mind. But others responded generously, and contributions rolled in from every part of the land.

As yet Emily had allowed Lord and Lady Hobhouse to think of her simply as the organiser of the fund, and now she had to break the news that she intended to go out to South Africa herself. It was the moment of collision between Emily, dutiful Victorian lady, and Emily, independent woman of the modern age. As she recalled the scene over twenty years later, "I yet did not feel justified in pursuing my long-nourished plan without the full acquiescence of my kind Aunt and Uncle. To obtain that was the hardest part of the enterprise. This cannot be realised by girls of the present day; to understand all that is to turn back to the ideas of the 19ᵗʰ Century, already so antiquated."

Nervously, she pressed her case with the doubting pair, explaining "the depth of determination which for months had been growing in me", but despite her best efforts received only a qualified assent. As the couple put it, "we do not ourselves believe strongly enough in the plan to give you any material help". Emily at once insisted she had never expected or wished for such a thing, though the refusal of money from her normally generous aunt and uncle surely was a disappointment.

Brother Leonard too urged her to reconsider, and warned of the danger of contracting a deadly disease in the camps like Mary Kingsley. The argument carried no weight with Emily. "For me Life has no attractions, Death a good many," was her theatrical response to all such strictures, and it was a theme she would harp on over the coming decades. Besides, it was vital that responsibility for distributing the fund should not be handed over to the authorities but be kept firmly in the hands of a *woman*. "By hook or by crook, I mean to go," she declared. "I wish an army of women could go. In my opinion, only women can end this war."

It was a view starkly at odds with Kitchener's idea that it was the women who were prolonging the conflict, and there were many on both sides who agreed that the Boer "Amazons" were far more intransigent than their husbands and sons.

Stories had gained credence that female crack-shots were joining the commandos, sometimes dressed as boys and sometimes undisguised. Reports circulated regularly of bodies of women being seen among the Boer dead on battlefields – along with a bizarre conflicting story that Boer men, due to a shortage of clothes, were fighting in dresses. In October, at the village of Jagersfontein, women were seen firing at British troops from their houses, and one of Kitchener's officers who witnessed their removal to a camp reported them as "mere girls and women so old that I wonder that they can be moved". His eye was held by "one magnificent handsome woman with a face exactly like Cruikshank's picture of Madame Defarge" in A *Tale of Two Cities*, and he was moved to record he had never seen so much hatred in a woman's face.

On November 29 Emily confided to friends that she had let the Chelsea flat. Nothing held her now and from her depleted resources she booked a second-class ticket for Cape Town. The few in the know were instructed to keep her departure secret, and at the next meeting of the Distress Fund Committee she handed over £300 collected by her own efforts. This was to be banked in Cape Town to pay for the first supplies of food and clothing.

*

Her steamer sailed on December 7. On board, but as first-class passengers, were the Quaker philanthropist Joshua Rowntree and his wife – in later life Emily always sharply contradicted reports that she went out to South Africa with the Rowntrees, insisting that in contrast to their superior accommodation her second-class deck was "crowded to discomfort". The novelty of second-class travel was beginning to wear thin.

On the voyage out Emily devoured book after book on South Africa and applied herself to learning Afrikaans, or as it was then called Boer Dutch or the Taal. Private tuition in London had given her a grounding but she struggled with the book-lessons because of baffling inconsistencies in grammar and spelling. Years later, in a letter to her greatest South African friend, Boer Dutch received a backhanded compliment: "Your language always attracted me, dear Mrs Steyn," she wrote. "It seemed to me such a perfect vehicle for all primitive and delightful things. What humour it can convey, what tenderness, what poetic feeling! How suited to intimate family life!"

And there was ample leisure to reflect on why she was sailing six thousand miles to face the uncertainties of wartime in a strange country, and to record her thoughts in the rolling periods of the Victorian pulpit: "Deeply I had felt the call. Passionately I resented the injustice of English policy. Wholeheartedly I offered myself for relief to the distressed. Carefully, step by step, I prepared the way. Sternly I economised and saved. Greatly I felt the wrench and anxiety for my aged relatives. But never did the vision fade of those desolate women and children, nor the certainty that I must go to them."

8 "WOMAN-HATER"

The steamship anchored in Table Bay an hour before dawn on December 27, 1900, and at sunrise Emily was stunned by the magnificent sight of Table Mountain. Impatient to be ashore, she left in the first tug among third-class passengers, crossing with an electric launch sent out for her by a reception party. Her first note dashed home to Leonard is full of the beauty of the scene – "brilliant weather, light bracing air and gorgeous flowers" – but also of the realities of a war zone, with long lines of military vehicles in the streets of Cape Town and "swarms of Khaki people everywhere". The warm welcome for the newcomer by a group of prominent Cape citizens known as Boer sympathisers was duly noted by the military authorities. The party included Mrs Caroline Murray, a descendant of Cape Colony's first prime minister and in her youth a renowned beauty, who was to call herself Emily's foremost friend in Cape Town.

Emily revelled in the hot climate. By the afternoon she was enjoying the Murrays' hospitality in the pretty suburb of Kenilworth, admiring the view of pure cobalt mountains from the garden, eating figs and apricots, and making friends with the family's pet meerkat. Feeling like a sponge continually sipping up new ideas and impressions, she was soon reduced to "a state of mental indigestion".

From the start she was bombarded with stories about the refugee camps springing up all along the railway network – not only the camps she already knew to exist inside Cape Colony, but others further north. Over the New Year she interviewed many women deported from the two republics after watching their homes destroyed. "It seemed almost impossible to credit the sad stories they had to tell, but the main features of these were again and again repeated," wrote Emily. The central fact to emerge was that, unknown to anyone in England, huge new camps were being set up. "I must get to them," she decided, "cost what it might."

*

Everyone agreed that the key man to see was Sir Alfred Milner, and here family influence paid off again. Emily had forearmed herself with letters of introduction from Lady Hobhouse and her cousin Henry the MP, both known socially to Milner in England – indeed, Henry was an old friend from Oxford days. But her first call at Government House was discouraging. Though the building itself looked welcoming – half country house, half country inn, as one recent visitor had described it – Emily's initial reception was less so. When Sir Alfred's secretary asked what subject she wished to discuss with him, she replied, "The condition of women and children". She was informed that His Excellency was unlikely to see her on *that* topic, but that she would be communicated with in due course. Emily went away depressed, but was contacted quicker than she expected.

"A kind invitation was send me to lunch at Government House yesterday, the very day the invitation was received," she wrote to Leonard on January 6, 1901. The short notice gave her no time to travel back from the wine-farm where she was staying with more of her new friends, and she was forced to write a letter of apology for delivery in person the next morning, asking for a meeting without lunch.

The next twenty-four hours were spent in "a blue funk". So much depended on Milner that the woman who habitually put on a fearless front was inwardly sick with terror. She later remembered: "As was (and is) usual with me in moments of mental or emotional strain, my heart beat so violently I could hardly breathe." Failure to win over the governor would wipe out all the months of toil and the chance to save countless lives.

On the morning of January 8 she set off for Government House alone, unable even to bear the company of the Murrays. On the train from Kenilworth, she opened her morning mail from England in the hope of distracting her tortured mind. What she found was a letter from Kate Courtney that ended with "a rare and very special thing" – a line from the blind sage in his own hand. Guessing Emily's likely state of agitation, Mr Courtney had written, "Be prudent, be calm". The message acted as both sedative and tonic, and Emily later acknowledged that those few words from Courtney's guided pen steadied her for the crucial interview.

Her fears seemed completely misplaced. She left Government House on cloud nine, having extracted from Sir Alfred almost every concession she could reasonably expect. She emerged into the blazing Cape afternoon, she wrote, "feeling as if wings were attached to my feet".

The governor had insisted on Emily joining his lunch party. She left no comment on the meal, though Milner rejoiced in a celebrated chef called Fauconnier; because of her inner turmoil, she probably failed to notice what she was eating. The other seven guests, all men, must have thought her "a strange animal and an awful bore", Emily thought, while she on her part silently branded them "inferior creatures". But the host himself turned on her a singularly charming and sympathetic manner and promised a short private interview after coffee. "Sir Alfred enquired kindly for Henry and asked to be remembered to you," Emily reported dutifully to Aunt Mary. He then led her into the cool and quiet drawing room and all at once her nervousness vanished. "We sat together on a sofa," she wrote, "and went at it hammer and

The influential Caroline Murray was the first South African to offer Emily hospitality.

tongs for an hour." This is not the only instance in Emily's letters when her turn of phrase may draw a smile from a low-minded generation like the present.

Milner struck her as "amiable and weak, clear-headed and narrow". In this Emily spectacularly misjudged her dapper, smiling host. Over the century since the Boer War, practically every commentator has indicted Alfred Milner as its evil genius, misleading even Chamberlain in his determination to engineer a conflict of arms. "Everyone says he has no heart, but I think I hit on the atrophied remains of one," Emily wrote to Lady Hobhouse, sounding a rather complacent note in her relief at getting a sympathetic hearing.

Milner, then a bachelor of forty-six, was strongly attracted to the sort of women who would nowadays be called feisty. Among those he was said to have courted without success in the past were the razor-tongued socialite Margot Tennant, who turned him down to marry the future premier Herbert Asquith, and Lord Curzon's racy, fur-loving mistress, the novelist Elinor Glyn, of whom it was famously asked:

> Would you like to sin
> With Elinor Glyn
> On a tiger-skin,
> Or would you prefer
> To err
> With her
> On some other fur?

There were also persistent whispers linking Milner and the flighty wife of Joe Chamberlain's brother Richard – a woman whose obsessive pursuit of men had more than once threatened to erupt into open scandal. Though the matter was hushed up, her sudden appearance in South Africa earlier in the war had given Lord Roberts a serious headache.

Whether Milner was attracted to the earnest Emily is a matter for surmise, but he certainly made all the right noises in response to her impassioned plea on behalf of the camp inmates. As a promising start, he admitted the farm-burnings were a mistake, and agreed something should be done for the displaced women and children. About these he was evidently uneasy, recorded Emily, "for with his own eyes he had seen some truck-loads of women when he came down the line, and it had occurred to him that it was rather terrible". Emily poured out stories of the suffering families – "and I did not mince matters" – ending with the heartfelt cry that "for the Honour of England we ought to mend matters in the camps".

Growing in audacity, she went on to offer the governor advice on how to deal with the Boers – at this point she had been in the country rather less than a fortnight as compared to Milner's three years – and informed him that a little kindness would work wonders. A picture of her childhood heroine must have flashed into her head: "I described to him the attitude and spirit of all the deported women I had met and asked him how he thought he was going to govern thousands of Joans of Arc."

Milner promised to do all in his power to get Emily into the camps along with the two trucks she thought she needed, one piled with clothing and one with provisions. He also agreed Emily should take with her "a Dutch lady" of her choice as translator and "representative of South Africa". Finding Sir Alfred so amenable, Emily silently resolved she would later push for a second assistant, having in mind her new friend Ellie Cronje. This was a daughter of the general who, at the battle of Paardeberg, had left the British Army with the highest casualties of the war and threatened to wreck Kitchener's reputation in the process. Emily never lacked for nerve.

Then came Milner's caveat – everything must first be referred to Lord Kitchener. However, as civil head of the country Milner would recommend and urge these measures on the commander-in-chief, and he thought the prospects good if only on the practical ground that the camps must be properly organised, and were likely to exist not for weeks but months, and possibly years. He promised personally to telegraph army headquarters in Pretoria and to let her have Kitchener's reply within a few days.

Milner was an exceptionally clever man – in his own way as clever as Emily's brother, and like Leonard a high-achieving Oxford academic. At the time of meeting Emily he was enjoying a close relationship, almost certainly adulterous, with Lady Edward Cecil, lively young wife of that Lord Edward Cecil who had served Kitchener in the Sudan. The Cecils had arrived in South Africa on the eve of the war, Lord Edward then going on to Mafeking as second-in-command to Baden-Powell while his wife stayed in Cape Town, riding and dining every day with Milner. It was said that when Lady Edward heard that Mafeking had been relieved, she retired to bed with a headache. Some contemporaries saw a hint of the Biblical story of David and Uriah in the dispatch of Lord Edward to Mafeking; and in the fullness of time the relationship between Milner and Lady Edward was to end in a denouement offering full satisfaction to the gossipmongers.

*

Emily rose from the governor's sofa in triumph. "We parted very good friends and I quite liked him and pitied him," she wrote home. "Now I wait on Kitchener and if he refuses, must attack again." Although she might be doomed to be "snuffed out" by the general, on the whole she felt sanguine: "The chances are that Kitchener, though a woman-hater, may welcome two women because of the difficulty (he has created himself) of dealing with thousands."

Besides, she was hearing some surprisingly good things about Kitchener from her Boer friends. For instance, the influential De Villiers family had a son-in-law who, while refusing to bear arms against the British, had served Boer militias as a despatch rider, and when captured had been deported to Ceylon. Lord Roberts had remained deaf to all pleas for clemency, but Kitchener ordered the man's release to England, where his wife was able to join him. As Emily wrote to Aunt Mary: "Kitchener, they say, has done a few kind things which gives me some hope for my bit of work. At any rate all agree that he seems and acts more as a man than Lord Roberts whose popularity seems to me chiefly a newspaper one."

Hope remained high when she received a very nice letter from Milner – a private one by his own hand – explaining that he had chosen to write fully to the commander-in-chief instead of telegraphing, as the wires to Pretoria were choked with urgent military matters. The fact was Milner strongly disliked sending telegrams – "it is so hard to establish an *entente* over the wires," he once told a female friend – feeling there was

A Mayfair hostess and accomplished string-puller, Aunt Mary was Emily's faithful correspondent throughout the war.

less likelihood of misunderstandings with a letter.

A few days had to be endured before Emily knew Kitchener's mind. In the meantime she continued to gather case histories that would eventually appear in her book *The Brunt of the War*, a narrative of the farm-burnings and of life in the concentration camps told chiefly in the words of the victims themselves. She also managed to secure a special permit to visit the nearby camp for wounded Boer prisoners-of-war at Wynberg, where family connections paid off once again. On hearing the name Hobhouse, the officer in charge introduced himself as a distant relation. "This may be very helpful to me because he is chief in regard to dealing out passes," noted Emily with satisfaction. The incarcerated Boers she found most interesting, as was news of another camp nearby where she might find fifty-seven captured enemy combatants aged between nine and seventeen – though the authorities had relented over one desperado of eight years, who was released to go back to school.

At last on January 17 came a letter bearing the Government House seal. To Emily's huge relief Milner enclosed a telegram from Kitchener giving permission to visit camps up the line as far as Bloemfontein, though no further. The general also objected to a Boer lady going with her – Sir Alfred in his private covering note placed a diplomatic gloss on the soldier's bluntness, suggesting "it would be better, no doubt, in discussing the matter with any of the Dutch ladies here, not to refer to Lord Kitchener's express reference to them". And he added: "I think those who know you will be satisfied with your going, and will not think it unnatural or unreasonable that the military authorities should be unwilling to multiply visitors to the seat of war."

The wording of Kitchener's telegram offers an insight into his way of thinking. He willingly agrees to the distribution of food and clothing among "Dutch refugee women kept out of their homes by the Boers" – such delicious self-deception, thought Emily – but of her request to be allowed a companion of her own choice he remarks "there are numbers of ladies in Bloemfontein who will give her every assistance", meaning ladies whose loyalty was to Britain.

Still, Emily told herself, half a loaf was better than none. It was already in her head that, once at Bloemfontein, she could somehow wangle permission to go further north. But Milner's request for silence regarding Kitchener's ban on companions caused considerable difficulties with her Cape Dutch friends. Some took the news very ill – "some indeed really stirred up bad feeling," she told Leonard, "accusing me of 'keeping in with Milner' and wishing to keep everything in my own hands." Alas, the row was "symptomatic of the excited and unreasonable state of mind prevailing".

But immediate practicalities dominated her thoughts. Using her influence with Milner, Emily met with the senior officer in charge of the railway line and secured the biggest available rail truck. A full day was spent loading it with six tons of foodstuffs purchased wholesale out of the £300 Emily had raised herself – the war had sent food prices sky-high – along with six tons of clothing sourced from sympathisers in England. Even so, the great truck was far from full, which seemed a pity considering the transport was free. One problem facing Emily is familiar to relief workers today – where to draw a line between what a distress fund should provide and what the authorities should be providing themselves. In any case, her stock would not last many weeks, and she hoped the committee back in London were urgently raising extra funds since "it would be horrible to be up there with empty hands".

To Lady Hobhouse, Emily wrote: "I want to make myself a big base of supplies in Bloemfontein and work up to Johannesburg from there as soon as I can wheedle Lord Kitchener into giving me a further permit." The state of the Johannesburg camp, she heard, was an absolute scandal, but in the first instance there were plenty of camps to target in the old Orange Free State, now Orange River Colony. Among those of which she had heard especially bad things were Edenburg, Kroonstadt, and Norval's Pont. Yet no one seemed to know exactly how many camps there were and how many people in them.

Emily's instinctive sympathy with the Boer cause shines out from these letters home. To her aunt on January 20 she repeats approvingly a friend's characterisation of the British army as "sick, weary, worn, spiritless, fit for nothing", whereas her own descriptions of the fighting men of the other side sound remarkably enthusiastic coming from a pacifist – "I think if you could see all these people you would see their spirit is wholly unquenchable, while the spirit of our soldiers is gone out like a candle," she says of one gathering of Boers who had solemnly sworn to fight to the death. And she writes excitedly of meeting a paroled commando leader who gave her "thrilling accounts of the early battles".

Her growing passion for the country is expressed again and again. Writing to Leonard two days later, she hopes his wife Nora will one day see the hedges of blue plumbago and pomegranates and the wild flowers which have ravished her eye. But for days there had been rain – "or as that is too mild a way to put it, I should say waterspouts" – and she remarks that no such downpours had been experienced during a South African midsummer since 1834, the year the slaves were freed.

That same evening of Tuesday, January 22, 1901, as Emily set off on her first journey, Queen Victoria died.

Emily's hostess at Bloemfontein, Caroline Fichardt was suspected of signalling to Boer commandos from her husband's grave.

9 "CRASS MALE IGNORANCE"

Victoria's health had been deteriorating steadily since her soldier grandson, Prince Christian Victor, died in Pretoria of typhoid, and grief and anxiety over the war had dominated the final days. According to her daughter Princess Beatrice, almost her last words were "What news is there from Lord Kitchener?" She died aged eighty-two having reigned an unprecedented sixty-three years.

Like many an activist since, Emily looked for any event to forward her own agenda. On January 20 she had written to Mary Hobhouse: "How grieved everyone here is about the Queen's illness; all wish she would express a dying wish that the war should end and that could be made an excuse for giving it up."

A deathbed peace gesture was hardly likely. In her letter congratulating Kitchener on his South African appointment, Victoria had warned that he would find the Boers "a horrid brutal people", and this was very much the received wisdom of the time. Lord Salisbury himself made up his mind about the Boers on a youthful visit to Cape Town some fifty years earlier. They were, he said, "as degraded a set of savages as any white men in the world", and had set up the Transvaal republic so they could "maltreat the natives to the utmost of their hearts' content".

When and where Emily heard of the Queen's death is unclear. Her next letter is full of the grinding two-day rail journey north to Bloemfontein and of what she found there. For over six hundred miles she had endured extreme heat followed by horrible dust-storms varied by thunderstorms. Sand constantly penetrated the closed carriage, filling her eyes and ears and turning her hair red. The desolate landscape rolling by seemed absolutely without life, its most striking features being animal carcasses, bleached bones, and refuse of every kind. "I saw a few burnt farms," she told Aunt Mary, "but those unburnt seemed still and lifeless also." Her great disappointment was that no Boer commandos had attacked and captured the train, which Emily claimed "would have enlivened the journey and been immensely interesting".

This was a show of bravado for home consumption. An attack was no idle thought as wrecking trains had become a favoured means of Boer warfare, and reached its peak at exactly this stage in the conflict. Long afterwards Emily confessed to falling into a state of miserable cowardice as the train moved off into "the strange hot war-stricken North with its accumulations of misery and bloodshed". At the frequent stops she found the stations thronged with British officers, but as "a mere woman, middle-aged, and somewhat dowdy at that", she was treated with little gallantry when trying to squeeze forward to order a meal. Fortunately her Cape friends had given her a giant tin of apricot jam and a kettle lamp for making tea and cocoa, so more often than not she fended for herself.

In letters of this time she vented her anger at finding Bloemfontein under army control, complaining that even the railway officials ranked as nobodies and that nothing was possible without military sanction. Like everyone else she was practically a prisoner:

The camps continue to spring up. Army-issue tents designed for active service are crammed with families and subjected to intense heat by day and bitter cold by night, along with high winds, floods and hailstorms.

"We cannot move without passes. Everything is censored – spies abound – barbed wire and picquets surround the town – newspapers nearly all prohibited."

Here Emily is being disingenuous. The town might have been in British hands for ten months but De Wet's forces remained a constant threat. Only a few weeks before the Boers had attempted an invasion of Cape Colony that was repulsed only at heavy cost. In recent days Kitchener had made a priority of guarding the two former capitals against attack, in Bloemfontein's case by enclosing a radius of twenty-five miles with defensive works. Emily must have known that relaxing the strict regime was not an option.

Finding the only decent hotel in town overcrowded, Emily was guilty of an act of remarkable indiscretion. The charming paroled Boer captain in Cape Town, with his thrilling tales of derring-do against Kitchener's soldiers, had urged her to seek the hospitality of his family when in Bloemfontein, and that is what Emily decided to do. Her stay with Caroline Fichardt, the captain's widowed mother, was to prove one of the most important periods of her life, though unknown to Emily Mrs Fichardt's immediate reaction to her guest's arrival was the fatalistic aside: "That's the end of us."

Certainly Emily could have made no more provocative start to her mission than to choose the Fichardts' mansion, Kaya Lami, as her base. Wealthy and influential, the family were viewed with deep distrust by the British as staunch Free State patriots and close friends of the fugitive President Steyn. Caroline herself was under military surveillance at this time, suspected of signalling to the enemy on her out-of-town visits to her husband's grave.

With the same unerring instinct, Emily also quickly sought out the president's wife, Isabella Steyn, then detained under armed guard. This was the start of another enduring friendship, perhaps the single most important of Emily's life with a woman. It is from correspondence preserved by Mrs Steyn that we are privy to many intimate thoughts of Emily that would otherwise be lost.

*

At first all seemed to be going well, and once again Emily had reason to bless her relations. Calling at Government House, she was warmly welcomed by the military governor, Major-General George Pretyman. A lanky figure whose waxed moustache was twirled to points in the style of the Kaiser, Pretyman recalled making the acquaintance of Emily's Aunt Catty and Aunt Eliza at Bournemouth. He regretted being unable to put her up at Government House because an outbreak of typhoid meant the place was overrun by doctors and nurses, but he issued a general invitation to take all her meals there. Astonishingly, no one had reported to him that Emily was being whisked round town in the Fichardt carriage, and when Emily blithely told him where she was staying, the general almost jumped out of his skin. When he protested that Mrs Fichardt was very bitter against Britain, Emily countered that her visit might have a softening effect on the lady. Happily Pretyman was favourably struck by this notion.

Emily found the governor "conscious of gigantic blunders" over the concentration camps, and harassed by problems he could not solve. "The more one talks to these men in power, the more one feels they are hopelessly on the wrong track," she decided. "The moral aspects of the question are wholly disregarded and they try madly to bring about their will by force and force alone." Wheedling permission to visit the camps in Pretyman's jurisdiction, she stood over him while he wrote out a permit.

This was a great coup. Pretyman was not only military governor of Bloemfontein but also controller of the civilian administration of the former Free State. The pass was pocketed with satisfaction, alongside Kitchener's telegram and Milner's letter. With the governor's blessing Emily met Major Cray, commandant of all the camps in the colony, who was soon pouring out a tale of woe – he had no money, insufficient transport, and lacked the authority to do as he wished. He ended by begging Emily to take her supplies into his camps, and the two agreed to put their heads together to concoct a letter seeking Kitchener's permission for Emily to go on to the camps in the north.

By now Emily was convinced that the authorities had no more idea of how to cope than the man in the moon. It was easy to identify the problem – "crass male ignorance, stupidity, helplessness and muddling". And she vowed she would "rub as much salt into the sore places of their minds as I possibly can, because it is so good for them". Even so, she couldn't help melting a little when they humbled themselves before her and confessed that the whole thing was a colossal blunder.

We know these thoughts from her letters home, every one of which borders on the reckless. Emily was perfectly aware that under prevailing martial law all mail was liable to be opened by a censor; perhaps even worse, the letters might have fallen into enemy hands, since around this time De Wet had profitably switched his attention to the mail trains. However, whenever possible she took the precaution of asking travelling acquaintances to carry her letters to Cape Town, and preferably on board ship. We can safely assume the stinging judgments on Kitchener's army never reached the chief's eyes or Emily might have found her first stay in South Africa a very short one.

Her letters enjoyed a measure of protection thanks to an unwitting Lord Roberts. During his time as chief, he reacted to a complaint against an over-zealous censor by quietly ordering that no letters were to be opened unless there was "good proof that they were from Boers", and indeed Roberts later recommended that Kitchener should get rid of the censor. By one of the ironies that pepper Emily's story, the original complaint had come from the influential C.F. Moberly Bell, a senior manager and future managing director of *The Times*, the newspaper soon to orchestrate a savage campaign against Emily and her works.

Emily was aghast at the filthy sanitary conditions she found at her first camp.

*

The first camp Emily visited was two miles outside Bloemfontein. Out on the bare brown veld, a village of bell-tents had been dumped down on the slope of a hill, without a tree for shade in any direction. To Lady Hobhouse in faraway Mayfair she wrote: "It was about four o'clock of a scorching afternoon when I set foot in the camp and I can't tell you what I felt like, so I won't try."

She found nearly two thousand inmates, all women and children except for a handful of the despised "hands-uppers". Inside suffocating, overcrowded tents, with black flies thick on every surface, she met woman after woman, "and they told me their stories and we cried together and even laughed together and chatted bad Dutch and bad English all the afternoon". While she was in the tent of a family called Botha, there occurred an incident that gives us one of the most vivid images of Emily Hobhouse: "While we sat there a snake came in. They said it was a night adder and very poisonous. So they all ran out to make room and I attacked the creature with my parasol." After a struggle Emily wounded the snake, then a man rushed in with a mallet and finished it off. It was later identified as a puff-adder.

The same letter gives harrowing details of sights in the camp. A child's corpse covered by a blanket, left stinking in the open under a cooking sun. A heavily pregnant woman trying to cope with six sick children, two of them with typhoid. Another woman laid on the bare ground for want of a mattress, pregnant with her seventh child, and in complete ignorance of the whereabouts of the others. These Emily said were quite ordinary cases among hundreds and hundreds. The latrines were without privacy and open to the sun and rain. "The effluvia is terrible," she wrote, "making it impossible to approach within fifty yards unless with nose and mouth tied up." Soap was unobtainable.

The filthy water was limited to two buckets daily for a family of seven or eight, for all washing, cooking and drinking. "As to the rations," adds Emily, "at first they sometimes had potatoes – seven potatoes for seven people – but that is now impossible."

Nothing in her previous experience had prepared her for this camp crammed with dying women and children. From that day forward she was a driven woman. Horrified by the callous stupidity of it all, Emily was now to plunge into the stormiest period of her career, buoyed up with righteous indignation. There was no conceivable excuse for what she had seen. A camp like this was a wholesale cruelty that shamed England, and to keep people in these conditions was simply murder.

For the time being she did what she could, sorting through her supply of clothes, making up little bundles for the most deserving cases, mentally listing the priorities for action. First, the camp needed a matron. Next, a mortuary tent. Next, more and cleaner water. Next, soap.

*

The home of Emily's hostess was a blissful relief after such horrors. Only two miles from the camp, Kaya Lami might have been on another planet. Not only beautiful, but large enough to have housed both Kruger and Milner with their retinues during the abortive Bloemfontein peace conference in 1899, the mansion was situated opposite the town's historic twin-steepled church, and figures in many memoirs of the time. Isabella Steyn, a regular visitor, recalled in old age how the smell of the violets of Kaya Lami's garden would drift across the street, while for Ella Fichardt, one of the daughters of the house, the mingled scent of fresh flowers, turpentine and beeswax was fondly cherished as the odour of her old home. Emily was to live on in her mind as "the sweetest guest" who sat with her on the hearthrug and sang old Cornish songs. Ella's sister Maude, a fine pianist, remembered Emily coming home exhausted from the camp, lying on the sofa with her eyes closed and saying, "Play to me, don't stop…"

Just as Emily was getting on so well with Major Cray, the man went down with gastric fever. Hurrying to Government House to beard General Pretyman, Emily found him in a half-crazed state and frantic to get away on leave. His stand-in, yet to arrive, was an unknown quantity called Hamilton Goold-Adams, but in the meantime Emily prevailed upon the harassed general to order the camp's temporary commandant "to do what I tell him". She even nagged Pretyman into handing over £50 of public funds and issuing a proclamation that all drinking water at the camp was to be boiled.

But the general's usefulness was nearly at an end. Though Pretyman was an old friend of Lord Roberts, the former commander-in-chief had not been blind to his deficiencies. Months previously he had privately said that Pretyman's governorship was a temporary one as the man lacked "the tact, temper, general knowledge and large-mindedness" essential to the position, while an agent of Milner's had reported his administration at Bloemfontein as "chaos pure and simple".

Emily's great immediate concern remained the water. The camp drew its supply from the Modder River, which was the same as swallowing typhoid germs whole; yet, in that treeless waste, no water could be boiled because of the scarcity of wood. Emily's idea was to get hold of a railway engine boiler for communal use and thus to economise on

Washday minus soap at Norval's Pont, one of the camps penetrated by Emily. Typhoid-infected water from the river was a major cause of epidemics.

fuel. Next on her shopping-list was forage for her cows – she had somehow acquired fifty but could get no more than four buckets from the poor starved beasts – while small boilers were needed for their milk.

Captain Albert Hume, the officer supposedly under Emily's orders, failed to live up to expectations, and made little effort to disguise his view that she was overly sympathetic to the Boers. He was soon to feel the power of Emily's wrath. Peering in one of the tents at the camp, she had found an emaciated four-year-old with "nothing left of him except his great brown eyes and white teeth from which the lips were drawn back too thin to close". She marched up to the officer. "Captain Hume," she said, "you shall look," and forced him into the tent to view the "child-skeleton". And then "at last he did say it was awful to see the children suffering so".

Emily packed Hume off to find fresh milk and had the child placed outside where it could catch the breeze that came up at sunset. To Lady Hobhouse she wrote: "I can't describe what it is to see these children lying about in a state of collapse – it's just exactly like faded flowers thrown away."

Captain Hume – "oh, how I want to box his ears!" – was far from being the only object of Emily's scorn. Bloemfontein's military officers and their hangers-on are constantly reviled in her letters as ignorant, hot-headed and of low character. At times Emily sounds like a stage duchess. "I have made it a rule," she informs Lady Hobhouse, "to talk politics to no one under a general or governor. They at least respect my views and even ask my opinion, but talk to these ignorant, narrow, heartless subordinates I will not." Indeed, Emily announces with a flourish, in future she will take orders from no one except Milner or Lord Kitchener.

Yet almost in the same breath she confesses that the atmosphere has made her paralysed and intimidated, and speaks of her dread of what she will find in the camps beyond Bloemfontein. "Some days," she says, "I think I must cut and run." And she can hardly have reassured her aunt in far-off London by adding: "Do not worry about me at all. I am perfectly well in body, only desperate in mind."

*

Far from cutting and running, Emily now embarked on a series of arduous journeys down the line to other camps, each time confronting the military controller with demands for passes and permits. Often her trains were delayed or simply never turned up. Once she had to sit bolt upright for fifteen hours alone in a guard's van, shunted to and fro in the dark all night long.

Yet now and then she would encounter an unexpected cavalier. One night, stranded at Norval's Pont Station, she had just reconciled herself to sleeping in the platform office when the railway staff officer gruffly offered to give up his own bed in a converted guard's van. Inside the van she found unimaginable luxury – a mattress and khaki blankets, newspapers, and a waiting bathtub *full of water*. Emily found herself so undone by this unusual and unlooked-for kindness that as soon as the officer left she collapsed in a fit of hysterical weeping. Knowing nothing of her benefactor beyond his surname and regiment, Emily wrote: "I have canonized him in my mind and he is St Bates of the Cheshires."

Another time she spent a ghastly night at a hotel where, having got "two black ladies" to wash her room out, she made a ring of insect powder in which to lie down. She later affected amusement at the memory of "my absurd hunger, thirst, fatigue, dirt, loneliness and general misery". The desperate tiredness brought on by her regime can be seen in the disjointed, rambling and repetitive passages in the letters. Emily admits to constantly falling asleep between writing sentences, heading one letter from "The Land of Nod", and adding question-marks to her date-lines.

In her impatience with the military, Emily gave little credence to what she heard of the progress of the war, though she was living through a particularly crucial period. As ever the great challenge to the British was De Wet, who launched a new attack on Cape Colony on February 10. But Kitchener had learned from the disastrous performance of independent commanders in the early days, and was now keeping the conduct of the war firmly in his own hands. From his headquarters in Pretoria, he would daily control the movements of seventy or eighty columns by telegram, moving them about on a map of South Africa as if in some great game of chess.

Yet unknown to Emily or almost anyone else, at this very time the British commander-in-chief was engaged in a remarkable secret initiative to halt the war. The success of the scorched-earth strategy had forced peace overtures from Louis Botha, the commandant-general himself, and Kitchener believed a personal meeting could end the war "if we are prepared not to be too hard on the Boers". Writing to St John Brodrick, who had replaced Lord Lansdowne as war secretary, he urged that it would be good policy to treat the enemy well, and sought permission to "do away with anything humiliating to them" in the terms of surrender.

The two opposing commanders parleyed on February 28 at Middelburg, north-east of Pretoria. Kitchener, wearing a black armband for the dead queen, was pleasantly struck by the Boer's unassuming manner, and over a long single day the two of them hammered out an outline settlement that Botha believed he could sell to the Boer leadership as a whole. Generous terms suggested by the British general included a million pounds for restocking devastated farms and an amnesty for acts of war, even those committed by rebels against the Crown. But if Kitchener thought he had found a formula for peace with honour, he reckoned without Milner. Setting his face against concessions, Milner cabled London with a stiffened version of Kitchener's proposals, and

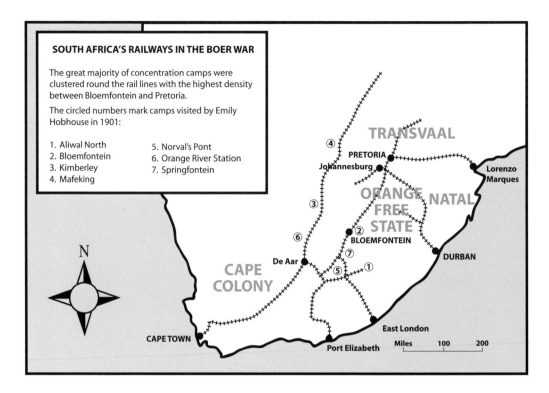

SOUTH AFRICA'S RAILWAYS IN THE BOER WAR

The great majority of concentration camps were clustered round the rail lines with the highest density between Bloemfontein and Pretoria.

The circled numbers mark camps visited by Emily Hobhouse in 1901:

1. Aliwal North
2. Bloemfontein
3. Kimberley
4. Mafeking

5. Norval's Pont
6. Orange River Station
7. Springfontein

even then stated his outright opposition. As his great sticking point he seized on the amnesty for Cape rebels.

In private the high commissioner was far from confident. As ever, he shared his most intimate thoughts with Lady Edward Cecil, writing on March 8 to admit deep perplexity over the way the negotiations were proceeding: "K affirms, though I do not know how much he means of this, or how far it is just said to frighten me into agreeing to a compromise, that our soldiers can't be trusted not to surrender on the smallest provocation, and that consequently disaster is not even now impossible if the Boers stick to it." Milner felt he could not afford to be branded as the villain of the piece – "could not afford it in the public interest, for it would not be possible to compel the army to fight on *against the wishes of its own Chief and the whole popular sentiment*, and an attempt to do so, which failed, would only encourage the enemy to still further efforts and demands, and end in a terrible fiasco".

Despite their differences Milner admired Kitchener the man. "I like the total absence of cant," he told Lady Edward, "the *clearness of vision*, and the immense strenuousness of his character. He may deceive others. I don't think he deludes himself. He *has not got* the 'lie in the soul'. And there is a kindly side to him too, shown in his remembrance of old friends and appreciation of good women" – a telling compliment coming from a man like Milner.

To Kitchener's dismay, Milner prevailed. Steered by Chamberlain, the cabinet insisted on surrender terms that everyone knew to be unacceptable to the Boers. Complaining to Brodrick, Kitchener called Milner's views narrow and vindictive, and expressed pained surprise that Britain was to continue a ruinous war "to put two or three hundred Dutchmen in prison". And with a characteristic eye on costs he added: "It seems to me absurd and wrong, and I wonder the Chancellor of the Exchequer does not have a fit."

*

So despite Kitchener's best efforts the war was to last a further fourteen months, with disastrous consequences for Britain's reputation throughout the world. For thousands of women and children in the swelling concentration camps, Milner's ascendancy was a sentence of death. Jan Smuts, one of the clearest-sighted of the Boers, would have endless occasions to offer up his favourite prayer borrowed from the Griqua tribe: "Lord, come to our help yourself and not your son, for this is no time for children."

In the meantime Emily fretted over the commander-in-chief's supposed inaction. "Lord Kitchener has twice distinctly refused me permission to go further north," she fumed to an unknown correspondent on February 25, as the elusive general was preparing for his secret meeting with Botha. Needless to say, the refusals failed to deter her, and she was now impatiently awaiting his response to her third appeal.

On March 4, as Kitchener himself was waiting anxiously for the cabinet's decision on his peace proposals, she wrote that Lord Kitchener was in her black books again over his latest rebuff. Had she known of his preoccupation, even Emily might have allowed that he had more pressing concerns than her latest letter. As it was, she simply settled down to plan her fourth attack. "If only I could catch him in the flesh," she sighed, "I am sure I could wheedle him round, but nobody ever knows where he is."

10 "THE WHOLE TALK WAS OF DEATH"

This was the defining period in Emily's life. All the contemporary fame or notoriety stemmed from her experiences travelling up and down the line between Bloemfontein and the other concentration camps she succeeded in penetrating, like Norval's Pont, Springfontein, Aliwal North and Kimberley. To the authorities she was rapidly becoming a thoroughgoing nuisance, and the camp at Bloemfontein witnessed her repeated clashes with the "insufferable" Captain Hume and the camp's new head, a "narrow, conceited and heartless" man called Macarty.

At the outset one or two camps surprised her by seeming to be reasonably well run, given the scant resources everywhere. The Aliwal North commandant especially came in for praise. At Norval's Pont she noted there had been no major outbreak of sickness, though all the cases nursed in the makeshift hospital had died. But Kitchener's sweeps were daily netting more people, and this made forward planning impossible even in the less bad camps. Useless to lay down a half-inch water pipe to supply a camp of two thousand inmates, protested Emily, if a fortnight later a one-inch pipe would be needed for four or even six thousand. That was what happened constantly, leaving her floundering in an ocean of misery.

The enormity of what was going on at the Bloemfontein camp sank in when Emily remembered that in her father's Cornish parish, with a population roughly the same as the camp, a funeral was an event, whereas here some twenty or thirty were dying daily. "The whole talk was of death – who died yesterday, who lay dying today, who would be dead tomorrow," she wrote. Here was a death-rate unknown except in the times of the great plagues.

Her mind dwelt obsessively on absent items like combs, needles and thread, candles, stuffing for mattresses, and above all soap. None of these needs occurred to the military mind, and the simplest necessities such as scissors and thimbles were like gold-dust, handed round from tent to tent. At one camp the arrival of Emily's rough deal packing cases created a sensation – not for what was inside, but for the cases themselves. All were gratefully seized as rudimentary bedsteads and tables or firewood.

She was desperately tired. In letters home around this time her words come tumbling out, with afterthoughts, asides, and inconsequential details mixed up with appeals for new supplies or polite commiserations over Aunt Mary's sore throat. Symptomatic of Emily's growing isolation and weakened grip on reality is her sudden bizarre decision to spend part of the distress funds on a boarding school education for "some of the higher-class girls" in the Bloemfontein camp. Belatedly realising the bewilderment this might cause at home, she then writes off asking for the executive's sanction – "as I am not sure you will approve, I will only begin with four girls," she says. In extenuation, she pleads with Lady Hobhouse in a separate letter, the committee should be informed that she has been very economical so far, always preferring to

*And still they come.
A camp's population might
double or treble in
a fortnight as
new families arrived
by open cattle truck.*

"squeeze the military" rather than spend the committee's money.

Predictably, the committee did not approve of her plans for the better-class girls and the boarding school scheme was dropped – though not before Emily had committed herself to completing the schooling of the four. Though bowing to the committee decision, in future times she would never tire of pointing out the success stories of the chosen girls. In another rambling letter of this time she writes: "I just want to say while it is on my mind that the blouses sent from England and supposed to be full-grown are only useful here for girls of twelve or fourteen or so. *Much* too small for the well-developed Boer maiden who is really a fine creature."

Emily never forgot the discomfort and hunger of her journeys through the "hot, dry, thirsty land" on a succession of dirty, uncared-for, endlessly jolting military trains. "I don't know how long my strength will hold out," she worried as early as February. All civilian travel was discouraged, so every journey was continually interrupted by officials with demands for this or that permit. Night after night was spent on board train or on the station with a "lullaby" of shunting goods vehicles in her ears. The great stand-by during these trials was her tin of apricot jam – "for days, even weeks together, bread and apricot jam was my only food three times a day with cocoa". That jam got her through, though for years afterwards she could bear neither sight nor smell of apricot.

Over the vast tawny desert of the Karoo, daytime temperatures at this time of year regularly hit 115 degrees Fahrenheit. Then tremendous rains would come, turning bone-dry land into a quagmire in seconds. One night, coming out of a camp following a downpour, Emily walked right into a bog, and was stuck fast up to the knees in solid black mud till someone came along and pulled her out. The extreme nature of South Africa's weather was illustrated one terrible night on the veld when six of Smuts's commandos were killed by a single bolt of lightning.

Her stays at Kaya Lami apart, only once in these months was Emily able to take a bath. It consisted of a hole dug in the ground, over which was draped a waterproof sheet, and a bucket of cold water thrown in. Emily remembered it as the most refreshing of her lifetime. There was space for this improvised tub as, to Emily's embarrassment, the camp commandant had put her into a large marquee instead of the usual bell tent. Overcrowding prevented the Boer women from adopting the same expedient, which explains Emily's indignation over the claim – commonly used by those seeking to justify the deficiencies of the concentration camps – that the Boers were naturally dirty people.

All the time she was taking down the women's stories for the book she meant to write. "Some are scared, some paralysed and unable to realise their loss, some are dissolved in tears," she wrote. "Some, mute and dry-eyed, seem only to be able to think of the blank, penniless future; and some are glowing with pride at being prisoners for their country's sake."

In an unknowing echo of Kitchener, Emily never doubted that "the woman rules the roost in the land", and she was fond of quoting a story about one burgher who surrendered and went home to his wife. Asked if he was wounded or ill, he answered no. "Then go away at once," retorted his wife, "and don't come near me again till you return with the freedom of your country."

Besides the women's testimony, there was the evidence of her own eyes. On March 15 she wrote of a distressing sight at the Kimberley camp – the corpses of three children being photographed "for the absent fathers to see some day". At least it was a relief to see that two of the children had been found coffins, as at Springfontein she had watched a family bury a young woman in a sack, "and it hurt their feelings woefully". Yet not every wrong could be blamed on the British military. Here at Springfontein the narrow-minded Reformed Dutch pastor refused to bury unbaptised babies in consecrated ground, and there was no shortage of them as the camp women were reluctant to christen in the absence of their husbands.

As Emily observed, births, deaths and marriages continued to occur, "for Lord Kitchener himself can't stop the course of nature". The plight of pregnant women and babies in the camps caused the greatest anxiety. The mother of one newborn child asked Emily to think of a girl's name appropriate to the times, and when Emily suggested Dolores or Hope, the sad, sick mother could see no reason to hope and chose Dolores. The letter relating this anecdote does not say so, but from this time one of the most popular names for girls born in the camps was Emily.

By now the acting governor, Colonel Goold-Adams, had settled in at Bloemfontein, and if he thought Emily an interfering busybody, he was gentleman enough to disguise his feelings. As Emily was inclined to do at first sight of one of these "men in power", she began by thinking well of Goold-Adams, seeing him as open and kind-hearted, "if not a man of any particular mental power". Further, she had the satisfaction of complaining loudly about Captain Hume and seeing that officer reduced to a state of abject deference after being bawled out by his new superior.

Goold-Adams went on to earn the good opinion of Briton and Boer, though Emily's combative style drove him to exasperation on at least one occasion. He gave great offence to local Boers by referring to her as a "hysterical lady" and was forced to withdraw the remark with apologies.

For weeks Emily had been demanding trained nurses for the camps, recruited either from the Cape or from England, suggesting a remuneration of five shillings a day plus tent and rations. The campaign finally bore fruit, but she was dismayed by an official

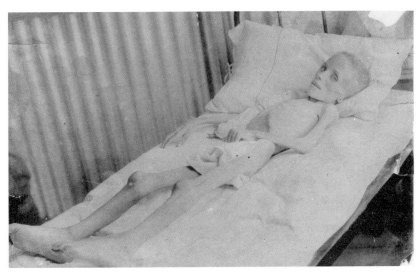

Lizzie van Zyl, aged seven, who died at Bloemfontein camp in May 1901. On her right arm is a doll given to her by Emily. On the back of the original photograph Emily wrote: "One of our little skeletons."

decree that all applicants for the nursing posts were to be vetted by Jane Waterston, South Africa's first woman doctor. Emily strongly disapproved of Dr Waterston because of her anti-Boer sentiments, and indeed all four of the nurses she endorsed to work in Bloemfontein turned out to be British refugees from the republics. The doctor's view of the camp inmates became crystal clear later when she wrote to *The Cape Times* complaining that "we fed and pampered people who have not even the grace to say thank you". Emily could not resist crowing when, of the nurses approved by Dr Waterston, "one drank and another was discovered to have been a forger".

There was of course another side of the coin. In the early stages of the war the medical care for wounded British soldiers too was desperately poor, with the total establishment of nursing sisters throughout South Africa standing at just sixty-eight. The shortage of professionals meant that a wounded man who survived between battlefield and base hospital would typically have endured a journey of several hundred miles by stretcher, primitive horse-drawn cart or ox-wagon, and the kind of military train that Emily found so excruciating. The patient was then liable to find himself at the mercy of the notorious self-appointed "Ministering Angels", ladylike incompetents who had travelled out from England to play at nurses. Some of the long-suffering soldiers took to hanging cards above their beds saying "I am too ill to be nursed today".

The flood of amateur nurses into South Africa had become a scandal early on in the war with Queen Victoria herself voicing disapproval of "the hysterical spirit" that moved such women to go where they were not welcome. Emily was fair-minded enough to recognise that on Lord Kitchener's arrival this sisterhood was rapidly disbanded and most of the ladies packed off home.

Yet, according to Emily, the War Office nurses who replaced the unwanted volunteers were little better. She was sharply critical of "their giddiness, inattention to duty, slovenly work and flirtations", and Kitchener came in for another word of praise when he clamped down on their gallivanting. "Serves them right," declared Emily, "for they have abused their privileges and disgraced the career which Florence Nightingale had made and ennobled." Of course there were splendid exceptions, but she thought the general quality of the nurses was amply illustrated by the fact that in one military hospital the milk for the entire establishment had been found on the windowsill of the typhoid ward.

*

By mid-March, still without the commander-in-chief's permission to go north to the Transvaal camps, Emily realised she might more profitably go back to England in the hope of mobilising public opinion. Towards the end of the month a change can be seen in the letters home as new and stricter censorship rules brought a greater circumspection. The private carriage of letters by road or rail was now prohibited under martial law, and Emily's correspondents were warned to take care how they wrote in future, while they in turn should expect nothing revealing from her.

The agonies caused by this enforced prudence can be imagined. Deprived of her accustomed outlet for raging against Kitchener and his works, Emily let off steam by keeping a diary. On Good Friday, 1901, she enters her impressions of a newly discovered camp at Orange River Station and of the "dreadful-looking creature" placed in charge. On Easter Day she tells the diary that not even tents can be found for the latest influx of six hundred people at Kimberley because Lord Kitchener had grabbed everything further up the line. She notes that her latest bundle of letters from home had taken a month to arrive and were mostly delivered censored, some twice over.

On April 9 – which Emily appears to forget is her forty-first birthday – she writes to her aunt from the famous siege-town of Mafeking after a particularly long and tedious journey. Despite succumbing to the temptation of buying a first-class ticket, she had been forced to travel second-class after all as "the officers crowd in and always get the best seats so that an unfortunate female had no chance". First class in South Africa was the equivalent of third at home, and anything below was "very dirty, smelly and disagreeable".

Stopping en route at a place called Warrenton, she had found over three hundred Boer women crammed into the village church and school owing to the shortage of tents, then the next day many hundreds more were dumped there. Mafeking itself was the end of the world, and the cart-trip out to the camp "like driving six miles into space". The eight or nine hundred inmates at Mafeking had better rations than at any other camp she knew, but were without blankets, candles and, inevitably, soap. It was at Mafeking, the first Transvaal camp she penetrated, that Emily collected one of her most vivid tales of the farm-burnings, told by an old woman who had thrown herself to the ground before the horse of General Lord Methuen and begged to be trampled to death. It was "a Job-like scene," Emily remarked. The old woman had brought no clothes to the camp but her white *dood-kleere*, or shroud.

Emily recorded a moment's soft-heartedness on the same general's part. At one of the farm-burnings, where as a rule all animals were confiscated, the lady of the house had confronted Lord Methuen with her ailing baby, which depended on a donkey's milk as she was unable to nurse it herself. Methuen relented and gave instructions that where the mother went, the donkey went also. But the story had no happy ending. Once the family reached camp, the donkey disappeared, and the commandant refused to help find it. Emily tried to save the weakening child, but one afternoon she was beckoned into the tent to see the tiny body laid out, a white flower in its hand – "a murdered innocent" aged three months.

Writing to her brother Leonard, Emily said she had resolved to buy mourning clothes for the child's mother, a Mrs Louew. "Don't think that foolish or extravagant," she begged. "You would not if you knew how much these people think of a bit of black and it seemed to me the best way to show sympathy." Though Emily hated mourning herself, the Boers were "like our Cornish folk" who would spend their last shilling on a piece of crepe. And so Mrs Louw's mourning would be "a present from England".

After four days Emily returned to Kimberley. At the Warrenton halt she saw two hundred and forty of the "so-called refugees" being sent on down the line unfed – "at the station were two trainloads of them, quite half in open coal-trucks, all piled up and wedged in with such goods as they had been able to bring". It was a scene burned into Emily's mind, with the truckloads of women and children hemmed in by flocks of frightened cattle and sheep – confiscations from the Boer farmlands – all "bellowing and baaing for food and drink". Truly this was "a picture of war in all its destructiveness, cruelty, stupidity and nakedness". The refugee trains followed Emily's slate-coloured armoured train to Kimberley, where just twenty-five bell tents awaited these two hundred and forty.

So the commander-in-chief was back in her black books. "I *thought* Lord Kitchener was considered such a great organiser," she wrote, "but is it good organising to have so little forethought and make so little preparation that thousands of people find themselves dumped down in strange places where there is *nothing* ready for their reception?"

Unpleasant news was waiting for her. Some weeks before, on a trip to Cape Town to collect the latest consignment of clothes from England, she had again met up with the philanthropist Joseph Rowntree, then on the point of sailing home. She spoke confidentially of her work in the camps, but the first account of her doings subsequently appeared in print in Britain and was then cabled back to the papers in South Africa. Though Emily declared Rowntree guiltless in the affair, the indiscretion meant trouble as the authorities were now wide-awake to her capacity to stir up trouble back home. She feared the publicity would cause the authorities in England to bar any successor being sent out by the Distress Committee.

Nor was this all. Some time before Emily had been invited to address the newly formed Loyal Ladies League in Bloemfontein, and had done so understanding the meeting to be private. A hostile report of her talk now appeared in the *Bloemfontein Post*, a newspaper printed under military auspices to replace a local paper closed down for refusing to toe the British line. The *Post* article hoped "that intense being" Miss Hobhouse, after presuming to instruct and correct ladies who had spent their lives in the town, would not make it her mission "to teach the refugees at the Refuge Camp, who have so much to be grateful for, to believe that they have grievances".

At first sight the episode seems to indicate a touching naivety on Emily's part in expecting a group calling themselves the Loyal Ladies to respect a notorious pro-Boer's wish for confidentiality. Alternatively, along with the Rowntree incident, it may simply point to the universal propensity for muddle and misunderstanding in times of war.

In her talk at Bloemfontein Emily particularly asked her audience to take up "the work of looking after the Native camps which have been formed and where I gather there is much sickness and destitution". The matter of these unexplored concentration camps for blacks weighed increasingly on her mind, and this was not the first time Emily pressed for action. Three times already she had written to the Distress Committee appealing for someone from London to come out to investigate. To Lady Hobhouse on March 4 she wrote asking if it was generally known at home that many large camps had been set up for the black population. These needed looking into very urgently as she understood that the death-rate in camps at Bloemfontein and elsewhere were very high.

*

Emily constantly set down her impressions of the country. The frequently-travelled railway line between Kimberley and Norval's Pont took her past some of the battlefields of Black Week, and she could see clearly from her carriage window the ridge at Magersfontein, where Highland troops had advanced under unrelenting Boer fire from that sinister innovation, a network of trenches. Nothing now marked the scene but the trenches and the graves. On the approach to Kimberley she noted – in rather the same tone in which the young Kitchener had disparaged the Cornish scenery compared with the Alps – that the mine heaps were not nearly as picturesque as those in Cornwall.

If her descriptions of the country are vivid, they are nothing compared to her wonderfully sweeping pronouncements on people, such as the doctor at Norval's Pont – "an insufferable cad and I pretty plainly told him so" – and the commandant at Kimberley, that "coarse, lazy, indifferent old man". And she takes a decidedly dim view of "the Baden-Powell police", otherwise the new South African Constabulary formed by the hero of Mafeking. Glimpsing a party on a passing train, she wonders: "Where on earth was such a low, rough, almost criminal-looking crew raked together?"

Emily knew her tongue made her enemies yet was unable to govern herself. General Pretyman, though now demoted to a post at Kimberley, was still a key figure, but he had begun to be "horribly cross" and "dreadfully testy" when harangued about the camps. He claimed to lack the authority to issue Emily with any more passes, while hopefully offering her one back to Cape Town. Relations at Norval's Pont reached a new low during one altercation in which Emily roundly informed the camp doctor that she would brook no criticism, interference or impertinence from a subordinate officer such as himself. She later confessed to her brother Leonard that she had mounted "a very high horse indeed".

Another high-horse incident blew up at her first meeting with a new commandant at the same camp. Fagged and dirty after two days travelling, she felt she had insufficient strength to drag herself the length of the platform to get her letters of introduction out of her trunk. When she explained her predicament to the officer, "he laughed at my plight and said he would believe me, but that did not suit me so I fetched the letters and then he would not look at them".

The perverse "that did not suit me" was now engrained in her character. Clearly these repeated confrontations with authority were not serving the best interests of Emily or the camp inmates and towards the end of her life she came to regret not only the practical consequences of her habitual outspokenness, but her "frequent misjudgement of men and things". In the light of riper experience she would remember incident after incident and "see in a flash how much better I could have acted – or written – or spoken". But such self-knowledge belonged to the future. In the meantime she limited herself to trying to exercise greater caution with new acquaintances, suspecting they might feign pro-Boer sympathies in the hope of egging her into indiscretions that could be reported. She longed to escape from the web of lies and horrors.

Emily did not have to fight every battle alone. At Bloemfontein she found valiant Sister Kennedy, daughter of a Devon clergyman, one of a tiny handful of volunteer nurses who were of actual use. When first met, sinking onto her bed in exhaustion, Sister Kennedy was trying to cope single-handed with seventy cases of typhoid besides epidemics of measles, pneumonia and tonsillitis. Then at Kimberley "a plucky little body of women" formed a committee of support for the activist from England. This deeply religious band opened their first meeting with prayers and a reading of the parable of the Good Samaritan, which it dawned on Emily was a reference to herself. This came as something of a shock, she told Leonard lightly, "but one gets hardened to everything, even to being publicly prayed over".

By late April she was back in Bloemfontein and again savouring the hospitality of Kaya Lami. She discovered that in the interval reprisals had been taken against Caroline Fichardt "for harbouring Miss Hobhouse", including the loss of the pass to visit her husband's grave. "Nothing daunted, she is harbouring me again," recorded Emily with pride.

In her absence the local camp population had shot up to four thousand, double the number she had left there only six weeks before. At Springfontein the once-manageable little camp of five hundred had swelled to house three thousand, and on a brief halt at the station on a bitter wet night Emily was shocked to see a further waiting trainload of six hundred, most of them in open trucks. A girl from the local mission house spotted Emily as her train was slowing at the platform and ran up with a can of hot coffee for her. This she gave to some of the women, as well as all the food she had for her journey. They had been travelling for two days without nourishment of any kind. Emily gave the mission worker money to buy all the food available at the station before jumping back onto her train at the last moment, as her permit was not stamped to break her journey.

At times she felt almost paralysed with despair. If only the camps had remained the size they were six weeks before! But the army sweeps were bringing in thousands more without any increase in rations or tents.[xv] The death rate was now rocketing not just at Bloemfontein but everywhere else, and two of the Boer girls Emily had trained as nurses were dead too. Emily lost her voice because of the constant arguing and pleading, but then all at once it seemed there was nothing left to say.

Colonel Goold-Adams, who had genuinely tried to persuade Kitchener to allow Emily into the camps further north, now admitted failure, and a telegram from Sir Alfred

Milner was unequivocal. Kitchener refused to budge. Emily made up her mind to return home instead and appeal directly to the British public.

*

On May 1, following daily visits to the local camp, Emily left Bloemfontein. As she did not expect to be able to secure a berth for England before mid-month, she broke her journey at Springfontein. To her horror, massed there at the side of the railway were the same unfortunate people whom she had seen when passing north ten days previously, and their condition beggared description. This was one of the most distressing of all Emily's experiences in the camps, and while still on the train she wrote a long and full account of what she had seen while it was fresh in her mind. The document was later posted to Lady Hobhouse, but for whatever reason never arrived in England.

What she remembered was painful enough. Without tents, the people could only shelter from the rain by crawling under rail trucks or begging bits of sailcloth from the soldiers who guarded them. Women clung to Emily, and she was led to one of the makeshift shelters to see a sick baby whose mother had nothing to give it. Emily thought a few drops of brandy might save its life but no brandy was to be bought, and when she sent a message to the camp a mile away, the superintendent refused to help. So there was nothing else to be done "and we watched the child draw its last breath in reverent silence".

To Emily it seemed that the essential elements of the great tragedy working itself out across South Africa had gathered under that old bit of sailcloth whose tattered sides hardly kept off sun, wind or rain. The mother, neither moving nor weeping over her dead child, was "far away into depths of grief beyond all tears", but a companion stood by calling on heaven to bear witness, and others crouching on the ground around her wept freely. This indelible spectacle was to have an aftermath. Years afterwards, when the South African government commissioned a national monument to the war dead, it was Emily's powerful description of this scene, with its echo of the Michelangelo *Pieta* at St Peter's in Rome, that would be the sculptor's inspiration.

Nor was this the only unforgettable incident of that day at Springfontein. Told that the aunt and uncle of Paul Kruger were there, Emily searched them out and found a couple nearly ninety years old, both veterans of the Great Trek of 1836. The woman was without a skirt, and Emily slipped off her own underskirt to cover her. These "brave and dignified old people" accepted the loss of all they owned as the will of the Lord. They would be dead and buried within a fortnight.

Emily stayed at the Springfontein camp till dusk, parrying repeated attempts by the superintendent to trap her into speaking out against official policy. Inwardly she rejoiced in the knowledge that she would soon be out of the country, free to broadcast to the world what she had seen. But when the train halted at Norval's Pont the next day, a further ordeal was in store for the shattered traveller. This was the last time she was stranded at night and the hardest to bear.

The train out of Norval's Pont was due at four in the afternoon but failed to appear. After dark came an announcement that no train would arrive until the following morning, but only military personnel were allowed to remain on the station. Worn out as she was, Emily had no choice but to climb the long road back to the camp, though she was utterly incapable of carrying her bag. Leaving it at the station office, she trudged off in the moonlight towards the camp, only to find her way barred by soldiers who demanded her pass. This was locked away back at the forbidden station. Summoning her last ounce of energy, Emily persuaded the soldiers to ignore their orders and let her creep into the camp, where she begged for shelter among the startled inmates.

Emily finally reached Cape Town on the morning of May 5, dirty, unkempt, and in the last stage of exhaustion. Even washing her face and hands had been impossible for days and her hair and clothes were stiff with red dust. She discovered that all ships for England were full except for a single berth. This was a cabin, first class, on the RMS *Saxon*, which was due to sail the day after next, and she reserved it gratefully. Booked on the same ship was Sir Alfred Milner.

11 "METHODS OF BARBARISM"

Once ensconced in the *Saxon* Emily displayed her usual lack of tact by making intimate friends of a Boer couple called Potgieter. The husband had been not only a leading light in the Transvaal republic but the last mayor of Pretoria, and she thought him by far the nicest man on board. The previous June it had fallen his lot to surrender the keys of the city to Lord Roberts, after which he refused to stay on in the occupied capital. The Potgieters helped Emily brush up her Afrikaans.

Milner kept himself aloof. A notoriously bad sailor, he recorded a feeling of mental torpor during the voyage. Emily's first attempt to beard him was foiled by the captain, who informed her that His Excellency did not desire to mingle with other passengers "nor speak to any lady", preferring to sit in solitary glory on a little raised dais in the seclusion of the upper deck. This did not suit Emily, and she continued to hover meaningfully; eventually Milner bowed to the inevitable and consented to exchange a few words at the railings. Emily at once plunged into her subject, whereupon the green-faced Sir Alfred gave the rough weather as an excuse for cutting the interview short. "I shall wait a few days and then bring him to book," Emily wrote to a friend from Madeira, adding that she hoped to seize her moment sometime between the extreme heat of the equator and the notoriously stormy Bay of Biscay.

A week into the voyage, she found her opportunity. As the rest of the passengers crowded the side to watch the receding cliffs of Madeira, Emily spotted her quarry alone and pounced. "We went rather fully into the matter then," she wrote, and Sir Alfred let slip the fact that during her weeks in the camps he had received some sixty-four reports on her behaviour. The number astonished Emily. Although she had been aware of spies dogging her footsteps, and of *agents-provocateurs* like the superintendent at Springfontein, all she could think was: "What an army of informers to pay!"

Unblushingly, Emily insisted she had always kept her bargain to steer clear of politics or associated matters, and chided Sir Alfred for his lack of trust. For good measure she spoke her mind about the low class of people he employed to act as his spies. For once Milner had no pat answers, but then as he admitted: "My brain is never worth anything on a voyage."

Emily thought there were two Sir Alfred Milners. One was a charming, sympathetic, gracious and cultivated man whose liberal leanings inevitably placed him at odds with the military figures crowded around him; the other Sir Alfred was the politician, bound in honour to do his government's dirty work. She felt that "the clash must have given him many dolorous moments of extreme agony". No doubt the third Sir Alfred, the masterful manipulator of men and nations who would enter the history books, would have filled Emily with horror.

But while Milner was being elusive, his private secretary was putting himself about in a decidedly obnoxious fashion. This was one Osmund "Ozzy" Walrond, who was heard to remark that Emily was wasting her time improving her Afrikaans as she would certainly never be allowed into South Africa again. Emily believed it was because of Walrond that she found herself much shunned on the ship, though her claim that she was only too glad to be left in peace rings a little hollow.

Also skulking on board was a particular bugbear of Emily's, the Reverend Adriaan Hofmeyr. A former minister of the Dutch Reformed Church, Hofmeyr had been suspended for immoral conduct with a member of his congregation, and had later found work as an agent for Cecil Rhodes. Despised by his fellow Boers for siding with the enemy, he had been feted in England during the Khaki Election, and throughout Emily's time in the camps was employed by the military in a vain effort to persuade the women inmates to induce their menfolk to surrender. Emily had refused to be introduced to Hofmeyr – "what a coarse repulsive-looking man he is!" – when he appeared at Bloemfontein in January. But he had the ear of Milner, and the esteem he enjoyed among the jingo party in England gave him power to harm Emily. How he would use that power was soon to be revealed.

Speculation had been rife over Milner's departure from South Africa, which left Kitchener as supreme head of both the military and civic authorities. Officially he was taking home leave after more than two years at full gallop, but pro-Boers like Emily's mentor Leonard Courtney believed and hoped he was being recalled in disgrace. Even one as high-placed as the chancellor of the exchequer, Sir Michael Hicks-Beach, saw something odd about Milner's return, suspecting that his nerve had gone after a fall-out with Kitchener.

The *Saxon* docked at Southampton on May 24 – propitiously, Empire Day – and the reason for the high commissioner's homecoming now became clear. He had been called back not in disgrace, but to be made a lord.

It is telling that on first receiving news that he was to be elevated to the peerage, Milner believed himself the victim of a hoax. In fact, Lord Salisbury felt his government's determination to stick to a hard line on South Africa could best be signalled by honouring the man who had torpedoed Kitchener's peace plan. The reception party waiting at Waterloo included Salisbury, Chamberlain and Earl Roberts, and Milner was driven in an open landau through cheering crowds to kiss the hand of the new king.

His choice of title was Baron Milner of St James's and Cape Town. Emily, with her inbred awareness of social niceties, must have allowed herself a derisive snort at the "of St James's", for the landless Milner was the first peer to name himself after his lodgings. As for the South African element of the title, his private villa there, "Sunnyside", lacked a sufficiently baronial ring, so he boldly annexed the whole city, rather as a victorious general like Kitchener or Roberts would take his designation from a conquered capital. This more sinister aspect of Milner's title would not have escaped Emily when she read the royal proclamation.

Emily had found the voyage tiring and the return to northern climes made her hands feel constantly frozen. Perhaps it had already crossed her mind she would never again feel really at home in England, a country she believed to be shamed by its war role, and where so many old friends turned their backs on her. Though soon reunited with her aunt and uncle amid the beauties of Crowsley Park, the borrowed gothic mansion in

Leonard Hobhouse drew up a list of key points for his sister's crucial interview at the War Office.

Oxfordshire, she was tormented by memories of the camps. She could know no peace until her story was told to all England. Distressing images rose constantly before her: the mother at Springfontein with her dead baby under a scrap of canvas; the tiny corpses lined up to be photographed for absent fathers; the old lady begging for death under the hooves of the general's horse.

At first Emily proceeded with uncharacteristic caution, no doubt under persuasion of the Hobhouse inner circle. She still entertained hopes of Milner, from whom she had extracted a promise to write very soon after reaching England.

It began to seem she would wait in vain. As man of the hour, Milner was being showered with congratulatory letters and telegrams and whirled from banquet to banquet as guest of honour. Hostesses vied to tempt the Empire's newest peer into the capital's grandest drawing rooms. He was sworn into the Privy Council and awarded the freedom of the city of London. On May 28 he went to Windsor at the invitation of the monarch and his queen, and was the first guest in living memory to be commanded to stay a second night, when King Edward introduced him to the new game of bridge. Perhaps Milner was tempted to sneak into Madame Tussaud's to view the new waxwork exhibit of himself, but if so his diary is silent on the fact. He did however find time for Lady Edward Cecil, who had departed from South Africa alone following an unsatisfactory reunion with her husband after the relief of Mafeking; he also visited, at a secret address in Brixton, a lady referred to in his diary only as Cecile D, his kept mistress of many years.

Brother Leonard and Uncle Arthur counselled Emily to seek an immediate interview with the war secretary, St John Brodrick. Of course it did no harm that he and Emily were related, Uncle Edmund the bishop having married a Miss Brodrick. A courteous reply came from the minister by return and an appointment fixed for noon on June 4 at the War Office, then housed in a rabbit warren of a building in Pall Mall. Leonard, fearing his sister's tendency to ramble into too much detail, drew up a list of key points to hammer home during the interview. Family influence also secured promises of appointments with other important figures, chief among them the Liberal leader, Sir Henry Campbell-Bannerman. Back in London, Emily spent a night at Cheyne Walk with the Courtneys before returning to the Chelsea flat, and braced herself for the all-important confrontation.

Writing to Leonard immediately after a meeting lasting two hours, Emily said she had come away from the War Office with a strong impression of Brodrick's "gentlemanly incompetence". She found him "slippery but pleasant, mediocre and agreeable; ready to listen, ready also to drift", but unfortunately convinced of the overall rightness of British policy in the camps. "Did not feel I got my claws into him *anywhere*," she noted despondently.

With his pompous manner and droopy moustache, Brodrick was not a commanding figure. Many believed he owed his appointment to the fact he was heir to a viscount. Contemporaries in government saw him as weak, vacillating, and prone to gaffes; nor was he helped by encroaching deafness. Emily's assessment of the man's powers might have been even dimmer had she known that on the outbreak of the war he bet his brother-in-law a case of champagne that it would all be over by Christmas.

The most sinister aspect of the interview was that she had picked up a strong indication that the government would oppose her return to South Africa. On the positive side, she managed to put across almost every point on Leonard's list, and the minister had asked her to put into writing her own suggestions for improving the camps. But true to form, Emily could not leave the man without an unwise dig: "Poor Brodrick! When I ended by telling him I should be obliged to make public his refusal to let me go again, he turned white as a sheet!"

Emily's initial requests were quite modest. She called for the release of any women possessing the means to support themselves outside the camps, for philanthropic societies to be permitted to organise distributions similar to her own, and for a resident minister of religion and a matron in each camp. She also wanted equality of treatment for all inmates, whether kin of fighting Boers or "hands-uppers". In the end, she came away from the War Office convinced that she had pleaded her case well despite her desperately-felt if invisible shyness: "The vision of the camps and suffering women was vivid and I felt myself the mediator between them and the Powers of England," she wrote.

Unknown to Emily, Brodrick's first step was to sound out Milner. Penning a lengthy private and confidential memo in reply, the new peer set out views that would have left her astonished and outraged. Most of her proposals he set his face against, or dismissed as purely military matters to be referred to Kitchener. While he conceded the government may have been too stingy over supplies for the camp inmates, the fact was "we don't want to make them too comfortable". But it was on the subject of Emily herself, and the prospect of her return to South Africa, that the smiling diplomat's mask fell away.

"I should advise her not returning and nobody else being sent," he wrote. "Of course, there will be a howl, but the pro-Boers will howl whatever we do." And he went on: "I have myself to write to Miss Hobhouse, and tell her whether she is to be allowed to return. If she does not she will doubtless make all possible mischief in England." On the one hand, "if we lay down the principle of allowing no more outsiders to meddle with the camps, and stick to it, we shall gain more than we lose"; on the other hand, "if for parliamentary or other reasons, it is thought necessary to allow such meddling, then Miss Hobhouse had better be one of the meddlers. As long as she is working in the camps she will not be able to carry on a crusade in England, though of course, she can *write* mischievously".

To another correspondent Milner said he never knew whether to laugh or cry when listening to deluded Utopians like Emily who believed that conciliation with the Boers needed only "a little more patience, a little more meekness, a little more of those gentle virtues of which I know I am so conspicuously devoid". The reality was that Britain's enemies in South Africa were lost to "panoplied hatred, insensate ambitions, invincible ignorance".

Those like Leonard Courtney he now hated with a passion. Endorsing a friend's remark that the great flaw of the English was their sham canting sentimentality, Milner complained of the pro-Boer Liberals' gushing affection for a people who trampled decency underfoot. And he declared: "Every crime against liberalism and humanity is pardonable in the eyes of these gentry on one condition, which is that it should be committed by an enemy of their country. That circumstance purified and sanctifies all." The more brutally the Boers treated the native population, the clearer became the rottenness, corruption, and barbarism of the whole Boer system, and the more the Courtneys seemed to like it.

*

Until now Emily had been a thorn in the flesh to the authorities in South Africa and a relatively minor irritant to a handful of politicians and officials in Whitehall, but she was not yet a household name. This was about to change.

Despite her resolution to squeeze the government for every possible concession before she went public, the temptation to tell all proved irresistible. Without waiting for Brodrick's promised reply, Emily handed the Distress Committee a forty-page report for publication, and on June 18 a shorter pamphlet based on her letters was circulated to both Houses of Parliament. The day after the electrifying document came into the hands of MPs, a noisy meeting was held at the Queen's Hall – scene of that "magnificent assemblage" of anti-war women just one year before – with Lloyd George predictably centre stage. With a contemptuous dismissal of a body of flag-waving jingoists struggling to gatecrash the ticket-only gathering, the Welshman brandished the report and bellowed that "the Herod of old sought to crush a little race by killing all the young children" and branded the government as "Herod's modern imitator". To the public at large, Emily's revelations came as a thunderbolt.

By far the most important repercussion followed Emily's interview with the leader of the opposition. Here at last she found a key political figure who was receptive – so much so that she poured out to him as to no one else the detailed horrors of the camps. For nearly two hours Campbell-Bannerman listened with rapt attention as Emily spoke of the wholesale burning of farms and villages, the desperate condition of a burnt-out population deprived of necessities like clothes, bedding and basic utensils, the semi-starvation in the camps, the fever-stricken children lying sick unto death upon the bare earth, the disease-laden atmosphere, the appalling mortality. As he listened, Emily would later say, the visibly moved Sir Henry repeatedly murmured "Methods of barbarism... methods of barbarism". These words would soon fly around the world.

That evening the Liberal leader was guest speaker at a dinner given by the National Reform Union. Here was his opportunity publicly to question the government's demand for the Boers' unconditional surrender and to denounce the inhumanity of the concentration camps exposed by Emily. "When was a war not a war?" he asked. "When it is carried on by methods of barbarism in South Africa."

The outcry was instant. Newspapers throughout the world printed the speech. At home the press denounced the Liberal leader for insulting the British Army and the British people, declaring him unfit to head a great national party. Lord Hugh Cecil, the prime minister's MP son, led the Tory counter-attack, sneering at Campbell-Bannerman for a pusillanimous assault on the government and asking why, if the accusations were true, he had not called for "at least the severe reprimand" of Lord Kitchener. As to the suffering involved in "devastating and concentrating", said Lord Hugh, babies had died for want of milk during the siege of Kimberley, but he had not blamed the Boers for the consequence of their operations.

Lloyd George returned to the offensive in the parliamentary debate, accusing the government of a policy of extermination. Campbell-Bannerman himself insisted he had never uttered a word implying cruelty or even indifference on the part of the army. "It was the whole system I consider, to use a word I have already applied to it, barbarous," he declared. "What I object to is the whole policy of concentration, the whole policy of destroying the homes of women and children, involving them in circumstances of considerable cruelty, certainly of unintentional cruelty." So why not act on Miss Hobhouse's advice? Why not send out properly trained doctors and nurses to deal with the epidemics? Why not free the women who could fend for themselves?

Emily watched despairingly from behind the women's grille in the Commons as her advocates were howled down. As she wrote afterwards: "In common with the Boer women, I felt sure that English humanity would not fail to respond instantly if the facts were clearly understood. I was wrong. No barbarisms in South Africa could equal the cold cruelty of that indifferent House."

It was now the personal attacks began. *The Times* fired the opening shots of a campaign against Emily that would last beyond her dying day. Initially the paper had printed a neutral account of Emily's published findings while casting doubt on the veracity of her Boer women's stories, remarking "it would not appear that the narrators were subjected to any searching cross-examination by Miss Hobhouse". After all, *The Times* correspondent Flora Shaw, perhaps the most influential woman journalist alive, had consistently presented images of order and even comfort in the camps, painting rosy pictures of the happy faces of children and the state of harmony existing between camp authorities and inmates.

With the Campbell-Bannerman speech the gloves came off. An editorial of June 19 dismissed Emily's claims and heaped praise on the government for refusing to let the camps be "turned into centres of agitation by the action, intentional or unintentional, of real or sham philanthropists, who write bloodcurdling descriptions and disseminate false and inaccurate stories". From now on the paper's Cape Town correspondents would dig up every possible anti-Emily story, leader-writers would vie in branding her an ignorant troublemaker or worse, and a host of readers would pen virulent letters to the editor.

A repeated accusation from Cape Town was that Emily's claims revealed her lack of knowledge of the country and of normal conditions of Boer life on the veld. This was the cue for Adriaan Hofmeyr to exact his revenge.

A letter of Hofmeyr's printed in *The Times* within days of Emily's report dealt a succession of shrewd blows. Here was a Boer, a clergyman too, who thanked God that England was so generous and kind to the women and children of his poor people, and who confirmed that the high mortality rate among his countryfolk was their own fault. The Boers were unused to "sanitary arrangements", he wrote, and in their little communities death from measles, diphtheria and the like was commonplace. Similarly with the general conditions in the camps, "what is apparently a hardship to Miss Hobhouse and other gently-nurtured English people we out there make light of".

When Miss Hobhouse condoled with the refugees, he argued, they made the most of their grievances, knowing that through this English lady they could damage the enemy England in the eyes of the world. The male inmates, more level-headed than the women, had told Hofmeyr how they longed for peace, "but everyone can understand how visits of such English ladies must unsettle their minds again". He knew from personal observation that Miss Hobhouse had filled their heads with stories about the Liberals coming to power and reversing South African policy, and had forecast intervention by a great power.

"I say that England's greatest enemies are in England," declared Hofmeyr roundly. But for the agitation of the pro-Boers, his misguided countrymen would long ago have sued for peace.

It was music to Emily's foes, and *The Times* weighed in with an editorial strongly endorsing the reverend correspondent's line: "Mr Hofmeyr has visited a great many more concentration camps than Miss Hobhouse ever saw. He knows much better than she does how to get the truth from people of his own blood and his own speech. He knows how they usually live, what are their habitual sanitary arrangements and standards of comfort, what epidemics mean in Boer families." Indeed, the inmates themselves "are eager to acknowledge the kindness with which they are treated, except when they see a chance to pour lamentations into the ears of sentimentalists in search of vituperations of their own Government".

The attacks gathered force. A Mrs Stuart of the Guild of Loyal Women of South

Africa claimed that Emily's report was "unintentionally a marvellous testimony to the exceeding care our military have expended upon the women and children of the very men who are shooting our brave soldiers down", adding the stinging remark that in her keenness for the Boers, Emily had ignored the suffering of the loyalists' children.

This was an argument developed by a well-known figure called Sarah Heckford, who had long ago earned the praise of Charles Dickens for her work among sick children. Recently returned to England after twenty years in the Transvaal, Mrs Heckford told *The Times* readers that when Miss Hobhouse "endeavours to harrow the feelings of others by describing what she imagines to be hardships to Boer women and children in the concentration camps, she provokes a smile from those who know the habits of the Boers".

Even Emily's adventure with the snake was ridiculed. A claim originating in the Cape's English-language paper, and gleefully taken up by the British press, was that the reptile in question had been no adder but a harmless house snake, easily recognised by a South African if not by an English lady – though the article failed to explain why all the South Africans present had instantly fled.

Punch magazine contributed with a facetious piece in which Emily's requirements for the camps were feebly parodied. In the *Punch* version of her list of necessities, Boer ladies were languishing in the camps for want of an adequate supply of hairpins and spirit lamps for heating their curling tongs, and British officers were castigated for their brutality in failing to appear for afternoon tea.

Vying with *The Times* in the ferocity of its assaults was the *Daily Mail*, owned by the future Lord Northcliffe, Alfred Harmsworth. Emily was an interfering woman who was not impartial, had no balance in her judgments, and knew nothing of war, editorialised the *Mail*. According to a Fleet Street legend, one brave journalist who protested over the proprietor's pro-war, anti-Emily stance was silenced by Harmsworth reaching down the circulation ledger. "Look," said the press baron, "here we began our campaign. See, up, up, up."

Emily affected unconcern at the attacks and the constant snubs she met with. The poet, traveller and notorious womaniser Wilfrid Scawen Blunt, meeting Emily at a lunch hosted by a pro-Boer, wrote in his diary that the poor lady was much persecuted on account of her stand: "People are rude to her, refuse to shake hands, and they get up to go when she enters a drawing room." However, Blunt was known for his unbalanced hatred of Lord Kitchener, and may well have led their conversation to a curious hobbyhorse of his, alarming Emily with a flat assertion that the general still possessed the Mahdi's head, having wickedly placed a substitute – "perhaps ham sandwiches" – in the container which was buried.

*

Emily now braced herself for her one-woman crusade, starting with public meetings up and down the country. Halls were booked at Bristol, Birmingham, Manchester, Leeds, and York; after proclaiming her message to the great cities, she planned to move on to the crowded seaside resorts. It was a remarkable undertaking for one who never overcame the agonies of stage-fright. She steeled herself to the task by addressing a large private gathering of ladies at Aunt Mary's house in Mayfair, where she later remembered telling her audience how hard she found it to speak to people as well-dressed and well-fed as themselves after leaving the Boer women in squalor and hunger. Clearly the speech did not make for comfortable hearing.

There was an unfortunate outcome to the rowdy Lloyd George meeting at the Queen's Hall. Emily had intended to make her public debut from the same platform, but she saw the authorities at work behind the scenes when the contract was broken at three days' notice. Next she tried to book Westminster Chapel, but the deacons cried off after a police warning that disturbances were likely. It was a bad start to the campaign. With the first meeting cancelled, the Bishop of Hereford, who had agreed to take the chair, wrote to *The Times* to complain of a new phenomenon in English life, "for such meetings to be rendered dangerous or impossible by a portion of the Press and the lawless and brutal element in the community". In Emily's eyes the ructions in London were proof that the government was scheming to undermine her appeal to the public and boded ill for the countrywide tour.

Brodrick's promised letter, when it came, was not as negative as feared. The government was now fully awake to the threat of a public relations disaster over the camps, and the accident-prone Brodrick was feeling his way with caution. Though evasive in its general tenor, his letter appeared to endorse the idea of letting solvent women out of the camps, and implied that other reforms were already in hand. Emily, still angling for War Office approval for a return to South Africa, took the minister at his word.

Others in her circle reacted as naively. Kate Courtney wrote to Leonard Hobhouse that Brodrick's response was "a great triumph, the Government really accepting your sister's suggestions, though their friends will probably continue to abuse her and us as traitors".

Behind the scenes Brodrick was seriously rattled. As early as April, he had alerted Kitchener to the private circulation of Emily's South Africa letters. Liberals and even some Conservatives were "hot on the humanitarian tack" but he still hoped parliamentary critics could be kept at bay. Secret correspondence then passed between Brodrick and Chamberlain, with the text of Emily's letters attached. Earl Roberts, copied into the exchange, urged the war secretary to telegraph Kitchener with the gist of the claims and ask for action "to render the life of the women and children as little irksome as possible". These memos highlight an important difference of opinion. Chamberlain thought the Boer families should be allowed back to their homes – the government could thereby wash its hands of the problem – while Roberts insisted that anyone leaving the camps would die of starvation. It was also in April that Brodrick first warned Kitchener to expect "a pretty hot time" over reports on the camps, and asked the commander-in-chief to feed him all that would help the defence.

By this time Brodrick suspected that Kitchener's instinctive reaction was to play down any question about the camps. As the furore over Emily's report mounted, he fired off no fewer than three cables to Pretoria in a single day. First, he asked Kitchener for monthly statistics on deaths, "white and coloured"; next, he belatedly itemised Emily's requests for the commander-in-chief's comments, repeating forlornly that the camps were exciting great attention; thirdly, he telegraphed to complain that the camps have become "the stalking horse of the opposition and I am pounded daily about them".

Kitchener took two days to reply. He seemed to wonder what all the fuss was about. Women, children, old folk and reliable male inmates *were* allowed to leave camp; each camp *had* a matron and a medical officer with trained staffs; ministers of religion *were* resident in or near all camps; separated families *were* brought together whenever possible. The harassed Brodrick cabled back the next day. In future would Lord Kitchener please provide statistics of camp deaths on a *fortnightly* basis?

As the telegrams continued to fly from Whitehall to Melrose House, the flamboyant Renaissance-style mansion that served as Kitchener's headquarters in Pretoria, something like panic set in. The opposition turned up the heat, continually pressing both war and colonial secretaries for some new statistic or clarification. Explanations were difficult because of the constant need to draw distinctions between the state of affairs in different camps at different times for different categories of inmate – the genuine refugees, the families of hands-uppers, and those classified as irreconcilables. Even Chamberlain, usually a masterful performer in the Commons, shifted his ground miserably when questioned about the camps.

The fact was that Milner's absence from South Africa had created a mountain of anomalies. In theory Kitchener had now relinquished military control of all camps to civilian superintendents chosen by Milner – Uitlanders to a man – and these had taken up post as long ago as February. But while they were responsible for the camps' internal management, the superintendents were tied to campsites established by the army, and no camp could be moved or extended, or a new one set up, without direct military approval. In practice this meant that any question of policy – for instance, whether families could be reunited – had to be referred to the commander-in-chief himself. So even a superintendent genuinely intent on improvements found himself hamstrung by military considerations. Worse, no civilian administrator had the slightest control over the numbers of people dumped at his gates, and precious little over supplies.

Kitchener tried to pass the parcel. In response to yet another query from Brodrick, he signalled plaintively: "I wonder you do not hand over the questions about the camps to the Colonial Secretary, they are entirely worked by the civil administration." The problem was that in Milner's absence, Kitchener *was* the civil administration. As Emily had pointed out from the outset, the interlacing of military and civil authority was the major obstacle to improving conditions. She was justified in her taunts against the "great organiser", since the difficulties had escalated hugely on the day that she and Milner sailed on the *Saxon*.

Kitchener had courted trouble by assuming the civil powers, rather than countenance the appointment of a stand-in for Milner. All the key political figures had counselled against the dual role, from Brodrick to Milner himself. Even King Edward expressed reservations over the increased burden on his commander-in-chief. Once again it was old Lord Roberts who had fought his protégé's corner and finally won the day.

Back on May 9, when Emily and Milner were still on the high seas, Kitchener had told Brodrick: "I wish I could get rid of these camps, but it is the only way to settle the country and enable the men to leave their commandos and come in to their families without being caught and tried for desertion." This was a reference to surrendered Boer emissaries, sent off by the British to persuade fighting Boers to give up, who were shot as traitors over their open graves.

By the time of the outcry over Emily's report, Kitchener was heartily sick of the camps. As if he hadn't enough on his plate with running the war and controlling the civic government of the whole sub-continent, he was now faced with a development demanding his most careful attention. On good authority, the Boer leaders were "nibbling at peace again", and the last thing he needed was this endless bombardment of Whitehall telegrams about the camps, with demands for pettifogging details about soap and bread and blankets.

On June 21, the day after the outlawed Boer leaders had gathered at an isolated farmhouse to decide whether to call off the war, Kitchener's temper finally snapped.

12 "TRAITOR TO HER COUNTRY"

S hortly before the furore over Emily's revelations, General Botha's wife Annie had been granted special permission to leave South Africa for Europe, and was widely believed to be carrying a message to the exiled Kruger declaring the Boer cause to be lost. A pretty woman of Irish descent, Annie Botha was regarded as relatively sympathetic to the British after acting as go-between for her husband's rendezvous with Kitchener at Middelburg. At the height of the previous year's fighting she had raised eyebrows by dining with Lord Roberts on what to the Boers was one of the darkest days of the war, the surrender of the commander-in-chief of the Free State, General Prinsloo, and more than four thousand men.

Both Roberts and Kitchener harboured a soft spot for the lady despite warnings from a Milner spy that she was in league with the enemy in the field. Roberts counted Mrs Botha among those who realised the futility of prolonging hostilities, and once wrote to Queen Victoria calling the enemy general's wife "a very nice person". After annexing the Transvaal, he sent a message to Louis Botha threatening to transport all families of commandos in open railway trucks but suggested that closed carriages might be found for the wives of Kruger and himself.

Four years Emily's junior, Mrs Botha was the subject of some fulsome and clumsy verse by her English friend – one of only two poems Emily is known to have composed – praising the "forget-me-nots from Irish streams" in Annie's eyes and the "wild roses, pink and white" of her complexion. The lines go on:

> Thy Irish charms 'neath Afric's sun
> To perfect ripeness grew;
> The veld its web of mystery spun
> And o'er thy spirit threw.

Landing at Southampton on June 8, the Irish charmer declined to talk to reporters but passing through London next day sought out Emily for a tête-à-tête. This was during the brief lull between Emily's interview with St John Brodrick and the thunderclap publication of her report on the camps. The two women were closeted for two hours before Annie continued on her way to see Kruger in Holland.

Fevered speculation surrounded Mrs Botha's objective. The Times initially claimed she was on a peace mission with Kitchener's blessing before more cautiously suggesting she might be travelling for health reasons. The Paris newspaper Le Matin insisted she was in Europe for her health but spoke of a widespread belief that she was the bearer of peace proposals. A Colonial Office minute at this time referred to "Mrs Botha's negotiations with Kruger", though a British intelligence agent in Holland reported the president as refusing to see Mrs Botha because of some private squabble; one of Kruger's inner circle poured scorn on the idea of a peace initiative by posing the question: "Is it likely that Lord Kitchener would employ a woman?"

What was the truth of it? A meeting took place between Mrs Botha and Kruger in Utrecht on June 14 – the very day of Campbell-Bannerman's sensational "methods of barbarism" speech – followed by a second interview the following morning. This opens the question whether Emily, buoyed by her meeting with the Liberal leader, had sought to influence the line taken by Mrs Botha with Kruger. Critics repeatedly accused Emily's circle of giving false hope to the enemy, and Campbell-Bannerman's speech certainly spread dismay among many on his own side. Suspicions that she was involved in some kind of intrigue would not have been confined to the Tories.

Emily touched on the matter in a letter to her brother but failed to clarify her role. "I fancy Mrs Botha's mission does not mean much from the Peace point of view," she wrote. "She needed change and only I think hopes to weld together the two parties among the Boers." And a letter from Kitchener, found long afterwards among Lord Roberts's papers, put a more prosaic slant on Annie Botha's goal. "She is hard up and cannot get funds out of her husband or elsewhere," Kitchener had informed his old chief as far back as April. "She told me she intends to ask Kruger to pay her Louis Botha's salary and meant to get it." Of his decision to allow her out of South Africa, he added offhandedly: "I do not see that she can do any harm at home or any good here."

*

As things fell out, Mrs Botha's visit to Europe came at a critical juncture for Kitchener, one which over the coming days would place an intolerable strain on his nerves. By the time her ship sailed, captured enemy letters had revealed that surrender was again on the Boer agenda.

How the letters fell into British hands became the stuff of legend. That stubborn bear of a man, Marthinus Steyn, the Free State's bald-headed, red-bearded president, had shared the roving life of the commandos since the fall of his capital, but on this celebrated occasion his camp had been surprised at night by British troops. While nearly all his band surrendered, the president himself escaped by a hair's-breadth, racing off on a bareback nag in his sleeping-cap and nightshirt. From letters in Steyn's seized baggage Kitchener discovered the Free Staters had been warned that their Transvaaler comrades-in-arms were secretly on the point of seeking terms. Their reasons included lack of ammunition, growing numbers of surrenders – these Kitchener attributed in part to the attractiveness of the concentration camps – and alarming signs of disaffection among the rank-and-file.

Also in the commander-in-chief's possession was a note to Steyn from General Smuts. He begged for peace before the Boer folk lost all faith, with the rider that the struggle could always be renewed in the future. Even better from the British viewpoint, reliable intelligence had now reached Kitchener that Louis Botha, the commandant-general himself, favoured a new effort to end the war.

The settled policy of clearing the country and herding the displaced into camps had now been in force for six months. Kitchener was convinced that these draconian measures had brought the Boers to the peace talks at Middelburg and were about to force the longed-for surrender, and once again the tantalising vision of India rose before his eyes. There was every reason to believe he would soon be following Roberts home to a hero's welcome, en route to Bombay.

Matters progressed encouragingly with the arrival of an official communication from the Transvaal leadership asking permission for Boer emissaries to leave the country in order to explain the present situation to the exiled president. Surely, faced with his people's desperate suffering, Kruger had no choice but to advise the generals to sue for peace? Yet again it seemed Kitchener would be thwarted. Out of the blue the cabinet denied him a free hand in any negotiations, insisting that his authority to deal with Botha covered only a cessation of hostilities. Also ruled out was any official recognition of a role for Kruger and his advisers. The instructions might have come from the cabinet, but they bore the unmistakeable fingerprints of Alfred Milner.

The Transvaalers were determined their president should not be sidelined. On June 3, using the Dutch consul in South Africa as intermediary, Smuts sent a cable in cipher to Kruger which painted the Boers' plight in the bleakest colours: "Most farms and most foodstuffs have been destroyed, almost all families are held in the camps where the treatment is not good and the misery very great. The two republics are a desert..."

Then came a breakthrough for Kitchener. The Smuts message was intercepted. At the War Office Roberts urgently demanded the deciphering of both the Smuts telegram and the expected answer from Holland. Roberts's old military secretary, now director-general of military intelligence, found a mysterious "someone in Ireland" who was able to crack the code.

Representatives of the two republics gathered on June 20 at a farmhouse at Waterval in the Transvaal to hear Kruger's reply. According to a later account by Smuts's son, the message from the sick old president, far away and out of touch with reality, was an uncompromising "Fight on!" What Kruger and his advisors actually said was that, mindful of the sacrifices already made, "we trust that the good cause will not be given up unless it becomes absolutely impossible to continue the struggle". Kruger claimed there had been a strong reversal of public opinion in England in the Boers' favour – a claim it is tempting to link with the interview with Mrs Botha and with the worldwide outcry over Campbell-Bannerman's speech. In fact these developments came too late to influence the exiled president, as the response to Smuts is dated June 11. His mind was made up before the meeting with Annie Botha.

Crucially, Kruger insisted that the chosen course of action must be endorsed by both republics. This effectively handed a veto to the obdurate Steyn, husband of Emily's great friend Isabella. The Free State might have been dragged into the war by its sister republic, but under Steyn's leadership had repeatedly stiffened Boer resistance when the Transvaal's will to fight began to crumble. Now once again, with the vehement backing of his charismatic general De Wet, Steyn harangued the assembled leaders until they agreed to fight on. It was a decision that would bring a further year's devastation to their land, an increase of one hundred million pounds to Britain's national debt, and many thousands more deaths, mostly of women and children in the concentration camps.

How quickly the decoded messages came into Kitchener's hands is unclear but Waterval dealt a shattering blow to his hopes which cannot be separated from his extraordinary emotional outburst on June 21. In a heated exchange of cables with St John Brodrick, he fulminated against the Boers as "uncivilised Africander savages with only a thin white veneer". Taking his cue from Smuts, he foresaw that it would be many generations before they forgot or forgave the war but would "bide their time and when we are least prepared for it, try the issue again".

The malign role of the female was not forgotten. "The Boer woman in the refugee camp," fumed Kitchener, "who slaps her protruding belly at you and shouts 'When all our men are gone, these little Khakis will fight you', is a type of savage produced by generations of wild lonely life. Back on their farms and their life on the veldt, they will be just as uncivilised as ever and a constant danger." On the same day, in a letter to his friend Lady Cranborne, frustration brought him close to self-pity: "I hope if they have anyone who can do the work better they will send him – it is not fair on the Army if anyone else could bring matters to a nearer end."

As the storm of criticism over the camps refused to die down, Brodrick seemed on the verge of losing his nerve. On July 6 he moaned about the endless queue of organisations now demanding to send people to investigate the camps – "we are refusing all," he added, "but think of sending some half dozen ourselves".

The problem was that the numbers in the camps were still shooting up. Back in March, the third of Emily's four months in South Africa, there had been a total of only 35,000 whites in all the camps; within six months there would be 110,000 with no proportionate increase in the number of campsites. Indeed, to the twenty-seven camps existing in March, only six new ones were added.

With greater overcrowding, the death rate soared. Emily had been alarmed at the increase during her time in the camps, which went from around 250 deaths over her first three months to 395 in April alone; and far, far worse was to come. Kitchener meanwhile doggedly continued to blame the Boer women themselves, particularly over the infant mortalities. To Brodrick he wrote: "It is impossible to fight against the criminal neglect of the mothers – I do not like the idea of using force but I am considering whether some of the worst cases should not be tried for manslaughter."

The widespread belief in the Boer women's culpability never ceased to infuriate Emily. She first heard the claim in her Bloemfontein days when harrying General Pretyman for passes. Pretyman became furious when tackled over deaths in the camps and his answer was to abuse the Boers as a whole, and the mothers in particular, as brutal, heartless, ignorant people who deliberately murdered their children with foolish remedies.

Two accusations were common, according to Emily – sick children were covered in "green paint" by their mothers, and were fed raw carrots. The so-called green paint was in fact a soothing ointment made of eucalyptus leaves and brought to mind her youth in Cornwall when, in the absence of a doctor, she had treated villagers with home-made herbal remedies. She saw nothing wrong with eating raw carrot but disbelieved the story as vegetables were almost unobtainable in the camps.

But there were other allegations, less easily refuted, which Emily ignored. Not all Kitchener's generals were unsympathetic towards the camp women, and during her stay in South Africa the army commander in the forbidden Transvaal territory, Sir John Maxwell, had personally opened a subscription list to provide "necessities" for the inmates; further, an appeal for funds by Maxwell's American-born wife was published in the *New York Herald*. Yet even General Maxwell joined the chorus of disapproval, telling his chief: "The Boer mother is greatly to blame, she insists on tending her children, refuses to obey the orders of the doctor or the advice of the nurse. The Boer remedy for measles apparently is a tea made from goat's dung, this is administered by the mother with deplorable results – another favourite remedy seems to be an absolute refusal to wash the children or any attempt at cleanliness."

*

Back in England, the stage was set for the nationwide campaign that would make Emily Hobhouse a household name. The tour was due to begin on June 28 at Oxford but the owners of the booked hall took fright and cancelled, forcing her to call smaller meetings elsewhere in the city. The *Oxford Times* denounced Emily's hour-long speech at the Master's Lodge at Balliol, her father's old college, as a wicked attempt by a pro-Boer to make political capital out of the suffering in the camps.

In the weeks following she was to address forty public meetings up and down the country – frequently from a platform found at a moment's notice – when the riotous scenes of Liskeard were repeated over and over, with minor variations such as peltings with sticks, stones or rotten vegetables. But as well as boos and hisses Emily found herself greeted with standing ovations, and she would later claim it was commonplace for a majority of the audience to file past the rostrum to shake her hand. Stumping the country she found an exhausting but exhilarating business. At least the rail journeys were relatively comfortable, as Uncle Arthur had come up with the money for first-class travel.

"I am always on the move now," she writes to a friend from Birmingham, describing her life as like a kaleidoscope – "daily a different town, a different audience, a different circle". And she adds with a touch of self-satisfaction: "The Government are *furious* with me."

In the first month alone she addressed twenty-six meetings. At Manchester she spoke with Leonard at her side, guaranteeing good coverage in the *Guardian* of July 3, but the next night at Southport the meeting was punctuated by cries of "Traitor to her country!" Emily had to be guarded by two policemen until her carriage drove away amid mingled boos and cheers.

The Times of July 5 described scenes of wild excitement at Holbeck Moor, near Leeds, involving several thousands: "The would-be speakers were completely routed, and a prominent tradesman of pro-Boer tendencies who drove by was chased by fully 3,000 persons to his residence. He had a very narrow escape. The police appeared on the scene, but judiciously refrained from exciting the mob." On reading *The Times* Emily fired off a letter to the editor vehemently denying that the meeting was pro-Boer, but simply the platform for a charitable appeal.

Within a matter of days no fewer than three venues had to be scrubbed. In Hull, after a cancellation forced a move to a small Quaker venue, Emily complained in her speech of a wave of moral cowardice sweeping the country. Soon after, at York, a meeting had to be abandoned at the insistence of the chief constable, while the council at Scarborough, "fearing that much disorder and destruction of property would result", called off a scheduled meeting at the town hall. But this was the home patch of Joshua Rowntree, and once again the local Quakers came to the rescue by offering their Friends' Meeting House.

In her book *The Brunt of the War*, Emily was to write that the spectacle of press and police affecting alarm at what she called her "quiet gatherings" would have been ludicrous "had it not been the outward sign of an inward intolerance, inhumanity, and pseudo-patriotism, lamentable to all who hold their country's true honour and dignity at heart". Ruth Fry felt that violent press propaganda had made Emily an outlaw in her own country.

Though several meetings were seriously disrupted by missile-hurling mobs, Darlington was the only one of her public appearances that summer where Emily was completely silenced. Here on July 20 her platform party and "a large audience of quiet thoughtful people" waited patiently while a group of a dozen or so ruffians howled and sang for an hour and a half. Although "the policy of non-resistance prevailed in this Quaker town", Emily told her brother, the outcome of the disturbance was that she never even stood up. Yet there was something extraordinarily impressive about that night, she felt, as the silent platform party faced a silent audience, "sitting out the time the speeches would have taken if delivered". In the midst of "this order and silence, this serious purpose and repose", the empty noise of the hooligans could be appreciated for what it was. There was something satisfyingly symbolic about the spectacle, she thought, so that in a sense it was the most wonderful and impressive of all her meetings.

Yet despite the fury Emily would remember the general run of meetings as "orderly, interested, and moved", and she often saw an audience in tears. And her eloquence was bringing in a steady flow of money to the Distress Committee.

A reporter present at the Friends' Meeting House at Leeds gave one of the few contemporary pen-portraits of Emily, describing her as a slight woman of medium height, with grey-tinged hair and a slightly aquiline nose and observing that her complexion had lost some of the bronze it must have acquired on her South African travels. With her great earnestness of manner, she gave the impression of being weighed down with the sadness of the scenes she had witnessed, and nearly an hour passed before she smiled. Then a wonderful change came about: "Her face is full of charm and sweetness when it is thus lit up, and she drew the audience a good deal nearer her after this." Despite her intensity, she demonstrated a sense of humour, and "the meeting was none the less successful because there were several outbursts of laughter once the ice was broken".

The Quakers provided not only venues but moral support. When Emily spoke at Bristol, every interruption from the gallery was met by a burst of hymn-singing from Quaker ladies massed upon the platform. A pained letter from an Emily supporter to the *Bristol Mercury* describes a noisy mob of forty or fifty "hobbledehoys" present for the express purpose of breaking up the meeting – "I myself think that the gang of disturbers were chiefly clerks," says the writer, with a turn of phrase worthy of Emily herself, "and some of those not yet out of their teens".

Though she never lost her dread of speaking in public, Emily was turning into an accomplished performer. Earlier speeches of the tour had suffered the same faults as her writing, being too packed with detail, too prolix, too dry. After hearing her at Manchester, her brother Leonard – always Emily's most constructive critic – advised a change of style. Perhaps, like her father in the pulpit, she had feared speaking from the heart in case her emotion got the better of her. After Manchester she followed Leonard's counsel to good effect.

Relations with the government had now deteriorated beyond the point where even the most influential of friends could render service. The Marquis of Ripon, a former viceroy of India and acting chairman of the Distress Fund, was clutching at straws when he wrote to Brodrick: "We have the pleasure to inform you that Miss Hobhouse has, with characteristic generosity and self-sacrifice, offered to proceed again at once to South Africa." Two ladies had gone out to Cape Town early in June on behalf of the committee – a Miss Monkhouse and a Miss Mellor – but the idea that Emily would be given permission to join them was hopelessly unrealistic.

She remained avid for news from South Africa. On August 15, writing to Caroline Murray from Manchester, and asking to be remembered to the household meerkat, she enquired anxiously for any sign of the concessions promised by Brodrick, in particular the release of women from the camps. In recent days she had been cheered to receive news direct from Bloemfontein which seemed to indicate an easing of the censorship regime.

Back home in Chelsea, she wrote again to Mrs Murray on August 29 exulting over a great success at Portsmouth: "Certainly, bits of vegetable marrow, etc, were thrown at me, but the cheering was greatly in the ascendant and quite deafening." She had even won over both of the local papers, one "Jingo Liberal" and the other Tory. The letter to Mrs Murray ends with a laboured joke, one of the few Emily put on record:

Question: why is a woman like a telegraph? *Answer*: Because her intelligence is always in advance of the male – i.e., mail.

Days later she was delighted by a letter in the *Manchester Guardian* from a retired field marshal strongly criticising the camps as a departure from the recognised laws of international warfare; soon afterwards she was cheered by a letter from Jan Hofmeyr, a leading Cape nationalist living in self-imposed exile in Holland, who praised the noble and effective work she had done in spite of what "that scapegrace of a cousin of mine" – the notorious sacked clergyman – was saying to the contrary.

*

During one of her breaks in London Emily persuaded St John Brodrick to see her again, but at their meeting on July 18 found him in no mood to reconsider the ban on her return. In Brodrick's view, Emily's crusade was prolonging the war and costing the country millions. "Government will *not* let me go," she wrote angrily to Leonard that night, saying of the confrontation with the war secretary that "we were both strong and furious but both civil".

Emily had left Brodrick "as white as a sheet" again and before quitting the office that evening he put pen to paper to prevent any possible misunderstanding. "While appreciating your offer of services in connection with the camps," he wrote stiffly, "we feel it is better not to accept them." The government was determined to send out "no one specially identified with any form of opinion".

As ever Emily was loath to take no as an answer, and replied by return post. By refusing to let her go back, she wrote, he was taking a very wrong step from his own point of view. Up till now she had studiously abstained from political remarks – "I have felt myself bound hitherto, but now I shall feel bound no longer, but quite free to say and do what I think best."

The claim that her campaign was prolonging the war she refuted entirely. On the contrary, the weekly death toll in the camps, and the sacrifice of Britain's own poor soldiers, lay at the door of the government itself. Then came an unexpected tribute to the man who had consistently thwarted Emily during her time in South Africa. "Only give Lord Kitchener a free hand to negotiate unhampered from home and he could end it," she declared.

With this letter Emily was again rubbing salt in sore places when it might have been wiser to resist the temptation. Writing to Leonard from Darlington, she delivered her final verdict on Brodrick. The war minister, she declared, was "a poor, poor thing". But her dealings with him were not yet over.

On July 22 Brodrick announced that a "Committee of Lady Visitors" was to go out to examine the South African camps, and to an outraged Emily the names confirmed that the government intended a whitewash. The leader was to be Mrs Millicent Garrett Fawcett, branded by the pro-Boers as "a hard and wicked woman" of extreme right-wing Imperialist sympathies, though she had always called herself a Liberal. This was the Garrett sister who had officially opened the Chenies Street Chambers of unhappy memory.

Named as assistants to Mrs Fawcett were Lady Knox, a general's wife who had nursed wounded soldiers in beleaguered Ladysmith, and Lucy Deane, a factory inspector with wide experience of special investigations concerning women and children. This Miss Deane was the single member of the commission who was not on record as supporting the war. Mrs Fawcett's team was to be completed by a nurse and two medical graduates already out in South Africa. One of these was none other than the Dr Jane Waterston who had been at loggerheads with Emily over recruiting nurses for the camps and who had publicly attacked the "hysterical whining" of pro-Boers in England. So far from being untainted by prejudice, as the government pretended, in Emily's eyes the commission were implacably anti-Boer – indeed, only days before her appointment was made public Mrs Fawcett had fired a broadside against Emily's report on the concentration camps through the columns of the *Westminster Gazette*.

Mrs Fawcett might have called herself a Liberal, but no one ever mistook her for the bleeding-heart variety. And once she had embarked on her own tour of the camps, many besides Emily would come to regard her as a monster.

13 "UNYIELDING AS A ROCK"

Brodrick's choice of Mrs Fawcett was a shrewd one. Like Emily, she is generally forgotten today, though it would be difficult to exaggerate her importance in the history of the feminist movement. Now overshadowed by later militant figures like the Pankhursts, at the time of the Boer War the name Millicent Garrett Fawcett was synonymous with the campaign for women's rights. She had been the youngest member of the first-ever women's suffrage committee formed in 1867; as a venerable dame of the British Empire, she would live to see the final victory of 1928, when parliament conceded the vote to women on the same terms as men.

If, in Emily Hobhouse, we see the strangely admixed elements of missionary, actress and political *bien pensant*, in Mrs Fawcett – destined to be Emily's arch-enemy among her own sex – we are confronted by an even more alarming combination of Lenin, Mr Gradgrind, and Bertie Wooster's Aunt Agatha.

Thirteen years Emily's senior, tiny in stature but supremely forceful in nature, this formidable character was a younger sister of Elizabeth Garrett Anderson, the first woman doctor to qualify in Britain, and the widow of a blind Cambridge professor and MP. Although her father had been an advanced thinker on education for women – as witnessed by his support of Elizabeth through thick and thin – money troubles in the family business had brought an abrupt end to Millicent's schooldays when she was just fifteen. This bitter disappointment meant that female education would vie with female suffrage as her life's consuming passion.

In the year the Boer War started, Mrs Fawcett became the first woman to be awarded an honorary doctorate by a British university in recognition of her pioneering work for women's higher education. She had also written a gushing biography of Queen Victoria and a bestseller on economics. To be appreciated in her full glory, Mrs Fawcett was best observed mounting a platform with her characteristic impatient step, with diamonds at her throat, lilies-of-the-valley at her bosom, and a speech on political theory in her velvet-gloved hand.

A great enthusiasm of Mrs Fawcett's was saving fallen women. Twenty years earlier she had figured as a stout supporter of W.T. Stead, the campaigning editor who exposed the scandal of Victorian child prostitution by purchasing a thirteen-year-old girl, and was gaoled for his pains. Despite official denials, Mrs Fawcett always believed that a private letter she sent to the Queen resulted in Stead being reclassified from "common convict-person" to a privileged grade of prisoner excused from hard labour. Soon afterwards, in a self-appointed role as vigilante, Mrs Fawcett arranged for the would-be seducer of a young servant girl to be harried in the streets with loud cries of "Scoundrel!" On another occasion she mercilessly dogged the footsteps of a parliamentary candidate who had ruined the reputation of a young lady of her acquaintance. Ignoring threats of a libel action, she toured the constituency informing

"A worshipper at the rich shrine, all that England stands for": Millicent Garrett Fawcett, head of the official investigation, believed it was her country's destiny to rule over others.

all and sundry of his misdeed, until the unnerved candidate withdrew from the contest. Mrs Ray Strachey, her biographer and friend, remarks that Mrs Fawcett always held "the strongest views as to the importance of uprightness"; on this issue, as on many others, she was "as unyielding as a rock".

Though neither left a record of an encounter, there is a strong possibility that Emily met Mrs Fawcett during the rectory years. As a Liberal MP, her husband Professor Henry Fawcett had been a close associate of the other notable blind politician of the age, Emily's future guru Leonard Courtney, both men having threatened to resign from a Gladstone cabinet over their leader's failure to champion women's rights; and Mrs Fawcett personally canvassed for Courtney in East Cornwall during the election campaigns of 1886, 1892 and 1895.

Nor was that the only connection with Emily's birthplace, since the affluent Fawcetts owned shares in the great Liskeard copper mine. Emily's father owned a substantial share in a tin mine which was leased to the Fawcetts from 1867 to 1879. Mrs Strachey tells a striking story to illustrate how the wife kept tabs on the family investment. In her keenness to check into the running of the business, Mrs Fawcett – a self-confessed "dragon over unnecessary expenditure" – would borrow the manager's overalls and descend into the bowels of the mine to inspect the workings by the light of a tallow candle stuck in her hat.

Though Mrs Strachey's biography emphasises Mrs Fawcett's fine complexion and shining brown hair, the striking features in her photographs are a tight mouth, gimlet eye, and remarkable high domed forehead. Unusually among early feminists, she took immense pains over her personal appearance. Her habit of dressing richly she ascribed not to any personal fondness for expensive clothes, but to a wife's desire to please a husband who, while sightless himself, enjoyed the compliments of his friends on her turn-out. That said, by the time of the Boer War she had been a widow for nearly twenty years, and still dressed as sumptuously as ever.

Setting aside their political differences, Emily must have incurred Mrs Fawcett's deep personal enmity in March 1900 when she launched her attack on the Chenies Street flats in the magazine *Nineteenth Century*. The article complained of bad management and overcharging and quoted one disgruntled tenant as saying she was treated "as a cross between a pauper lunatic and a rebellious schoolgirl". By her own admission Mrs Fawcett was "not a forgiving person", and Emily's disparagement of a cherished family project would not have been forgotten.

Millicent Fawcett made a fearsome foe. She was quite as brimful as Emily of moral certitude and just as given to outbursts of righteous indignation. On the other hand, the frostiness of her demeanour was legendary, with no hint of Emily's excitability in her nature, and stout pillars of the Establishment were known to quail at her glance. As Ray Strachey puts it, Mrs Fawcett never really tried to be tolerant of people whose opinions differed from her own, "and if, added to their wrongheadedness, they were active in retarding or injuring the causes which she upheld, then they were entirely beyond the pale"; in fact, "after affixing the black mark against them in her mind, she would wholly disregard them". And by the time of the Boer War, no name bore a blacker mark than that of Emily Hobhouse.

In her disappointingly tepid autobiography, *What I Remember*, Mrs Fawcett does not once deign to mention Emily's existence, though the pro-Boers as a breed are given short shrift as espousers of "that perverted form of patriotism which extols every country but its own". For a gauge of her special detestation of Emily we must turn again to Mrs Strachey, who labels Miss Hobhouse "violent", "unscrupulous" and "quite lacking in patience or restraint". Moreover, Emily was easily deceived by agitators and impostors, and since she was ready to believe all good of one side and all evil of the other, many false and exaggerated stories lodged in her mind. Because of this, "the demonstrable untruth of some of her statements and the excessive bias of others", combined with her warm friendship for the families of the Boer leaders, "led her to be regarded almost as a traitor to her own country".

In different circumstances Millicent Fawcett might have figured among Emily's heroines. Feminist credentials apart, the two were alike in many respects. Each set out in life resentful of a lack of formal schooling but went on to make a mark on the world through sheer determination. Each was addicted to declaiming on the honour of England. Neither was ever troubled by the idea she might be wrong; neither gave quarter to opponents of a cherished cause. Like Emily, Mrs Fawcett steeled herself to become an effective public speaker, yet would be physically sick in anticipation of mounting the platform, where she too was accustomed to being pelted with all manner of missiles by "hooting hooligans". Again like Emily, she had a savage tongue and alienated potential supporters without number. Each was estranged from old friends over the Boer conflict – not least among them, in Mrs Fawcett's case, W.T. Stead and Leonard Courtney. In the eyes of these former intimates, admits Mrs Strachey, "her attitude towards the war seemed monstrously wrong, and her activities harmful and pernicious".

Her private name for the pro-Boers was "the O lot", the O representing a propensity to whinge and wail. It remained Mrs Fawcett's favourite term of abuse for people like Emily, rivalled only by "the screaming sisterhood". Mrs Fawcett also resembled Emily in her tendency to judge works of art in the light of her politics. Applauding the first London performance of Wagner's *Ring*, for instance, she declared enthusiastically that the opera cycle had a wonderful bearing on the woman question.

But in political outlook, as in temperament, the two differed profoundly. Where Mrs Fawcett parted from Emily irreconcilably was in her fervent Imperialism, grounded in the conviction that the British were a very great people with a mission to rule others. She saw herself as "a worshipper at the rich shrine, the holy of holies, all that England stands for". Gladstone had been the great bugbear of her younger days, blamed for a string of humiliations beginning with the death of General Gordon and the first Transvaal war, and never forgiven for his conversion to Home Rule "to catch the illiterate Irish vote".

Her sweeping racial and national stereotyping is guaranteed to shock today's right-thinkers. The Irish character, for instance, she described as weak in honesty, industry and self-reliance, while in any Celt like Emily or Lloyd George she discerned a genius for destructiveness. On the other hand, her belief that the United States was "on some other planet" might still strike a sympathetic chord with many.

Mrs Fawcett's rigorous logic carried her to opinions unpalatable to many other Liberals. The law of supply and demand was her god. She set her face utterly against any concession to her own sex on account of physical unsuitability for heavy or unpleasant work, and led the opposition to a campaign to exclude women from pit-brow labour in the mines. Of these pit-women she remarked that it was "quite picturesque to see their rosy faces shining through the coal-dust". In the celebrated 1898 strike of London match-girls she backed the match manufacturers without hesitation, fiercely attacking the "drawing-room philanthropists" who sought to ban the use of phosphorus in matches. In Mrs Fawcett's view, match-girls who succumbed to phosphorus poisoning did so through their unclean personal habits. It was entirely typical of the woman that, throughout this long and bitter controversy, she saw no reason to shrink from public comment simply because she owned shares in Bryant and May.

On the surface the lady was ever icily serene and her voice calm but emphatic. Never in her life did she appear to experience a moment of self-doubt. Yet according to Mrs Strachey, she was "at all times exceedingly afraid of showing emotion and almost passionately reticent", so that only her closest friends ever detected the "desperate and rigid self-control" behind the mask.

*

Mrs Fawcett jumped at the opportunity to head the commission to look into the concentration camps. With a longstanding interest in South African affairs – her cousin Edmund Garrett had edited the *Cape Times* for years after serving an apprenticeship on Stead's *Pall Mall Gazette* – she saw a clear parallel between the voteless status of the Uitlanders and the plight of women at home. What Mrs Fawcett advocated, however, was the vote for Britain's *property-owning* women, then totalling fewer than two million. On the question of universal suffrage, whether for men or women, she would always remain an arch-sceptic.

It is likely that Mrs Fawcett's name first entered St John Brodrick's head as the ideal leader of his ladies when he read her letter in the press disparaging Emily's report, though she had unfurled her colours plainly much earlier in the war. Incensed by the widespread anti-British feeling in Europe, she had organised a distribution of pro-government leaflets throughout Germany and Holland as a counter to Boer propaganda.

At that time, for any official body to include a single female was remarkable. For a government committee, almost a royal commission, to consist exclusively of women was unprecedented. Mrs Fawcett had spent her whole life notching up firsts for women, so was a highly appropriate figure as chairman, or, as she was later more grandly called, president.

Four days after Brodrick announced the committee, Emily made a last despairing effort to induce him to relent. "I am continually asked on all sides when I am going out again," she wrote, and repeated the familiar disclaimer of personal political bias. The ladies selected were too few for the work entrusted to them, she insisted, and her own acquaintance with the camp women and their language would make her useful.

The war minister remained adamant. By return of post he again refused her services, claiming that the only consideration in the choice of ladies, beyond their general capacity, was that they were "removed from the suspicion of partiality". One can imagine Emily's furious snort as she read this. All sorts of philanthropic agencies were clamouring to send ladies of their own, Brodrick went on, and it was impossible to accommodate her while declining others, "the more so as your reports and speeches have been made the subject of so much controversy".

Though desperately disappointed, Emily made an effort to put on a philosophical front. Breaking the news to her brother she remarked: "Brodrick is a gentleman undeniably – alas! that he is not also something of a man."[xvi]

Inevitably, the chief targets of her fury over what she called "the whitewash committee" were Mrs Fawcett and Dr Waterston, for at the time she seemed unaware of the very decided views of the second South Africa-based doctor, a peer's daughter called Ella Scarlett. A few years younger than Emily, Dr Scarlett boasted a pedigree studded with eminent military men, among them the Crimean War hero General James Scarlett who fifty years before had led the successful action of the Heavy Brigade which was instantly overshadowed by the charge of the Light Brigade. Writing to the War Office to accept a place on the committee, Ella Scarlett too had displayed her colours: "The refugees are ungrateful, dirty beyond description, and never speak the truth; they have heard something of the pro-Boer agitation at home, and try to be impertinent."

The home-based commissioners were ready to sail within ten days. Generous terms of employment agreed by the government included a daily payment of up to four guineas each with an extra guinea a day if a personal servant was taken – Lady Knox for one declared it impossible to do without a maid – plus a clothing allowance of one hundred pounds.

To put this into context, one of the civilian medical officers belatedly being recruited for the camps around this time could expect to earn two pounds five shillings a day; a Colonial Office advertisement for concentration camp nurses in 1902 offered a year's contract at a monthly salary of ten pounds, or twelve in the more expensive Transvaal, and a one-off outfit allowance of ten pounds, with rations, tent and tent furniture provided. This was actually a marked improvement on the terms set in the early stages of the war, when a fully trained nurse was expected to go out to South Africa for forty pounds a year and, to quote a sarcastic editorial in the *Nursing Record*, "the wicked and lavish luxury" of a uniform allowance of four pounds.

Emily, already smarting at being excluded from the body set up wholly as a result of her investigations, must have cast a green eye over the financial terms granted to the Fawcett committee. The miserable conditions under which she herself had travelled from camp to camp would have come vividly to mind as she read that throughout their stay in South Africa the ladies were to live on a special private train, or Mrs Fawcett's "almost royal train" as Emily immediately dubbed it. This was to be equipped with a sleeping carriage, a saloon car, and a kitchen staffed by a Portuguese cook; two saloon attendants would be at their beck and call, plus "a boy". Most enviable of all was the commissioners' unchallengeable right to passes of every kind and the guaranteed freedom to go where and when they chose.

According to Ruth Fry, Mrs Fawcett refused a meeting with Emily before sailing. It was then that Emily, distraught over the latest death statistics from the camps, was moved to compose an open letter to Brodrick, penned in what she later admitted to be "a white heat of feeling". This highly emotional rebuke of the war secretary, almost incoherent in parts, protested at the commission's tardy departure and ended: "Will you not now, with the thought before you of those 3,245 children who have closed their eyes forever since I last saw you, on their behalf, will you not now take instant action, and endeavour thus to avert the evil results of facts patent to all, and suspend further enquiry into the truth of what the whole world knows?"

No answer came.

*

Mrs Fawcett kept a special diary on her South Africa appointment from the day of her interview at the War Office. Mr Brodrick warmed immediately to the candidate when she volunteered her opinion that the high proportion of very young and very old in the camps would lead naturally to high mortality – "he seemed struck by this point and had not thought of it before," she noted with satisfaction. Rejoicing in her robust unconcern at the prospect of baying critics on "the humanitarian tack", Brodrick knew he had found his ideal committee leader.

Rather unfairly, Emily criticised the ladies for delaying their departure for Cape Town. Considering all the arrangements to be made from scratch, a gap of ten days between their appointment and embarkation hardly seems unreasonable. Mrs Fawcett, who always prided herself on getting things done without vacillation, neither forgot nor forgave Emily's claim, and dismissed out of hand her central idea that "a large band of kindly workers" should be sent to work in the camps.

Instead of a personal servant Mrs Fawcett chose to take her only daughter as a companion. A great bluestocking, Philippa Fawcett had made up for her mother's educational disappointments with an unprecedented triumph in the Cambridge mathematical tripos of 1890, scoring higher than the top man. Yet despite her academic triumphs, Philippa, then aged thirty-three, came across to many contemporaries as a strangely colourless creature, eternally in the shade of a mother bent on achieving her thwarted ambitions by proxy. Determined that Philippa should be "something which no woman had ever been before", Mrs Fawcett never ceased to scheme for her daughter to batter down the walls of some male bastion or other. Philippa herself seemed rather less keen.

The voyage to South Africa did not prove the sybaritic progress of Emily's broodings. Standards on board the Orient Line's *Oratava*, which sailed from Southampton on July 22, appear to have fallen short of those on the rival Union Castle ships patronised by Emily, and soon after leaving port Mrs Fawcett was woken in her berth by a rat jumping on her from the bunk above. Fortunately the phlegmatic Philippa was not disturbed by her mother's great yelp. The captain later informed his distinguished guests that the crew had killed around eight hundred rats as the vessel lay in dock.

Mrs Fawcett's diary during the voyage yields a number of vintage lines. Nearing South African waters, she expresses her dissatisfaction with the eagerly-awaited Southern Cross in the night sky – "a more second class constellation I have never seen," she writes crossly – and goes on to complain of an evening when, packed in like herrings to listen to the chief engineer's gramophone records, mother and daughter find the promised sacred music replaced by vulgar music-hall ditties. The Fawcett ladies are also bothered by the attentions of a fusilier, "a well-known bad lot" observed loitering near their cabin. Mrs Fawcett was a particularly bad sailor, which may have contributed to the acidity of the entries. But when the *Oratava* nears Cape Town, and she savours the magnificent view of Table Mountain, her mood briskly changes: "It looks like a country worth fighting for."

The commissioners' train, their home for four months, turned out to be special principally for the many discomforts it offered, and the diary's account of the cramped conditions endured by the ladies prompts a shudder at the idea of Emily and Mrs Fawcett cooped up in the train together. "We each have a little hole of our own, but it is a very small one," she wrote home. "An equable temper is of primary importance for getting on in such a life." Equably or otherwise, she did not hesitate long before getting rid of an "abominably bad-tempered male servant" on board.

On inspecting her first Boers, Mrs Fawcett decided they were far more reasonable than the pro-Boers back home, though predictably "the O lot" had put them up to complaining. Friends of Emily, including Caroline Murray, hastened to meet the commissioners in Cape Town but reported that talking to Mrs Fawcett was like talking to a stone wall. Admittedly the commissioners were polite, said Mrs Murray, but wholly without heart or sympathy. Mrs Fawcett struck Emily's old hostess as "an able woman but cold and hard" while the "quite commonplace" Lady Knox stuck in her memory chiefly for the remark that she would give the camp children sweets provided they washed their hands and touched their caps. The commission firmly declined an offer for any of Emily's friends to accompany them on their travels.

Mrs Fawcett for her part was infuriated by what she saw as the South African women's melodramatic point-scoring. When asked to suggest the most useful commodity that could be taken to the camps, they replied: "Send them calico to wrap their corpses in." During all the months the commissioners spent among camp inmates, she later wrote, "never once did a single human being utter a word which justified the Cape Town ladies' insinuation". Mrs Fawcett blamed Emily's circle for portraying her as a Herod-like monster, "presiding and gloating over a deliberately planned massacre of the innocents".

The journey from Cape Town to the first camp on Mrs Fawcett's list, Mafeking, took five days. At the famous siege town some of her companions developed a taste for collecting war souvenirs such as shell cases and bullets, though she herself disdained such fripperies. In general the ladies rubbed along well together, though Mrs Fawcett's favourite was clearly Dr Waterston – "an out-and-out Britisher," she declared, as the highest possible form of compliment.

Echoing Lord Kitchener, Mrs Fawcett decided that the people who had not fought were far more vindictive than those who had. She convinced herself that the savage criticism of the camps "was induced by race and party feeling, and by propaganda", with the critics "more anxious to have a stick to beat the government with than to help the camps".

An achievement of Millicent Fawcett's that Emily had laboured for in vain was a face-to-face interview with the commander-in-chief himself. Kitchener, according to Mrs Strachey, was notoriously abrupt and difficult and was said to have the very lowest opinion of the female sex, but with some reluctance he agreed to talk to the commissioners about the camps. Mrs Fawcett in turn bowed to his request that only two of the committee should go to his headquarters at Melrose House, and chose Lady Knox as her companion. On entering Kitchener's room Mrs Fawcett was amused to overhear him ask how many ladies had appeared – "I think he was very much alarmed" – but both parties found the discussion that followed satisfactory and businesslike.

Of Kitchener she later wrote: "I liked him far better than any of the politicians I had gone to on deputations in London. I always say that Lady Knox and I, after this interview with Lord Kitchener, received the compliment of our lives, for after sampling two of us he invited the whole six to dinner!"

Despite Emily's scornful dismissal of the committee, the members set about their task in earnest, inspecting thirty-three camps out of the thirty-four they knew to exist, in some cases making repeat visits. Their arrival was often without warning of any kind. Though the ladies as a body sometimes dodged investigating the sanitation and slaughtering arrangements – only Dr Waterston steeled herself for these – they were no stooges. Mrs Fawcett further showed her mettle by refusing to play along when Lord Milner tried to wheedle her into endorsing the camps' administration. In her letter of reply, she flatly contradicted Milner's bland assurances and spoke out forthrightly of the evidence she collected of poor organisation, lack of foresight, inadequate food allowances, and dreadful administrative blunders.

Indeed, the Fawcett report compiled during the tour, a blue-book style publication of some three hundred pages, was packed with damning statistics. It berated the camp authorities for failure to implement the most elementary rules of sanitation, failure to foresee the consequent spread of disease, failure to deploy medical staff properly, and failure to provide proper rations – all these deficiencies being needlessly magnified by red tape. Long before the report was released, the ladies' trenchant comments on the spot led to marked improvements and the sacking of the worst camp officials. At Mafeking, for instance, while Mrs Fawcett engineered the dismissal of the superintendent, the hands-on Jane Waterston cleaned latrines and set up a soup kitchen. But the camp inmates did not escape criticism either. In Mrs Fawcett's view the Boer women, like the London match-girls, brought much of the evil on themselves through unsanitary customs.

When Ruth Fry read the Fawcett report, she decried its unemotional tone – "a bare recital of facts," she complained, "which has no room for any expression of human sympathy with those who were suffering, but on the contrary, is very conscious of their shortcomings, such as their addiction to most questionable remedies, their hatred of fresh air and their dirty habits." Nevertheless, even this staunch ally of Emily's admitted that the document overall was extremely thorough and granted that the commissioners had not shrunk from highlighting cases of gross carelessness and neglect.

Mrs Fawcett herself would have refuted indignantly that it was any business of hers to indulge in sympathetic noises.[xvii] She left that sort of thing to sentimental hysterics like Emily and just got on with the job. Even so, the document amounted to an exoneration of Emily Hobhouse, though her name was never mentioned.

14 "A LITTLE BLUFF NOW WOULD FINISH THE WAR"

Kitchener agreed to meet the commission ladies with a bad grace, grumbling that there was little for them to do as the camps were so well looked after. But in a private letter to Roberts he hoped the visit would calm the growing press agitation in England, which he believed could be traced to money laid out by Kruger in Holland.

Although the often-repeated claim that Kitchener never visited a concentration camp is untrue – there is ample documentary evidence that he did, and the anecdote about the belly-slapping *vrou* has the ring of a nasty personal experience – there is no record of an inspection during Milner's absence from South Africa, when the death rate peaked. From first to last, he never questioned that his military role should have absolute precedence over all other calls on his time. The camps were a distraction which he left in trusted hands – the newly-knighted Sir Hamilton Goold-Adams in Orange River Colony, Sir John Maxwell in the Transvaal.

Furious that Milner's interference had prevented him from ending the war, Kitchener determined to revert to the well-tried iron fist. It was entirely in character that, once denied his first preference for magnanimity towards the enemy, he should advocate striking with shattering severity.

Kitchener was now in whole-hoggish mood. Among proposals he cabled to London around the time of Mrs Fawcett's appointment were the shooting out of hand of all Cape and Natal rebels, the confiscation of all property owned by Boers who failed to surrender, and the permanent banishment of prisoners-of-war and those still in arms, along with their families and dependants. Plucking countries out of the air, he talked of packing them off to Fiji, Madagascar or the Dutch East Indies, as well as to existing POW camps as far apart as the West Indies and Napoleon's isle of exile, St Helena.

"We have now got more than half the Boer population either as prisoners-of-war or in our refuge camps," he reminded his political masters, and urged that the whole lot be shipped out so that South Africa could be made safe for British colonists. One great advantage he saw in a wholesale removal was that the concentration camps could be emptied and closed down.

In Downing Street the cabinet were taken aback by Kitchener's vehemence. All at once the commander-in-chief himself seemed to be the main problem. Even his old champion Lord Bobs realised there was no chance of such drastic measures being approved, while Joseph Chamberlain questioned the commander-in-chief's mental state. "I do not blame him for these absurd proposals," he told St John Brodrick, "but they show that he was too much occupied with military matters to be able to give his mind to other things, and we poor civilians have therefore to think for him."

Milner, who had long since realised that South Africa was not big enough for the two of them, seized the opportunity subtly to undermine his rival. First he told Chamberlain: "It is a good thing if we can do something which Kitchener wants. It may steady him and give him fresh hope. His tendency to discouragement is to my mind one of the most serious features of the situation."

So "the cheering up of Lord K" became official government policy. One sop thrown to him was approval for a plan to place prominent Boer civilians as hostages on board trains liable to attack. Kitchener already had a list of nominees – many of them relations of Boer leaders – to which one of his junior officers thoughtfully added the name of a clergyman with the remark, "in case of any deaths he could conduct the funeral". It was the kind of touch the chief appreciated.

The cabinet also approved a proclamation threatening Boers in the field with banishment and with charges on their property. Unfortunately the vague wording of the authorisation led Kitchener to believe he had been handed the necessary power to seize the property of commandos and sell it off to meet the rocketing cost of the camps. While grumbling this did not go nearly far enough, he was mollified by the thought that he could at last target the assets of the Boer leadership. When it became clear there had been a misunderstanding – in fact the property charges could only be levied for the upkeep of identified dependants – he was incandescent.

As he saw it, the only Boers he could punish were the poor and insignificant. So the very men to blame for continuing the war, above all Botha and Steyn, were to escape his grasp – despite their wives and families being granted concession after concession, including permission to live outside the camps and even to jaunt off to Europe. Kitchener fulminated against the pettifogging lawyer mentality that could dream up such injustice and clung stubbornly to his initial idea. "If I could threaten them with being all permanently banished from the country they would I believe give in," he persisted. "A little bluff now would finish the war."

Brodrick set out his objections in a letter of July 26. What Kitchener now promised from a policy of confiscation the government had earlier been promised from the farm-burnings, he chided gently, "but we were led quite wrong in this". Besides, Europe would be needlessly scandalised by such a development.

Kitchener showed signs of buckling under the strain. Sometime in July his younger brother Walter, now a major-general chasing De Wet in Eastern Transvaal, had noted worrying symptoms of a breakdown, and decided to alert Roberts. Walter was not the only senior officer who believed the chief's health was seriously impaired. On being transferred from South Africa to India, Lieutenant-General Bindon Blood told the viceroy, Lord Curzon, "that the strain has told severely on him, that he takes but little exercise, that he is very thin and of a bad colour, that there is probably something the matter with him". Curzon was already having second thoughts about a masterful figure like Kitchener taking the Indian command, and reported Blood's words to the cabinet.

With his state of mind causing concern at the highest levels, fate now dealt Kitchener another blow, this time within the family circle. Back in England that autumn, Walter Kitchener's wife Caroline found herself unable to throw off a debilitating illness, and on consulting a doctor was told she had only a short time to live.

119

Determined to see her husband one last time, she travelled secretly to Cape Town on a troopship and set out on the gruelling train journey north, getting as far as Johannesburg before her strength gave out. She was on her deathbed when reunited with Walter, and died in his arms.

Kitchener felt his sister-in-law's death keenly, and by immediately dispatching Walter home to care for the motherless children lost his one family link in the country. Around the same time the commander-in-chief learnt of the first call for his dismissal in the British press. It appeared in *The Spectator*, edited by a close friend of Milner's. This critical period coincided with the commission's tour of the camps and it was within days of Caroline Kitchener's death that he had to meet Mrs Fawcett.

As the commander-in-chief's black moods became more frequent, Roberts offered to return to South Africa but Kitchener insisted he would see things through to the end, while admitting he "hated the country, the people, the whole thing more every day". Even Roberts could not ignore signals of this kind, writing to Brodrick on November 2 that Kitchener was obviously overworked.

Milner, now back in Cape Town, decided it was time to play his hand. In a private letter sent to Chamberlain around the time Caroline lay dying, he urged that Kitchener be relieved of his command. He was now convinced there could never be "co-operation between Lord Kitchener and any other man who was not either distinctly his subordinate or distinctly his superior". The letter was shown to the prime minister and discussed in cabinet. With the cabinet evenly split, Lord Salisbury came down on Kitchener's side, but it was a close call – Chamberlain, now heading the anti-Kitchener party, happened to be absent that day due to illness, or his persuasive tongue might well have altered the outcome.

The ever-reliable Bobs came up with an idea. Kitchener was notorious for his reluctance to delegate, and on assuming supreme command in South Africa had appointed no chief of staff – his own role under Roberts. Kitchener was persuaded to take on Sir Ian Hamilton, a trusted comrade-in-arms of Roberts then on leave in England. Technically Hamilton would go out to South Africa as chief of staff, but in reality his task was to lift Kitchener from depression. The first of a series of lively reports to Roberts was posted when Hamilton's ship called at Madeira. "My first, my most important, my most easy business," he wrote, "will be to cheer up Lord K and make him understand that he continues to be thoroughly well appreciated by all his old backers at home." He would also try to persuade Kitchener to let him share his burden.

Ian Hamilton, knighted the previous year, was a lieutenant-general only three years Kitchener's junior, and he turned out to be just the fillip the beleaguered commander needed, while keeping canny old Roberts informed of goings-on at Pretoria headquarters. Kitchener was constantly surrounded with hero-worshipping young aides, but here for the first time was a man more of his own standing, yet posing no threat. Roberts's plan worked and the newcomer was soon invited to move into a room in the chief's own house. "Perhaps for the first time in his life, he appears to feel the want of some senior officer to help him," Hamilton reported, while still confessing misgivings over discussing Lord Kitchener behind his back.

Sir Ian's memoirs offer an insight into the routine at Melrose House. Lord K was always down in his dressing-gown around five-thirty and at work by six. He would first digest the operational telegrams from fifty or sixty column commanders, crawling over the huge map laid on the dining room floor and planting it with little red flags. Terse orders would then be dictated, leaving little discretion to the commanders in the field. He then disappeared upstairs to shave, returning for breakfast at eight.

A typical morning would be taken up by departmental heads of the general staff and the military governors, and end with what to Kitchener was the particularly uncongenial task of briefing the press. After dealing with correspondence he would go out for a ride. Dinner with his personal staff was followed by a game of billiards; he then returned to work alone, often far into the night.

Hamilton is worth listening to on Kitchener's personality. Although his superior always maintained a rock-like impassivity in appearance, below the surface he was "a bundle of sensitive and highly-strung nerves kept under control 999 hours out of 1000 by an iron will". Hamilton relieved Kitchener of many time-consuming tasks, among them the refugee camps. In view of Kitchener's attitude, it is no surprise to find this was one of the first responsibilities passed over to the newcomer, who fortunately found it "an interesting job".

Milner too, on his return, found the concentration camps monopolising his time to the detriment of all other business. As he reported to London, "I should be very glad if someone else could take it over but I do not see who there is". The writer John Buchan, who joined Milner's staff at the time of the Fawcett commission, wrote to a friend: "The camps have made my hairs grey. When we took them over they were terrible – partly owning to the preoccupation of the military with other things, partly to causes inherent in any concentration of people accustomed to live in the sparsely populated veld."

Having failed in his manoeuvrings to have Kitchener sacked, Milner faced the prospect of seeing out the remainder of the war with a rival harbouring a diametrically opposed view on practically every issue. Every initiative of his own, Milner complained to Chamberlain, "has to be fought for inch by inch, and watched with ceaseless vigilance, else some fresh obstacle is improvised while your head is turned". Kitchener likewise felt that Milner and the people around him were too hasty with their reforms: "Nothing I can say will check the civil element in thinking because they do not hear guns firing around them that the war is over," he grumbled to Roberts.

*

But there were lighter moments, and none made greater efforts towards the cheering-up of Kitchener than the devoted staff he had gathered at Melrose House. Perhaps the most attractive personality among Kitchener's ADCs was young Frank Maxwell, an Indian cavalry officer who had won the VC during the march on Pretoria and whose boyish looks inspired his nickname of "The Brat". Letters to his parents bear out Maxwell's reputation as a charmer with a sunny sense of humour and throw unexpected lights on his chief's character, including his fondness for animals of all kinds.

One morning the Brat entered Kitchener's room to find him still in his dressing gown, hair unbrushed, darting to and fro trying to catch two young starlings that had come down the chimney. The "poor little beggars" were secured after a heated chase

Kitchener with his favourite aide, Frank Maxwell, VC – "the Brat" – who chronicled his chief's obsession with two starlings that came down the chimney.

andTdeposited in a pigeon house in the garden. "Then there was much fuss all day about their food," Maxwell wrote home, "and the good man would leave his important duties every half hour to see if I had given them meat or procured succulent worms, and bustle in and say they were starving." Eventually the parent birds discovered their whereabouts and began to feed them through the wire, "which interested the Commander-in-Chief so much that the operations in South Africa received no attention most of the remainder of the day".

Visits to the starlings continued over succeeding days with Kitchener chirping at them through the wire, and Maxwell got a rise out of him by sneaking a four-foot-high model of a stork inside the cage. One of the starlings survived to be a treasured pet but, when Kitchener was away on tour, it escaped while being fed. Informed by telegram, he rushed back to Melrose House, summoned all his ADCs, servants and orderlies, and directed a painstaking search of the grounds. The usually immaculate general became dishevelled from his frequent falls into wet flowerbeds. In the afternoon the search was widened until the starling was eventually recaptured in the chimney of a neighbouring house. Kitchener remarked that he had never been so fond of the bird as when it was lost.

But such light-hearted moments were increasingly rare in Lord Kitchener's life, and a new trouble was on the horizon. Emily Hobhouse, provoked beyond endurance by being sidelined, was secretly planning her return to South Africa.

15 "AN HYSTERICAL SPINSTER OF MATURE AGE"

E xactly when Emily resolved to flout the ban on her return is unclear as she confided in no one except intimate friends and family. Almost certainly her mind was made up by the time of Mrs Fawcett's sailing. In the years ahead Emily would steadfastly deny she ever dreamt of disobeying Brodrick, yet as her goal was to go on working for the camp women and children it is difficult to see how she could have done this without defying the War Office.

The matter of intent is important in view of her later protestations of innocence, but such claims were inevitably open to challenge from the moment she booked her passage to Cape Town and asked that her name be omitted from the passenger list. Even more tellingly, Leonard in a memoir of Lord Hobhouse privately printed in 1905, begins an account of his sister's second sailing to South Africa with the sentence: "Miss Hobhouse determined to make a final attempt to reach the camps again."

On September 27 the Union Castle line's head office confirmed Emily's first-class berth on board the *Avondale Castle* sailing from Southampton. Also confirmed was the desired anonymity. The confirmation came two days before the date of her last appeal to Brodrick, in which of course no mention was made of the booking. In her dealings with the line, Emily would have made no secret of the fact that Percy Molteno, who was married to the Union Castle heiress, was a great friend of hers.

In later days Emily explained the ruse by saying she needed rest and quiet. Certainly she was in a poor state following months of stress, and she took the precaution of engaging a capable young nurse called Elizabeth Phillips as her travelling companion. Miss Phillips came highly recommended by the wife of a clergyman friend and was encouraged by Emily to settle in South Africa and work in the camps.

Leonard Hobhouse ran down from Manchester to see his sister off, though his mind was not fully focused on her business. Out of the blue had come a trouble of his own, for the mill owned by his wife Nora's family had got into serious financial difficulties and he was one of three guarantors responsible for its debts. The timing could hardly have been worse. Leonard had just announced he was leaving the *Manchester Guardian* to concentrate on writing his books on philosophy; these, though well received, could never pay the bills of a growing family. Even so, he was ready as ever with practical advice and warned of big problems ahead should martial law be declared in Cape Town.

Emily was as usual dismissive of arguments counter to her wishes, despite the strains she was placing on her family. As soon as the *Avondale Castle* had sailed on October 5, Aunt Mary confided to Leonard that in addition to the deep anxiety she felt over Emily, she had doubts about her own nerves standing "this continued atmosphere of excitement".

On board ship Emily was once again superbly inconsistent. Despite the demand for anonymity, she immediately claimed her place of privilege at the captain's table, and few were unaware for long that their fellow passenger was *the* Miss Hobhouse.

As on her doomed bridal voyage to Mexico, Emily seemed morbidly on the lookout for bad omens, and when a great storm blew up Captain Brown jokingly compared her with the biblical Jonah. Two days before the ship was due to put in at Las Palmas there was high drama when one of the passengers threw himself overboard as Emily and the captain were taking after-lunch coffee together; despite an hour-long search the man was not recovered. Emily believed the unfortunate has become deranged by the great heat and the incident cast a further gloom over the ship. Any hopes of a relaxing passage were fast disappearing – "It was a dreary voyage and, far from resting me, made me very unwell," she wrote.

Only one passenger struck her as a fellow soul. This was a Miss Steedman who was travelling out to take up a new post as principal of the school for girls in Bloemfontein. Though Miss Steedman had "the usual newspaper view of me" prior to their meeting, said Emily, before long the two became fast friends.

Then on October 9, unknown to anyone on board, Leonard's prophecy was realised.

*

One month previously the Boers had launched a small-scale invasion of Cape Colony. In what came to be hailed as an epic trek, a commando force under Jan Smuts forded the Orange River and during the weeks following criss-crossed the territory in a game of hide-and-seek with the British Army, recruiting rebels as they went. Military historians would later judge the incursion as a nuisance to Kitchener rather than a serious danger, but in the short term it bore fateful consequences for Emily.

For some weeks now, with the support of Bobs in London, Kitchener had been urgently demanding authority to extend martial law. Four days into Emily's voyage, the uproar over Smuts finally gave him an excuse to impose martial law on all Cape ports. The invasion renewed fears of an uprising by Boer sympathisers in the colony – always Britain's worst nightmare – while at the same time the tranquillity of Natal was shattered by Louis Botha at the head of a thousand-man commando. This was the time of great personal strain for Kitchener. Faced with a double threat from the Boers, and with his sister-in-law dying in a Johannesburg hospital, he brooded angrily over the cabinet's obstructive behaviour. Then on October 10 came unsettling news from London. The latest victim of a long-rumbling feud within the War Office was Sir Redvers Buller, who had been nursing an outsized grievance since losing the South African command; now he had been sacked from the army. As public disquiet over the war continued to spread, Kitchener worried that a new scapegoat would soon be needed.

On top of everything else, the controversy over the concentration camps would not go away. For it was during this same month, as the lady commissioners were poking disapproving noses into anything and everything, that the death rate of inmates reached its absolute zenith. Emily had left South Africa in May, her mind reeling at a monthly mortality rate in the low hundreds; during Mrs Fawcett's travels around the camps, the figure rocketed – 2,666 deaths in August, 2,752 in August, 3,205 in October.

This was the background to the painful scenes which were about to enacted on board the *Avondale Castle*.

Back in England, Emily's secret was out of the bag. Even before her ship left home waters, a ferreting journalist had discovered the identity of the nameless first-class passenger on board. In Whitehall the news quickly buzzed around the Colonial Office and created a stir among Chamberlain's gaggle of frock-coated advisers. One argued that the fact Emily was travelling under an assumed name – this was not actually true – proved she meant mischief, while another suggested she "wanted to be martyred".

The colonial secretary ordered that the authorities in South Africa be cabled with the news but remarked in his strange metallic voice that for his own part he did not believe the Empire was threatened by this "hysterical spinster of mature age". It is tempting to picture "Pushful Joe" assuming one of the poses loved by the cartoonists, polishing his trademark monocle or sniffing the orchid in his buttonhole. He had always made clear he had no time for "rabid do-gooders" of Emily's ilk, yet at present he thought it would be foolish to take any notice of her; but alas, he added, the military were "terribly afraid of women".

As it happened, the first direct telephone line had been installed between Milner's office in Cape Town and Kitchener's Pretoria headquarters shortly before this time. Its advent robbed posterity of what must have been a fascinating exchange between these bitter rivals, temporarily united against a common enemy. Had they still relied on the telegraph, archive copies would have recorded what was said; as it is, all that survives of their conversation is the outcome, a terse order from Kitchener passed down the chain of command: "High Commissioner and I are agreed that Miss Hobhouse should not be allowed to land."

We need not depend on Emily's version of the events that spanned the next six days. A vivid and detailed picture of the unfolding drama can be patched together, in part from a witness statement by one of Emily's Boer friends, who might be suspected of bias, but also from notes by Kitchener's subordinates, who carefully filed the written orders and reports passing between them. Clearly much of the documentation was meant to cover the writers' backs, for it was rapidly dawning on those concerned that the affair might have serious repercussions. After all, the lady involved had split public opinion in Britain, and if her supporters were in a minority they included powerful political figures, among them the likely next prime minister of Great Britain. At the same time, there is no difficulty in reading into the actions of every officer concerned, from lieutenant to general, a nervous awareness of their chief's reputation. It was received wisdom throughout the British Army that anyone who failed to carry out Lord Kitchener's orders to the letter need not look for a second chance.

As the *Avondale Castle* neared port, messages continued to fly between Whitehall, Pretoria and Cape Town. At this point in the story the waters were muddied by a curious and completely unfounded report that Emily was travelling in the company of Maud Gonne, a firebrand Irish socialist, now best remembered as the muse of W.B. Yeats. Kitchener signalled his personal interest with a telegram to the senior officer at the Cape, Major-General Arthur Wynne: "Has *Avondale Castle* arrived and have you any news of ladies?" Wynne passed the message to the commanding officer of Cape Town district, one Colonel Cooper, who in turn informed the docks commandant that neither Miss Hobhouse nor Miss Gonne would be permitted to land.

The *Avondale Castle* dropped anchor in Table Bay at four in the afternoon on October 27. After twenty-two miserable days at sea with the vessel grinding along with an asthmatic engine against strong currents and headwinds, Emily was dressed and anxious to be ashore. "All was calm and lovely as we glided into the Bay," she wrote, but then a steam tug drew alongside and "I saw with horror the Khaki in it and knew at once the worst had come".

The khaki figure in question was a lieutenant called Lingham. Once on board Lingham settled himself in the smoking room and announced his intention to interview every one of the four hundred and fifty passengers. Emily's heart beat faster as she moved up the queue. Presently her turn came and the officer when he digested her name said that he would prefer to take her last. This Emily realised boded ill, "but I bowed and withdrew still expecting only a more detailed and reaching examination". Not till the dinner bell rang did Lingham come for her.

To take up the story from Emily's later letter to Leonard:

"I took him to the Captain's cabin for I had an instinctive turning to the Captain at that moment, as the only man to stand by me. He welcomed us in and was himself withdrawing when the officer stopped him saying that the matter concerned him also. He, Lingham, then turned to me and informed me I was placed under arrest, that I should not be allowed to land in South Africa anywhere and that I was to have no communication with anyone on shore by word or letter."

Emily drew herself up and asked from whom he had received such an order. Lieutenant Lingham replied that he was acting on behalf of Colonel Cooper, but when pressed to identify Cooper's superior declined to name anyone higher. At this point Lingham turned to Captain Brown, now looking "horribly miserable", and said the lady was placed in his charge and he would be held responsible for her. Emily was then given the choice of returning home on the *Carisbrooke Castle*, a steamer due to sail on Wednesday – it was now Sunday – or remaining on board her present ship.

To return on the *Carisbrooke* Emily declared out of the question as she felt wholly unfit for another voyage so soon, and she asked the lieutenant to take letters from her to his superiors. This he agreed to do, promising to collect them the following morning. "Altogether I kept my head fairly well," she told Leonard, "but I was so taken aback that I could hardly at the moment think what was best to do."

News of the arrest spread through the ship like wildfire and wherever she went on board Emily could feel eyes boring into her back. Even so, she determined to keep up appearances, steeling herself to walk down to dinner with a display of unconcern and chatter away merrily throughout the meal. Then she went to pour out her woes to the astonished Miss Steedman. Between them they composed letters to everyone of importance they could think of – Colonel Cooper, Lord Milner, Sir Walter Hely-Hutchinson as governor of the Cape, and Kitchener himself. Emily's hand was afflicted by cramp and had to be massaged by Nurse Phillips.

All that night, she told Leonard, "I lay awake shuddering from head to foot with the effects of the shock, for oddly enough it was a shock and unexpected in that form. Then I began to see my way and brace myself to the battle. I shall be very polite, very dignified, but in every way I possibly can a thorn in the flesh to them. I see already many ways of being a thorn. For instance, *they* don't want it much talked of in Cape Town and I mean that it shall be."

In letters like this, Emily confessed later, she was putting on a brave face. In fact the shock to her system was "far greater than I myself knew"; a quarter of a century later, in a fragment of autobiography written for Mrs Steyn, a sense of outrage still burned over finding herself arrested and imprisoned. "Brought up as we were in strict obedience to the law and enjoying freedom as the breath of life," she declared, "this illegality stunned me."

On shore, Colonel Cooper opened Emily's letter. "It cannot but seem to me," she had written, "that the summary arrest of an Englishwoman bound on works of charity without warrant of any kind and for no stated offence is a proceeding which requires explanation."

The letter again flatly denies any political motivation – her works being "purely and consistently philanthropic in character" – then boldly recasts the nature of her mission. "I have been urged from end to end of England," she tells Cooper, "to ascertain the exact needs of the British refugees of whom so much had been heard, and I have come here simply for that purpose." Here Emily is being less than candid. But having set off this smokescreen, she says that if the government objects to such useful work she is perfectly willing to submit, but what objection can there be to her living quietly in Cape Town where she has many friends? And might not her nurse be allowed to land as the bearer of a letter from Lady Ripon to Lady Hely-Hutchinson?

"I have been out of health and shrinking from the cold of an English winter come to this warm climate," Emily goes on. "I do not feel equal to the strain of an immediate return journey such as you offer me nor the alternative of remaining a prisoner on board the *Avondale Castle*. If, however, it is felt necessary for the honour of England that I should be imprisoned, I am perfectly willing and happy to forgo it, but I do pray that I may be imprisoned on land. I do not care how small the cell or how bare the diet, so long as it is only on terra firma. In making this request I do not think I am unreasonable, as I cannot sleep on board."

Emily then demands that a guard be set over her. A guard, she says, would not only give Colonel Cooper himself peace of mind, but would be a witness of "my adhesion to your regulations, until such time as you see fit to intern me in a land prison". This Emily evidently believes to be a well-placed thrust since, as she later tells Leonard, "soldiers hate guarding women". A final gibe comes as a postscript. Is she allowed to communicate with a washerwoman or is *uncleanliness* part of the regime to which she must submit?

The letter to Cooper is a gem of self-dramatisation, seamlessly running in a few lines through a protestation of innocence, a play for sympathy, an outburst of indignation, an appeal for gallantry and an embrace of martyrdom, not to mention a thrust or two of sarcasm and a choice example of name-dropping. When Emily says she is going be a thorn, she means it.

After the exasperation of seeing the other passengers land, the first day of detention seemed endless. The second was as bad, and as the continuing gale kept the ship out in the bay she attempted to divert herself by sketching, her chosen subject a panorama of the Cape mountain range. "The wind was terrific," she would remember, "but I pinned my paper onto the deck itself and did it lying down" – surely a curious undertaking for an invalid.

In a letter to Leonard dated October 29 Emily speaks of gathering strength by thinking about their ancestors who had suffered imprisonment – one Hugh Hobhouse, imprisoned for adherence to the Quaker faith around 1660, and of course the great Bishop Trelawny. "I wonder if 20,000 Englishmen 'will know the reason why' about poor me!" she remarks wistfully, echoing the words of the Cornish hymn.[xviii] Finding Macaulay's *History of England* in the ship's library, Emily looked up the bishop's story "hoping to get some wrinkles for my own guidance". And she found one. The imprisoned Trelawny had refused to pay for his board in the Tower and Emily resolved to follow his example on her prison ship. Here was another way of being a thorn, for she could refuse to pay the ten shillings a day for her keep. And she ends the letter: "No more tonight. I am too weak in the hand to wield the pen any longer."

Emily's demand for a guard rattled the military. That evening Colonel Cooper ordered Lingham to go back and demand Emily's word that she would not escape. In reply Emily said that giving her word was tantamount to keeping herself in prison, and why should she do that? "He said parole was the usual thing, and I answered I believed that was so only in quite different cases, for I understood people were let out of prison on parole, not detained thereby." Warming to her line, Emily pointed out that the authorities were refusing to trust her to keep her word on shore, so how could they trust her word afloat? "Mr Lingham appeared to have no answer to this argument, but pressed for parole, though sorry to trouble me."

Poor Lingham was clearly out of his depth. With a pang of pity Emily assured the man she attached no blame to him personally, "regarding him merely as mouthpiece of a tyranny and injustice higher than himself". Whatever comfort Lingham derived from this, he floundered again immediately when Emily asked what he meant to do if she continued to refuse parole. At this juncture she decided to compromise, agreeing not to escape until she received replies from Lords Kitchener and Milner. The relieved lieutenant hurried off, thankful for this small mercy.

That night Emily was again unable to sleep until Elizabeth Phillips mixed a draught to calm her. It is typical of her contrariness that, as she noted later, "in spite of my parole a detective was left who watched me closely, so next day I asked for his withdrawal".

Meanwhile, dismayed friends on shore considered what to do. Miss Steedham had broken the news of the arrest to Emily's old hostess in Cape Town, Caroline Murray, who was waiting vainly at the Union Castle office. Concern over Emily's health had exercised her South African allies long before the voyage; Mrs Murray herself had written in July begging Emily to scale down her campaigning for the sake of her health, adding: "If you knew how gratefully people look to you here you would feel you could best help them by reserving your strength."

Mrs Murray's consternation over the arrest was not shared by the lady commissioners in far-off Bloemfontein. Picking up the rumour about Emily and Maud

Gonne along with a premature story of deportation, Lucy Deane wrote to her sister: "We were all much amused to hear of Miss Hobhouse's ignominious defeat at Cape Town. How that woman can be so silly as to have associated herself in such a matter with Miss Maud Gonne of all people in the world!"

The supposed deportation of the pair was welcomed by Miss Deane: "Had they landed they would certainly have wanted to see us, and in my opinion it would only have been right and just to see them and hear what they have to say, but certainly Dr Waterston and Lady Knox would have kicked up a silly womanish row and refused to see them and thus put themselves or rather the commission in the wrong." On the other hand, she added, "it would have been most dangerous and mischievous to have them running loose about the country here".

Lord Kitchener, keeping in touch from Pretoria, repeated to General Wynne that Emily must not land. Wynne looked over the fast-expanding file on the unwelcome visitor and found a report from Lingham reporting Miss Hobhouse to have vowed that England would ring with the infamy of her arrest. Clearly the woman was determined to make trouble, and the matter could no longer be left in the hands of a mere lieutenant.

Colonel Cooper now went on board himself to confront Emily. He offered a launch to take her out to the *Carisbrooke*, which like the *Avondale* was delayed in the bay. This she declined, again complaining of fatigue and ill health before launching into another grand remonstrance about the honour of England. Cooper was not the kind of man to cope with a woman prepared to make a scene. Far from overawing Emily, he was obliged to beat a baffled retreat. Only when back in his office on the docks was he struck by the need for more forceful action. This meant summoning the hapless Lingham again. At least Cooper was then able to send General Wynne a confident-sounding assurance that he had "directed that Miss Hobhouse should be informed that I would have to send her home in the next ship sailing for England."

By a written order marked *Pressing and Confidential*, Lingham was instructed to go out and tackle Emily once more. "Impress upon her," said Cooper, "the inadvisability of remaining on the *Avondale Castle*. I would much prefer that Miss Hobhouse should consent to move voluntarily. In the meantime, she is not to land and visitors will not be allowed to see her without a special pass from this office. Please give strict orders to ensure that she does not attempt to escape. Several very decided Pro-Boers have paid her visits today and it is as well to be on guard."

This was an oblique reference to an embarrassing slip-up by Cooper himself. Without thinking through the likely consequences, he had earlier agreed to Emily's request to forward a letter to Caroline Murray, which led to an unfortunate scene when the *Avondale Castle* finally tied up on October 30. The moment the gangplank was lowered, a party of Emily's friends marched on board bearing fruit and flowers, the redoubtable Mrs Murray leading the way.

Within hours, at his desk at Government House, Lord Milner was leafing through reports from his spies. One claimed that the real reason for Emily's visit was to smuggle out of the country a dossier of concentration camp atrocity stories destined for use as propaganda by Boer exiles in Holland – "I am positive of this," added the informant, "as I was one of the men detailed to collect stories and was told I must get the correct names of the British officers and the names of the women and children who suffered." Another agent listed the names of Emily's friends who had made their way on board and referred darkly to various "papers" which Emily was observed to carry off to her cabin.

One of those prevented from boarding the ship was a plain, forthright English spinster of forty-three called Alice Greene, who had gone out to South Africa fifteen years previously as a short-term teacher at a girls' school and stayed on to became a fervent pro-Boer. Miss Greene, who had rented rooms in Cape Town for Emily, was suffering strained relations with her family back home in Cambridge. They complained of the increasingly anti-British tone of letters while she was dismayed by their repeated assertions that Milner was "such a wonderful man". Like her inseparable friend the school's headmistress, Alice Greene had been eased out of her job in recent days for addressing a protest rally against the war. But the two women meant to carry on their fight to see their friend.

*

It was a pillar-to-post sort of day for Lieutenant Lingham. Returning defeated from his latest trip to the *Avondale Castle*, he was immediately called to the telephone to speak to Colonel Cooper. He was ordered to go back yet again and this time to hand Miss Hobhouse a copy of the telegram confirming her immediate deportation on the personal orders of Lords Kitchener and Milner. The lady was also to be told to hold herself in readiness for transfer to another ship, the *Roslin Castle*, which was to sail for England either that day or the next.

Back came Lingham bearing a short message scribbled in pencil: "I have been very unwell ever since I saw you," she wrote to Cooper, "and it is quite impossible for me to contemplate the proposed voyage. I am, yours truly, E. Hobhouse."

By this time Lingham too was committing every detail to paper. "Acting on your orders by telephone," he minuted to Cooper, "I informed Miss Hobhouse that she must embark on board HM Transport *Roslin Castle* that same afternoon, to which she replied that it was quite impossible as she was much too ill… I then wrote to you submitting that some medical man be requested to come and see her, in answer to which I received a telephone message from you." The burden of Cooper's message was that a senior medical officer would be sent, but that the transfer of Miss Hobhouse to the *Roslin Castle* need not be delayed.

"I then went back and requested Miss Hobhouse to have her luggage packed up by her attendant," noted Lingham doggedly. "Miss Hobhouse forbade her attendant to do anything in the matter and I then ordered two of the stewardesses of the ship (through the Chief Officer) to pack up Miss Hobhouse's luggage, which was done in the presence of the lady's attendant."

The dawn of October 31 found Emily exhausted from lack of sleep and sustenance. Sick and frightened yet bolstered by a burning sense of injustice, she braced herself for the battle of her life.

But the immoveable object was about to meet an irresistible force.

16 "THEY WILL CARRY YOU AWAY LIKE A LUNATIC"

At around ten-thirty that morning a severe-looking lady of forty-nine with oddly drooping eyelids appeared at army headquarters at the docks and asked for the officer in charge. She announced herself as Miss Betty Molteno, and the name Molteno was not one to be ignored in Cape Town. The lady was the elder sister of Emily's special friend, Mrs Murray; their father had been the first prime minister of Cape Colony and the tentacles of family influence reached far and wide. Miss Molteno herself had been headmistress of Alice Greene's school, but like her had recently lost her position for espousing the Boer cause. She was ushered in to see Colonel Cooper, who after some dithering handed over a permit to board the *Avondale Castle* so that she might say goodbye to Emily. Pushing her luck, Miss Molteno then requested another pass for Mrs Murray but this was refused, as was a request for a laundress to be allowed on board. Cooper then made small talk in the course of which he asked uneasily about the relationship between Emily and Lord Hobhouse.

Emily had spent the morning dozing fitfully in her cabin between hazily-remembered interviews with a procession of officers and officials, all of whom urged her to accept the inevitable. Among these was a flustered Lieutenant Lingham, again tediously pleading that he was acting on orders and warning that force would be used if she remained obdurate. Emily roused herself long enough to berate him with renewed fury. "Why not take me on shore and hang me? Why torment me so?" she cried; and again Lingham retreated in confusion. In her overwrought state, Emily seems actually to have thought she might face execution. According to Alice Greene's diary, she chose "a black silk gown to be hanged in".

Betty Molteno boarded around noon. In a statement written when events were fresh in mind she described finding Emily leaning back with closed eyes in her deckchair, apparently asleep. Miss Molteno quietly seated herself beside her friend and after a while Emily opened her eyes with a great start. She looked utterly exhausted and spoke in a whisper. A large official envelope lying on her lap contained official notification that "a free passage had been granted her in the *Roslin Castle*".

The visitor sat with the drowsy invalid until the luncheon bell when Emily stirred herself to insist that her visitor went down to eat. She herself stayed in the cabin and took a little broth. Soon after Miss Molteno's return they were joined by the nurse Miss Phillips, who had been ashore on some errand.

Betty Molteno records the last appearance of Lieutenant Lingham. His plea for cooperation being refused by Emily "with restraint but under great excitement", the officer turned abruptly and left them. Nurse Phillips was then called away, returning to say she had been ordered by the military to pack Emily's boxes. This Emily forbade, only relenting when the ship's first officer came to say his stewardesses had been told to pack, and the nurse's presence was requested "as a protection to the stewardesses". Emily consented to Miss Phillips standing in the doorway while the packing was done.

A new player in the drama was now waiting nervously to make his entrance. This was Lieutenant Colonel J.F. Williamson of the Royal Army Medical Corps. A bachelor in his late fifties, Williamson was a veteran of Lord Roberts's Afghan campaigns, "an awfully good fellow, a thorough gentleman", according to friends, but notoriously shy with women. Williamson sent in his visiting card with a request to see Miss Hobhouse.

Betty Molteno takes up the story:

"Miss Hobhouse asked Nurse to say that she was quite unequal to seeing a stranger and must ask Colonel Williamson to excuse her. Nurse returned with a message that Colonel Williamson was a medical man and wished to see Miss Hobhouse professionally. Miss Hobhouse told Nurse to say that she did not wish to see a strange medical man and must beg to be excused. Colonel W then approached himself and said: 'Miss Hobhouse, I am the chief of the medical staff and am ordered to see you professionally.'

"Miss Hobhouse replied: 'I am exhausted by the voyage I have made and the shock I have had, but a strange medical man with whom I am not totally acquainted cannot help me in any way. What I need is rest and quiet.'"

Emily continued to refuse to be examined until he cannily remarked: "I may find you too unwell to sail at present." At this she finally consented and allowed herself to be helped to the smoking room where Williamson examined her heart and tongue, and asked Miss Phillips to take her temperature.

What Emily needed, he announced, was a stimulant, which he would prescribe. He left the room with Miss Phillips and Emily's hopes rose. When Miss Phillips returned, she asked excitedly: "What does he say, Nurse, am I to stay?" Nurse replied that Williamson said her heart was all right, and she would be well enough to sail when she had drunk some champagne or brandy. Emily burst out indignantly: "I never supposed I had a diseased heart! What did he expect to find? It is my nerves and the exhaustion and shock I have had that I am suffering from."

The scene now becomes agonizingly protracted. First the ship's chief officer puts in a sheepish appearance to say that he has been unable to prevent the removal of Emily's baggage, and that a cab is waiting for her. "They make take my luggage," declares Emily, "but they will not take me." Williamson then reappears. "Miss Hobhouse," he says, "everything is arranged; will you kindly prepare to come." When Emily refuses, he adds: "I am acting under orders and if you will not come voluntarily, force will be used."

"I do not believe," flings back Emily, "that any English gentleman will carry out such an order." Williamson says two nurses will be called to remove her, and she repeats: "I do not believe it. Women will not do the dirty work that men refuse to do themselves. I shall appeal to their sex and their womanhood; I know they will not touch me."

To continue Betty Molteno's testimony:

"Two women burst into the smoking room. They were not army nurses but wore what looked like an attempt at a uniform. They were large, stout women... they approached and took up a position on either side of Miss Hobhouse. I was ordered to move from beside her and crossed to the other side of the room. Miss Hobhouse appealed to their womanhood, to their sense of responsibility to a Higher Power, addressing them as Sisters whose mission was to succour, aid and bless, not to use violence."

What follows is pure theatre:

"After listening silently for a while the women who had placed themselves in a resolute attitude – with bodies stiffened and arms akimbo – gradually relaxed their faces; their arms dropped and finally they turned and quietly went out. Miss Hobhouse said as they moved away: 'Thank you both, Sisters, I was sure you would not do it, I knew that women would not so disgrace their womanhood.'" According to Miss Molteno, Emily remained throughout the scene calm and collected, "speaking quietly but with penetrating intensity and resolution which the women seemed wholly unable to resist".

Drained by the contest, Emily took a little tea to husband her strength for the next bout. It was not long in coming. Nurse Phillips went out to see how things stood, returning to report: "They say they are going to send for a stretcher and bearers and that they will carry you away like a lunatic."

Emily sent for Captain Brown and the chief officer, who protested they are powerless to intervene. Soon after the two army nurses came back and tried gently to persuade Emily to leave, one of them whispering: "It will be so horrible for men to touch you. We are volunteer nurses. We are free. We can refuse to touch you, but the stretcher-bearers dare not." Emily only shook her head.

Colonel Williamson tried again: "Now, Miss Hobhouse, come quietly with these sisters and do not give us so much trouble." Still she refused, saying she would do her best to be fit to travel in a week or so, and he broke in: "I am acting under instructions. You will have to go today."

The scene, said Miss Molteno, became "inexpressibly painful", and when Williamson stalked out of the room she followed, hoping one more appeal might tip the scales. The officer was pacing the deck in deep perplexity, but when she begged for a week's reprieve he replied: "Impossible. We are acting on orders direct from Lord Kitchener."

By this time the exhausted Emily was scarcely capable of speaking. Shortly before seven o'clock, when she said she might go to bed, Nurse Phillips came in to report the stretcher-bearers were on board, and Miss Molteno urged her not to abandon Emily if she was sent back to England. At this point Colonel Williamson re-entered.

Two stretcher-bearers took up position at the cabin door – "square-looking men," in the words of Miss Molteno, "not tall, but heavy and stolid, their faces absolutely expressionless as though they wore masks". Williamson came close to Emily and said: "Now, Miss Hobhouse, you have had your will, you have had the scene you wanted. I will touch you on the shoulder, that will be sufficient for your purpose, you had better come quietly."

"You have no right to do this," insisted Emily. "Martial law has reference to taking steps against the enemy. You have no right to interfere with private individuals."

"I am not here to argue," Williamson broke in. "I cannot listen. I say, will you come quietly?"

Emily appealed directly to the men: "You will not do this thing you are asked to do. You would not treat your mothers or wives or sisters so. There is a Higher Law – you cannot, you dare not obey these orders."

The eyewitness of Emily's deportation, Betty Molteno, left, with her bosom friend Alice Greene, who wrote of Emily choosing a black dress to be hanged in.

Williamson gave the signal. Emily continued to harangue the stretcher-bearers – "the laws of God and humanity forbid you" – as they seized and lifted her. She broke free and planted her feet on the cabin floor. According to Betty Molteno, Williamson deftly slipped out "a long black band" and tied it round the struggling woman's waist as the men took hold of her. Between the three of them they succeeded in lifting her off her feet again, at which "she lay all her length like a baby, helpless in their arms". Emily burst out: "You brutes, you brutes, you touch me." As they lifted her through the doorway, with Williamson repeating, "Be careful, be careful, don't hurt the lady", she gave "a great terrible heartbroken cry".

Betty Molteno went on: "They placed her, still struggling, in a Madeira chair on the deck and quickly lifted it... she struggled free of the chair and succeeded in planting her feet on the deck. Again Colonel W placed his arm round her from behind and the three men seized her at the steps leading to the lower deck. I heard Colonel W say repeatedly: 'Be careful, don't hurt the lady.'"

As she was carried off the ship to the waiting carriage Emily called out goodbyes to Captain Brown and others who had shown her kindness. But her humiliation was not yet over. As Betty Molteno panted down the gangway after them, she was surprised by "sullen horrid hisses and hootings and low growls as from savage beasts". This was the reaction to Emily's appearance from an "ill-looking little crowd" on the quayside. A high shrill voice called: "Canting old hypocrite – serves her right! A sousing in the saltwater would do her good!"

Emily was thrust into the carriage. Running after it, Miss Molteno was in time to see one of the nurses inside put a comforting arm round Emily, and was relieved to see Nurse Phillips on the seat opposite. Miss Molteno pressed a basket of fruit and flowers for Emily into the coachman's hands and, as the carriage passed by, her distressed friend caught a glimpse of her and called goodbye.

Betty Molteno insisted that Emily "was extremely dignified and mentally collected" throughout what seemed an interminably protracted ordeal, but this is not quite how Emily comes across in Colonel Williamson's version of the story.

*

The morning after Emily's removal from the *Avondale Castle* Williamson breakfasted with a friend, the Cape attorney-general Sir James Rose Innes, and treated the table to a blow-by-blow account of the incident that kept his listeners in stitches.

"Old Williamson is much put out about the whole affair and takes it *very seriously*," chortles Sir James in a letter dated November 4 to his wife Elizabeth in which he predicts there will be a great fuss in the English newspapers.

The Rose Innes account does not differ materially from Miss Molteno's except in the picture it paints of Emily's demeanour. According to Williamson, in the course of the struggle Emily had not only continually harangued him and the nurses in a passionate manner but "fixed herself in a corner of the saloon behind an immoveable table, from which retreat she defied everybody".

Sir James's letter goes on: "In the middle of it when he was telling how the orderlies were obliged to carry her out I said, 'Williamson, I hope what Elizabeth calls her *frillies* were all right.' Without a smile, and very earnestly, Williamson said: 'I am an old hand; I had thought of that; and when she was picked up I threw a shawl over her feet.'" The straight-faced delivery struck the listeners as so droll that Sir James laughed till he was helpless and feared a guest sitting opposite would have a fit.

Repeating Williamson's assertion that it took over four hours to get Emily off the ship and into the carriage, Sir James added: "A small crowd had assembled and the poor woman, beside herself with excitement and anger, shouted and screamed at them also. The only result was loud laughter and coarse remarks; and thus amid the jeers of the dock loafers the unfortunate lady made her exit. Whatever may be thought about the wisdom of sending her back, there can be no two opinions about the want of self-restraint and dignity on her part."

Sir James believed Lord Kitchener had blundered in sending express orders for Emily's deportation: "I should have thought the wise course would have been to let her land and not to have let her go up-country, where *everything possible* is now being done for the people in the concentration camps. However, thank goodness, we, the civil authorities, have no responsibility."

In Emily's own account of the incident, we find well-turned little speeches unrecorded by other witnesses. In this version Emily has all the best lines and dispenses withering put-downs to her tormentors. A good example is when Williamson asks her to go with the stretcher-bearers, and she answers: "Sir, I cannot and will not give other reply than what I have said from the beginning. My refusal was based on principle, and principles do not alter in a day." Or again, when he asks if she wishes to be taken from the ship trussed like a lunatic, she ripostes: "Sir, the lunacy is on your side and with those whose commands you obey."

The temptation to improve one's words in memory is always strong and perhaps inevitable in circumstances like Emily's on board the *Avondale Castle*. As she repeatedly declared herself to be sick and confused, it would be remarkable if she had retained the presence of mind to deliver such polished retorts, and the ability to recall them verbatim.

The divergence of opinion over Emily's behaviour must be examined in detail as it was of paramount importance to herself. Her insistence that she remained "very polite, very dignified" throughout agrees with Miss Molteno's statement. However, some differences emerge between the versions of Emily and her friendly witness. At odds with the Molteno account, for instance, is Emily's description of the stretcher-bearers as hesitant and reluctant – one, she claimed, actually turned and made for the door before being ordered back by Williamson. And she makes no mention of putting up a struggle and twice breaking free of her captors.

Williamson in his official report says Emily resisted violently and screamed loudly; Sir James Rose Innes, on the basis of the breakfast conversation, told Lord Milner the following day that Emily "lacked dignity and self-restraint", adding that "she harangued everyone on the way, nurses, stretcher-bearers and dock loafers". This contrasts with Emily's recollection that "I spoke a few words to the men who bore me, otherwise there was silence".

Military censors blanked out news of the deportation in the mainstream Cape press, but some weeks later a scurrilous account of the event surfaced in a satirical local journal called *The Owl*. By this time Emily's removal from the *Avondale* was claimed to have entailed "the services of a stretcher, body straps, a file of Tommies, half-a-dozen nurses and a few other people", and Emily was said to have "kicked, scratched and yelled worse than any coloured woman ever run in for drunkenness". The language she hurled at the British officers, added *The Owl*, "proved that in her time she must have frequented places just as filthy and quite as crowded as she alleged the concentration camps were".

Emily's resistance was a difficult issue for the Quaker Ruth Fry. In the carefully chosen words of her 1929 biography she admits two separate problems, these being "the wisdom of the actions of the Government and those of Miss Hobhouse". Judgment on Miss Hobhouse's conduct, she suggests, should be informed by understanding the experience "as it presented itself to her" in the absence of capable advisers; therefore "if her actions be deemed undignified, it must in fairness be borne in mind, that not only was she overwrought by long-continued strain, but she was firmly, though erroneously, under the impression that if she did not offer physical resistance, she would be held to have acquiesced in the proceeding". It is hardly a ringing endorsement of her friend's behaviour.

Tellingly, the deportation is skated over in the three-volume *Life of Lord Kitchener* by his friend Sir George Arthur. The single reference to Emily comes in a dismissive footnote of four lines beginning: "A lady called Hobhouse, whose zeal outran her sense of propriety, was forbidden to land at Cape Town."

Milner, in a letter to a friend describing Emily's "exportation", seems anxious to dodge his share of responsibility for the painful scene: "Of course it was most stupidly mismanaged by the officers in Cape Town, who were simply told not to let her land, and should never have moved her by force from one ship to another. Still, her own conduct was childish and disgraceful in the extreme." He was willing to defend his own part in the prohibition on landing: "We have a witches' cauldron here already and cannot afford to admit mischief-making busybodies, who at a less critical time one might simply be content to laugh at."

As Ruth Fry discerned, the stress of the previous months had evidently told on Emily's judgment as well as on her physical state. Her own story suggests that, despite the attempts to justify herself, she fears her conduct had been unbecoming. Certainly the scene would have rendered her father speechless with horror, and she must have feared that Uncle Arthur would deplore any hint of exhibitionism. Perhaps she was angry with herself for giving way to sheer frustrated rage, and preferred to draw a veil over the unladylike details. Betty Molteno, on the other hand, lacked Emily's pacifist scruples, and failed to grasp that her friend would be distressed by her emphasis on the physical struggle.

Even so, Emily was left with an abiding sense that the sanctity of her person had been violated. Nothing in her experience, not even in lawless America or Mexico, had prepared her for a manhandling. Almost certainly this was the first time in her life she had been subjected to physical force; even during the furious scene at Liskeard, rioters like Wyndham Childs had fallen back in confusion under her haughty glare. With hindsight, she probably realised that submission to a tap on the shoulder as urged by Williamson, technically an exercise of force, offered a more dignified exit than the sensational scene that delighted her enemies and troubled many friends.

The closest Emily ever came to acknowledging regret was in a memoir written over twenty years later for Mrs Steyn, in which she wrote: "Ill as I was – prostrate from shock – every power of mind and body was concentrated on the effort to stand firm in the non-acquiescence which I believed my duty, and for the sake of the sufferers whose champion I had become." Alas, it was a far cry from the long-ago daydreams of Joan of Arc.

So how ill was she? As Ruth Fry said, the past months had taken their toll, and Emily had chosen a trained nurse as a travelling companion. Yet friends conceded she was disposed to milk illnesses for advantage as well as dramatic effect, and it would certainly have been in character to exaggerate her condition on board ship in her efforts to get her own way. This is not to say she did not make herself genuinely ill in the process. On the other hand, Emily's life story is peppered with wonderful recoveries from desperate maladies, and no doubt a swift revival would have followed had she been allowed on shore.

*

Betty Molteno and Alice Greene were among the many friends refused permission to see Emily before the *Roslin Castle* sailed, but they went to the dockside on the off-chance of catching sight of her. At first they could see nothing but hundreds of figures in khaki from stem to stern but suddenly Betty cried out "There she is!" Alice craned forward and made out Emily in a deckchair with Betty's flowers on her lap.

"I should not have known her, she looked so ill and altered and utterly exhausted," Alice wrote in her diary. "How unlike the brilliant, beautiful, indomitable Miss H of five months ago! But the face to me more beautiful than ever, full of a new wistfulness, yearning tenderness and sympathy. With the shawl over her head and the broken heart-stricken look in the eyes she looked like some old medieval picture of the Mater Dolorosa, bearing in her heart the sorrows of the world. She gave us a beautiful, loving smile."

*

Before the ship sailed Emily rallied sufficiently to fire off furious letters to her persecutors. Nothing useful could come of such protests but, as she put it, "my feminine desire to speak my mind was strong". The first letter, confused in wording and pathetically scrawled in pencil, was addressed to Lord Kitchener, and would have reached him the day before his sister-in-law Caroline died:

"Your brutality has triumphed over my weakness and sickness. You have forgotten so to be a patriot as not to forget that you are a gentleman. I hope that in future you will exercise greater width of judgment in the exercise of your high office. To carry out orders such as these is a degradation both to the office and the manhood of your soldiers. I feel ashamed to own you as a fellow countryman."

Milner was next. "Your narrow incompetency," she declared, "is leading you to such acts as this and many others, staining your own name and the reputation of England." She had actually started out liking him, but "now I see you more clearly as you really are and can believe it is true what a man once said to me: that you have 'the soul of a spy'."

Hely-Hutchison too came in for a blasting. "It seems to me," she wrote, "if I were a Governor without power enough to protect one sick Englishwoman from torment and brutality I would resign from a post so useless." Signing off "in bitter shame for England", she added: "Excuse the pencil scrawl but I am weak and exhausted."

Nor did Colonel Cooper escape. "I write to tell you it will be my duty to make this whole affair very public in England," Emily promised. "I shall be obliged to mention your name, as well as Lingham's, and that *xxxxx* Williamson." On second thoughts, she wrote in explanation of the crossing-out, it was better to erase the epithet he deserved.

*

An intriguing postscript to Colonel Williamson's part in the story comes in a letter written by Mrs Murray to her brother Percy Molteno. The officer, she says, had found Emily "a very charming woman he could not but admire" and remarked wryly that she "had the face of a Madonna, but she fights like the devil."

A much praised beauty in her youth, Caroline Murray retained a knowing interest in matters of romance, and despite the painful nature of the deportation seems

138

to have been tickled by the idea of the bachelor Williamson being smitten by her friend. Writing later to Emily, she was unable to resist repeating his tribute to the Madonna-Devil, though coyly adding "perhaps I ought not to tell you this".

Over sixty years later the letter was discovered among Emily's private papers.

17 "CARRION CROWS WILL TEAR AND REND ME"

T he voyage back to England was every bit as bad as Emily dreaded. Incapable of sleeping, she refused for seven days to touch any food except the fruit and bottled peaches from her Boer friends; her only solace was that the flowers Miss Molento had thrown to the coachman kept fresh all that time.

Emily documented the shipboard horrors in a rambling letter written for Mrs Murray over the early stages of the voyage and posted at St Vincent, the first port of call: "The smells are horrible. Fancy 700 men always smoking. I can get no square inch safe from tobacco anywhere and it makes me sick, this coarse tobacco." Ten days later her complaints centred on the vibration of the ship's propeller, and she admitted to striving constantly against hysteria. On the outward journey Emily had injured her side in a fall during a storm, and the sickening pitch and roll of the *Roslin Castle*, the smallest and oldest troopship in service, brought the pain on again. And all the time the trauma of the arrest and manhandling was going round and round in her head. "The men hurt me a good deal," she wrote, "their hands are so rough and strong and I am much bruised."

The ship's commander meant to be kind, enquiring after her each day, but Emily now shrank instinctively from anyone in British uniform. Both she and the loyal Miss Phillips dreaded the three-week ordeal before them. In the draft autobiography compiled years later, the number on board would go up to eight hundred; as she would then remember, there was dirt and disorder everywhere, and the pervading smell was not of tobacco but of rotten onions. To add to the foul stifling atmosphere of the cabin, the cold weather was increasingly a trial as the ship ploughed on northwards since neither Emily nor Miss Phillips had imagined a need for winter clothes; but at least Emily could see this particular discomfort as "a slight realisation in my own person" of what tens of thousands of South Africa's women were enduring.

Indignation over the deportation burned as fiercely as ever, shot through with misgivings about her personal behaviour. In her best theatrical style Emily told Mrs Murray she would have gone quietly to any prison or to be hanged, but in the face of "so insensate an order as the one carried out by brute force against a sick woman", it had seemed her duty to resist being seized "in justice to myself, to Nurse, and to all concerned" – the peroration is predictable – "the honour of England included".

Emily was also in another muddle about money, and had to save her few remaining shillings to cable home once the ship reached St Vincent. At the same time as bracing herself to ask Uncle Arthur for some ready cash, she prepared instructions to her bank to transfer hundreds of pounds in committee funds direct to South Africa.

Meanwhile back in England confusion spread among family and friends. As the press had been effectively muzzled on Emily's fate, the Courtneys' enquiries at the shipping office met with a blank wall. A well-intended act by Alice Greene in Cape Town only served to add to the mystification. In an effort to outwit the watchful army censors, she cabled the message "TELL NORA GAINED PRIZE" to Leonard Hobhouse's sister-in-law. This was based on a secret code previously agreed between Emily and Leonard but was initially misinterpreted to mean that Emily had been thrown in prison.

Kate Courtney gave vent to her outrage in her diary: "Surely, things have come to a pretty pass when an Englishwoman can be imprisoned and not allowed to communicate with her relations, her uncle a Lord of the Privy Council too!" When Leonard himself examined the cable he correctly decoded the message as "deported" and decided that the real threat to his sister's liberty might come when the *Roslin Castle* docked in England. Uncle Arthur, who at eighty-two had recently resigned from the Privy Council, hurried anxiously to make enquiries at the War Office and was promised any news that might come in.

Aunt Mary wrote to commiserate with Leonard, though her words reveal a distinct coolness over the whole adventure: "I suppose E was prepared for this abortive end to her journey whose object I never clearly understood, but I knew her heart and interests were there and that she would not settle down here till she had made the attempt." Kate Courtney too detected a reserve in Lady Hobhouse when she called at Bruton Street, later telling Leonard that his aunt was disposed to wait a day or two before pressing the War Office for more information, "and she evidently does not want to hurry Lord Hobhouse".

But the next day Uncle Arthur could restrain himself no longer, writing to the War Office that an obscure message had reached the family that Emily was "departed" or "deported" and demanded clarification from the war minister himself. Curiously no one had thought to put St John Brodrick in the picture, and he was forced to send a secret telegram to General Wynne on November 7: "It is alleged that Miss Hobhouse has been deported from South Africa. Is this correct? What is the cause?"

Rather than allow Wynne to respond, Kitchener sent his own explanation: "Milner asked me about Miss Hobhouse being allowed to land at Cape Town," he told Brodrick, "and we agreed that considering the attitude she had taken up and the untruths she had published that it would not be desirable in the present state of the colony for her to do so." He enclosed copies of Emily's emotional letters to himself and Lord Milner, adding: "I daresay if they were published in the press it might give the public a clear insight into the sort of lady she is."

That same day, November 8, the news broke in the English papers. Again Emily's name was at the centre of a major political storm. Joshua Rowntree expressed astonishment that martial law had become so naked and unashamed; one MP branded her arrest "a shameful indignity to a noble-hearted woman" and called the deportation the meanest of all the acts in a disgraceful war; even the government of Crimean War times had stopped short of arresting Florence Nightingale, he cried, overlooking in his excitement that the Lady with the Lamp had not gone out to minister to the enemy side.

Though the press generally remained hostile to Emily, the *Daily News*, newly converted to the anti-war cause, carried an editorial calling the deportation a "lawless outrage" and fiercely attacking the war minister by name. Had Brodrick acted sooner on

Emily's revelations, claimed the leader, "many hundreds of lives might have been saved, and the public character of England would not have suffered an ineffaceable stain".[xix]

Once again, the most important intervention came from Campbell-Bannerman. Speaking at a party meeting in Bath, the Liberal leader launched a blistering attack on the government's war policy and paid tribute to "the noble lady, Miss Hobhouse". The name brought the audience cheering to its feet. To Emily, declared Sir Henry, belonged the credit of having first called attention to the concentration camps, and she had now heaped further honour on herself by being deported. Cries of "shame" mingled with cheers as he added: "As if, forsooth, the power of this great Empire was too weak to stand the presence of a woman."

Hobhouses and Courtneys urgently debated what should be done when the *Roslin Castle* arrived at Southampton on November 24. Leonard Hobhouse and Uncle Arthur thought the government might have Emily re-arrested once she set foot on English soil. But Leonard was discouraged from meeting his sister and decided to remain in Manchester; in the event of her arrest, remarked Aunt Mary sensibly, Emily would want no help in protesting. The Courtneys were at first ambivalent about travelling down to Southampton themselves – "my husband doubts if we are the best people," remarked Kate, meaning as notorious pro-Boers – but in the end it was these trusty friends rather than family who were waiting at the dockside.

Leonard composed a careful letter of instructions for Emily to read while still on board, telling her to avoid talking to the press until the inner circle had agreed on the best course of action. Clearly, political capital was to be gained from the affair; already there was much talk of legal redress, with one MP writing to the papers suggesting a public subscription list to pay for the action.

Among the flood of letters waiting for Emily perhaps the most treasured one was signed with love and kisses from her favourite nephew Oliver – Leonard's nine-year-old son, and a replica of the golden-haired cherub who had won all hearts at St Ive Rectory. He asked: "Did you really get put in prison?"

One note that seems strikingly light on sympathy came from Emily's sister Maud, once her cherished confidant. "Do hope you will take up something a bit less notorious," wrote Maud, adding that she understood the infant mortality rate "in Battersea, etc" was quite as bad as in the South African camps, so she thought that henceforth Emily should busy herself in the London slums instead. The remainder of the letter was devoted to wistful twittering about a costume of Emily's left in Maud's care, and a none-too-subtle hint: "It fits me exactly but hearing you were returning I *never wore* it."

Taken as a whole the family letters appear remarkably devoid of the explosions of indignation and tender enquiries that came from friends like Lady Ripon and Isabel Rowntree. No one could accuse these Hobhouses of being sentimentalists; Leonard's wife Nora too, after the rather perfunctory statement "we are so glad to have you safely back", continues her short note: "Here you will be of great use. Already you are being used as a handle to hit the Govt. with." Near the end of her life, re-reading these letters, Emily would remark that she had been glad her personal welfare was regarded as of secondary importance compared with "the public honour"; yet one senses that a little more solicitude from her relatives, and less political calculation, might have been welcome at this most stressful of times.

The Courtneys meanwhile were shocked by their friend's physical and nervous state after the punishing round-trip of forty-eight days, and found her too exhausted to give a lucid account of her ordeal. Avoiding a scrum of reporters, they hurried Emily from the dock. Yet several of the *Roslin Castle* officers made friendly goodbyes and Kate Courtney noted in her diary that no one was uncivil except three smartly dressed ladies. Emily was taken to a quiet hotel room nearby so that she could rest before boarding the London train that would take her to the haven of Bruton Street.

Once there, fortified by beef-tea, hot milk and a strong tonic prescribed by Lady Hobhouse's doctor, she dashed off a note to assure her brother that his instructions would be heeded: "I will be very wary of my words and of pressmen who are upon me as thick as a swarm of bees in May," she wrote, promising to do "nothing unauthorised". Commiserating over Leonard's continuing financial difficulties – for he and Nora were now facing the trials of life without a housemaid – Emily offered to go to Manchester once she was well enough, so long as she was allowed her fair share of the housework.

In this letter Emily adds interestingly to the deportation story. "I was removed by force, bound in a shawl," she says, "and carried by 8 soldiers like a corpse." Her mode of resistance she describes as "polite but passive"; the officers and men involved clearly loathed their task, she claims, and "I told them quietly what I thought of it and them". And she insists: "I made them respect me and I considered that though finally worsted, I triumphed morally."

*

As controversy over the deportation raged, *The Times* weighed in with a leader inevitably critical of Emily's physical struggle against her captors: "She had only herself to thank if she was thereby placed in an undignified position or has to suffer any other inconvenience than the sacrifice of some project of officious interference with what is none of her business."

Uncle Arthur was prevailed upon to write to the press in Emily's defence, though he surely realised that a newspaper was no fit platform for a judge's scrupulous musings on the abstract principles of liberty balanced against the exigencies of military law. *The Times* came back with a dig at Lord Hobhouse, suggesting he had not grasped "the simple proposition that civil liberty in the full sense is only possible when obedience is given to the civil power". In the view of *The Times*, when civil liberty was being used to fight the enemy's battles, then civil liberty must be curtailed or altogether suspended – an argument as familiar today as during the Boer War.

It was in this fraught atmosphere that Emily determined to sue Lord Kitchener, along with Lord Milner, Colonel Cooper and Lieutenant Lingham, for assault and false imprisonment. The eminent solicitor chosen on her uncle's advice was Sir George Lewis, whose roll of past clients included the King himself when Prince of Wales. Among Lewis's advisers was Sir Edward Clarke, solicitor-general under the previous Conservative administration, but of known pro-Boer sympathies; as leading counsel Emily retained Rufus Isaacs, KC, later to become the first practising Jew in a British cabinet and, as Lord Reading, a viceroy of India.

Curiously, the name of her admiring handler Colonel Williamson was absent from the papers served on the War Office by Emily's lawyers, despite the specific threat against him in the last note she scribbled in Table Bay. Emily's explanation was that the legal action centred on "the act of arrest and subsequent deportation, and not the mode in which the intermediate agents behaved", though this seems hard on Cooper, who no less than Williamson was following Kitchener's orders, and on the junior officer Lingham, who for all his badgering of Emily never laid a finger upon her.

The public was much excited about the case, Emily wrote to Caroline Murray, "but for myself I am still suffering so much from the shock that I feel callous – only dimly conscious that my carcass is thrown into the public arena and all legal and political carrion crows will tear and rend and devour me". She believed the action might lead to a change in English law, but added that "being only a female, and not deeply interested in an abstruse legal point", she felt much more strongly about "the personal-outrage side of the question".

Lord Hobhouse loyally backed his niece, though not without a private grumble or two. The great stumbling block in the case, he knew, was finding a defendant to proceed against in England. As to the cost of the action, he confided glumly to a friend, "I prefer to bear on my shoulders the expense of the suit, as well as the odium and ridicule which its failure will bring down". The financial sacrifice involved clearly rankled. It would prevent his usual donations to political causes, he said, but he would have to put up with that. The truth was he felt too old and worn out for "newspaper warfare"; he had never wanted to write the letter to the press in the first place, only yielding to urgent pressure from others.

Emily was determined to put forward her own account of the deportation. A full week was taken up preparing her statement for publication, but then every word had to be checked out and argued over by her brother, uncle, various axe-grinding acquaintances, and a whole team of lawyers. Emily began to see the authorised version of events as "a mosaic of everyone but myself". Though written in the form of a letter to the Distress Committee, the report which finally emerged was intended for the widest possible circulation. It was printed as a pamphlet and sent out to the press with a covering letter in Emily's name; it was advertised for sale to the public at the price of a halfpenny. On the day the corrected proofs were delivered she told Leonard: "Now I have done my part and hope I may forget the weary story which goes round and round my brain in a continual wondering how else I could or should have acted."

As the government feared, the sensational elements of the story were seized upon by England's enemies everywhere, and for a second time in a year Emily's name was trumpeted all over the world. But there was a difference. Six months before the great controversy had been over the concentration camps; now the story was Emily herself.

Fan mail poured in from every part of the globe. A meeting of an international women's peace movement in Paris voted unanimously to express their warmest sympathy and admiration for Emily's "sublime and charitable action"; from Philadelphia in the United States came a call for her to act as patroness of a fund dedicated to the camp inmates; the president of the Women's League for the Promotion of International Disarmament wrote admiringly from The Hague; in Switzerland a committee of anti-war ladies was formed, and in Basle alone collected twenty thousand signatures to a testimonial saluting Emily's valiant fight for the Boer women.

Among famous foreign writers inspired by her story was Edmond Rostand, author of *Cyrano de Bergerac*, whose *Ballade de Miss Hobhouse* was rushed into print in Paris. With a refrain of "*Miss Hobhouse est un coeur charmant*", it was set to music and performed throughout France and translated into Italian and Dutch; a prize-winning English version published in South Africa ended each verse with the words "*Emily Hobhouse, noble heart!*" Another French poet began his homage with the line: "*Dans le camp, une ange a passee...*" In Holland, the bard L.S. Leipolt penned the tear-jerker *An 'n seepkissie* – addressed to a soapbox used as an infant's coffin in a concentration camp – which would still be recited by Dutch schoolchildren fifty years later.

Meanwhile in South Africa, the canonisation of Emily began in earnest. Her fervent admirer Alice Greene published a highly emotional composition entitled *Miss Hobhouse* which begins:

> *The Terror reigns! Our lips are dumb:*
> *The Terror reigns! Our hands are tied:*
> *Yet hither did a woman come*
> *Across two oceans wide.*

It goes on:

> *O Englishwoman, tall and fair,*
> *O Englishwoman, calm and brave*
> *Within the breach thou standest there*
> *Those innocents to save!*
> *Thou standest there with outstretched arms,*
> *Like some Madonna, strong to bless,*
> *To soothe their childish wild alarms,*
> *And comfort their distress.*

And so on for sixteen verses, ending with the lines:

> *She, star-like, shines, and in our souls*
> *She lives for evermore.*

At home, now partially recovered, Emily was feted at a dinner at the New Reform Club. Presided over by the legendary editor of the *Manchester Guardian*, C.P. Scott, it was an unprecedented honour for a woman, though her pleasure in the occasion was tempered by private knowledge that Scott had recently tried to re-employ her hard-pressed brother Leonard on inferior financial terms.

But in England the antis continued to outnumber the pros. Among new detractors was Arthur Conan Doyle, world-famous as the creator of Sherlock Holmes, whose bestseller on the South African War branded Emily as politically prejudiced. Thanks to a demonstrable error of detail in Conan Doyle's account, Emily was able to force a reluctant apology from the author, and the offending passage was struck out of later editions.

The legal preliminaries against Kitchener and the others rumbled on. At first Emily pinned high hopes on clever Sir George Lewis – "a darling," she enthused, "with a face like a cameo and brilliant dark eyes" – and observed approvingly that her solicitor longed to get his claws into the government and into Joe Chamberlain especially. But matters were not proceeding well.

The opening move in the campaign, a letter dated December 3 from Lewis to St

John Brodrick, announced Emily's intention to bring an action against the four named men; the war secretary was asked to instruct a solicitor to appear on their behalf. The War Office took over a week to respond, and then merely stated that the minister declined to take the suggested course on behalf of the four, who were all serving their country in South Africa.

In the New Year – almost a month after the initial approach – Lewis reported that Brodrick was still stonewalling. A further fortnight went by, then in an effort to provoke a response Uncle Arthur agreed to make public all the correspondence between Emily's solicitors and the War Office. "The delay in instituting legal proceedings is not due to Miss Hobhouse or her advisers," he insisted to the Press Association, while admitting failure in finding someone willing to accept responsibility for his niece's arrest and seizure.

Heated debates continued in both Lords and Commons. Reassembling for the first session of 1902, the Commons had their first opportunity to debate both Emily's deportation and Mrs Fawcett's blue book. "I say every visitor to the camps," cried Chamberlain, "with the exception of Miss Hobhouse, has recognised the efforts of all concerned to do their best for the poor people in their charge." In response, the Irish Nationalist firebrand John Dillon declared that history would honour Emily, "although her name was jeered at in this House today".

Brodrick accepted responsibility for the deportation but stuck rigidly to his script on the legal issue. After this a number of sympathetic MPs began to murmur against the way Emily's case was being handled, leaving her with nagging doubts about the wisdom of the course set by Uncle Arthur and Lewis. In her commonsense way she wondered why her lawyers had asked Brodrick to accept service of the writ, instead of simply serving it; but then Uncle Arthur was paying the bills, and she did not wish to appear ungrateful. Perhaps divining her difficulty, a group of pro-Emily MPs took the initiative and referred the essential question of law to no fewer than five counsels. Unfortunately the legal opinion was unanimous. If the case went to court, Emily would lose.

The leading counsel, Arthur Cohen, softened this bald statement with a private letter to Emily in which he thanked her "for allowing me the privilege of advising you without accepting a fee". But after stating his strong view that the authorities had committed a stupid and offensive outrage upon her, he could only repeat that the advice to drop the case was good. He promised however to keep a close eye on the expected passage through parliament of an act of indemnity relating to the war, and "to consider carefully whether its terms are so framed as to deprive you of all chance of success in maintaining an action against Lord Kitchener on his return to England".

The decision was a bitter disappointment to Emily, though surely welcomed deep in his heart by Uncle Arthur. News that the case was to be abandoned was a relief to Brodrick too, for soon after admitting responsibility in the Commons he had written to Kitchener – it is unclear how much in jest and how much in earnest – informing the commander-in-chief that "Miss Hobhouse is panting for your blood" and warning that on his return to England he might find himself in Newgate Goal.

Emily herself felt "something like a broken motor car left in a ditch". Her health simply refused to mend. Despite her doctor's assurance that she would pull round after a few weeks of rest, she believed the marks of the ordeal would be on her for the rest of her life. The collapse of her legal action only added to the strain.

What she needed, Emily decided, was sun and silence away from England. She started off alone for France, but travelled via Brussels to meet up with Annie Botha. She found her friend looking refreshed – "so different from the harassed war look she had worn when passing through London" – but in great distress over the latest news from her country, where many Boers were reported murdered by hostile blacks.

Emily went on to find a solitary spot on Lake Annecy in the Savoy. There, as the only guest at an old inn at the village of Talloires, she remained completely undisturbed for eight weeks, speaking only to an occasional peasant. This beautiful place, with its views of the snow-capped Alps, had once been dismissed by the painter Cezanne as lending itself admirably to the artistic efforts of "young English misses", but Emily thought it perfect. For her it was the greatest possible contrast to the horrors of the concentration camps she now forced herself to relive.

However desperately she needed rest, a greater need was to tell the story of the women whose cause she had embraced. With her to the lakeside retreat had gone all the papers amassed on her travels, including those observed by Milner's spy being smuggled to Emily on board the *Avondale Castle*. From this harrowing material she wrote the book she would call *The Brunt of the War*.

She finished the manuscript on Sunday, June 1, 1902, unaware that late the previous night, at Melrose House in Pretoria, the leaders of the Boer nations had finally gathered round the table to sign Kitchener's terms. The war was over.

18 "WE ARE GOOD FRIENDS NOW"

The peace was hailed as a personal triumph for Kitchener, yet only weeks before he had suffered a complete nervous collapse over news of the Boers' last major success of the war. This was the humiliating defeat of a British force at Tweebosch and De la Rey's capture of the wounded Lord Methuen, the most senior British general in the field. The crisis threw the commander-in-chief into a depression of such paralysing intensity that for forty-eight hours he refused to leave his bed or eat.

As so often before, he was nursed back to equilibrium by the cheerful chivvying of Frank Maxwell and what the young VC tactfully referred to as "a slump in spirits" ended with a hearty breakfast downstairs. Soon Tweebosch was seen in perspective, a mere setback in the inevitable march to Britain's victory. Just as importantly, many influential Boers saw it that way too.

At the end of March Kruger's stand-in president, Schalk Burger, signalled his willingness to discuss peace terms and under a safe-conduct from Kitchener began a search for his Free State counterpart, the roving Steyn, in order that the two Boer leaderships could agree a course of action. Despite previous disappointments Kitchener again bubbled with optimism, though he knew that Steyn had always proved fanatically intransigent compared to Transvaal figures like Burger, Botha and Smuts.

Sixty representatives of the two republics finally met up on April 9 – Emily Hobhouse's birthday – and secret talks followed between a small Boer delegation and Kitchener. The Marthinus Steyn who stumbled into the conference room at Melrose House was evidently a very sick man, plagued by double vision and constant shooting pains in the legs. Even so, he acted true to form and with magnificent audacity ignored the desperate straits his people were in and stuck out for independence. But this time the Transvaal leaders were determined to avert a breakdown of negotiations. For a month the Boers argued among themselves at a tented camp obligingly set up for them by the British at Vereeniging, a riverside village on the border between the Transvaal and the old Free State. Kitchener waited with what patience he could muster.

Deneys Reitz, one of Smuts's tiny retinue, vividly described the contrast between his Transvaal commandos – "starving, ragged men, clad in skins or sacking, their bodies covered with sores from lack of salt and food" – and the dreamlike apparition of Lord Kitchener riding out to greet them on a magnificent black charger, followed by a glittering and numerous suite, including turbaned Pathans in Eastern costume with gold-mounted scimitars.

The gorgeous display was not meant to rub salt into the wound. As Kitchener foresaw, the Boer delegates, clinging to their remnants of self-respect, appreciated the many acts of courtesy he ordered, such as the turn-out of a guard of honour at their every appearance. Even a man like Reitz, who was to chose exile rather than remain in South Africa as a subject of the Crown, was moved to call the British a generous people because

*President Steyn showing
signs of the mysterious
illness that struck him
down during the
peace negotiations.*

of what he saw at Vereeniging – "throughout the time we were amongst them," he wrote, "there was no word said that could hurt our feelings or offend our pride, although they knew that we were on an errand of defeat."

But it was not over yet. Milner arrived on the scene and again threatened to wreck Kitchener's strategy. Notionally partners in the talks, the two Britons were working to very different agendas – Kitchener seeking an accommodation with the Boer moderates, Milner in his eagerness to continue the war finding common cause with Steyn's bitter-enders. Kitchener confided to his friend Lady Cranborne that the Boers' deadly loathing of Milner presented huge difficulties, while Milner on his part told his intimates that Kitchener was giving away too much in his haste to be quit of South Africa.

This time the soldier proved the more astute. "Kitchener practically held all the strings throughout," conceded Milner glumly in a letter to Chamberlain. "He was in constant communication with the Boers and steered them into the paths he chose." To one of his own staff he remarked: "I feel as if I were negotiating with Kitchener, whilst the Boers look on."

149

Throughout it all Milner never lost a grudging admiration for the man. As he admitted to his special friend Lady Edward: "He is fearfully wrong-headed at times, but he is always *homme serieux*, practising himself, and enforcing upon others, the highest standard of *workmanlike* strenuousness, indefatigable industry and iron perseverance. Great qualities these in a wishy-washy world…"

At the resumed conference at Melrose House the Boer delegates and Milner haggled through the night, and towards morning Kitchener gently touched Jan Smuts on the arm and whispered to him to go outside. For a while the two future field marshals paced up and down in the dark. "Look here, Smuts," Kitchener burst out, "there is something on my mind that I want to tell you. I can only give it you as my opinion, but my opinion is that in two years' time a Liberal government will come to power. And if a Liberal government comes to power it will grant you a constitution for South Africa."

This was the moment that tipped the scales. At last Smuts saw a straw to grasp at, a hope that independence could be lost in the short term but regained. Soon afterwards the Boer representatives returned to Vereeniging to begin what had to be positively the last round of arguments, for now they faced a deadline. Milner demanded a final answer to the British terms – no more counter-proposals, just a plain yes or no – by midnight on May 31.

Though the arguments had been raked over countless times, there was yet more passionate oratory from both moderates and bitter-enders, thick with biblical quotations. As Deneys Reitz remembered, "even in adversity the Boer instinct for speeches and wordy wrangling asserted itself".

Those favouring peace spoke of a land close to total ruin. Starvation was widespread; fewer and fewer men were willing to carry on the struggle; no hope remained of foreign intervention or of a rising of the Cape Dutch. And then – it was an irony that no one present appreciated – hostile natives increasingly posed a threat to Boer womenfolk, who had been left exposed on the veld because Kitchener refused new admissions to the concentration camps. On the other side of the argument were ranged those who would not, could not believe they were beaten. For the sacred cause of independence the fight had to go on to the last man, the last woman, the last child.

Two factors decided the outcome. The first was Kitchener's forecast that the next Liberal administration would return South Africa to self-government. For despite prosecuting the war against them with unflagging ferocity, despite the long and bitter controversy over the "murder camps", the Boer leaders still saw Kitchener as, in Smuts's words, essentially kindly and understanding, a soldier who appreciated the feelings of a vanquished foe. Unlike Milner, Kitchener could be trusted.

The second development was a turn for the worse in President Steyn's mysterious illness, later diagnosed as botulism caused by eating a bad sausage. This was the one man on the Boer side who gave Kitchener sleepless nights – "I only fear that Steyn, in his ponderous way, will make a patriotic speech at the meeting and turn them all round," he confided to Brodrick. But a spreading paralysis meant Steyn was incapable of attending the later debates. Lying helpless in his tent, he was forced to resign the Free State presidency to his great general, De Wet; and De Wet, to his later consuming regret, was at last prevailed upon to opt for peace. The final vote on the British terms was fifty-four in favour, six against. But everyone knew it could have been a very different story had

Steyn remained an active force.

An hour before the deadline expired, the delegates gathered at Melrose House. The terms before them, typed on parchment, were little different to those rejected at Middelburg so many thousands of lives ago. In return for laying down their arms the Boers were guaranteed liberty and property; they would be spared special taxes to pay for the war; the Dutch tongue as well as English would be taught in schools. Despite Britain's earlier promises to cooperative blacks, the extension of the franchise to the country's vast majority was to be deferred. An extra sweetener for the Boers, pushed through by Kitchener in the teeth of Milner's opposition, was a £3 million contribution from the British exchequer towards the restoration of their devastated lands. By signing the document, the Boers acknowledged King Edward as their sovereign.

As the ink dried on the last of the twelve signatures – Kitchener's own – there was a prolonged silence. Kitchener attempted to lighten the atmosphere by moving from one delegate to the next, shaking his hand and saying "We are good friends now." It was General de la Rey who provided the touch of pawky humour that momentarily lifted the gloom. Looking round the long faces, he remarked in his heavy accented English that they were "a bloody cheerful-looking lot of British subjects".

Long before midnight the paralysed ex-President Steyn had been driven to the station and carried on board a homeward train. His extraordinary career was over. His cause was lost, his health wrecked, his fortune gone. From the carriage window his swimming vision could just make out the tents of the Vereeniging concentration camp, one of the many forbidden to Emily on her previous year's travels. If there could be one consolation for Steyn, it was that the document of surrender did not bear his name.

*

Emily was sitting beside Lake Annecy when she read in her paper that the treaty had been signed. Till that moment, she said later, she hardly realised the strain she had been under, and there at the waterside she cried her heart out. Being able to cry, she was fond of saying, was one blessing of being a woman. Of course there was overwhelming joy and relief than no more lives would be sacrificed to the struggle, but reading the detailed peace agreement she "could not forget how bitterly the brave women in the camps would feel its terms and the crushing of the hopes that had borne them up though loss and pain".

In Britain rejoicing crowds swarmed into the streets to repeat the scenes of Mafeking Night. In Pretoria a great peace parade of five thousand troops and eleven bands was ordered, followed by a thanksgiving service celebrated by an archbishop, two bishops and parsons of all denominations. The commander-in-chief pinned medals on nine new VCs.

Kitchener was showered with congratulations, promoted to full general, and raised in the peerage as Viscount Kitchener of Khartoum, and of the Vaal in Transvaal. It was at this point he asked for his honours to pass, in the absence of a direct heir, to one of his two brothers in the armed services – a third, civilian brother he wished excluded from the succession. There was bemusement in Downing Street when Kitchener wired Lord Salisbury to accept the viscountcy with the proviso that "I do not

151

A pensive Emily in 1902, the year the Boer War ended. Her favourite photograph.

want at all in order to keep title in family to have to take a permanent encumbrance". The aged prime minister wrote in the margin of the telegram in his shaky handwriting: "Does he mean a wife?" Garter King of Arms dreamt up new embellishments to add to the coat of arms originally devised for Kitchener after the Sudan campaign, among them an orange tree allusive to his triumph over Steyn's Free State. A parliamentary grant to the hero of £50,000 – the equivalent of £2,500,000 today – was quietly invested in Rand gold.

Milner too was promoted to viscount, though his patent was dated a few days later than Kitchener's to give the soldier a nominal seniority over the civilian.

The Boer signatories to the treaty faced scorn, bewilderment and bitter recriminations from many of their people, not least from the women in the concentration camps. But the war was lost, and for the twenty thousand remaining in arms against Britain the choice was between exile and acknowledgement of Edward VII as their king. Men who had endured almost three years of appalling hardship without complaint met the news with hysterical weeping or even fainted away. Smuts was called a traitor by his own followers. To the diehards, only Steyn had kept the faith.

When Mrs Steyn heard the terms of Vereeniging, she changed into mourning. For the next forty years she wore nothing but black.

The final death toll in the white concentration camps was almost 28,000, virtually all of them women and children. The figure far exceeded that of the fighting men lost by both sides. Despite Emily's urgings, no reliable record of the deaths in black camps was compiled at the time, but later estimates would range from 13,000 to 20,000. The war had cost the British taxpayer £250 million, not including the promised funds for reconstruction.

At least the map was now red from the Cape to Cairo, though Cecil Rhodes had not lived to see it. Weeks before Vereeniging he died of heart disease. His last words were: "So much to do, so little done!"

*

On her return home from France Emily enlisted Uncle Arthur to help correct the proofs of *The Brunt of the War*, which had been taken on by the London publisher Methuen. Six years previously, Methuen had brought out Leonard Hobhouse's critically acclaimed if poorly selling first book, *The Theory of Knowledge*; the firm's star author, however, was Rudyard Kipling, who had set Methuen on the road to success with titles like *Barrack Room Ballads*. The link with the Empire's favourite poet did not prevent the acceptance of a controversial work on the concentration camps, and it was probably through Emily's introduction that the following year the same house brought out *Through Shot and Flame*, the wartime memoirs of the Rev John Kestell, chaplain to President Steyn and General de Wet.

Leonard hurt Emily's feelings by his lack of interest in her book. "I gathered my brother thought it badly put together from a literary point of view," she wrote plaintively to Mrs Steyn, "but I was only a novice unversed in the art of presentation. All I wanted was to put down the facts as plainly as I could. And I am quite sure it wasn't the inferior literary merit that made the authorities suppress it, but those very plain facts."

Despite the historical importance of *The Brunt of the War* – it is still an indispensable source on the camps – Leonard was justified in criticising the manuscript as poorly organised. The skilful marshalling of facts which distinguished his own works was absent, and Leonard lacked either the time or inclination to help knock it into shape. Lord Hobhouse on the other hand made an over-scrupulous collaborator for Emily. He could be relied on to warn tirelessly against any hint of sensationalism, to point out a con to balance every pro, and at every turn to reinforce his niece's tendency to wordiness. Understandably, but to the detriment of the narrative, Emily played down her own part in the story, including the deportation, no doubt fearing a charge of self-dramatisation. To the shocking facts she added too many dry appendices, too many

OCCUPANTS AND FURNITURE OF ONE BELL TENT SOON AFTER ARRIVAL FROM THE FARM. NOV. 1900

later this family was pitiable in the extreme

Omitted by Printer

An illustration from a presentation copy of "The Brunt of the War". Below the printed caption Emily has handwritten a line left out by the printer.

lengthy excerpts from official documents, but no index. Even before reaching the introduction, the reader had to wade through articles of The Hague Convention and an extract from a manual of military law. Not until page 93 do the words occur "I determined to go to South Africa", and it is page 116 before she visits a concentration camp. Nor did it help that Methuen refused to publish the most distressing photographs collected by Emily, such as that of a skeletal seven-year-old called Lizzie van Zyl who died at Bloemfontein. Inmates instinctively tried to look their best for the camera, with the unintended result that some of those who appear in the book look relatively well-fed and dressed.

When Emily writes from the heart, as in her tribute to Boer women which ends the book, the prose is moving, yet overall lacks the spirit and immediacy of her committee report of the previous year. Perhaps she was too tired to do herself justice, for given the original material she had collected – the eye-witness accounts of suffering in the camps, the extraordinary catalogue of official incompetence and worse – *The Brunt of the War* is a strangely unimpressive book. When she delivered the corrected manuscript to Methuen she must have known she had let slip a great opportunity. Professionally edited, with the kind of powerful introduction, eye for telling detail and lucid summary which were the hallmarks of Leonard's writings, it might well have become an enduring classic.

Leonard's indifference calls for comment. Around this time he was facing new claims on his time and energy through the formation of the Sociological Society. Mounting financial problems had forced him to accept an uncongenial paid post with the Free Trade Union, an organisation set up to combat an imperial protectionist campaign launched by Joseph Chamberlain, while at the same time he had to continue to freelance for the *Manchester Guardian* on poorer financial terms. And as ever he was feeling unwell. In any case, his journalistic instinct told him that, quite apart from his reservations about Emily's style, the concentration camps were now a stale issue. Perhaps his restless intelligence insisted on moving on to matters he thought more pressing; perhaps like so many of his countrymen he had simply become bored with the subject.

As will be seen presently, Emily was to have further reason to complain of a lack of brotherly support once she was back in South Africa.

*

The pro-Boers had not been alone in suffering ostracism while the war was in progress. Millicent Fawcett on her return from South Africa found that the praise heaped on her in the House of Commons merely fuelled the hostility from other quarters. "Several pro-Boer people who used to be quite good friends of mine now cut me dead," she wrote, "and turn their backs if I am coming towards them. I don't exactly like it; but I try to bear it with patience. It takes a many people to make a world."

For Mrs Fawcett the treaty of Vereeniging changed everything: "Hatred and evil feelings died down, and animosities gradually weakened; and before long nothing but a faint echo of the controversy remained alive." For Millicent Fawcett fresh challenges lay ahead. There were new causes to take up, new bestsellers to write, new honours to have heaped upon her – for she was to become the first woman to address the Oxford Union, one of the first women magistrates, one of the first dames of the British Empire, and much more besides.

Not so for Emily. Everyone else might want to forget the war, but for the woman who had exposed the camps the suffering of the Boers remained the all-consuming issue, and she knew the best place she could keep her campaign alive was South Africa. Once her book was printed Emily determined to return and see the extent of the devastation for herself. In the meantime her fund-raising effort for war victims was hampered by Chamberlain's constant harping on the British taxpayers' generosity towards the beaten enemy. As her friends the Boer generals were soon to discover, the stream of private charity had all but dried up.

19 "THEY WILL NEVER FORGET HER"

That August a trio of famous Boer commanders arrived at Southampton on board the *Saxon*, the mail steamer on which Emily had waylaid Milner during her first return voyage. They were Botha, De la Rey and De Wet. Their immediate mission was to seek an increase to the three million pounds promised by Kitchener, but they also planned to cross to Europe and milk the widespread anti-British feeling there for extra funds.

With many thousands of their countrymen and women destitute, with thousands more about to emerge from the concentration camps, the generals braced themselves to set foot on the land of their conquerors – a humiliation spared the now completely paralysed Marthinus Steyn, who had been forced to seek medical help in Europe. When his ship put in at Southampton weeks before, he had been immediately transferred to another bound for Holland, thus avoiding what Emily called "the physical and mental strain" of landing in England.

When the *Saxon* docked, the trio's staunchest English champion was waiting. Emily had recently been reunited with her Cape Town hostess Caroline Murray, who had hurried to England as soon as peace was signed; the friends travelled to Southampton together to welcome Mrs Murray's sister Betty Molteno, the eyewitness to Emily's deportation and now a fellow-passenger of the generals.

The two ladies talked their way onto the Union Castle tug sent out to meet the *Saxon*, a lovely sight emerging from the silvery morning haze in its striking livery of lavender-grey with red funnels. Emily then heard news that made her cheeks change colour. On the Royal Navy vessel lying alongside was none other than Lord Kitchener, newly returned to his hero's reception in England. In company with Joe Chamberlain and Earl Roberts, he had been about to join the Spithead naval review, but delayed the ship's departure to see the *Saxon* into port. It was now nine months since Emily's deportation, six months since the collapse of her law suit.

Kitchener, keenly watching the arrival of the steamer bearing the most formidable of his former enemies, must have trained his binoculars on the welcoming tug. If so, this seems to have been the only time in his life he set eyes on Emily Hobhouse. For Emily and Kitchener belong to that select band of historical pairings, like Queen Elizabeth and Mary Queen of Scots and Wellington and Napoleon, who never actually met face to face. Kitchener's one chance to gaze on the woman who had caused him such grief occurred as she became the first person to welcome the Boer commanders to England – though it is open to conjecture whether any of his entourage could enlighten him as to the identity of the erect, well-dressed lady climbing the *Saxon*'s gangway.

The "Glorious Trio" stood at the head of the gangway to receive Emily and Mrs Murray while hundreds of khaki-clad servicemen on board looked on. Emily thought the three "perfectly sweet" as they returned her greetings with old-world courtesy.

The "glorious trio" of Boer generals – from left to right, De Wet, De la Rey and Botha – refused to join the King at the Spithead review but accepted supper invitations to Emily's flat.

Gen. Christiaan de Wet.   Gen. Louis Botha.

Chamberlain sent the generals an invitation to his ship, and Emily noted with satisfaction that they stayed on board only five minutes. The Boers greatly annoyed the colonial secretary and Kitchener by refusing to attend the royal naval review – they would have seen the immense fleet assembling as the *Saxon* entered Southampton Water – using the excuse that they lacked appropriate ceremonial uniforms. Instead they departed with Emily on the London train. Emily was widely blamed for advising them to decline the invitation, suggesting they would look like captives in a Roman-style triumph. If this was so she dealt a blow to their mission, as stories quickly appeared in the press that the Boers had snubbed the King. The British public had been anxious to fete the former foes and their stand over the naval review did not go down well.

With the war safely over, there was an almost universal desire to regard the war as a kind of gentlemanly falling-out, and commentators liked to dwell on such episodes as De la Rey's gallantry in returning the wounded Lord Methuen to the British lines, along with a respectful note to Lady Methuen. The prevailing British attitude of the time was summed up by a chilly rebuff delivered to Kate Courtney by her husband's former friend the Earl of Mount Edgecumbe, Lord Lieutenant of Cornwall. In response to a hint from Kate that they should let bygones be bygones, Mount Edgecumbe insisted that Courtney's speeches had encouraged the Boers to prolong the war, and on that account he refused to make up. "One can shake hands with an enemy if he is fighting for his own people," said the earl, "but not if he is one's fellow countryman."

Before leaving South Africa, Kitchener had fantasised that the Boer leaders might be induced to take part in the procession for Edward VII's coronation. The ceremony had finally taken place days before on August 9 after a postponement caused by the King being struck down with acute appendicitis; the three generals had timed their fund-raising visit to avoid the expected orgy of imperial self-congratulation, and the delay almost caught them out. It was the first coronation for sixty-four years; London, flushed with victory and gaudy with flags and bunting, could hardly have offered a more poignant contrast to the ruined Boer homelands. The generals did however feel constrained to accept a private invitation to go on board the royal yacht at Cowes the following Sunday, when Kitchener presented the top-hatted and frock-coated trio to the royal family. The Prince of Wales, later George V, observed to his wife that they seemed quite decent people "but distinctly common".

Emily formed a very different picture of the three. Botha she saw as "a kingly person with very courtly manners and commanding air", De la Rey as "a patriarch, very gentle and quiet", and De Wet as "enigmatical but stamped with the responsibility and the sorrow of war". Their dignity astonished observers, she thought, and seemed to carry a rebuke.

*

Emily in her turn had recently found herself in a position to glare at her great adversary. The coronation procession appears to have been the only occasion when she set eyes on Kitchener, though like him she had no chance to speak. It is a strange coincidence that the single opportunity each of them had to glimpse the other should occur in a matter of days and so far from South Africa.

As she wrote: "Someone gave me a ticket for a seat on the grandstand flanking St Margaret's Church where I had a fine view of Parliament Square and the crowd, always itself the most thrilling thing at these public events. Conveyances were few that day, so I walked from Chelsea, going by the river, and found the streets quiet. One never sees much of the chief actors on these occasions, and the only figure remaining in my mind was that of Kitchener on horseback keeping order or something of the kind in the open space below." Emily being Emily, she cannot resist a dig: "He seemed quite unable to manage his horse; the animal would only walk sideways or backward. It was very funny and undignified."

The new viscount's place of honour in the procession to Westminster Abbey was a little ahead of the golden coach, behind the royal ADCs – three of them Indian maharajahs in exotic garb – and immediately before Lord Roberts, the most senior officer in the British Army. Emily seems to have been the only witness to comment on Kitchener's difficulty in controlling his horse, other accounts stressing the loud cheers from the public as their hero rode by.

*

When the Boer generals travelled up to London with Emily, she sat between Botha and

De Wet with De la Rey opposite. She was dismayed to find all three "*wholly* ignorant of English politics and affairs", and later mused in a letter to her brother that they would benefit from talking with "someone not in official political life who knows all the ropes". As it was, they seemed scarcely to know who Mr Courtney was, and muddled up other leading champions of the Boers like W.T. Stead, the campaigning journalist, and John Morley, the radical parliamentarian. Here Emily entertained unrealistic expectations of the trio, forgetting they had spent the previous three years in circumstances allowing few opportunities to peruse *The Times* or *Manchester Guardian*.

While pursuing their business over the next couple of months the generals were all Emily's guests in Chelsea. Each accepted a separate invitation to supper at her flat, and each shot up in her estimation by declining to smoke the fat cigars she got in specially – "my first and last attempt to buy tobacco in any form," she recorded primly.

The three Boers went to and fro between England and the Continent. In London, while continually lobbying for more money, they were lionised in Aunt Mary's drawing room by the likes of the Courtneys, and both De Wet and Botha stayed with Leonard and Nora Hobhouse at their new home in Wimbledon. This visit led to a favourite family story. When the great commando leaders tried to hire mounts at the local livery stable, the manager eyed them up and down doubtfully and asked: "But can the gentlemen ride?" All three, and Emily, were painted by the noted Dutch artist Antoon van Welie, though Emily exposed her streak of vanity by complaining bitterly when "the crude unfinished portrait of myself" was put on show. It is perhaps the most striking study of Emily extant, with no attempt made to disguise her imperious nose.[xx]

At the Dutch seaside resort of Scheveningen the generals paid their respects to the immobilised Steyn, now kept in a permanently darkened room on doctor's orders, before moving on to the Kruger court at Hilversum. The meeting resulted in the release of an ill-judged "Appeal of the Boer Generals to the Civilised World" aimed at raising money by playing on anti-British sentiments. The Europe-wide campaign raised a derisory £105,000 to weigh against the three million from the British taxpayer and moved the normally Boer-friendly *New York Evening Post* to brand the demands of the generals "extraordinarily presuming, puerile and preposterous". In Germany the trio were dealt a further blow when the Kaiser declined to meet them. Chamberlain was thus handed a golden opportunity to call for Kruger to return the "missing millions" to his suffering countrymen and women, and in the end the chastened generals sailed home almost empty-handed.

Emily later conceded the appeal was a tactical mistake while insisting that the Boer leaders had no choice but to launch it. The question remains whether her influence helped shape the appeal. The autobiographical notes she wrote long afterwards for Mrs Steyn throw no light on the matter, but Emily comes across as decidedly defensive on the subject. Certainly such advice as the generals received in Britain would have emanated from Emily and her immediate friends.

*

Shortly before the coronation the pro-Boer circle were involved in a charitable gesture that would one day have important personal repercussions for Emily. When ex-President

The queenly former First Lady, Isabella Steyn. She never forgot Emily's efforts to raise money for the life-saving medical care of her stricken husband.

Steyn's baffling illness compelled him to seek expert treatment in Europe, Emily had joined with Kate Courtney and other well-wishers to organise a secret subscription fund. Over £1,500 was raised quickly including £1,000 wheedled from the American millionaire Andrew Carnegie. And it was Emily who was consulted on the question of how a man of notoriously prickly pride could be induced to take the money. This delicate task Emily delegated to the philosopher Herbert Spencer, a long-time friend of Kate Courtney and her sisters.

A tactful letter persuaded Steyn to accept. Even Steyn's opponents, wrote Spencer, freely admitted the heroism of his sacrifice of position, property and health. This was certainly true of Kitchener himself, who even when living in fear that Steyn would wreck the Vereeniging talks had remarked that he was "head and shoulders above the others".

Steyn travelled from his homeland on the *Carisbrooke Castle*, the ship Emily refused to board before her forcible deportation. Returning to England on the same vessel was the Miss Greene who had sent the mystifying telegram to Emily's anxious family, and she was to leave an account of visiting Steyn's flower-laden cabin and watching Mrs Steyn "tenderly stroking his beard". The man who still called himself president had not been expected to survive the voyage.

Writing to Kate Courtney from Scheveningen, Mrs Steyn poured out heartfelt thanks for the money. She never forgot the generous, unlooked-for gesture to her stricken husband, who would certainly have died without constant medical supervision. Over twenty years later, when Emily herself would reach one of the lowest points in her life, Mrs Steyn was to pay back the gift in kind.

*

Emily missed the opportunity of a reunion with Isabella Steyn at Southampton through an unfortunate misunderstanding. "No other woman in England knew you and I felt sure you would feel very strange and lonely and in need of a woman's help," she told Mrs Steyn long afterwards. But having arranged to go down to Southampton to meet the *Carisbrooke Castle*, she was dissuaded by a well-meaning South African acquaintance who insisted the president's wife had expressly stated that she wished to see no one. To her distress, Emily learned too late that her friend always meant her to be the exception to the rule, and was much hurt over her failure to appear.

There was some consolation for Emily three weeks later when the same acquaintance wrote contritely from the ex-president's bedside in Scheveningen. Steyn, flouting doctor's orders to keep absolutely quiet, had insisted on sending a message to Emily expressing his deep personal gratitude for all she had done for the suffering women and children and added: "Tell her Afrikanders can never repay her but they will never forget her."

Yet in a way neither could anticipate, repay her is exactly what the South Africans would do.

20 "CAN THESE DRY BONES LIVE?"

Now the war was over, no one could prevent Emily's return to South Africa. But her health had not recovered, and even when *The Brunt of the War* had been seen through the press there were exhausting speaking engagements to honour. Before steeling herself to go back to the shattered Boer homelands, she took another holiday in France with her brother and his wife. Leonard too craved rest from all the pressures upon him. And though there was still cold hostility at home, in Europe the great Miss Hobhouse was feted wherever she went. When she travelled home from Lake Annecy by way of The Hague, the Dutch prime minister himself had called at her hotel to pay his respects. Now, in Paris, Emily was guest of honour at a banquet and the celebrated dramatist Paul Loyson expressed his admiration by dedicating his latest play to her.

Not until April 1903 did Emily brave the long sea voyage to Cape Town, booking a first-class passage on the *Carisbrooke Castle*. The sight of the ship lying at Southampton brought back a flood of disagreeable associations but in terms of physical comfort it turned out to be her best-ever passage. First class was Emily's natural habitat, and the neuritis that had long plagued her began to ease as the vessel steamed into balmy southern waters.

Once again she asked for her name to be kept off the passenger list but her identity quickly became known. Most people refused to speak to her. One gentleman maintained friendly relations for ten days before discovering she was *that* Miss Hobhouse, whereupon instead of turning the expected cold shoulder he whipped out an autograph book and demanded that she sign her name next to Lord Shaftesbury's under the heading *Philanthropists*.

Writing to her sister-in-law Nora, Emily crowed of making a conquest of the chief engineer, who confessed he had heard of her deportation with great satisfaction. When Emily asked why, he said he had believed what he read in the newspapers – "but now," he added, "as soon as I saw your face I knew you were genuine". But the majority on board decided she was to be ostracised and on hearing her name would instantly present their backs. Against what she called "this insolence" Emily had no weapon.

The *Carisbrooke Castle* reached Cape Town on May 12. In her delight to be back Emily thought even the dirty docks looked like a fairyland. She became agitated over a delay in disembarking but at last descended the gangway to find a waiting reception party led by loyal Mrs Murray. It was "rather fun" at the customs house. Officials inspected the notorious arrival with curiosity and suspicion, and one of them made her laugh out loud by demanding to know whether any of her boxes contained firearms. But another customs officer stood by and stared at Emily till she felt "quite hot" before he gasped out: "Beg pardon, but *are* you the original Miss Hobhouse? Sorry to ask, but you see I've read your book." On Emily admitting she was the genuine article, he lifted his cap and remained bareheaded until she left the building.

Emily made conflicting statements about the South African reception of *The Brunt of the War*. She recorded frequent encounters with people who had read it and took undisguised pride in letters of congratulation, yet repeatedly referred to its suppression. Rykie van Reenen, the editor of Emily's wartime letters, has observed that the book was apparently widely read in South Africa and believes that considerable numbers were shipped into the country. Emily herself wrote: "The first consignments got in, but they are quietly squashed now, though if any bookseller chose to bring the matter into court the prohibition would be removed."

All facts and figures relating to the book's publication – costs, print run, and such details as the number of copies despatched to South Africa – appear to be lost for good. Most of Methuen's archive was destroyed in the bombing of its Essex Street premises during the Second World War or lost as a result of numerous changes of ownership.[xxi] Copies of *The Brunt of the War and where it Fell*, to give its full title, are now extremely rare, whether in the bottle-green binding for the home market or the scarlet "colonial library" livery. Certainly in Britain many copies were bought purposely to be burnt and the major distributors flatly refused to handle the title. Emily promised the South Africa distress fund all royalties from the sales and was dismayed when these amounted to a mere £30 or £40.

In Cape Town Emily stayed with the wealthy De Villers family at their pleasant house in the elevated Gardens district and enjoyed ample opportunity to savour her fame among the Boers. Though her friends were supposed to keep quiet about her arrival, word spread and "all that day Dutch ladies toiled up the hill in succession and I sat on the *stoep* and received and talked to them". The spontaneous act of homage would be repeated on innumerable occasions.

The first unpleasantness occurred when she visited the bank to ask if there were any letters for Miss Hobhouse. The bank clerk replied with disgust: "Miss Hobhouse! You don't mean to say that Miss Hobhouse is coming to South Africa again?" According to Emily he looked "quite evil with concentrated Jingoism", so she made a little bow and introduced herself, causing "complete collapse of clerk". Some time later the bank manager heard that one of his staff had been rude to her and apologised handsomely. However, Emily told Aunt Mary she refused to identify the culprit, and "now it is lovely to see how they run to serve me in the bank". The episode confirmed Emily's conviction, typical of her class, that while an underbred subordinate might give trouble, as a rule she could rely on his superior being a gentleman.

Emily stayed in Cape Town for several weeks to enjoy the company of old friends. There was a good deal of interesting gossip to catch up on. At the time of her deportation to England she had found Nora Hobhouse preoccupied with the loss of a maid, and this was clearly on her mind in a letter to her sister-in-law. "If the servant problem is felt a little in England," she wrote, "be assured that it cannot bear comparison with the woes experienced by housewives in and around Cape Town… This scarcity of servants is largely brought about by the war, for coloured men received then such high wages that their womenfolk no longer care to earn their own living."

Matters had reached such a pass that a special government-backed scheme was launched to pay the passage to South Africa of British female servants. The idea was that

Emily takes leave of Kaya Lami for her tour of the ruined farmlands. A member of the Fichardt family and house servants say goodbye as her guide Mr Enslin grips the reins.

the immigrants would marry and boost the non-Boer population, but according to Emily the sort of girls brought over tended to find shipboard lovers and vanished into "low inns" immediately on arrival. "Cape Town rings with stories of this kind," Emily added, declaring it shameful that such girls were being sent out in batches "to almost certain ruin".[xxii]

Emily's host in Cape Town was John de Villers, who as the colony's chief justice secured her a ticket to attend the opening of parliament. It was here she saw again her old adversary Lord Milner. Since the end of the war Milner had assumed the governorships of the Transvaal and the old Orange Free State as well as that of the Cape. In theory if not in fact, he held in his hand the entire power for which Kruger and Rhodes had contended. This subtle schemer, Emily had long since decided, was the root of all evil in South Africa – "better Kitchener with all his brutalities than Milner with his duplicity."

Now the new viscount sat under Emily's gaze in his splendid uniform and cocked hat and read out "a very dull speech full of nothing". But Emily was impressed by the way ladies were allowed plenty of space in the Cape parliament building, as they were able to watch the proceedings from the main floor and balcony while the men crammed onto side benches. It was a far cry from the grille through which women had to peer at Westminster.

At last Emily tore herself away from the pleasant society of Cape Town and set to work in earnest. Her plan was to travel by rail between major towns and then trek into the barren veld to see how the ordinary country people were faring. Once her presence was noted by the authorities there were predictable difficulties over travel passes, but on June 6 she boarded a train for the first stage of the long journey north. At Bloemfontein she was reunited with her old friends the Fichardts and happily installed in her old room at Kaya Lami. It was the last taste of luxury for some time.

*

Emily set off on the first of her treks in a hired wagon pulled by four mules. As guide she chose a penniless Boer veteran called Enslin, until recently a prisoner-of-war in Ceylon, and as her mulateer a jolly-looking black called Jacob. The wagon was just big enough to carry the three of them plus Emily's small stock of relief supplies. With his bleak Boer humour, Enslin gave all the mules the names of prisons. The animals' tendency to stampede quickly forced a switch to horsepower, a move that caused Emily considerable embarrassment because of the burden it imposed on local farmers. These unstintingly provided the necessary relays of horses but despite their poverty refused payment from the revered Miss Hobhouse. In a mad moment she even contemplated continuing the trek by bicycle.

These next few months Emily would remember as the most exhausting period of her life, leaving her drained physically, mentally and emotionally. The concentration camps might now be closed, but she found despair and near-starvation everywhere, confirming the rightness of her instinct to work among the scattered farmland communities rather than in the many relief camps which the authorities had been forced to open. Most houses on the veld were charred ruins with the families crowded into stables or outbuildings. The contrast between Kaya Lami and the burnt-out farmhouse where she spent her first night was a poignant one. "I write by the light of the cart lantern with my feet upon my rolled-up bed," she told Aunt Mary, describing a floor covered with sacks and scraps of goatskin and a ceiling patched together out of reeds. Even so, she said she was comfortable enough, "if being kindly treated makes you comfortable".

Emily's return to South Africa coincided with a drought of biblical severity. Lasting until early in 1904, this natural disaster added hugely to the problems of reconstruction confronting Milner. Lack of rain meant the staple crop of mealie, or Indian corn, was almost totally ruined, and the wheat crop proved nearly as bad. Plagues of locusts and caterpillars devoured what survived, and for the first time in living memory the Caledon River ran dry. In Orange River Colony, every soul who lived on the land was forced to beg for government assistance.

At the outset all Emily had was £200 raised in England. In the face of appalling cases of hardship her initial supplies of rice and meal quickly disappeared, and the remaining cash trickled away on scarce, highly-priced local purchases – materials to mend a farmer's roof, a sewing machine for a widow with five children, a pair of bellows for a destitute blacksmith. Here she would give a live sheep or goat or chicken, there a tin of bully beef or loaf of bread. At one country orphanage she paid for a treat of jam and cheese for all the children, at another pairs of stockings for the girls.

Travel by cart was agonising. Within days of leaving Kaya Lami, with a face torn to ribbons by sunburn, she swore never again to brave the South African climate without learning how to protect her complexion. Yet each new day of blistering heat began with thick ice underfoot, and the wagon would set off into a cutting wind with Emily huddled inside her fur coat. Halting at a country parsonage not long into the first trek, Emily failed to recognise herself in the mirror – the reflected face looked like *biltong*, the tough raw springbok meat that had sustained the Boer commandos. Then there was the constant feeling of being bloated due to misguided hospitality – she was drinking unwanted mug after mug of coffee from her hosts' scant supplies, fearing that refusal would give offence.

Food was a different matter. So meagre were the meals offered in the distressed Boer households that Emily was racked by constant pangs of hunger and took to raiding a private hoard of *biltong* and dry bread in the night when no one could observe her. The guilty secret was confessed in a letter to Aunt Mary.

Nearly half a million horses, mules and oxen had been killed in the war, besides the Boer flocks and herds deliberately slaughtered, and the roadside presented an endless vista of bleached animal bones. The sight brought vividly to Emily's mind the description of the Valley of Dry Bones in the Old Testament, and she must have recalled her father preaching from the Book of Ezekiel, his voice breaking as he reached the question that haunted Victorian England: "And can these bones live?" In one almost hallucinatory passage in a letter to her aunt Emily wrote of trying to count the skulls of "disdainful" goats and of sheep gazing at her reproachfully "through their hollow eyes". Wherever she went, the hollow eyes seemed to follow her.

Arriving at a forsaken spot called Hoopstad, she recorded wearily a drive of seventy miles that day, from sunrise to sunset: "I came fast, over no sort of roads, with relays arranged in advance, and only five minutes' pause to change the cart and horses here and there." It had been "drive, drive, forever drive," and she only hoped she could hold out, "but the jolting tires one so that at last you fall asleep over the endless tales that everyone wants to tell". Time and again her letters end with the same words: "Too tired to write more."

Throughout her tour Emily found a crop of "peace babies" to rival the famously large number of war babies born to Boer women who had stayed out on the veld dodging Kitchener's soldiers instead of being swept into the camps. It was a sign of the growing reverence in which she was held that many of the girls were being christened Emily, or even Emily Hobhouse. "So you see," she wrote to her brother, "I am multiplying in this uninteresting way, and wretched babies are being saddled with my very ugly name." In the famine-stricken town of Lichtenburg Emily was prevailed upon to stand godmother to one of these namesakes, the newborn granddaughter of old Piet Joubert, first commandant-general of the Boer republics. Here was another unwanted link between Emily and her arch enemy, whose victories in South Africa resulted in countless British baby boys being christened Herbert or Kitchener.

*

The first trek ended late in June. There was another blissful break at Bloemfontein, where Caroline Fichardt instructed Emily how to shield her skin during the South African winter before packing her off on the next stage armed with provisions "of Kaya Lami munificence". By July she was in the Northern territory forbidden to her during Kitchener's time. As guest of the Potgieters, the friends made on board the *Saxon*, she

Emily laden with shawls and basket during her trek of 1903. The strain of listening to endless horror stories proved more than she could bear.

heard claims of wartime atrocities she later reported to both War Office and Colonial Office, though without tangible result.

Images from the endless horror stories of murder and mutilation kept her awake night after night. Among them was a detailed account of the infamous case of "Breaker" Morant, an Australian officer controversially sentenced to death by Kitchener for ordering the shooting of eight Boer prisoners. A German missionary who stumbled on the scene of the killings had himself been murdered, leading many to regard Morant as a scapegoat who was executed not for killing Boers, but as a sacrifice to a furious Kaiser. Certainly at the time of the outrage Kitchener was well aware of the British government's jitters over the possibility of intervention by its most powerful continental rival, with St John Brodrick voicing his fear that "a torch might be put to the German powder magazine". Emily's on-the-spot sleuthing threw up a Boer claim that British agents had kept the missionary's widow quiet with a pension and £5,000 in cash.

Emily's fame was now such that she complained of being "dreadfully snapshotted" everywhere she went, and there are photographs from this time of a string of receptions in her honour. At Heilbron, in the north of Orange River Colony, a party of ladies and gentlemen greeted her in their finest clothes, with a brilliant display of pink feather boas, while Emily stood wretchedly before them covered head to toe in the red dust of the veld. An even grander reception waited at the garden of the parsonage, where a hundred more had gathered to honour their "highly esteemed friend".

In Pretoria the leading lights of Boer society threw a private garden party for Emily when use of the public park was vetoed by the British authorities. Here she was presented with an address defiantly embellished with the old Transvaal wax seal, along with a flag of the extinct republic. Once again she wrote home bewailing her embarrassment at appearing in shabby travelling clothes and peppered with red dust, though in surviving photographs of these events the guest of honour invariably appears to be regally turned out as she gracefully accepts tributes of roses. There were valuable gifts heaped upon her too, including a gold brooch and a costly carriage rug made of the skins of the rare silver jackal, and Emily's letters home do not conceal her delight at receiving two magnificent diamonds from wealthy admirers – one in the Free State, one in the Transvaal.

Wherever Emily went, everyone seized her by the hand. Even in the orphanages every tiny child expected physical contact with the heroine. It was the same at each farm, she wrote home, where "even babies of one and a half years will solemnly walk up and put out their wee hands." Like royalty, she learned to keep her gloves on.

Emily sometimes felt utterly at a loss to know what to say to the people she met, every one of them bearing a burden of want and debt and barrenness, and she never got used to the spectacle of starvation, especially that terrible kind which was combined with perfect respectability. Whenever she took her leave of a place, the people would crowd around and "kiss and cry over me".

The stress was becoming unbearable. She wrote to Leonard: "To continue smiling on everyone in every town who crowd round you with their tales of sorrow is a tremendous strain." If one story went on too long, its teller would be pushed out of the way by the next in the queue, who would launch into some terrible new tale which would go on until he or she was shoved aside in turn. At last the ordeal of listening to them all became too much and Emily set herself a limit of twenty horror stories a day. Even then, "excessive fatigue made me stupid" and her brain would refuse to take in any more.

It was in the market square of the hill town of Heidelberg that Emily witnessed the first great Afrikaner political rally since the war. Two thousand had come to hear Louis Botha speak, and Emily was profoundly struck by her first sight of a large gathering of Boer men, remarkable for their seriousness, silence, and orderliness. All that day she had felt ill and giddy, and the sensation that everything around her was swaying made her cling to a tree as she watched the proceedings. When during the three hours of speeches Botha introduced his famous English guest the crowd broke into cheers, and she had to stand to hear the customary hymn of praise, clutching her little tree for support. The two thousand screamed with delight when she responded briefly in their own tongue.

In mid-July, when Emily arrived at Pretoria for a second stay, a waiting telegram from Kaya Lami brought shocking news of the sudden death of her great friend Caroline Fichardt, so recently left in apparent health. As the telegram had lain unread for ten days, the anguished Emily was too late to return for the funeral.

From Pretoria she planned treks into deepest Transvaal, though after thoughtlessly mislaying her fur coat at the railway station she dreaded the extreme conditions of the high country. The fear proved justified, for once in this most exposed part of the veld she was assailed by bouts of neuritis she likened to hellfire inside her. Then there was the acute pain in her arm, the result of an earlier mishap. The sufferings were greatly increased by the jolting of the unsprung cart. One particular August day seared into her memory was spent with one of the commandos who had captured Lord Methuen. This veteran drove her over the veld in a wreck of a mule-cart, "like the wind, up hill and down dale, over the bumpiest and stoniest roads imaginable, so that I shrieked aloud with pain and fright all the time".

Her relief activities, not to mention the renewed links with leading nationalists like Botha and De Wet, were once again annoying the British authorities. The appearance at the Heidelberg rally was a typical provocation. Nor were relations likely to improve while she kept up a constant barrage of criticism of the army's tardiness in processing claims for compensation, or dismissed Chamberlain's £3 million grant as "a joke", or lambasted the government loan scheme for impoverished Boers as "worthless".

Matters threatened to come to a head with an unauthorised visit to the relief camp at Tweespruit, where her old colleague Mary Monkhouse was at work on behalf of the committee in London. Here Emily was accosted by the superintendent, whose "extreme insolence" led her to reflect on what curious people were given positions of power in wartime. The fact she was driven into camp by a well-known Boer general may have played some part in the manner of her reception. After Tweespruit the warning signals were flashing unmistakably and on receiving a stiff official rebuke from Milner's deputy Emily took the precaution of devising a new code for messages home in the event of a second deportation.

None of this stopped her from castigating the authorities as lazy, complacent, incompetent, and worse. To the Boers, she claimed, the very word British had come to mean "unjust, dishonest, grasping and oppressive". To take just one instance, she had not met a single man who had received proper payment of his signed wartime receipts from the military.

Her antagonism towards authority was noted with dismay by a well-connected English Quaker, Lawrence Richardson, who sought out Emily that October while on a fact-finding tour of South Africa. They had first met the previous year in Chelsea. Richardson wrote in his journal that Emily needlessly and foolishly picked fights with officials over trivial matters. "I fear Miss Hobhouse is overwrought and suffering from 'swelled head'," he said. But he added: "I have always had a high opinion of Miss Hobhouse, but am *very much impressed* with the amount of trekking she has done and what she has accomplished in distributing relief; also with her judgment and business ability and absence of anything hysterical."

It was during these travels in 1903 that Emily collected new women's stories that would be published after her death as *War without Glamour*. At the village of Hartebeestfontein an old Boer lady called Alida Badenhorst handed over a fascinating diary of her wartime hardships, later translated into English by Emily under the title *Tant' Alie of Transvaal*. A number of watercolour sketches she made at the time, including views of a ruined church and the concentration camp cemetery at Middelburg, would appear as illustrations in *War Without Glamour*, and though no one would claim them as works of art, Emily's bold sense of colour lends each scene a power and immediacy that is absent from contemporary photographs.

She was able to step up relief work after Heilbron because of a further £560 wired from London, but funds quickly ran low again. By August she was resorting to direct appeals to newspapers in South Africa and Britain, while at the same time bombarding friends at home like the Courtneys with demands that they prod the government into action.

So the storm clouds gathered again. Soon Emily was writing home that the newspapers of Johannesburg and the Cape were all on fire against her for saying the people were distressed, while in England each new attack on her was eagerly reprinted by *The Times* and others. The *Birmingham Daily Mail* said her claims were "all too transparently those of a credulous lady who went forth to discover evidence of Boer suffering and hardship, and who was too ready to believe anything that a Boer with a grievance cared to tell her". Unlike the Quaker observer Richardson, the leader-writers almost invariably labelled her hysterical.

This was the one insult that really stung Emily. The term hysteria, much bandied about in her time, was firmly associated in the public mind with women's frustrated desires. Freud himself believed the condition to be rooted in trauma, usually sexual, and often springing from the wish for a father's death. To one Johannesburg audience Emily declared: "Calling a person hysterical because you have no knowledge with which to deny their facts is the last refuge of the unmanly and the coward."

But though the personal attacks harmed her fundraising, she was still able to collect remarkable sums, the newspaper appeals alone netting over £8,000 – though no doubt she could have raised even more had she avoided antagonising so many editors.

*

During her tours of the ruined districts Emily was troubled by contact with the poorest class of whites, known as the *bijwoners*. She especially took against their daughters – "big strong girls with nothing to do," as she described them. In England they would have gone uncomplainingly into service, she thought, but in this country they refused to do what they called "Kaffir work". Such people Emily flatly refused to help.

By contrast, she was full of sympathy for the plight of the black population and collected evidence of widespread starvation. Even before returning to South Africa her failure to reach any of the concentration camps for blacks had weighed heavily on her conscience and during her talks with Lawrence Richardson in Chelsea she had pleaded that any Quaker relief workers sent out should concentrate on helping the Africans.[xxiii]

From Kroonstad, a large railway town halfway between Johannesburg and Bloemfontein, Emily wrote of her perplexity when missionaries implored her to feed eleven thousand blacks who had crowded into town in a search for work. She provided food from her own resources – "they need it sorely," she said, "young and old" – and went on badgering the authorities to take action. As a result she found herself assailed in the *Rand Daily Mail* for saying there were blacks in distress.

At Hartebeestfontein she was delighted by a Zulu evangelist preacher named Alexander Tschwangtwe, a man with a wonderful profile, who came to call on Emily at the home of her host. "He called in the kitchen," she wrote to Lady Hobhouse, "as it appears a Kaffir should always use the back door." The visitor said he had heard "the English Missis" had come to see the devastation, so he wanted her to view the ruins of the church, school and huts of the blacks. "So I said I gladly would," Emily went on, "and much to the surprise of the Boers I deserted them all and walked off with Mr Tschwangtwe and enjoyed his society very much."

Emily documented the travails of Hartebeestfontein's blacks in detail. While escorting her home the Zulu preacher told her that during the war he had been called to a great black camp at nearby Harrismith where inmates were dying at a rate of between thirty and fifty a day. As they returned to the house where Emily was staying, her companion left her at the front door and entered by the kitchen door to say goodbye.

*

In her efforts to help both black and white, Emily was aided by the appointment of a sympathetic newcomer, Patrick Duncan, as South Africa's colonial secretary. As she put it, Duncan had the sense "to make use of me, and work with me, instead of insulting me", which meant that from the time of their first meeting this future governor-general of the country was constantly bombarded with her pleas and demands.

One of Emily's most inspired ideas was to purchase teams of oxen which could be sent from farm to farm throughout the country districts, ploughing for one and all. Late in October, when the longed-for rain had fallen in parts of the Transvaal, the first of Emily's teams were set to work, and by mid-November nearly thirty were in action. She calculated each team to be worth more than £1,000 to the district where it operated. "Barring disease, the oxen will make money by transport after harvest and be there to plough again next season, for it will be long before the country is stocked again," she reasoned.

Emily left a touching account of how she attended a farm auction to buy oxen, and how no one would bid against her once they knew who she was. In this manner a superb team was knocked down to her for the bargain price of £15. Then as the price was being entered in the auctioneer's book one of the farmers came up and contributed ten shillings towards each beast, and a second offered free transportation. On that occasion alone her admirers saved her £50.

But the teams could plough only in places where the drought had ended. In parched Bloemfontein the authorities ordered a Day of Prayer for Rain, and when twenty-four hours passed with no divine response, tried for a military solution – "twelve-pounder guns were called out and marched up the hill whence they attacked the heavens, firing at the clouds till they had all retreated and the skies were clearer than ever," Emily wrote acidly to Aunt Mary.

*

By the time of this second visit to South Africa Emily seemed to be avoiding religious services whenever she could. The church might have dominated her life until her mid-thirties, and she might have gone out to America blazing with missionary zeal, but the influence of religion was now distinctly on the wane. Though she left no record of a spiritual struggle, she was clearly disillusioned. Ruth Fry thought her friend had been disappointed by her unfortunate experiences of clerical figures, no doubt having in mind such bugbears of Emily's as McGonicle in America and Hofmeyr in South Africa, while in England she had been disgusted by the refusal of leading Anglican churchmen to support the distress fund. The Bishop of Chester's nonchalant remark to her, "There are worse things than war", seemed to summarise the attitude of the established church. Even among the Quakers, many had sided with the government during the South African conflict. But it was the experiences in the camps that underlined the change in her outlook. During the visit of 1903 Emily could summon scant sympathy for any organised form of Christianity, though she stopped short of the open agnosticism of her brother Leonard.

Her near contemporary Sir Edmund Gosse, whose memoir *Father and Son* described his own upbringing by an unbending clerical parent, identified the period coinciding with Emily's philanthropic activities in America and South Africa as that in which an introspective, metaphysical form of religion was overtaken by an objective kind based on strenuous labour for the good of others. Certainly Emily Hobhouse exemplified this trend by granting no distinction between philanthropy and true religion.

She got on well enough with most pastors of the Dutch Reformed Church, whose standing among the Boers had been greatly enhanced by their work in the camps, and on her post-war treks the local Boer dominee would frequently offer her bed and board. But she could no longer endure those who "walked hand-in-hand with the Almighty". One minister encountered at Klerksdorp she found so objectionable that she had to let off steam in a letter to Leonard. This particular gentleman, seethed Emily, was so overbearing, autocratic, dogmatic, conceited and narrow, that when he launched an attack on Chamberlain she was horrified to find herself siding with "Pushy Joe".

The most irksome receptions organised for her were odious affairs held in churches, she said, where the proceedings were "half-service, half-laudatory of me, which I loathe", followed by the usual presentation of illuminated address and solemn orgy of hand-shaking. "Oh," she wailed in a letter home, "I get so cross!" At Middelburg, desperate to avoid being trapped for hours in the rectory as guest of honour, Emily proposed instead a visit to the nearby camp burial ground. She sent Aunt Mary a memorable account of the trip, describing how she had paced by bright moonlight among the rows upon rows of children's graves, each bearing a name and date of death on a scrap of paper inside a glass bottle.

The harrowing letters to brother and aunt continued unabated, but as the weeks turned into months those to Leonard went largely unanswered. Emily, increasingly disgruntled over her brother's silence, seems to have been unaware that he was exhibiting the first signs of a serious breakdown. Letters to Bruton Street on the other hand were answered faithfully each week, though Aunt Mary dropped increasingly pointed hints about the poor state of health of herself and Uncle Arthur. In September Emily wrote to commiserate over an accidental knee injury suffered by Lord Hobhouse and was moved to add a line of apology: "I am afraid my letters are not calculated to cheer or enliven you, being all about sad and desolated things." But she went on posting more of the same.

Aunt Mary was assiduously feeding titbits from Emily's letters to the press. However, on one occasion she was forced to make an embarrassing retraction after she misread a reference to starving Boers eating meerkats, and solemnly informed a newspaper that the population was reduced to eating mice and cats. Mary's slip was understandable. As the treks took their toll, Emily's handwriting, formerly so beautiful and clear, deteriorated badly due to desperate tiredness and cramps in the hand.

"Rumour says you are in Cornwall," she wrote to Leonard in August, and playfully pictured him struggling with picnics under umbrellas and catching cold by sitting on the damp grass of a make-believe summer. Two months later, she had taken to complaining to friends that Leonard never wrote, and warned that she would "economize gratitude" in her brother's direction.

At the end of October Emily called a halt. She had absorbed as much suffering as she could bear. Short rest periods apart, she had spent five months on the veld. "Everyone wants me to go everywhere, and flesh and blood won't and can't do it," she wrote to sister-in-law Nora, despairing of a reply from Leonard himself. She bade an emotional farewell to Kaya Lami, where the younger Fichardts had tried to fill the void left by their mother's death. Returning to the Cape, she revelled in the contrast between the verdant colony and the parched landscape of the defeated republics. Even after a full month's rest, she could not face a planned return to the north, confessing to an Edwardian version of compassion fatigue: "My nervous system won't do it any more."

There had been a whiff of calculation about a letter to Aunt Mary late in September, when for the first time Emily broached the subject of coming home, and sighed that lack of funds would condemn her to a second class cabin on an inferior boat. Shortly afterwards she wrote again with gushing thanks for the money from Uncle Arthur to cover the upgrade to first class. As it happened the plan to return early fell through, and Emily remained in South Africa a further three months.

In a letter of November 23 to Kate Courtney she mentions her growing anxiety over Aunt Mary, who has not sounded like herself since Emily left. Yet come December Emily is still sitting amid sunshine and flowers and ripening fruit and shuddering at the thought of the intense cold and fogs of London. The letters of this time are full of the passion for flowers which Emily could indulge properly only at the Cape. She has come to the conclusion that, compared with England, country life in South Africa is perfect, "barring a cobra or two in your rose garden", and thinks it is a pity that Uncle Arthur and Aunt Mary at home are forced to keep indoors.

But the recent letters from Bruton Street had increased her sense of guilty unease and finally dictated her return. As she admitted long afterwards, she felt her aunt had put pressure on her. "Without wishing to injure my work, she too evidently felt her failing powers and wished to have me near her," she wrote. "My uncle's health was causing her great anxiety." Even so, she believed she was bound to complete the distribution of her remaining funds, and it was not until Christmas week that she tore herself away from the sunshine and boarded a ship for home.

Shortly before sailing-day there was another health scare. Emily had seized a long-coveted opportunity to scale Table Mountain, joining a party of friends who set off at sunrise in order to approach the summit before the hottest part of the day. "The climb was more difficult than I anticipated, the heat near the top terrific, and indeed I was in no state of health to have attempted it," she wrote later. "But I did not then know it. If the climb was a tax on the heart, it seemed to me the descent after we crossed the summit and came down the further side was even more painful. The declivity was so steep that it shook one painfully, and any attempt to steady oneself by clinging to the rock and boulders was only to scorch one's hands with their burning heat."

Nor was this the only mishap of the last few days. Staying at a wine farm near Stellenbosch, Emily wandered some distance from the house and all at once found herself sinking into a bog. She sank quickly to her knees but in the struggle to get free was sucked in deeper. It was a ridiculous but highly dangerous position to be in, the more so as darkness was falling. "I was planted like a tree and immensely tickled at the humour of the situation," was her unconvincing claim.

She called and shouted for what seemed an age – in reality perhaps twenty minutes – varying her notes to find the one that would carry furthest, and pausing at times to husband her strength. Eventually her cries attracted the attention of a passing "boy", who roused the household. The farm manager supervised the laying of a path of corrugated iron sheets over the bog, and from this platform the distinguished visitor was dug out, mustering what dignity she could. To her annoyance a garbled account of the incident got into what she called "the comic press", but she never found out who leaked the story.

It was a wholly characteristic Emily misadventure.

21 HIGH-SOULED, HIGH-THINKING FRIENDS

E mily Hobhouse was always short of close friends, as distinct from overlapping circles of co-activists, political fellow-travellers, and awestruck admirers. Most of the intense friendships formed in her youth were lost in the wake of the Liskeard riot, and her abiding sense of class and position tended to discourage new relationships, as well as to blight her romantic prospects. Then there was her fault-finding nature, unhappily combined with a marked sensitivity to criticism of herself, which must have strangled many a latent intimacy at birth. Yet during this South African visit of 1903 Emily was able to forge two personal friendships which would prove among the most significant, enduring and cherished of her life.

The first was with Olive Schreiner, celebrated novelist, women's rights campaigner, and child of the veld. Five years older than Emily, short, dark and voluptuous, Olive was in certain respects as unlike her new friend as it was possible to be. Violently demonstrative about her feelings, and by the standards of the time sensationally outspoken about her sexuality, she seemed always, as one observer put it, "in the sort of state that other people get into after a bottle of champagne". Certainly one is hard pressed to imagine Emily imbibing heavy doses of bromide to curb a frantic sex drive, or asking men for their views on masturbation, or nonchalantly walking round her lodgings stark naked – all documented acts of her new friend. Havelock Ellis, the pioneering writer on sex who was involved in an intense relationship with Olive lasting thirty-six years, wrote wistfully of his inability to satisfy "her elementary primitive nature".

Olive's permanent state of emotional turmoil had not discouraged eminent admirers from many walks of life, among them Gladstone, Bertrand Russell, Oscar Wilde and W.B. Yeats. Predictably, that aficionado of forceful women Alfred Milner, on first landing in South Africa, expressed his keen desire to meet the fascinating Olive Schreiner. Her best-selling first novel, *The Story of an African Farm*, is a study of two orphaned sisters growing up in a Bible-dominated household on the veld. By coincidence, one of the girls is called Emily, though hardly from the same mould as her Hobhouse namesake. The fictional character is a kind-hearted, obedient, domesticated creature who acts as a foil to the proud, avid, rebellious heroine based on Olive herself.

Whatever the differences between the new friends, their similarities were as remarkable, and went far beyond a common interest in women's rights and pacifism. The two shared many facets of character, and a striking number of Emily's formative experiences were mirrored in Olive's own life history, if never in such luridly heightened colours.

Flamboyant, fiery and startlingly frank about sex, Olive Schreiner was South Africa's most famous woman. Like Emily, she bore the scars of an unhappy love affair.

Both women were gifted with great intelligence yet denied all but the most rudimentary education. Both endured an unhappy, repressed childhood in a home ruled by religion – Olive's father, a stern protestant missionary, laboured long to make Calvinists of the black tribesmen of the remote Cape frontier country. Both bore the scars of unhappy love affairs while continuing to yearn after some will-o'-the-wisp ideal romance. Like Emily, Olive was drawn to deeply unpopular causes and was branded a traitor to her own country. Both pined for Africa when in England, for England when in Africa. Heroines of the Boers, they went on to dismay the Boers by championing South Africa's blacks. For the rest of their days, Emily and Olive would be chronically hard-up, and martyrs to intense physical sufferings that not only detractors but many friends believed to be largely imaginary. Restless, lonely and impulsive, the two together created a sisterhood of suffering. Today, both would surely be diagnosed as manic depressives.

Like Emily, Olive was obsessed with pains in the chest, perspiration, palpitations, and a recurring feeling of suffocation; indeed, their relative states of ill health would remain a subject of lively correspondence between them until Olive's death. In one important respect their experience differed. Both longed for children, but unlike her English friend Olive had borne a child, a daughter who had died within hours of birth.

What the two shared above all was a passionate partisanship for the Boers, and they sealed their first meeting with fervent declarations of friendship. Olive praised *The Brunt of the War* in characteristically extravagant style and claimed that every South African household was acquiring a copy. Such an endorsement from a world-famous writer must have worked wonders for Emily's morale after her brother Leonard's damning faint praise. "You have saved not hundreds but doubtlessly thousands of lives," Olive enthused in her first letter to Emily, and in this at least she did not exaggerate. Nor was she wrong to warn her new friend that the noble self-denying work would leave "injurious and lasting scars" upon her system.

Olive was the sister and wife of prominent Cape politicians. Her brother Will had been elected Cape premier in 1898; her husband, the rather creepy Samuel Cronwright-Schreiner, sold up his ostrich farm to go into politics and had become a leading member of the colony's legislative assembly. He added the Schreiner to his own name in deference to Olive's views on equal rights for women, though the two only occasionally lived together.

In her retreat from religion Olive was streets ahead of Emily. At the age of ten she had watched a beloved younger sister die and had slept all night with the little corpse. She never recovered her belief in God. At sixteen she had been seduced by an older man, an experience which left her prey to unresolved emotional conflicts for the rest of her life. These inner tumults caused Olive to abandon most of her writing projects, political as well as fictional, though her tract *Women and Labour* was to be hailed by later feminists like Vera Brittain as the Bible of the women's movement, while *African Farm* would remain in print more than a century on.

One of the earliest conversations between the new friends must have brought to light a curious link between them. On her first visit to England in the 1880s, carrying in her suitcase the unpublished manuscript of her great novel, Olive had been one of the original tenants of Chenies Street Chambers in Bloomsbury – the same block of flats from which Emily was ejected a decade later. Stranger still, both rented Flat 22 on the top floor. There the South African had hung her greatest treasure, a jewel-like little picture of a place she had never visited – the Cornish beauty spot of St Ives where Emily would one day make her home.

Emily always cherished as one of her happiest memories of South Africa a week she spent with Olive at her tiny one-roomed house of corrugated iron on the open veld near the ugly little railway town of De Aar. "There was Olive Schreiner, hidden from the world, like a diamond in the desert," she wrote. The week passed in a flash, the two women roaming the veld together or playing with Olive's pet meerkats. "Olive did all the talking and I asked nothing better," said Emily. "The large mind and fertile imagination seemed inexhaustible. She refreshed one like bathing in a sea."

*

The second of Emily's new friendships was with Jan Smuts. The two established an instant rapport during a first meeting at Pretoria and they were to stay in touch for the rest of Emily's life; indeed, their correspondence would provide an unrivalled insight into the sad, fluctuating state of Emily's mind in her latter years. For despite stormy ups and downs in their relationship, almost always provoked by Emily, their close relationship was to survive Smuts's rise to affluence and great power, and her own descent into poverty and discredit.

Smuts had been an altered man since those few whispered words from Kitchener on the eve of Vereeniging. It was as if the scales had fallen from his eyes and opened up an instant vision of a union of Boer states within the British Empire. As he confided soon after to the Reverend John Kestell, President Steyn's chaplain: "The idea of the *imperium* grips me. It is something wonderful." In these early days he did not care to share his vision with the violently anti-imperialist Emily, or it is difficult to see how the friendship could have blossomed.

By the time of their first meeting Smuts, still only thirty-two, had cultivated his trademark pointed goatee, then known as a French beard. He was building up a lucrative law practice in Pretoria but still craved the power only politics could offer. He pleased Emily by refusing a seat on Milner's new legislative council in order to become the right-hand man of General Botha, recently elected as leader of a new nationalist political party called Het Volk, or The People.

As in the Kruger days, canny observers saw Smuts as the real power behind a figurehead leader. British intelligence kept a careful eye on the ambitious young lawyer, one secret report speaking of him as "pleasant, plausible and cunning". Though years would pass before she grasped that Smuts harboured long-term objectives diametrically opposed to her own, Emily wrote to her brother prophesying a great future for this very charming, clear-headed and clever man, and was moved to proclaim that only "high-thinking" Jan Smuts and "high-souled" Olive Schreiner could properly express the moral and political sentiments of the Boer people.

In parallel with his careers as lawyer and politician, Smuts was quietly pursuing the scientific and philosophical studies that would lead him to the theory of holism – the word was of his coinage – and worldwide academic honours. A revealing anecdote tells of a distinguished American woman botanist who on a field trip in Durban asked an equally distinguished South African colleague to name a grass unknown to her. "I don't know," said the professor, "but ask the General over there." Smuts stepped forward and not only promptly identified the grass but gave a scholarly exposition of its distribution and ecological significance. When the American expressed her amazement at such learning in a military man, Smuts replied: "But my dear lady, I'm only a general in my spare time."

For all his philosophical bent Smuts was ever the pragmatist, and over the next half century would show an astonishing talent for political survival. But in the immediate postwar period he concentrated on making himself financially secure, and all he earned as a lawyer was invested in land. Within six years of Vereeniging he owned six farms, eventually increasing his holdings to over fifty thousand acres. Emily was to benefit personally from her friend's growing wealth.

Once he knew her well, Smuts almost always acted contrary to Emily's advice, for the truth was she would have made a terrible politician. The word compromise did not figure in the Hobhouse dictionary, and the long game at which Smuts would prove a master was completely alien to his English friend's impulsive nature. Smuts quickly divined that for all her practical experience at relief work, for all her genius for improvisation when galvanised by the sight of suffering, Emily was hopelessly unworldly on the broader political issues, as she was at managing her own life. Yet though he would learn to discount her opinions, in these early days she was highly valued for her contacts with Britain's brokers of power. No one else of Smuts's acquaintance could offer such an entrée to the society of influential Liberals.

Despite the worldwide celebrity that would stem from his imperial conversion, and the bitter enmity he inspired among some Boer factions, Smuts remained at heart a man of his people. Thirty years after the fateful stroll in the garden of Melrose House he could still let slip the remark: "I keep believing in God, but I don't forget that He favoured the English rather than the Boers."

Emily's friendship with Jan Smuts ripened into an intimacy with the whole Smuts family. She became a regular visitor to their home, was invited to join the clan on their seaside holiday, and even invented pet names for the Smuts children. Most remarkably of all, she made a conquest of Smuts's wife, notorious for her deep hatred of the English. Later on, a rash act of Emily's would turn Isie Smuts against her, but in 1903 the angel of the camps was an honoured guest and cherished friend.

In December, when Emily decided she must return to England and Aunt Mary, Smuts wrote that her departure would create a void filled only by the memory of her good works and selfless devotion. He added: "To me, who learned to know you better than most, you will always remain a bright figure on a sombre background." And he vowed that in the little homesteads on the veld Emily's name would always be woven into daily conversation, inspiring selflessness and charity, and dissipating race prejudice.

Perhaps more than anyone else, including her own family, Olive Schreiner and Jan Smuts would be trusted with the secrets of Emily's heart. Yet the great irony of these two South African friendships is that Olive would one day break with Emily because of Emily's refusal to break with Smuts. Olive, baffled by how her pacifist soul-mate could remain on affectionate personal terms with an authoritarian general while differing on every political issue, would in her dramatic way demand that Emily choose between the two of them. But this was in the unknowable future, and for many years the two women would remain bosom friends.

*

Emily's farewell speech to her Cape friends came at a reception hosted by the Dutch Reformed Church. At this gathering fraught with emotion, the ovation was so overwhelming that for some time she struggled to regain sufficient composure to speak. When she did, a tense silence fell, and in the name of all those in England who thought like herself, Emily apologised for the indignities, sufferings and death inflicted on the Boer nations. "Forget you never can," she said. "These things are laid by as sacred memories in your hearts. But – I ask it of you here and now – forgive us if you can."

Emily was in no forgiving mood herself. Speaking bitterly of her arrest and deportation two years before – "the great insult practised on me by my own countrymen" – she declared she had not forgotten and would never forgive. And she attacked by name those she held responsible – Milner, Brodrick, and Kitchener. "Something more is due to self-respect," she declared. "For myself, the time to forgive will come when public apology has been made me by the authors of the deed."

22 MISS HOBHOUSE'S UNPARDONABLE INDISCRETION

The sea voyage home from Cape Town turned into another great drama. In her exhausted state Emily did not cope well with the motion of the vessel, suffering headaches so agonising that concerned fellow-passengers urged her to disembark at Lisbon and complete her journey overland. This proved to be very bad advice indeed.

She knew she had insufficient ready money for the extra expense involved but was told that the British consul at Lisbon would cash a cheque – indeed, she wrote later, everyone assured her it was a consul's duty to render such help to his fellow-citizens. It is a plaintive cry echoed by countless stranded holidaymakers to the present day.

Lack of funds was not the only pressing concern. On landing she discovered that passengers coming from ports with a history of plague had to undergo examination, and while Cape Town had long been plague-free the Portuguese officials proved over-zealous. Local regulations demanded the fumigation of soiled linen, and instead of quietly throwing hers overboard like everybody else, Emily innocently owned up to possessing such articles. She was immediately ordered into a boat, rowed across the river Tagus, and landed at a distant place of quarantine where she found "huge furnaces and fumigating erections". These were all unlit, and even after Emily had prodded idle officials into kindling a fire, she was informed the fumigation of her smalls would take at least four hours. Only then did it flash upon her unworldly mind that a bribe was being solicited. At the first gleam of silver a furnace flew open and she was able to dash back to the boat for Lisbon in the nick of time, though the boatman too exacted a heavy toll on Emily's shrinking purse.

When she announced herself at the British consulate next morning her plea for cash was met by "a blank and very curt negative" from the consul himself, who said he had never heard of Emily Hobhouse. After she was turned away by a local bank, visions loomed of being marched off to a Portuguese gaol once her hotel bill was presented, and more time was lost when a cable to Barclay's, her London bank, went astray. "I saw then all it means to be in a foreign country without money," she wrote forlornly.

Her last resort was predictable. Emily wrote urgently to Uncle Arthur, who cabled money immediately, and at the Lisbon bank where she had known only chilly disdain she was now received with bows and smiles. A week of rest restored her sufficiently for the journey to London, where she could depend on a period of recuperation with Lord and Lady Hobhouse. As the lease on the Chelsea flat had expired the previous year, Bruton Street was now the only place Emily might call home, as Aunt Mary constantly urged her to do.

Her aunt and uncle she found greatly aged and enfeebled. But much as she loved and valued them, Emily confided in a letter to Mrs Steyn, she felt they were looked after very well by their household of servants, and before long she was fretting for an outlet for her recovered energies. With the winding-up of the Distress Committee, her restless mind was working overtime on South Africa's problems, and the idea of organising some kind of cottage industry for Boer girls began to obsess her.

Lace-making and needlepoint seemed the most suitable occupations to promote and Emily was soon plaguing lace collectors and haunting shops selling lace, teasing out every scrap of information about its manufacture. Her investigations were pursued in the usual exhaustive manner with a fact-finding visit to Venice, cradle of European lace-making, and further studies at Brussels, Ghent, and Bruges.

Lace-making appealed to Emily because she saw it as "refining and educative", demanding patience, extreme cleanliness, absolute thoroughness, delicacy of workmanship, and an appreciation of design – all qualities she had discerned in South African households. Then on a trip to Ireland she suddenly changed her mind and decided that spinning and weaving were more appropriate occupations for the homely Boer womenfolk. The early Dutch and French settlers were said to have taken spinning wheels and looms to the Cape, and Emily thought that some remnants of such handicrafts might still exist.

*

The Venice interlude was memorable for a detour to spend a week with the Steyns, then wintering in a borrowed house at Cannes. It was the first face-to-face encounter between Emily and her hero the ex-president, and he was now sufficiently improved thanks to the "electric baths" recommended by his doctors to rise painfully from his chair to welcome his English admirer. Emily was always to remember the moving spectacle of "the combination of that unbroken moral and mental vigour with the sad bodily incapacity" in Steyn, peering at her through his blue-tinted glasses, and the watchful tenderness of his wife.

During her stay with the Steyns Emily also had her first and last sight of that other exiled president, the decrepit Paul Kruger, then nearly eighty and living in a cheap little villa at nearby Mentone. The meeting impressed her deeply. As she was ushered into the hall by Kruger's secretary, Emily glanced through the open door of the parlour. "And there, clothed in sombre black, was the old man, solitary and absorbed. He sat before a table on which rested a high brass reading stand which in its turn supported a heavy folio Bible. Paul Kruger was reading and was evidently so withdrawn that he was impervious to sight or sound."

Their conversation was brief. Emily saw that "already his mind was elsewhere and the world ended for him", though he was anxious to know whether Emily had ever met his dead wife. When told no, he seemed too disappointed to make further effort to speak and Emily stole out of the room as "that medieval and puritanical figure" returned to his Bible. Less than four months later he was dead.

The rail journey from Mentone to Venice was marked by another of those mishaps that were something of a speciality of Emily's. At Alassio she left her train for a few minutes in the vain hope of finding a relation who was staying there, and returned to find her bag rifled and her purse gone. As she had already noted the train to be crowded with "questionable people" perhaps the theft should not have surprised her greatly. Fortunately she had the foresight to carry a reserve bag of banknotes round her neck, but as she had also chosen to wear a blouse with its fastenings at the back – a stupid fashion, it struck her in retrospect – she was unable to get at her remaining funds. Emily draws a veil over how she finally managed to retrieve the moneybag, recording only that "they cheated me horribly" on her midnight arrival at the Milan exchange.

Determined to be look on the bright side, Emily felt compensated for her nightmare rail journey by the magical sight of Venice at dawn from a gondola – "in the western sky the moon hung silver while the glowing of coming day was brightening in the East" – and wrapped in a silence broken by bells for the first mass of Easter.

*

Over this period began the remarkable correspondence between Emily and Jan Smuts that was to continue to the end of her life. By then the "Dear Miss Hobhouse" and "Dear General Smuts" of the early exchanges had warmed to "Dear Missus" – the revived nickname of her nursery days – and "My dear dear Oom Jannie", Oom being an affectionate term in Afrikaans for an uncle-like figure. During 1904 the Smuts letters which followed Emily on her travels throughout the British Isles and Europe kept her up to date with South Africa's political affairs and laid the foundations for a strange intimacy that would survive two decades and a hundred upsets.

Smuts, at that time professing to hanker for a quiet life, contrasted his own longing for peace with Emily's inexhaustible pugnacity. "You seem made for battle, for the excitement which accompanies great endeavours and achievements," he wrote, and went on to claim in self-pitying terms that the Boers had little heart left for a struggle. "But," he added, "belonging as you do to a conquering, a victorious race, and just now refreshed with Italy's magic air, you would probably laugh at all these dismal croakings."

Emily was having none of that. "You say I belong to a conquering race," came the reply from Bruton Street, "but only half of me is Anglo-Saxon; the other half is Celt, pushed away by the conquerors into the remote Cornish hills where, ever since, my family in unbroken line have lived, never feeling one with the rest of England. So you see I have, by inheritance, sympathy with those who love liberty and independence."

While scolding Smuts for pessimism and lack of ambition, Emily sympathised over his difficulty in keeping alive "the high aspirations". In this revealing passage she went on: "I used to feel like this during the long years I lived alone in a Cornish village, growing up alone, dreaming of what could be and should be, full of unattainable ideals, and I know by experience it is almost madness to have no scope to work out your ideals, and to feel the years slipping past bearing one's youth and strength with them, dreading that one's life will be only dreams and never *acts*. One can only go back to that sort of existence when every shred of active power is consumed."

The claim of "growing up alone" would have dumbfounded her four surviving siblings, and the lines that followed would have surprised and pained her doting aunt and uncle. "Curiously enough," she wrote, "I am just now contemplating my final settling down in life – or, at least, the place where I shall finally settle down. I am thinking of buying a cottage residence somewhere in the country and so establishing a base to retire upon in sickness or old age… I think I have another five years' active work left in me." That "in the country" could mean either England or South Africa, and Smuts was asked to be on the lookout for a suitable plot for a "cottage on the veld" to be purchased with a recent windfall of £500.

"I am myself swayed from side to side by varying interests and emotions," Emily admitted, "one day deciding for England and the next for Africa. It seems as if the physical side of me clings here to all that is familiar and comfortable in climate and material things, and where, if sickness or trouble come, here are those to whom I have a right to turn for help; while the mental and soul side of me finds no life here and turns to the country and people with whom I have been so strangely linked."

Of one thing she was certain: "I cannot go on living this dual life with my body in England and my mind in South Africa. I must cut myself free on one side or the other."

Smuts initially welcomed the idea of Emily spending her "far-off old age" among the Boers but sounded a cautionary note: "I do not know whether it is right to uproot you at your time of life from your native country. You know, in old age (which to you will come as to all) we turn back to our youth and relive the beginnings of our life. In youth we want to get away from it, in mature years we smile at it, in old age we return to it with its hallowed associations… I think you will be happier in that England of yours than you will be here."

As so often, Emily asked for advice only to ignore it. In the same manner she sought his help in identifying an appropriate site for her great new project, a spinning school for Boer women – the first of many she envisaged opening across the country. It was while Emily was engaged in planning the home industry enterprise that a serious indiscretion of hers almost wrecked Jan Smuts's political career overnight.

*

Early in 1904 a major crisis blew up in South Africa over the issue of Chinese labour. Because of postwar difficulties in attracting black labour back to the Johannesburg gold mines, the recruitment of large numbers of low-paid workers had begun in China. The policy quickly became South Africa's hottest political issue. Conditions for the immigrants were certainly appalling. Not only did they have to work long and dangerous shifts for six days a week, but when not underground were confined to compounds; worse, many were subject to summary beatings. Boers, already hugely outnumbered by blacks and a discontented Indian population, were appalled by the introduction of yet another racial group. In England Liberals like Lloyd George and Campbell-Bannerman spotted an opportunity and launched a blistering attack on the "Chinese slavery" supposedly backed by the Tories.

Smuts unburdened himself in a bitter letter to Emily. South Africa, he wrote, was "merrily spinning to perdition" as Milner's government pursued a criminally foolish policy that amounted to a sacrilegious plunder of the Boer heritage. The Rand capitalists he declared to be mostly swindlers who had turned the Transvaal into "the happy hunting ground of the fraudulent company-promoter".

Emily herself spoke out publicly on the Chinese question from the platform of

Caxton Hall, appearing alongside Leonard Courtney and other Liberal luminaries. Then, in a moment of breathtaking thoughtlessness, she decided to press her case by sending a copy of Smuts's private letter for publication in *The Times*. Choosing the paper with the most consistent track record against her causes was not so much tempting fate as poking it in the eye with a stick, and her want of judgment brought down a hornet's nest on Smuts's head.

As the controversy raged he warned Emily that any further disclosure of his private thoughts could well end with exile from South Africa on the orders of Milner. After her fashion Emily was contrite – "I am deeply, deeply sorry if I have vexed or injured you" – and promised not to be so reckless again. Typically, she could not resist adding: "And yet I *can't* feel sorry that it *is* published, for continually I am thanked for it – and everyone seems to think I did right."

Smuts had had a nasty jolt. Only a strong instinct for self-preservation saved him from destruction. Fifty years later, his son would still be referring to "Miss Hobhouse's unpardonable indiscretion" and darkly alluding to other hasty things said by Emily "for which my mother has never forgiven her". Smuts himself merely begged Emily to exercise some prudence in the future, before resuming the stream of letters. But he never quite forgot her loose-cannon moment.

As matters fell out, the great casualty in the Chinese slavery controversy would eventually turn out to be not Smuts but Lord Milner himself. His initial approval of imported labour and, more damningly, his authorisation of "light corporal punishment" to deal with outbreaks of violence among the Chinese, would one day come back to haunt him and help to put Emily's Liberal party into power.

*

Emily returned from Venice in time to join her aunt and uncle on their annual visit to Oxfordshire. The old couple revived in the fine May weather to the point where Emily suspected that the long walks with her uncle, then nearing his eighty-fifth birthday, were less taxing on his strength than on hers.

That April the family mourned the death of Arthur's brother Edmund, the former Bishop of Nelson. After the glittering years at Oxford and a rapid rise in the church hierarchy, Edmund's life had been marred by disappointment and scandal. Over the years he had succumbed to the negative traits in the Hobhouse character, turning by degrees into a mirror-image of Emily's father – austere, humourless, and unbending. Edmund's episcopacy in New Zealand had combined a grim conscientiousness over matters of liturgy with a spectacular insensitivity in his dealings with people. At loggerheads with clergy and laity alike, he had fallen into a deep depression and had finally resigned his office after the shock arrest of his cousin Henry, who had joined him in Nelson as bishop's assistant, on a charge of sodomy. Edmund's remaining years in England had been marked by those repeated breakdowns in mental health which increasingly appeared the lot of Emily's family.

Her own physical health, however, continued to improve all summer, and by August she would think nothing of cycling twenty-five miles to meet her brother for tea. But the cramps in her right hand refused to improve, and it ended with the momentous decision to purchase a typewriting machine. Throughout her life Emily deplored modern inventions with a passion, always excepting the bicycle and the typewriter.

Later in 1904 a sudden whim of Lord Hobhouse to repeat a boyhood climb to the highest points of his native Mendip Hills proved too much for himself, his niece, and his little dog Meg. Emily recorded the outing in miserable detail. "Exhausted by the work of the past three years I found the climb worse even than Table Mountain," she wrote. "In addition I had every few minutes to rescue the dog who in her blindness repeatedly plunged into clumps of gorse which pricked her nose and entangled her long hair. It ended by my having to carry her. To crown all I was filled with anxiety lest my uncle should collapse. His breathing grew laboured, and every few minutes we had to rest, but plucky to the last he refused all suggestions to be content with anything less than the summit."

The Mendip adventure sealed her uncle's fate. In November his condition took a turn for the worse and Emily hardly knew which needed the greater care, "he in his weakness or my aunt in her utter desolation". Lord Hobhouse died at Bruton Street on December 6. Most unusually for the time, his body was cremated, the practice having been legalised in England only two years before. A memorial service was held at St Margaret's, Westminster, and in the absence of Aunt Mary – too broken in spirit to attend – Emily acted as chief mourner along with her cousin Henry Hobhouse, the Hadspen squire.[xxiv]

These were desperately sad weeks. As Emily remembered it, her whole being was absorbed in helping her aunt to bear her loss. Arthur and Mary Hobhouse had rarely been apart in their fifty-six years of marriage, and in Emily's view had enjoyed "that special possession in each other of those who have no children". Mary was facing the world alone for the first time, and in need of her almost-daughter as never before.

Yet it was now Emily decided that her place was in South Africa rather than in Bruton Street. After all, plans were well advanced to open the first spinning school at the small town of Philippolis in the old Orange Free State; as a result of Emily's latest campaigning, funds for the project were pouring in from the Liberal great and good, with crates of spinning wheels and looms already on the high seas; her berth to Cape Town was booked. Twenty years later Emily would insist that she told her aunt she had only to say the word and she would stay, while admitting that "sorely I felt she needed me". But Aunt Mary was too proud to speak, and Emily determined that "the wisest thing" was to go as arranged.

*

By the time of his death Uncle Arthur was a wealthy man, leaving an estate worth over £92,000. Emily must always have known she would benefit handsomely from the will. Lord Hobhouse had felt honour-bound to care for his dead brother's daughters, and for many years previously had paid an annual allowance of £40 to Emily and each of her sisters. A will dating from 1897 had earmarked the sum of £10,000 to be divided equally between the three girls and their two brothers, with a similar bequest favouring the children of the other brother, Bishop Edmund. Significantly, Uncle Arthur signed this version of the will soon after Emily's disastrous speculation in Mexico, but before her engagement with the American adventurer was broken off. In his lawyerly way Arthur stated his desire "that my niece Emily's share shall be held to her separate use for life".

By a codicil dated July 23 1901, when Emily was working in the camps, the legacies to all nieces and nephews were increased, boosting Emily's share to £3,720. Two years later, at the time she was touring the ruined districts, the financial plight of his favourites among the children was clearly troubling Arthur and the frail old peer signed a second codicil by which, on Mary's death, a further £2,500 would go to the hard-pressed Leonard and an extra £1,000 to Emily.[xxv] So when Emily left England in January 1905, a few days after the will was proved, there was some relief in sight to the money worries that had dogged her since the Jackson affair. Further, Aunt Mary seemed to be reconciled to Emily's departure, and pledged financial support for the spinning enterprise.

Emily could not hide her longing to be gone, and there was the additional excitement in prospect of returning to Cape Town in the company of the man regarded by many Boers as the only untainted hero of the war. Instead of sailing from Southampton, Emily crossed to Antwerp, where she had been invited to join the indomitable Marthinus Steyn. For though still an invalid, "the uncrowned king of South Africa" had at last received his doctors' permission to end the years of exile. In the words of his biographer, Johannes Meintjes, "the smart and lovely Emily Hobhouse" figured among the presidential entourage who saw Steyn carried through cheering crowds to board the German steamer *Kronprinz*, a brave sight with its flutter of bunting from stem to stern in his honour.

But she was never to see Aunt Mary again.

23 "A BLANK NOTHING COULD FILL"

Unusually, Emily kept a diary during the voyage. Perhaps she sensed that the era when Aunt Mary acted as her chief correspondent and archivist, diligently preserving Emily's letters for posterity, was drawing to an end. The diary begins with the sailing of the *Kronprinz* on January 27, 1905 – that first evening she decided against attending a ball in honour of the Kaiser's birthday because of the cold – and goes on to paint a picture of her growing intimacy with the Steyns.

The President – Steyn was addressed thus by admirers like Emily for the rest of his life – proved to be the great and good man she had expected. He held gratifyingly liberal views on issues dear to Emily's heart, such as female suffrage, and the two soon settled into a routine of cosy chats in his flower-filled cabin. Almost every day she read to him for two hours, keeping a careful record of her selections which included More's *Utopia*, Boswell's *Johnson*, Sidney's *Arcadia*, novels by Dickens and Samuel Butler, and what she vaguely referred to as "various books on co-operation, banks, and co-partnership". Steyn reciprocated with lessons in Dutch. Yet there was always a curious ceremoniousness about Emily's relations with Steyn's wife Isabella, who was known to all her other friends as Tibbie but "Mrs Steyn" to Emily to the end of her days. Perhaps it was her way of making up for the indignities the Orange Free State's First Lady had suffered at the hands of the British.

Emily's diary of the voyage highlights a growing preoccupation with the state of her health. In Mrs Fawcett style, she complains of being kept awake at night by the carousing of tipsy men outside her door and of nursing a "somewhat turnippy head" the next morning. The President kindly orders his private masseur to work on her neuritic arm while the solicitous Mrs Steyn, noting signs of fatigue, insists on Emily lying down to rest in her cool cabin. The pages are dotted with phrases such as "very poorly" and "head still bad" and references to feeling giddy and shaky. Before long, everything involving stooping becomes a trial.

Emily was not travelling alone. Sharing her cabin was an idealistic, toothy young Quaker from Somerset named Margaret Clark, of the wealthy shoe-making family, who had volunteered to help out with the spinning school. Among other impressive credentials, she was a granddaughter of the radical MP and peace campaigner John Bright, one of Emily's heroes. While Emily read to President Steyn, Margaret Clark applied herself zealously to learning to spin and card. Emily vowed she would never ask the Cambridge-educated Margaret to do anything she would not do herself, a promise the younger woman was to recall with a rueful smile as she mixed urine with indigo for the dyeing vats.

Overshadowing the voyage are nagging doubts about the prospects for the school. "Shall we succeed or fail?" asks Emily in the diary. "From such talk as I have had with Boer friends on board I fancy that they all think us doomed to fail."

At last on Saturday, February 18, the two women stood on deck to watch a glorious dawn break over Table Mountain. As the *Kronprinz* glided into port Emily was able to point out to her companion the dock where she had suffered the traumatic imprisonment on Kitchener's orders. On board came a gathering of Boer leaders to honour the invalid on his return after nearly three years – "and me too, they kindly said," Emily wrote to Aunt Mary.

As the presidential entourage departed, Emily and Margaret were left in the care of General Smuts and the three chatted merrily on the dockside as fifty cases of looms and spinning wheels were unloaded onto African soil. A round of visits followed to old friends, among them Emily's especial favourites the Moltenos and Murrays. The first night she hardly slept and lay awake thinking of her tumultuous past and uncertain future.

On landing Emily had found only two letters waiting. "Aunt Mary's was *very* short," she notes in the diary.

Emily and Margaret Clark rejoined the Steyns for a two-day rail journey north to Orange River Colony. The President's return to his native land was a triumph, though in Boer style a curiously muted triumph. Wherever the train stopped on the journey from Cape Town to the Steyn farm near Bloemfontein, crowds gathered in silent homage. Steyn vetoed any great receptions in his honour, in the same spirit that he had refused to draw on Free State funds during his exile – "let it go to the destitute, the widows and orphans," he declared – and had declined his presidential salary in wartime, in case anyone saw him as profiting from his refusal to make peace.

Emily had long agonised over where to site her school before the issue was settled by the offer of a free house and workroom by Mrs Steyn's father, the local pastor at Philippolis. But the town, reached at the end of February, turned out to be far from ideal for Emily's purposes. Perpetually short of water despite its situation on the Otterspoort River, Philippolis was remote from vital supplies of coal and timber, and the premises themselves were rickety and cramped.

"Every night I am possessed by fears that I have attempted a task wholly beyond my powers and my means," brooded Emily a week after arrival. "My heart nearly failed me and weakened my belief in my own scheme." Between furious bouts of activity to make their little house inhabitable, she and Margaret Clark seemed to take turns to fall ill and be nursed by the other. The diary catalogues every woe of these days – "feet ache unmercifully", "dead beat", "felt as if I must break down", "very poorly", "voice gone", "very low physically", "more dead than alive".

The squalor of their surroundings depressed both women and they soon began to fear their task was hopeless without expert help. And – a sore trial for one with Emily's hunger for the latest on world affairs – weeks went by without sight of a newspaper. But there were good days. Early one morning Emily's soul was "refreshed by a glorious cactus flower", the gift of a neighbour. The occasional newspaper began to appear. There was consolation in seeing the workroom start to look shipshape, and the paid help arrived. There was a black "boy" called Moses to hew wood and fetch water, and a Boer cook, known as the Widow Boshoff, who immediately won her new employer's sympathy by saying she could cook far better before the English burnt her recipe book. Then a helpful local magistrate provided assistance in the shape of a troop of convicts, instantly set to labour by a grateful Emily. "Ups and downs about our enterprise, one day all hope, the next all despair," she wrote.

Emily's view of the Boers was no longer entirely rose-tinted. As in America, hard experience had dented her initial wide-eyed enthusiasm. But in these days the Boers would do anything for Miss Hobhouse. As Margaret discovered, "the Englishwoman who had crossed the seas with mercy at the time of their great distress, wore in their eyes a halo". As in Minnesota, she found it was possible to subsist almost entirely on gifts left by well-wishing locals – one day eggs or butter, the next day figs or melons.

March 13 was celebrated as a red-letter day with the arrival of the school's first six pupils, most of them orphans, whose working day began at 8 am and ended at 6 pm. One month into the project, Emily declared grandly: "In fact, I am not living in Philippolis but in an Idea." As the weeks went by more girls were admitted, with sixteen at work by early April.

A curiously poignant comic scene was recorded on March 14 when Emily entered the house to find Margaret stamping wildly on a copy of the *Manchester Guardian* which she had thrown down on top of an intruding snake. Emily calmly finished off the reptile, not with a dainty parasol this time but with a heavy umbrella inherited from Uncle Arthur. By now she was well prepared for serpents in the South African Eden.

*

Emily and Margaret were both amateurs and it showed in their clumsy first efforts. A supposed expert brought over from England proved useless, and did not long endure Emily's reproachful eye. Unexpected problems arose because South African sheep proved very different animals from those in England. Most available wools had a short staple which made a fine-drawn thread difficult to achieve, while the yarn tended to be thick and heavy. Then the red dust and grass seeds blown in from the veld stuck stubbornly to the fleeces and the first of the home-made dyes faded quickly. The fluctuating extremes of dryness and moisture brought a host of difficulties.

But determination paid off. The girls took to the work and in a remarkably short time Margaret was writing home that Emily felt confident of success, "thanks partly to her own energy, thoroughness and resourcefulness, and to her powers of leadership". As the Philippolis products reached acceptable quality, Emily judged the time right to open a second school in the Transvaal.

Packing a sample bale to show to Smuts, she set off for Pretoria but found property prices there prohibitively high. She had almost lost heart when a clergyman suddenly appeared and offered space in an orphanage he had established at Langlaagte, a village fast being swallowed by Johannesburg. A respected pastor of the Dutch Reformed Church, Abraham Kriel had rescued several orphan girls from the concentration camps, and these he offered as the first pupils. Despite the premises being cramped and spartan, a new workroom was set up in a corrugated iron shed with a mud floor, where Emily and her helpers were to endure plagues of flies from neighbouring pigsties. Rats would scuttle eerily over the roof at night. But in October came a morale-boosting visit from President Steyn, who despite his poor health insisted on making the journey to see the new project for himself.

It was while Emily was staying with the Smuts family at Pretoria, on May 2, that a cable arrived with news of Lady Hobhouse's death.

*

Earlier the same day Emily had sat down at her writing-desk to book her passage to England. She had promised her aunt to be home before June, she told Mrs Steyn, adding plaintively that no one had written to tell her that the old lady's condition was serious, while Lady Hobhouse's own letters had made light of her deterioration.

In Emily's later words, the death left "a blank nothing could fill". The indefatigable campaigner was once more her private and vulnerable self, faced with a sudden chilling realisation: "I was absolutely alone for the remainder of my life". To the end of her days Emily would insist that Aunt Mary had supported her decision to return to South Africa, though the repeated assertion had a defensive ring. "Whatever might happen, I was to remember she would rather think of me as useful in Philippolis than present at her bedside," was how Emily would express the dilemma twenty years later.

The fact remains that on February 23, a matter of days after Emily's arrival at Cape Town, Lady Hobhouse had called her solicitor to Bruton Street and changed her will. Under a new codicil witnessed by her cook and butler, existing bequests to four other nieces were increased to £2,500 apiece while Emily was left just £200 – the same sum bequeathed to the Hobhouses' Indian friend, Cornelia Sorabji. Nor was Emily to share in the contents of her aunt's wardrobe or jewel-box, these being split between other nieces.

Though Uncle Arthur had left Emily the substantial sum of £4,720 to be paid on Mary's death, it must have come as a blow to receive so little from her "almost mother" at the same as her monthly allowance was ended. It seems reasonable to speculate that, had she decided her first duty was to stay at Bruton Street, a much larger share might have come her way from Lady Hobhouse's personal estate of over £26,000. It might be argued that in favouring her blood family over her husband's kin, Aunt Mary was following custom, but on the other hand Uncle Arthur's settlements on Emily and her sisters were actually less generous than one he made on a niece on his wife's side. As it was, the loss of financial support, coupled with the severance of the former annual allowance of £40 granted under Lord Hobhouse's will, dashed Emily's hopes of a comfortable old age and dictated a radical change to her plans.

Without breaking into her capital, she felt it was impossible to underwrite the spinning school enterprise for more than three years. To Emily's way of thinking, there was only one answer to that – she would just have to work harder to accomplish her aims inside that time. The great ambition, to have flourishing home industries ready to hand over to self-governing states in the Transvaal and Orange River Colony, was not to be abandoned.

By forcing the pace, Emily stored up future troubles. The work she set herself was simply beyond her strength, as she would be obliged to admit years later when it became clear that the exhaustion brought on by unaccustomed physical labour at high altitude had damaged her heart to the point of permanent disability.

*

Among brighter developments around this time was the arrival from England of a trained teacher of spinning, a Miss Picard, whose practised eye instantly detected where Emily and Margaret had been going wrong. She was appointed head teacher at Philippolis. And an appeal by Emily for spinning wheels to meet the expanding needs of the schools brought a ship-load from well-wishers throughout Europe, especially in Switzerland, Germany, and France – many of the gifts proving to be heirlooms of magnificent workmanship.

At the end of the year Margaret Clark went on extended leave to England, her own health injured by her labours. It was uncertain whether she would ever return. The loss of her great friend and helper left Emily desolate, and at the approach of Christmas, unable to face the pigsty smells of Langlaagte alone, she took a decision which, in its sheer perversity, foreshadowed a kind of behaviour that would exasperate all who cared for her in the years to come, and to a present-day psychologist might suggest a tendency to self-harm. In a country where countless friends and admirers would have fallen over themselves to invite her to stay, she resolved to spend the festive season in a tent on nearby farmland, "alone with Black Joanna". Her reason for doing so was never made clear. The inevitable chapter of accidents meant the ordered tent did not arrive in time, and Emily and her servant ended up celebrating the holiday in a borrowed garden summerhouse open to the four winds, with corned beef and rice for their Christmas dinner.

A stand-in for the absent Margaret was found in Marion Rowntree, a member of the wealthy Quaker family headed by Emily's friend Joshua. A Cambridge contemporary of Margaret's – like her, she arrived in South Africa at the age of twenty-seven – the robust, down-to-earth Marion took over at Philippolis early in 1906 and quickly won golden opinions among the local Boers by bicycling out to their farms and conversing in German with a strong Yorkshire accent.

A tower of strength in the schools, Marion proved less of a starry-eyed devotee than Margaret. Writing home to England after several months of close observation of Emily, Marion commented appreciatively on her zeal for work and masterly attention to detail, and remarked pityingly of how the rough work of the schools left ugly bruises on her sensitive skin. But "personal love" for Emily was a different matter.

"I love her character at a distance as it were," she wrote, "and agree with her in all things that matter, but in the things that don't matter – the little everyday ways you like your bread buttered – that seem to me to call for love or aversion, and somehow our instincts about the punctilious are different." All the same, admitted Marion, "her character and unfailing range is a study more absorbing every day".

Between Emily and the practical, unromantic Yorkshirewoman there could be nothing like the intense relationship she shared with Margaret Clark. Certainly the new helper was never complimented on possessing what the Germans call *Schone Seele* – beautiful soul – that Emily said she saw shining out of Margaret's face. And ever wistful for love, Emily was shocked when Marion spoke in complacent terms of her fiancé, a York solicitor. On being asked the colour of his hair, she said offhandedly that she could not remember.

Emily had not entirely abandoned her own dreams of finding a partner and

Jaap de Villiers, briefly known to Emily as "His Majesty", the eligible bachelor whose visits set tongues wagging.

perhaps even of becoming a mother. Though now forty-five, while at Langlaagte she formed a romantic attachment with a much younger man, a well-connected Johannesburg lawyer called Jaap de Villiers. In letters to intimate friends she went through a phase of referring to De Villiers coyly as H.M. – for His Majesty – and local gossips observed how the eligible bachelor's regular horseback visits to the spinning school alternated with dinners for two at his fine residence in the city suburbs. Emily must have pondered that women tended to marry late into her own family and still produce children – Uncle Edmund the bishop, for instance, had chosen as his bride the thirty-nine-year old Mary Brodrick, who bore two live children before tragically dying in childbirth at forty-five; and Emily's own mother was almost forty-four when she had Leonard.

Only the previous year, in terms that would have scandalised many a feminist then as now, Emily had confided to Isie Smuts that she only threw herself into public affairs – "Chinese labour and the rise and fall of governments and parties and the well-being of colonies" and suchlike – to fill the blank caused by the absence of a home and children. "I deem the rearing of one baby far more important and infinitely more interesting and satisfying than all those other things piled together," she wrote, and roundly declared that domesticity and babies were "the greatest subjects".

But whatever hopes she may have entertained fizzled out within months, and subsequent references to young De Villiers were couched in less than flattering terms. A year later he married a fashionable twenty-year-old beauty dismissed by Emily's friends as a ninny. "I think the standard of masculinity is low at present," she remarked stiffly not long afterwards. "So many girls are telling me there are no men they meet worth marrying." In the same vein, having inspected Marion's choice of partner following their marriage, Emily would remark to Smuts: "Somehow the husbands of one's friends *are* disappointing".

If the relationship with Jaap de Villiers deserved the name romance, it was her last. After this episode she seemed to accept that she was fated, in the words of Marion Rowntree, to be "loved at a distance"; in future she would have to make do with Leonard's boy, Oliver, as an "almost son". But the extinction of this last faint hope of marriage, so soon after the loss of Margaret Clark, brought on one of the worst spells of depression in Emily's life. Nothing could lift her spirits. Some of the blackest passages to be found in her letters date from the end of 1905 to early 1906 and conjure a picture of a woman trapped in never-ending brooding over life's losses and defeats. Writing to her brother she said bluntly that she did not wish to live any longer, and Margaret too had her share of Emily's dismal musings.

"With no interest in the present and no hope for the future," she wrote, "I find thoughts turn backward very much during the solitude and I again live through the long succession of sorrows that have gone to make up the story of my days. I can honestly say that not one single day of it would I care to have again."

*

But at least she could console herself with a home-life free of the noisome stenches of Langlaagte. She had finally decided to press ahead with the long-discussed project to build herself a cottage, choosing a plot in the Johannesburg suburb of Bellevue. However, it was to be a temporary refuge and investment for the future rather than the retirement home she had talked about with Smuts. From Bellevue she could travel into the school just three times a week and leave the day-to-day business to assistants in preparation for what she called "a gradual withdrawal of my own personality" and an eventual return to England. That at any rate was the original plan.

True to form, Emily built her house nearly six thousand feet above sea-level where the thin air was guaranteed to worsen the strain on her heart, and where she soon became "a martyr to nose-bleeding". In self-dramatising mood she called her new home Mara, meaning bitterness – presumably having in mind the passage in the Book of Ruth where Naomi says, "Call me Mara, for the Almighty has dealt bitterly with me", or possibly the bitter waters of Marah in Exodus.

Despite the lugubrious choice of name and the long-term effect on her health, Mara was to prove one of the few sound investments of Emily's life. The plot with its glorious views of the Magaliesburg range was purchased with the small legacy from Aunt Mary while the building work was paid for with £500 of her savings and a loan of the same sum. By the time she left South Africa, booming Johannesburg had seen property values rocket and in future years of impoverishment Emily would increasingly depend on the rent that Mara brought in.

The Langlaagte experiment did not end well. After five months of observing the neighbouring orphanage at close quarters, Emily decided the time had come to hand Pastor Kriel a memorandum pointing out how badly he was running the place. High words ensued, whereon the incensed clergyman withdrew all his orphans from her school.

At first sight here is another example of Emily's high-handedness. A man apparently after her own heart, Kriel had been on commando during the war, had distinguished himself working in the camps, and earned a reputation for acting decisively while others just talked. His orphanage was praised to the skies by the Quaker fact-finding delegation from England headed by Lawrence Richardson. But like Emily he could brook no criticism, and a terrific falling-out was always on the cards. Richardson, a great admirer of Kriel, referred in his South African journal to "an intelligent Boer source" who told him Emily was a credulous woman who judged too much by English standards, and it is very likely that the pastor was his informant.

Taken aback by Kriel's explosion, Emily complained bitterly of not being appreciated and declared she should linger no more in his "very dirty and depressing village" once the agreed year's lease was up. On the advice of Smuts she began a search for new premises in Johannesburg and lighted upon much superior accommodation within a stone's-throw of Mara. Invigorated by a fortnight's rest at the Steyns' farmstead, she successfully removed the school and the remaining pupils from Kriel's baleful sight. The new workplace suffered endless invasions by armies of mice, but these were an improvement on Langlaagte's rats and flies.

Despite all the setbacks, the fame of the spinning schools continued to spread. An exhibition of products at Johannesburg in April 1906 offered for sale not only bales of cloth but brightly coloured items such as rugs, tapestries and blankets. Thereafter the successes multiplied. A great discovery was a Danish lady living near Langlaagte who turned out to be an expert on tapestry, while a new arrival from England, a professional weaver engaged by Margaret Clark, oversaw improvements to the dyeing techniques.

In May 1908 a great three-day exhibition of work was held at Cape Town. "It was quite a revelation to the Cape people how far on our girls have got, and the artistic work was greatly admired," preened Emily. Demand was so high she felt obliged to turn down a chain of outfitters who wanted to buy the entire stock of tweed, rather than disappoint the eager crowds packing into the hall. Members of the Cape parliament who bought cloth to be made into suits included the prime minister and the speaker. Yet the triumph was not as complete as she might have wished.

"Miss Hobhouse considered the menfolk very feeble who found it scratchy and uncomfortable," noted Ruth Fry, while Emily herself admitted that her tweed was worn in the Transvaal "as a patriotic duty with a very bad grace". The more stoical customers seemed to regard her garments as the saints did their hair-shirts. The tailor of the Cape's speaker seemed to voice a universal fear rather than hope when he remarked that the Boer tweed would *never* wear out. Smuts too felt constrained to wear the itchy philippolis tweed while privately complaining that it made him feel like an ostrich.

24 "A LITTLE WORM OF DOUBT"

The yearned-for day of the fall of the Conservative government in Britain, to be replaced by the Liberals under Campbell-Bannerman, had come in December, 1905. The Chinese labour controversy helped to undermine the exhausted administration, now led by Lord Salisbury's nephew Arthur Balfour, and internal divisions finally finished it off. Joe Chamberlain, the political giant of the time, waived his claim to the premiership in order to pursue his hobbyhorse of trade protectionism – the very issue that was exercising Leonard Hobhouse on the opposite side of the fence.

Chamberlain's enthusiasms bored the new prime minister, an insouciant, porcelain-collecting aesthete who would cycle to Downing Street wearing pince-nez. Balfour also resisted "Pushful Joe"'s other pet scheme, a formal alliance with the dominant Continental power, Germany. Instead he pressed ahead for a new understanding with France, the *Entente Cordiale*, with all its implications for future generations. Perhaps as the crowning achievement of his almost forgotten premiership, Balfour also began a radical overhaul of Britain's armed forces whose faults had been exposed by the Boer commandos.

Emily's delight at the Liberal landslide was marred by its timing. Political triumph for her party, promising self-government for South Africa as prophesised by Lord Kitchener, coincided with the personal losses of Margaret Clark and De Villers. So her greatest depression coincided with the fulfilment of her political ambition – and that too was quickly to prove a disappointment.

As Campbell-Bannerman began to wrestle with the problems of Boer independence and Chinese labour, Emily rushed off a letter of advice to Downing Street, "ten sheets and feminine". Leonard Hobhouse happened to meet the harassed premier soon afterwards, and was told in terms of mild reproach: "I had a letter from your sister the other day." As Leonard recorded, "I could only look my sympathy."

Impatient as ever, Emily expected South African self-government to be granted instantly, and was soon complaining fiercely to her old mentor, Leonard Courtney, over what she saw as the new government's tardiness. In reply the blind sage rebuked her gently. "Things will go better, and are indeed moving towards a better condition in spite of everything and everybody," he wrote. "We may be vexed with delays, we may be irritated by the incompetence of one man and the stupidity of another, but larger causes are at work, and if we have a little patience we shall see the end."

Courtney was right. Within days of taking power Campbell-Bannerman won his cabinet's backing for the defeated Boer states to be returned to self-rule at the earliest date possible, and the policy was made public in the King's speech on February 19. Self-government was granted to the Transvaal before the end of the year and to the Orange Free State a few months later.

One of Campbell-Bannerman's early acts in office was to acknowledge his debt to Leonard Courtney, sending him to the House of Lords as Baron Courtney of Penwith. Emily was gratified by her old ally's return to the political scene, though it is likely she ribbed him unmercifully about becoming a lord; for though she never lost pride in the Hobhouses' exalted connections, her political ideas were becoming ever more radical. Friends who accepted new titles found themselves on the receiving end of unwelcome jibes.

"Chinese slavery" had played a key part in the election. Lord Milner was vilified from platform after platform, with one Liberal candidate employing a party hack to dress up as a Chinese and to rattle about in chains during fiery denunciations of the former high commissioner. Soon afterwards Milner was censured in the House of Commons for authorising summary flogging. A speech by Winston Churchill, now a Liberal MP, was particularly resented by Milner's friends as ungenerous, patronising and tactless bearing in mind Churchill's slavish admiration of the proconsul at the height of his power.

Embittered, Milner went into what seemed at the time a permanent retirement from public life, buying a secluded manor house in Kent and consoling himself with his books, a clutch of lucrative directorships, and the continuing liaison with Lady Edward Cecil. No one, least of all Emily, could have dreamt that a turn of fortune's wheel would one day thrust him back into the innermost circle of power, bringing renewed contact not only with old Boer foes like Smuts and Botha, but with Lord Kitchener and the Hobhouse family.

*

Jan Smuts was in the meantime immersing himself in a remarkably intense correspondence with Margaret Clark. The leathery general and the radiant pacifist, whose first meeting on the Cape Town quayside had been limited to polite chit-chat, found themselves sharing the same boat to England – she returning home to Somerset worn out by the hardships of Emily's spinning school, he on a political mission to remind the Liberal victors of their lavish promises to the Boers when in opposition. Thrown together during the voyage, they had recognised each other as soul-mates. So as Emily was eating her corned beef Christmas dinner with Black Joanna, her two great friends were discovering a mutual love of nature, religious mysticism and "soul analysis". When the ship put in at Las Palmas, the pair spent what Smuts called "one of the most pleasant and beautiful days that I have had in my life" exploring the lush countryside together, even as he was writing home to wife Isie to complain of the unpleasantness of the voyage.

The friendship with Margaret and her family would last the rest of Smuts's life. When in 1909 Margaret married the banker Arthur Gillett, just as Smuts was planning a trip to England, he wrote hoping that Mr Gillett would not be jealous "to see on what terms we are". The intimacy of her friends might have put Emily's nose out of joint, but Smuts need not have worried about Arthur Gillett. The two men came to a close understanding of their own and Margaret took to complaining when letters from Smuts were addressed to her husband instead of herself.

*

Emily Hobhouse's stock among the leading Boers was still sky-high. When Het Volk triumphed in the first South Africa elections held in February 1907, a powerful group headed by Marthinus Steyn decided that the premiership should go to the reluctant Louis Botha. It was Emily, with her unique prestige and moral standing, who was chosen to persuade him to accept. Her account of the mission, written for Mrs Steyn, displays Emily at her most persistent as she buttonholes the agitated general:

"He was very much put about. I had not anticipated such strong opposition. He refused even to consider the idea. Again and again he asseverated: 'I will not be prime minister, Miss Hobhouse; I cannot and I will not.'

"'But General Botha, President Steyn says you must be.'

"'Nothing will induce me, you must not ask me; I would rather go over the border.'

"'But the President says there is no one else... He says you must put personal disinclination aside and you must be premier.'

"'Miss Hobhouse, you must tell the President that he must not ask it; that I cannot and will not.'

"'I can't take him that message; if you think it over you will see there is no one else.'"

The persecuted general retreated, still swearing he would never be prime minister, whereon Emily continued her assault by letter, and soon afterwards Botha bowed to the inevitable. Emily encountered him in the street the day after his acceptance of the premiership had been announced. "Perhaps, knowing his feeling, it was ill taste of me to congratulate him," she told Mrs Steyn. "It was too soon; he could not speak and, breaking down entirely, burst into tears."

*

This was by far the longest of Emily's South African sojourns, lasting from February 1905 to October 1908. It was broken only by a short visit to England in 1906 when she stayed with her brother Leonard at Wimbledon. There followed a flying trip to deliver her personal thanks to the Swiss organisers of the spinning wheel appeal, when despite a warm welcome she felt out-of-sorts and spoke lamely, unable to rise to the occasion. Only much later did it dawn on her that the recurrence of her illness was connected to the high altitude of Switzerland.

During this visit she acquired a dog, a pure-bred St Bernard she called Caro, the same pet name once bestowed on her fiancé Jackson. This creature she took back to Johannesburg. A St Bernard was a rare sight in South Africa – understandably, considering the animal's thick coat and the country's extreme heat – and Caro created a sensation wherever they went. The doting Emily turned down an offer for the dog of £1,000, an enormous sum at that time, and over the next few months lavished on Caro all her frustrated love. At last the desperate depression brought on by the loss of Margaret Clark and De Villiers seemed to have lifted.

Predictably, heartbreak was in store. Writing to Mrs Steyn, she described how

Caro had suddenly caught fever and how she had nursed him without stint day and night, administering beef-tea, eggs or brandy every two hours. On the fifth night she brought a bed into the dog's room but in her exhausted state slept through the time for his beef-tea. "I awoke with a start, feeling something was wrong," she wrote. "Caro had raised his head and was looking at me with reproachful eyes. The effort was too great, and before I could reach him he fell back dead."

A week later she poured out her anguish over "my one friend and close companion" in a letter to Ruth Fry, then treasurer of the London committee supporting the spinning schools. "I should never have believed a dog could be so much to one or fill so big a space in one's heart and life," she wrote. "The house is desolate without him and every room haunted by him. I see him everywhere." She swore she would write nothing more of Caro as nobody else could appreciate what he had been "in my solitary life". Yet she seems never to have questioned her judgment in taking a dog bred for the Alpine snows to a city where winter temperatures approached 30 degrees.

Her friend Olive Schreiner would have commiserated. Olive too had lavished unbounded love on a dog, a fat little fox terrier bitch called Nita, who only months before had gone under the wheels of a cab. Needless to say, Olive's grief scaled more extravagant heights than Emily's. Thereafter, whenever the Cronwright-Schreiners moved house, Nita's coffin would be dug up and taken with them; Olive wrote a will decreeing that, on her death, Nita was to be exhumed again and reburied with her mistress.

*

By the time Emily returned from Europe the promised representative governments of South Africa were in the saddle and arrangements could be made for the home industries to be taken over. No fewer than sixteen spinning or weaving schools had now been established throughout the Transvaal with a further dozen in the old Free State, and a special board was appointed to administer the hefty public subsidies voted to support them.

Emily had always said she would retire from the scene after three years, and she knew she was near the end of her strength. Yet despite profound relief at shedding personal financial responsibility for the schools, a worry since she had been told about Aunt Mary's will, "a little worm of doubt" began to gnaw at her heart. She realised she did not wish quite yet to relinquish the power "to initiate, guide or restrain". As she saw it, the infant industry still cried out for "the fostering care of one who had studied the matter for years and was conversant with every detail". In the event, she could not bring herself to accept that dignified surrender of control envisaged only a few months previously, for that would leave nothing else in her life.

Smuts, now the Transvaal's colonial secretary, tried earnestly to reassure her, but Emily and the board were on collision course. As a sop Emily was given the title of adviser and supposedly kept a position of authority, but the board members had definite ideas about who was now in charge.

By August Emily was talking emotionally of having to resign because the governing body neither sought her advice nor took it when offered. At meetings she felt her remarks were waved aside like buzzing flies, so it was becoming "more and more impossible" to remain. To Kate, now Lady Courtney, she fumed at watching "an incapable but pig-headed board slowly poison my only child". The choice of word is telling. So taken was Emily with this dramatic figure of speech that she would still be tweaking it two years later, telling Smuts how it had broken her heart "to see my only child slowly murdered by ignorant officialdom combined with officious ignorance".

Ruth Fry for one judged the board members to be in the right, believing that Emily in her "over-strained condition" failed to acknowledge their positive qualities or their genuine appreciation of her past efforts. The very fact that Emily had given her all in setting up the schools explained why fresh brains and ideas were now needed, in the view of that uncompromisingly honest Quaker lady. In battles with the board Emily was increasingly isolated, for not even her great lieutenant Margaret Clark could offer the unconditional support she craved. None of her circle seemed fully to grasp Emily's frantic need to fill the void in her life.

Margaret's return to South Africa, after a year-long see-saw of anxiety over whether ill-health would force her to stay in England, registered only as an anti-climax. Emily later admitted that the eagerly-awaited reappearance had scarcely made an impression and blamed the absence of any clear memory of the event on "brain fatigue". Though they would remain friends, the intensity of the earlier relationship had been lost for good. Margaret was now much closer to Smuts, and in future the pair would always temper their mutual declarations of fondness for Emily with wry asides about her contrariness. Neither made any serious effort to dissuade her from returning to England; indeed by this juncture many were clearly relieved to see the back of her. All in all, it was a sad end to a magnificent enterprise.

In a farewell speech in her honour, Smuts the rising statesman was generosity itself, offering thanks for Emily's self-sacrificing labours and calling her part of the history of South Africa. On behalf of admirers he presented the departing heroine with a painting of herself by the Cape artist Hugo Naude. An over-life-sized, soft-focus representation of a tall, slim, elegantly-dressed and ladylike figure, the Naude oil would remain Emily's favourite among her portraits. "Of course, one cannot judge oneself – but it is certainly *like* and is dignified," she told Kate Courtney, while admitting that it might lack a certain force. Her pleasure in this conventional, flattering piece of work was in contrast to her strong dislike of the characterful study dashed off by Van Welie in London five years before, which represents Emily with a beaky nose, heavy-lidded eyes and determined mouth; but then, it is a rare sitter who enjoys the attentions of a warts-and-all painter.[xxvi]

25 "HOLDING ON TILL DEATH"

L ife without a cause was nothing to Emily, who immediately on reaching London threw herself into the campaign for women's suffrage. This was an abiding interest of Emily's rather than a devouring passion, and always took a back-seat to works of practical philanthropy. In Cape Town Olive Schreiner had talked her into addressing a suffragist group and she had chaired a feminist gathering in Pretoria, but these were minor affairs compared with her doings in London. When Emily walked onto the platform at an Albert Hall rally that December, over eleven thousand were there to applaud her.

The British political scene had been in ferment during Emily's absence. The thirty Labour MPs who won seats in the 1906 general election had seemed harbingers of a new age that would secure the vote for women. Just three months earlier, to the disgust of the orthodox suffragist organisations led by Millicent Garrett Fawcett, the Pankhursts had committed their rival suffragette movement to open militancy.

Emily Hobhouse's title of Most Hated Woman in England had now passed to Mrs Emmeline Pankhurst, whose daughter Christabel appeared at Bow Street police court in 1908 on a charge of inciting a mob to invade the House of Commons. Inevitably, Mrs Fawcett loudly deplored the Pankhursts' popularity among "the lowest classes of London roughs and the dangerous hordes of unemployed". But the genie was out of the bottle and not even Mrs Fawcett herself could push it back. The suffragettes would go on to wage an increasingly bitter campaign of arson, street protests and hunger-strikes right up to the outbreak of the Great War.

As a pacifist Emily never identified herself with violent protest, but the women's movement as a whole she hailed as glorious. The male-dominated political scene she declared odious, sealing her disillusion with the Liberal government. The unexpected death of Henry Campbell-Bannerman some months before had handed the premiership to Herbert Asquith, who as a supporter of the South African war and opponent of votes for women was no friend of Emily's. In any case, she announced in one of her letters to Smuts, she no longer called herself a Liberal as the scales had fallen from her eyes on reading *Justice and Liberty* by the Cambridge don Lowes Dickinson. "It has bowled over my remaining difficulties," she enthused, "and made me a complete Socialist" – a curiously late declaration of faith for one who had helped John Burns win Battersea at the Khaki Election. Her letter was the first of many futile efforts to convert South Africa's foremost imperialist to her new creed.

These letters to Smuts – "so vibrant with feeling, intelligence and wit", in the words of Sir Keith Hancock, the foremost authority on the statesman – provide by far the best evocation of this relatively unrecorded period of Emily's life. At intervals they recall the tone of joyous optimism that had enlivened her early American correspondence. Though these were intensely unhappy years for Emily, in the Smuts correspondence the old spirit and verve flash out again and again. To open her heart to Oom Jannie must have been one of the few pleasures left during times that brought so many disappointments and so much physical pain.

Settling down to write, Emily might be in a mood to scold, flirt, reproach, or moralise. Fascinating details of her domestic affairs alternate with unsolicited opinions on great matters of state, and wails of indignation over the wicked home industries board give way to exhortations to read her latest discoveries in poetry or fiction. Punctuation and spelling are forgotten as she teases, lectures, and cajoles, flitting breathlessly from one enthusiasm to the next in a shower of capital letters, underlinings and exclamation marks. Tedious harangues are interwoven with delightful jokes, high politics, money troubles, health scares, flights of fancy, bugbears.

Nearly all of Smuts's letters to Emily have been lost – a strange fact, given how industriously she squirreled away trunk after trunk of papers throughout her life – but hers to him are preserved in the Smuts archives, offering a vivid picture of what Hancock called "their pathetic and glorious friendship". Most begin with the familiar "Dear Oom Jannie", though a variation of address will often signal her preoccupation of the moment. It might be a peremptory "Oom!" to launch an attack on some political act of his of which she disapproves; or "Dear, dear Oom Jannie" as a lead-up to asking a favour; or "My dear generous but ever naughty Oom Jannie" when she discovers that Smuts has secretly paid out for work on her Bellevue cottage, now rented out to boost her dwindling private funds. Even when lost for words, Emily contrives to express herself with force and charm: "I can't write much for I feel so strongly, but oh!"

One typical outburst when we seem to catch Emily's speaking voice is over Smuts's purchase of a motor car. Urging him to return to the healthier exercise of the saddle, she writes: "Motors are so modern and I think on the whole degenerating physically and mentally. In our crowded Europe motorists become quite inhuman, and to the poor of all classes they are a pest of noise, dirt, danger and smell. Don't be spoilt, mind and body, by a mere motor, a horrid monster of tubes and oil."[xxvii]

Above all, Emily used her letters to denounce the new South African regime's policies and appointments, and with striking frequency takes Smuts to task over his countrymen's treatment of blacks. She complains of the unhealthy conditions faced by "the poor Kaffirs" in the mines and urges the case of Harriette Colenso, spinster daughter of the controversial Cornish bishop, and like him a passionate champion of the Zulus. Emily asks Smuts to aid Harriette's campaign to free a son of Cetshwayo, the warrior king, imprisoned for high treason.[xxviii]

She also sides firmly with Gandhi's Indians, again on strike over grievances against Smuts's government. Comparing Gandhi's struggle in South Africa with Mrs Pankhurst's in Britain, Emily declares that governments cannot prevail against "a great moral and spiritual upheaval", underplaying the suffragette leader's relish for the battlefield. On a personal note, she compares her present unsatisfactory servants with the excellent "boys" she employed in South Africa.

Without a trace of irony she writes that "we the *people*, we *democrats*" should refuse to leave power in the hands of autocrats like Smuts. "You see," she says elsewhere, "I am always in opposition to you now, and take the line you used to take in the good old days when Milner and Crown Colony Government reigned." She gaily compares herself to the Irishman who defined his politics as being "always agin the government", and to underscore the point parades her Cornishness: "No government pleases me, for I am a Celt."

Ever the pacifist, she ridicules Smuts for fearing the Kaiser's ambitions to extend his African empire – "I suppose most of your time will be spent riding up and down that border in the Kalahari pretending to study locusts' nests but in reality thinking how to guard against German invasion" – and demands that all South Africa's military spending be banned henceforth and the money devoted to industries and arts. Oom Jannie would best defend his country by not defending it, she declared, reminding him how the Boers without a standing army had withstood the British for nearly three years.

Smuts bore the attacks with good grace. Neither of them allowed the yawning gulf between their political beliefs to disturb the bedrock of friendship, though Smuts now wisely refrained from expressing his political views too openly. Who knew when his excitable friend might take it into her head to broadcast them to the world?

*

Most of the last few years before the First World War were lived abroad. Emily was now homeless in England, as on Aunt Mary's death the Bruton Street property had gone to her cousin Henry Hobhouse of Hadspen, along with the bulk of Uncle Arthur's fortune. The Christmas of 1908 was spent miserably at Wimbledon contending with her brother Leonard's pipe smoke, and Emily soon found herself on the move again, parcelled out her time between friends' houses and lodgings up and down the land. The Courtneys urged her to find a permanent place near to them in Chelsea – Lord Courtney wanted her help with his latest hobbyhorse, proportional representation – but the conviction took root that England could never truly be her home again.

Nor could she pretend that things remained unchanged *vis-a-vis* the friends who had laboured alongside her in the spinning schools. Margaret Clark, whose intense relationship with Emily had cooled since the shipboard soul-mating with Smuts, had recently acquired her banker fiancé; Marion Rowntree had never been so close, and in any case was now married with a baby. Emily had already met and pronounced her disappointment in Marion's husband; now Margaret's intended likewise struck her as just another amiable mediocrity rather than the god she had been led to expect. So far as she herself had an object of affection, it remained Leonard's good-looking son Oliver, now sixteen. This nephew, who in time came to be Emily's "almost son" and the main beneficiary of her will, was to cause Emily much grief in later years, but in that he was no different to anyone else she loved.

Past disappointments and despair over the future came crowding in during that first Christmas back in England when she wrote to Smuts thanking him for the gift of a book of fairy-tales. Reading it made her feel young again, she said, taking her out of "horrid practical life" and into those realms of spirit and fancy "where indeed my reallest self always abides".

*

Early in the New Year, 1909, Emily travelled to Italy with Ruth Fry. Ostensibly for further researches into lace manufacture, the trip had a more immediate aim. Emily had at last made up her mind to settle abroad, and she had cherished the Italian climate and people since the family holidays of her distant girlhood. Moreover, Italy was cheap, and the state of her funds presented a compelling reason for leaving England.

By this time Emily was reduced to a physical wreck, worn out by the incessant demands on her strength. Apart from the long-standing heart complaint she had been diagnosed as suffering from arteriosclerosis, uraemia, and more recently rheumatoid arthritis. This last condition, which she believed to have its origin in a childhood fall, was to add crippling back pain to her woes for the rest of her life.

Ruth Fry was a pitying observer as Emily moved painfully from place to place in search of a home. Being the woman she was, Emily refused to acknowledge that her disabilities placed any limitation on her, and on finally deciding to settle in Rome chose a flat at the top of ninety-six steps. Every time she went out she had to be carried up and down the steps by a man hired for the purpose; but as she liked to say, her view of the Forum was really quite charming. Ruth Fry realised her old friend was unfit for the cares of everyday life. Emily was hopelessly inconsistent at the best of times, and increased physical suffering had so warped her judgment that she rushed into schemes even more thoughtlessly than usual, only to find herself thoroughly embarrassed or uncomfortable, and then forced to make fresh arrangements after much expenditure of time, trouble and money. It piled pathos upon pathos, wrote Ruth, to reflect on "the very many discomforts and difficulties she might have been spared, had she had the knack of seeing what house or what plans would really best suit her needs". She badly needed someone to look after her, but she had no one.

To her correspondents Emily told contradictory stories. To Smuts in these early Roman days she boasted of an exciting social whirl, liberally sprinkling her letters with the names of titled ladies who invited her to their palazzos and of charming and sophisticated gentlemen like the professor who read Dante to her. Oddly enough, it was to Smuts's wife Isie, still seething over the release of the infamous letter to *The Times*, that her first open play for sympathy was directed. "The isolation is terrible," wrote Emily, "and I don't quite see yet how I shall bear it. When days pass together without my speaking to anyone I feel the solitude almost driving me mad, and I am not strong enough to do much reading or writing." It was a terrible thing to be a solitary invalid woman, she said, "but there are thousands of us in the world and it is a mere matter of holding on till Death".

Before long she found the heat and dust of Rome as insupportable as the cold and fog of London. She would lie awake all night struggling for breath and worrying about money. With costs mounting for the man to carry her up and down the steps and with a cab needed to undertake even the shortest journey, Emily was forced to ration herself to one outing a week, and for the rest of the time would lie on her sofa, a prey to anxiety and idle grief.

Even so, she refused to admit her most obvious mistakes. Desperately inconvenient as it was, the flat near the Forum would be kept on for two years before she could be persuaded to change quarters. Even then, one unsuitable home was exchanged for another, then another, and one unsatisfactory maid for the next – for whatever her circumstances, Emily was rarely without a personal servant. "Undoubtedly her slender income was strained to the utmost to keep up with her demands on it," Ruth Fry would write in her memoir, reflecting sorrowfully that a woman with a genius for helping others had no facility for managing her own life.

There were occasional visits from friends and relations, best of all from favourite nephew Oliver and her cousin Eleanor Hobhouse of the Hadspen branch. Eleanor, warm-hearted and adventurous, was a girl after Emily's heart, and was destined to spend much of her life in relief work for sick and starving children. There was even a visit from Emily's once-close sister, the ever-impecunious Maud Hebblethwaite. Nor was there a shortage of reverential South African visitors to toil up the ninety-six steps to the door of the great Miss Hobhouse, each offering a temporary distraction from her lonely troubles.

Late in 1909 she felt well enough for a trip to London. Once again she tried to immerse herself in the suffrage movement but in the English weather "neither heart nor limbs would work". One of her doctors insisted that she drop her vegetarian diet, return to the warmth of Italy, and take no baths until spring. In the meantime she had gone to the futile expense of renting and furnishing a house in Westminster, where she was visited several times by one of her old English friends from South Africa. "She is just very ill and very lonely and no wonder," wrote Alice Greene. "She has broken down her health for the sake of others and I doubt whether there is one person both able and willing to help." Alice saw Emily for the last time on a freezing cold day on the eve of her return to Rome when, "stiff and lame with pain", she spoke wistfully of Cornwall and reminisced about her ancestors, among them a Trelawny who fought at Agincourt. "Miss Hobhouse herself is a splendid woman that England cannot afford to lose," lamented Alice.

By March the following year Emily's heart was giving serious trouble and she no longer attempted to disguise her deterioration. One attack was of such severity that she thought death a certainty. "During the choking spasms my thought was of my many friends in various parts," she wrote later, "and my one wish to have bidden them a farewell." When her Roman doctor insisted that her active life must cease, she told Smuts that her "poor stupid heart" was not diseased but worn out: "I think South Africa would be found stamped on it for South Africa wore it out. Nevertheless one often loves the very thing that kills."

In June 1910 she remained ill and suffering on her invalid's sofa and could only get about by being pushed in a bath chair. Nine months later she wrote of having to abandon even her rare efforts at walking, but said that the approach of spring helped her cling to hopes of a return to health.

Money troubles resurfaced early in the summer of 1911 after Smuts, now acting as Emily's trustee, invested £2,000 of her savings. "You must not think," she wrote, "that I doubt your kindness or that I think my *capital* insecure. I know that is safe. What worries me is when my income is seriously curtailed by the money lying idle. Then I get really frightened, because I am too weak to earn my living in any way, as once I could cheerfully have done."

Smuts offered an immediate loan but it was not until September, when Emily faced an expensive move to Florence for new medical treatment, that she swallowed her pride and took his money. Women, she remarked, were always being accused of changing their minds, but in this case the *circumstances* had changed rather than the woman. "I have found that in spite of every care the expenses of this illness and having to live in Florence will run me very near, too near, the edge of my income," she wrote. But she insisted on strict conditions before accepting the needed £50. As protection for Oom Jannie's heirs, the loan had to be subject to the full interest rate charged by the Transvaal banks, and its repayment written into her will in the event of her sudden death.

Emily called the loan "a most brotherly offer" on Smuts's part, but one that she could not ask of her real brother, who remained absorbed in his own concerns. And she went on: "With some measure of health next year, I have plans to make money *in my way*, which is by saving it. I could probably let my Roman flat for a good sum and go myself to live in a place I hear of which is very cheap, providing I am strong enough. Also next year if my brain works again I can earn something by writing."

Jan Smuts must have shaken his head in sorrow as he read this, knowing all such schemes were doomed to failure. He at once sent his personal cheque for £100 as a gift and declined to cash the cheque that Emily posted back during a temporary improvement in her finances.

The move to Florence was momentous. Emily had heard exciting tales of a Dr Carloni there, the inventor of a novel treatment for heart patients. As explained to Smuts in elaborate detail, this involved the use of a special electric inhaling machine which worked by pumping air into a large cylinder – "the compressed air passes through the iodine or other liquid necessary in a bottle and boils it," Emily wrote, "and the fumes from this pass into a tube the end of which, terminating in a glass mask, the patient holds over mouth and nose."

When Smuts wrote back dismissing Carloni as an obvious quack, Emily mounted an indignant defence. The doctor had thrown up a brilliant appointment in the Italian navy after falling in love and being refused permission to marry, she replied, adding that "the girl was American but he won her and now they live in Florence and have three little children". With her weakness for a romantic story, she seemed bemused that everyone else was not instantly convinced of the man's greatness.

But Emily had her triumph. After two months inhaling Dr Carloni's fumes she was able to write from the Florence clinic crowing that her heart had now reduced to half its former size. "Iodine," she lectured, "is a specific for rendering arteries elastic and for liquefying viscous blood." Apart from the fumes, carbolic acid baths were doing her good, and soon she could boast of having at least the *appearance* of radiant health, her cheeks "as rosy as a Dutch doll's". With a little help, she was now walking a third of a mile in forty minutes.

By this time her faith in Carloni knew no bounds. "He is no quack," she insisted, "but a highly diploma-d doctor, very up-to-date, though deeply imbued also with the knowledge of the very learned herb-loving doctors of the fifteenth and sixteenth centuries." And not only did the great man excel at hearts and lungs and diabetes, but he could also cure asthma like magic: "That is why I *long* to see Olive Schreiner under him, *and* he is far cheaper than English doctors are."[xxix]

While in Florence, Emily haunted the picture galleries of the Pitti. To nephew Oliver, now an undergraduate at Oxford, she wrote that her favourite Botticelli in the

A pencil sketch of Emily dated 1912, the year she submitted herself to the "electric inhaling machine" of a controversial Italian doctor.

palace was a painting of Minerva, "the most beautiful female figure in the world". If this seems an odd and even embarrassing observation for a fifty-one year old maiden aunt to address to a young man, the choice of subject matter is a significant one.

Botticelli's *Minerva* is nowadays displayed alongside other Medici treasures in the Uffizi Gallery. It is a striking and mysterious painting of the goddess of war seizing a centaur by the hair, while clasping a battleaxe in her other hand. Painted as a companion piece to the more celebrated *Primavera*, it is an allegory of the triumph of female chastity over male brutishness. According to James Hall's *Dictionary of Subjects and Symbols in Art*, the centaur, half-man and half-beast, personifies man's violent lower nature, in contrast with the higher wisdom symbolised by Minerva. Though first appearing as a warlike figure, Minerva evolved by degrees into "the patroness of many household crafts, especially spinning and weaving", notes Hall, while her special attribute changed from a spear to an olive branch.[xxx]

Emily's ideal of female beauty is suggestive. This Minerva does not belong among the melting, doe-eyed Botticelli beauties typified by the Three Graces of the *Primavera* or the shell-borne nude of the *Birth of Venus*, but possesses an altogether firmer, fuller figure. Instead of the golden hair of the average Botticelli nymph or goddess, she has long wavy tresses of auburn. The face is handsome rather than pretty, with a larger nose and heavier eyelids than usual, and the expression is uncompromisingly stern. It does not seem fanciful to detect a resemblance with Emily in her prime; it is also worth remarking that, to one of her cast of mind, physical beauty cannot escape a moral or political

207

dimension.

Emily's strict regime under Dr Carloni made her conscious of her own shapeliness, prompting the remark that her figure was becoming very elegant thanks to the diet; to regain her former trimness was some consolation to set against the prospect of living the rest of her life subsisting on the tiny portions of food prescribed by Carloni and entirely without wine, tea or coffee. Even so, the conviction that the good doctor's treatment had saved her life did not prevent her from spurning his advice to give up the Roman flat of ninety-six steps, and she returned after five months of the iodine cure, saying the Florentine winter was too cold for her.

And so the pattern was set. She had uprooted herself too many times to settle anywhere. In England she fretted for Italy, in Italy for England; in both she pined for South Africa, despite her one lengthy sojourn there having ended in bitter recriminations. By the summer of 1912 she was temporarily back in London, and on hearing she had been taken very ill there Olive Schreiner sent a note of commiseration.

"Dear," she wrote, "I know what this long stretch of unbroken physical suffering is – no one knows or can understand who has not lived through and is not living through it. When I think of you so beautiful and strong and stately as I first saw you in Cape Town, and then even as you were when you spent that time at De Aar with me, my heart aches…

"And oh, dear, remember all you did in the cause of justice and mercy in South Africa. You have not lived for nothing. You were the only one who really succeeded in saving thousands from just that terrible physical suffering which has you now in its grasp. Let that thought comfort you in all your terrible pain and weakness, dear brave woman."

But Emily's life was still far from over. She would return to South Africa one more time. Earlier visits had ended in defeats which were moral victories, and the last one would be no different. In true Emily Hobhouse style, it would be a glorious, inspirational failure.

26 "BURY UNFORGIVENESS AND BITTERNESS"

During her frequent stays at the Steyn family farm, Emily heard the President speak of his cherished scheme to raise a national monument in honour of the concentration camp dead. Progress since then had been painfully slow, but in March 1913 – almost eleven years after the end of the Boer War – she received a letter confirming that a great cenotaph was at last being built on a site south of Bloemfontein. Emily, an Englishwoman, was asked to perform the unveiling ceremony. The invitation had her at sixes and sevens, and she dashed off a letter to Smuts.

Even as she declared her wish to consult him, she explained that she used the word consult in a feminine way, meaning she wanted his advice without binding herself to follow it. Smuts must have smiled as he read this, for when had she ever done otherwise?

There was danger in travelling to South Africa in her poor state of health, but Emily's main anxiety was whether the planned ceremony of dedication would be truly national or a partisan affair. Might it revive animosities between Boer and Briton? Did General Botha intend to be present, and if so would he appear in his capacity as premier or as a private citizen? She had heard of bitter divisions arising between the leaders of the erstwhile republics and demanded that Oom Jannie take on the role of peacemaker. "To give this function its really solemn and representative character *all* must sink their differences, personal or political, that day, and meet to do honour to the dead heroines," she wrote.

Smuts did as she asked. Reassured that Botha and Steyn would share the platform with her, Emily excitedly began her preparations for what she guessed must be her last time in South Africa. The honour of unveiling the monument had given her a new lease of life. Her health took a decided turn for the better, and she wrote to her intimate Cape friend Mrs Murray that for the first time in four years she felt full of vitality instead of at death's door.

The upbeat mood survived a negative letter from another old friend whose opinion Emily had canvassed. Olive Schreiner warned of an unpleasant atmosphere in South Africa since Emily was last there and worried in case the Boers had forgotten the great debt they owed her. Emily, characteristically ignoring unwelcome advice, decided that Olive's outlook had been soured by her state of health and the lonely life she led. In any case, she told Mrs Murray, "I do not think that a cold, callous, forgetful or even adverse attitude to those who stood by them in trouble either will or ought to influence my present decision". Emily believed that unveiling the monument was her "Sacred Duty with a big D", providing only her health held out.

The visit was already mapped out in her head. The day chosen for the ceremony was December 16, that date of great resonance for every Boer. As the anniversary of the Voortrekkers' victory over the Zulu leader Dingaan, it had been selected for the state funeral of Paul Kruger nine years before. Emily planned to stop off in England, take ship in October, stay a month with friends at the Cape and a week or two with the Steyns before performing the ceremony, then escape from South Africa before the summer heat became too trying. She turned down Smuts's wistful suggestion that Margaret Gillett be asked to accompany her.

The saga of the memorial had begun two years earlier, in the summer of 1911, when the Dutch-born sculptor Anton van Wouw was commissioned to create a group of figures at the base of a 120-foot sandstone obelisk, and he immediately announced his intention to travel to Rome to ask Emily's advice. She wrote back agreeing to help all she could, but Van Wouw soon had cause to regret his initiative. Emily's own description of their meetings, garnered from waspish letters to Mrs Steyn and Smuts, offers a cameo of the strained relations that frequently develop between artist and patron, the role she quickly appropriated. Reading the correspondence, it is difficult to keep in mind that Van Wouw was no tyro but an established sculptor aged forty-three who had already won loud acclaim. His was the statue of President Kruger, then as now one of the sights of Pretoria; his the famous Voortrekker monument; his also the group of statues controversially carried off from South Africa by Lord Kitchener as personal trophies.[xxxi]

In January 1912 Van Wouw toiled up the steps to the flat near the Forum for the first time and presented a clay model for Emily's approval. The interview was not a comfortable one. "I did not like it and had to tell him so," she informed Mrs Steyn. The Dutchman's abilities were compared unfavourably with those of Italian sculptors she knew, whom she described as better able to express their ideas and more skilled in composition.

With her own idea of what the monument should look like, Emily had no intention of letting any notion of Van Wouw's get in the way. What she had firmly in mind as the focal point was a group of figures based on the unforgettable spectacle she had encountered at Springfontein station at the height of the war – the mute and motionless mother "beyond all tears" sitting with her dying daughter in her lap, while a companion cried on heaven as witness. As inspiration for the mother and child, Emily directed Van Wouw to St Peter's to study Michelangelo's *Pieta*; she may not have been able to resist pointing out that Michelangelo had completed his masterpiece when half Van Wouw's age.

"It is a great subject – a grand opportunity – and since he has appealed to me for help I shall do my utmost to keep him up to the pitch and not let him be satisfied too easily," she wrote to Smuts, adding cuttingly: "Of course he may not have *greatness* in him."

One month later, Emily was still treating the sculptor like a novice, reporting that he was "finding the full difficulty of his task". Having asked her to visit his studio to view his second effort in the clay, a model three feet high, Van Wouw must have listened crestfallen as she pronounced it *some* improvement on the first but insisted it was "very far from what it should be and must be". Nor was his self-esteem improved by the suggestion that he should ask one of her Italian sculptor friends for "professional hints".

Emily returned to the studio and found the group of figures somewhat improved, though she continued to remark critically on the lack of realism in both the mother – "still far from satisfactory" – and the child who appeared neither sick nor dead. She directed Van Wouw to the local hospital to acquaint himself with one or two real corpses.

A month later Emily had more or less reconciled herself to the monument being no more than a provincial effort. In any case, she wrote to Smuts, the sculpture could not possibly be finished and transported to Bloemfontein in time for the proposed December unveiling in December 1913 – "Van Wouw told me the central group was to leave Rome before the end of April, but it is still being cast at the foundry and hardly likely to get off before June" – while the bas-relief panels intended for the monument's base had failed to progress beyond the clay stage.

What the job required was "real artistic genius", she lamented, and poor Van Wouw did not possess it. He was "an inferior though painstaking artist and quite devoid of genius". She went on grumbling that the South Africans had awarded the commission in too much of a hurry and wanted it on the cheap; as she later remarked, her own choice for the job would have been Rodin. But she was wrong in declaring that Van Wouw would miss his deadline.

*

Preparations for leaving Rome were already well advanced before Emily informed Smuts of her formal acceptance of Steyn's invitation to unveil the monument, adding that in view of the sorry state of her finances she was forced to accept the Bloemfontein committee's offer to pay travel expenses to South Africa for herself and her maidservant. After a stay in London and the inevitable chopping and changing of her plans, she boarded the *Garth Castle* at Southampton on September 13 to endure what turned out to be yet another "hateful" voyage.

Once in Cape Town she rested with friends. Doctors insisted that the translation to the high altitude of Bloemfontein must be by slow stages and on the eve of the rail journey north she wrote to Mrs Steyn expressing the wish that she could set off lying on a featherbed in a traditional Boer ox-wagon, or at least in her own rail van so she could stay a few days at different levels, thus avoiding the fatigue of getting on and off trains. Whatever Emily's intention, Mrs Steyn took the fancy literally and made enquiries with a view to placing a private coach at the invalid's disposal.

Emily thereupon declared herself "horribly ashamed and unhappy" over the misunderstanding. But after insisting it had been a joke about having a carriage of her own, she went on to deliver a stinging rebuke to the host country. Every slight, ingratitude and injury suffered at the hands of South Africans, above all the ever-festering grudge of her departure from the spinning schools, must have boiled over as she took up her pen. "I assure you," she told Mrs Steyn, "nothing would have induced me to *ask* any favour of any *public authority*, and *certainly* not from this Government from whom I have never received the slightest recognition or even civility. I feel dreadfully hot and unhappy about it and hope at least that such a request did *not emanate from me*. If they had wished to *show* me civility they would certainly have offered it, especially as they must be aware that I am an invalid."

Arrangements were hurried through to soothe the distinguished visitor's hurt feelings, though with limited success. Thanks to Smuts's intervention, the minister of railways offered a private carriage but spoiled the gesture by remarking ungraciously that Emily would be expected to pay her maid's fare. Fiercely resenting his comment that the favour was "so difficult and so unusual", Emily snapped that but for her weak state she would certainly refuse it. To Isabella Steyn, however, she conceded that the private coach was "an immense physical relief to me".

As it turned out, all the efforts were in vain. Emily had travelled no further than Beaufort West in the Western Cape – less than half the distance to Bloemfontein – before the strain of the journey started to tell, forcing her to seek refuge at the local parsonage. On Sunday November 30 she wrote to Mrs Steyn that the rapidity of her pulse had made her send for a doctor who immediately insisted that the only thing for her to do was to turn round. Still she refused to bow to the inevitable: "I replied I was bound to go on and only needed his advice how to do it with the least danger." So the doctor urged her to rest at Beaufort West till the last possible moment, dash up to Bloemfontein in time to stay in bed or on a sofa undisturbed for one or two clear days before the ceremony, then immediately go away.

With apologies for "being such a plague", Emily went on: "Believe me, if my body will do it, I shall come on – but there is a point at which the body *won't* and *can't* and if I reach this point, please assure the committee I shall repay the journey money." The idea of letting down the organisers continued to nag her, and in a second letter to Mrs Steyn that same day she wrote: "Tell the committee to rest assured, I will not fail them unless *I know my presence will be worse than my absence.*"

Thoughts of death were constantly with her. Since arriving in South Africa she had received shocking news from Cornwall that her eldest sister Carrie – another heart sufferer – had dropped dead in church; now here was the Beaufort West doctor warning that any sudden dilation of her heart would be fatal. To Smuts she wrote telling him where to find her will and assuring him there was enough money in the bank to bury her. She felt ready, "almost anxious" for death, but wished to perform the unveiling first rather than disappoint President Steyn.

Days later all hope of reaching Bloemfontein were abandoned and the special carriage, wrested from the government with such humiliating effort, bore Emily back to Cape Town. So on December 16 the guest of honour was to be at the ceremony in spirit only while her exhausted body lay more than six hundred miles away.

Emily gleaned what comfort she could from the fact that the decisive action had been taken by others – "each day, each hour at Beaufort I grew weaker till at last the moment came when the decision was taken out of my hands". To Oom Jannie she wrote that the old horse, still in harness, had fallen at the very last. "They brought me here," she said, "and put me to bed where I must bide awhile to see if my heart regains what it has lost or is, as the doctor half fears, permanently injured and enfeebled by this great strain."

Utter exhaustion did not prevent her firing off lengthy letters to various correspondents or ordering an urgent printing of the speech she had prepared for the unveiling – four thousand copies each in English and Afrikaans – and making arrangements for their distribution among the crowds at Bloemfontein.

To Mrs Steyn she wrote: "The pain is so great around my heart, and I am entirely in my bedroom, can hardly crawl across it without the pulse racing. But relief came the moment I got south and perhaps with time and completest cessation of effort, of voice in particular, I may pick up a bit once more." Smuts in the meantime was on the receiving end of one of her feminine scoldings. "Here I am, held up by that incapable organ, my heart," she mourned. "Why oh! why did you urge such a derelict, such a broken-up wreck to come so far?"

Oom Jannie responded with tender assurances. "I know you have an iron constitution and I think even the heart will pull right with rest," he wrote. "I do indeed feel most bitterly sorry and disappointed for your dear sake." He himself would still go to Bloemfontein, he said, but would miss "that face and figure which represent the noblest message of the Englishwoman to the Boer woman."

*

Barely a week before the ceremony on December 16, now officially declared *Vrouwen-Dag* or Women's Day, Emily suddenly set her heart on her speech being read out by John X. Merriman, the most respected of South Africa's elder statesmen. It was a bitter disappointment when Merriman firmly declined not only to read the speech but even to be present at the ceremony. Nine years previously he had been incensed by the highhanded way Emily had released Smuts's private letter to *The Times*, and had written to commiserate with the general for being "scurvily used". Like Mrs Smuts, Merriman seems never to have forgiven Emily's indiscretion, though the reason he gave for his refusal was the fear, widely shared in advance, that the event would only stir up dormant grievances – that initial anxiety Emily had been able to stifle.

Emily's first reaction was to declare that if Merriman wouldn't read it, no one else should, and to stipulate that the eight thousand copies be scattered among the people present instead, to be digested in silence. In the event calmer counsels prevailed. She agreed that the speech would be read aloud in both languages by one of her oldest Boer friends, Charlie Fichardt, while her choice as stand-in to unveil the monument was, inevitably, Mrs Steyn.

When the day of the ceremony came, it confounded the doubters by briefly reuniting the feuding factions of Afrikanerdom. All three of the world-famous generals were there. Over a thousand mounted men took part in a procession to the obelisk along with hundreds of women and girls in white bearing white flowers. People afterwards remarked of the ceremony that, addresses apart, nothing broke the uncanny silence except for the thud of horses' hooves and the crash of the artillery salute. In the view of Sir Keith Hancock, the speeches of Jan Smuts and the absent Emily "together raised the ceremony at Bloemfontein to the level of spiritual greatness".

In a speech reckoned one of the best of his career, Smuts pointed out that the women and children who died in the camps were well over a tenth of the entire white population of the old republics. Yet those who like himself had fought in the war knew that almost without exception their womenfolk had made no attempt to persuade them to give up. "On the contrary," he said, in a striking echo of Lord Kitchener, "burghers who lost their courage and surrendered were received with contempt and scorn by these heroines. I myself know of many such instances where the men, out of shame at this reception, rejoined their commandos."

The monument was the nation's homage to these heroic dead – "a homage that is paid, so we hope, without bitterness in the heart and only out of pure love and respect for the noble women and their children who were the victims". He paused before thoughtfully repeating the words "without bitterness", and acknowledged how much he was asking of those for whom the list of dead included wives, mothers, daughters, children. Yet it was their duty to harbour no bitterness or hate. "Our task is different," he said. "We may and we must honour these noble women. We may and we must preserve the story of their passing as a priceless jewel in our history. We may and we must teach our children to try to be worthy of such mothers."

Steyn, by now a wreck of a man, was helped to his place of honour at the base of the canvas-draped monument. His arms hung limply at his sides and swollen eyelids reduced his eyes to slits. In the emotional turmoil of the moment, he too had to ask someone else to read out his words, and the crowd of over twenty thousand, many in tears, stood to hear the former head of state's tribute to the stricken Emily. "We know," he had written, "that she from the outset virtually risked her life to pay her last respects to the women and children of our people for whom she suffered so much. The effort and self-sacrifice she took upon herself for our people awaken in us feelings of profound respect and heartfelt gratitude."

Emily's address opened with a quotation from Euripides:

> *Would ye be wise, ye cities, fly from war!*
> *Yet if war come, there is a crown in death*
> *For her that striveth well and perisheth*
> *Unstained.*

She confessed a sense of personal pride: "From ancient times men have pronounced eulogies over the graves of their fellow men who had fallen for their country. Today, I think for the first time, a woman is chosen to make the commemorative speech over the national dead – not soldiers but *women* – who gave their lives for their country."

Privileged as she was to have known many of those being honoured, there had come into her mind Jeremiah's prophetic vision of the mourning Rael being comforted: "Refrain thy voice from weeping and thine eyes from tears; they shall come again from the land of the enemy; thy children shall come again to their own border."

The speech spoke of poor souls stripped bare in the camps, torn from familiar family life, plunged into sickness and destitution, surrounded by strangers: "The sight was one to call forth pity, yet pity did not predominate. Quite other feelings swallowed that. Even throughout the greatest misery the greater pity was needed elsewhere: Christ, I have read, had pity for the poor, the lowly, the imprisoned, the suffering, and so have we, but remember that He had far more pity for the rich, the hard, those who are slaves to their goods, who wear soft raiment, and live in kings' houses. To Him riches and pleasures seemed greater tragedies than poverty and sorrow.

"So, as we turn our minds back thirteen years to dwell on the stormy past, pity enters in, but who is it that we pity? Surely, had you seen the inward and spiritual graces that shone forth from that outward and visible squalor you yourselves might have felt that it was not the captives in those foul camps that were most in need and pity. The rich and highly placed, the financiers who wanted war, the incompetent statesmen who were their tool, the men who sat in the seats of the mighty, the blundering politicians of that dark story… these needed and still need our deepest pity." The women and children who had died towered above pity, so those with pity to spare should give it to those still living who "must ever carry in their hearts the heavy memories of the blundering wrong by which they wrought the war".

Out of charity to Van Wouw, Emily departed from strict truth in describing the making of the sculptured group for the monument: "Far away in Rome I have been privileged to watch its creation. I noted its conception in the sculptor's thought. I saw it first issue in the common clay; moulded by his hand it passed into the pure white plaster; at length chastened in his mind and meet for the supreme ideal it was cast into the pit of burning metal whence issued the perfected work.

"Even so did Destiny, the mighty Sculptor, like clay in his hands take those simple women and children from their quiet homes, mould and chasten them through the successive stages of their suffering, till at length, purified and perfected to the Master-mind by the fierce fire of their trial, they passed from human sight to live forever a sacred memory in your land."

Like Smuts, she insisted on forgiveness: "As your tribute to the dead, bury unforgiveness and bitterness at the foot of this monument forever. Instead, for you can afford it, the rich who were greedy of more riches, the statesmen who could not guide affairs, the bad generalship that warred on weaklings and babes – forgive – because so only can you rise to full nobility of character and a broad and noble national life."

It was a long speech, charged with emotion from beginning to end, if in places uneven, wordy, and repetitious; yet audiences of that long-gone world had a strong appetite for public speaking. There were also passages of great power which have stood the test of time, affecting descriptions of what she had seen with her own eyes, and trenchant reminders that the Boer side too could not escape censure over the conduct of the war. For all that, the present-day reader of the *Vrouwen-Dag* speech may wish Leonard had materialised at his sister's sickbed to strike out the odd infelicities and reduce the reading time, which is around thirty-two minutes when spoken at the "sermon-pace" recommended to the clergy.

Or was the speech read to the crowds indeed shortened, but for the wrong reasons? On a platform crammed with bitter-enders, Charlie Fichardt must have been loath to give utterance to several remarkable passages critical of the Boers' treatment of blacks. There was Emily's rebuke to South Africa's whites that they were "withholding from others in your control, the very liberties and rights you have valued and won for yourselves". There was her lament over "the unlearned lesson, that liberty is the equal right and heritage of every child of man, without distinction of race, colour or sex". There was her appeal that simple justice required white people to remember "how many thousands of the dark race perished also in concentration camps, in a quarrel that was not theirs". Faced with twenty thousand Boers at Bloemfontein on December 16, 1913, Fichardt is thought to have hurried over certain lines and missed others out.[xxxii]

Emily's speech went on to recall her days trudging daily to the camp nearby – "I moved from tent to tent, witness of untold sufferings, yet marvelling ever at the lofty spirit which animated the childhood as well as the motherhood of your land" – and asked her listeners to imagine an Englishwoman witnessing such horrors. Did they ever wonder why she had come among them? She had never seen their country nor known any one of them; she had no personal ties with South Africa. She had come, quite simply, "in obedience to the solidarity of our Womanhood and to those nobler traditions of English life in which I was nurtured, and which by long inheritance are mine".

So for the women gathered beneath the monument she had a stirring message. It was for them to purify the body politic and guide the helm of state: "The dead have won for you a lofty place in the life of your nation, and the right to a voice in her counsels. From this sacred duty you surely dare not flinch." And so to Emily's ringing climax: "My friends, throughout the world the Woman's day approaches; her era dawns."

When the speech ended, Steyn could no longer rest silent. As Mrs Steyn, in a full-length black gown, moved across the platform and pulled the cord to release Van Wouw's sculpture from its white muslin cover, a flock of white doves was released and the old man struggled to his feet, lifted his hand and cried out: "Birds of peace!" Then the silent women and children in white approached the monument two by two to lay their wreaths and posies in a steadily growing mound of white petals representing the women and children who perished in the camps – each tribute completely white until the last, a wreath of blood-red roses laid by the Steyns' own granddaughter.[xxxiii]

*

Olive Schreiner's state of health during 1913 had kept her constantly in fear of sudden death, and not long before the Women's Day ceremony she finally gave in to the pleas of Emily and others to seek medical attention in Europe. The organising committee's failure to invite South Africa's most famous woman writer to the unveiling at Bloemfontein had profoundly shocked Emily, as she told Mrs Steyn: "It is almost impossible to conceive such a day, such a memorial, such a gathering and yet that Olive Schreiner should not be a speaker, if not the foremost speaker. I suppose South Africans have *no* idea of the position she holds in the world at large." Alas for Olive and Emily, the organisers were intransigent. Formerly a heroine to her people, Olive had outraged the government by her vociferous stand against the racially discriminatory measures in the Natives Land Act passed earlier that year.

By the day of the ceremony Olive had made her will and burnt many of her papers and letters, including all those from Havelock Ellis. She booked a passage for Southampton but her ultimate destination was Florence, where she intended to submit herself to the Carloni "electric heart treatment" as recommended by Emily. Her husband Cronwright-Schreiner would later go to considerable lengths to avoid mentioning Emily's name in his biography of Olive, writing only that she decided to subject herself to Carloni's cure because of its success in the case of "a woman friend of hers". In this he set the pattern for other contemporaries, old friends as well as foes, who would strike all reference to Emily from their memoirs.

For Olive there remained a problem over money. Even more than with Emily, it was an article of faith with Olive Schreiner to assert her financial independence. But the earnings of her early writing successes had long since disappeared, and Olive had always strenuously resisted offers of aid from both her hard-up husband and her well-to-do brother. When finally forced to ask for her boat fare from her brother Will, she insisted on handing over the rights to her latest unfinished novel so that he would have a chance of recouping his money, and in the end she appears also to have accepted a grudging advance of the outstanding funds from Cronwright-Schreiner.

Two years earlier Emily had conceived the idea of quietly raising the necessary £350 to pay for Olive to be treated in Italy, but on hearing talk of a subscription fund Olive had vetoed the proposal. "Somehow I fancy one can err by being *too* proud," the thwarted Emily mused in a letter to Isie Smuts, "and thus debar one's friends of what is a real joy, the joy of giving presents and of helping those in sickness and trouble. And when it means actually the prolongation of a valuable life and preserving unique powers it seems a duty to accept help from those who love us."

Did Olive still resent Emily's interference, however well-meant? A telling remark is buried in the archives of Will Schreiner preserved in the library of the University of Cape Town. When urged by her brother to travel to Italy in Emily's company, Olive adamantly refused. Her old English friend might be a dear good soul, she wrote back, but that did not alter the fact she was "one of those masterful women who quietly crushes everyone who comes near her".

With one incisive observation Olive seems to sum up the experience of so many who had found themselves drawn into Emily's orbit, and many more who would do so in the future. Yet for others she would always remain beyond a breath of criticism, and among them was one of the greatest names of the century. He was then called Mohandas Gandhi, and Emily was about to meet him for the first time.

*

In the days following the Women's Day ceremony Emily had "hardly come back from the brink of the grave", as she put it, before being called upon to perform another service for South Africa. Out of the blue she received an appeal for help which brought her face to face with Gandhi, her ardent admirer of many years.

Then aged forty-four, and at the height of his campaign of civil disobedience called *satyagraha*, Gandhi had thrown up his lucrative law practice in Bombay twenty years before, moving to South Africa to oppose discriminatory legislation against the 100,000-strong Indian population. He had been profoundly impressed by Emily's exploits during the Boer War and in more recent days had acclaimed her work in the spinning schools. During later years in India, when he was venerated as Mahatma or Great Soul, he would always insist on the importance in his creed of the spinning wheel, in symbolic as well as practical terms. For this he acknowledged Emily as an inspiration.

At the time of their first meeting – or to quote his own words, when Gandhi first enjoyed "the privilege to be known to Miss Hobhouse" – he had just completed a sentence of hard labour for leading the famous march of four thousand. During his time in gaol unrest had spread like wildfire and, in the largest general strike ever seen in South Africa, many Indians had died in confrontations with the army, police and Zulu guards employed by the owners of mines and plantations.

Following world-wide protests, the South African regime had been forced to set

Grateful for the aid of "one of the world's greatest women", Mohandas Gandhi wished to nurse the ailing Emily with his own hands.

up a commission to examine Indian grievances, but Gandhi was appalled when the government appointed two notorious anti-Indian agitators. He vowed to resume the struggle with a new mass march on New Year's Day 1914 unless the objectionable members were removed. Botha and Smuts refused to back down, and it was at this crucial juncture that Gandhi wrote to Emily asking her to intervene.

Two days after Christmas, Gandhi received a telegram in reply from the convalescent Emily asking "as a humble woman" that he postpone the march for fifteen days. The Indian leader replied that he had no choice but to agree because of his esteem for her. Emily roused herself from her bed and set to work on Oom Jannie, penning a long letter offering herself as intermediary in the dispute.

Emily wrote that as a woman without a vote she could sympathise with Indians who were denied the franchise. On the other hand, she sympathised with South Africa over the unwanted influx of immigrant workers, and added an uncomfortable aside for future generations to ponder: "I never weary of asking English folk what they would say and do if Indians in a like proportion took possession of England – one-sixth, say five millions. I guess tall talk of free Empire and free entry etc would go out like a candle. I tell them you can't force your own altruism on other countries."

Gandhi clearly trusted her, she argued, since he had personally asked for her intervention. And here, cannily if uncharacteristically, she swallowed humble pie. Alluding to her great blunder in handing his private letter to *The Times*, she wrote: "Also I think *you* might trust me, though I am not so sure about that, for I once sinned didn't I? And you, like the wise burnt child that dreads fire, have never forgotten though you forgave so sweetly." Whatever his decision, she added, "I am too old and benumbed to mind throwing myself down as a paving-stone and being trodden upon as a result". It was an appeal the gallant Smuts could not refuse.

In the early days of the fateful year of 1914, Emily and Gandhi met face to face at Groote Schuur, formerly the mansion of Cecil Rhodes and now official residence of South Africa's prime minister, where Emily was staying as the guest of General and Mrs Botha. The introductions were made by Betty Molteno, the witness of Emily's forcible removal from the *Avondale*, now a convert to Gandhi's cause. The Indian leader had written many times requesting an interview with Botha without success, and this was the breakthrough. Emily insisted that they meet; she and Gandhi then went on to see Smuts, and formal negotiations between the two sides began on January 13, two days before the postponement of the mass march granted to Emily was due to expire.

Emily's intercession averted further bloodshed, probably on an unprecedented scale. After failing to reach Bloemfontein for the Women's Day ceremony, it was a consolation to have played a peacemaker's role with signal success. For this was one of the rare occasions when an act of Emily's earned praise from every quarter. A clergyman who accompanied Gandhi as an adviser during the talks wrote that there was no doubt her sway over the Boer leaders paved the way to reconciliation between the two sides. A provisional agreement was reached on January 22, and Gandhi himself paid tribute to Emily, saying: "She played no mean part in the settlement. Hers was a name to conjure with among the Boers. And she made my way smooth among them by throwing the whole weight of her influence with the Indian cause."

Confirmed in his view of her as one of the world's greatest women, Gandhi likened a visit to Miss Hobhouse as "a perfect pilgrimage". But he remained anxious over Emily's poor state of health and invited his "dear friend" to continue her recuperation at his movement's headquarters village at Phoenix on the Natal coast, writing: "I venture to think that you will find loving hands to administer to your wants, and nothing would give me personally greater pleasure than, if I were free, to be able to wait upon you and nurse you." He also wrote to Betty Molteno offering heartfelt thanks for bringing him in contact with "that noble soul". To be in Emily's presence, he said, was "a spiritual uplifting for me".

Soon afterwards, when Emily sailed for England, it was Gandhi who saw her off.

27 "THE GERMANS, POOR DEARS"

Many of Lord Kitchener's countrymen saw the hand of fate in the great man's presence in England in August 1914, when the nation faced the greatest challenge in all its history. Unusually, Kitchener had elected to come home for his summer leave, and spent the sunset hours of the old world on a shopping spree, compulsively buying antiques for his recently-acquired country seat in Kent.

The years since the Boer War had consolidated Kitchener's reputation as Britain's greatest soldier. Taking up the coveted Indian command in October 1902, he had acquired perhaps the most resounding of the exotic titles conferred upon him – *Jang I Lat Sahib*, or Lord of War. Over the next seven years he introduced long-overdue military reforms, but his stay in India would be remembered chiefly for a deadly struggle for power with the Viceroy, Lord Curzon. Both men were driven by ferocious ambition, and both were determined to dominate the other. It was Kitchener who emerged the victor, engineering Curzon's resignation in 1905.

Yet in the meantime a close friendship had sprung up between Kitchener and Lady Curzon, the daughter of an American millionaire. The Viceroy believed his rival was half in love with his wife, and Mary Curzon on her part was hugely flattered by Kitchener's affection. "There is a sort of bracing north wind of resolution and strenuousness about him," she wrote, "and a gentle spot about a woman which a woman is always quick to find." She even entertained a fleeting dream that Kitchener might propose to her sister Daisy, a flighty young creature who broke countless hearts when on a visit from Chicago.

Kitchener got on well enough with Curzon's replacement, Lord Minto, but the fall of the Conservative government at the end of 1905 was a serious blow to his influence at home, while his relationship with the new secretary of state for India, John Morley – a personal friend of Emily Hobhouse and Lord Courtney – was doomed from the start. One of the most radical of Campbell-Bannerman's appointments, Morley had been a leading opponent of the Boer War, and constantly interfered with Indian Army reforms. In 1909, when Kitchener's Indian command expired, the Liberal administration offered him a relatively unimportant appointment based in Malta, which he was induced to accept in the belief it would help him achieve his new overriding goal to succeed Minto as viceroy. But this was an ambition too far, thwarted by Morley against the wishes of King Edward and the new prime minister, Herbert Asquith. Kitchener was consoled by promotion to field marshal and, in 1911, by his purchase of Broome Park near Canterbury.

There had always been something obsessive about Kitchener's accumulation of treasures. There was now in store a gigantic hoard of pictures, furniture, armour, porcelain, carpets, icons and gewgaws without number, the gifts of monarchs, sheikhs, maharajahs and lord mayors, along with bargains picked up over four decades in eastern bazaars and costly acquisitions from London antique shops. The ill-disposed used to whisper it was advisable to hide prized possessions when Lord Kitchener came calling, as they had a way of disappearing into his pockets. Certainly the scale of his collecting amounted to a mania. After one visit to Japan, he left with twenty-five crates of porcelain alone. It was as if Kitchener was trying to assemble single-handedly the kind of legacy he felt he should have inherited from a long ancestral line, the like of which he would eye longingly during visits to grand acquaintances like the Cecils of Hatfield.

All that was missing was an impressive mansion as a setting for his treasures, and this he found at last in Broome. That his choice fell on this particular house may be explained by one architectural historian's description of the vast Jacobean pile "with its disciplined regiment of queer gables and gigantic coupled chimneystacks like guardsmen arm-in-arm". Moreover, the spacious gardens were ideal for showing off Kitchener's set of enormous *Voortrekker* figures by Anton van Wouw, that same sculptor whom Emily had terrorised in Rome. The figures had been removed, some said looted, from South Africa in 1902 and hidden in storage ever since. Broome had been placed on the market by a hard-up baronet, and determined haggling by Kitchener, second nature after his years in the east, brought the purchase price down to a remarkable £1,400. As soon as the property was signed over, the new owner embarked on extensive alterations to house and parkland. It was a programme that would remain unfinished at his death. As master of Broome, Kitchener became the last of the victorious British warriors whose promotion to the landed class was funded by a grateful nation. At sixty-one he seemed reconciled to his honours passing to a brother's descendants, and must have reflected that if he had no son to inherit estate and title, he was no different from the first Marlborough and Nelson.

After Malta, Kitchener briefly visited Australia and New Zealand to advise on reforms to the armed services, but with the accession of George V he found himself back in favour and soon after the coronation went off to Cairo as consul-general. At the time of his return to England in 1914 he had been in Egypt for three years, but his rule had not been universally acclaimed. Rudyard Kipling when visiting Cairo painted an unflattering picture of "a fatted pharaoh in spurs, gone to seed awfully" and "garrulously intoxicated with power". And he was still a prey to disabling depressions which devoted aides like Lord Edward Cecil contrived to keep secret. Not long before his summer leave the consul-general had suffered a complete nervous breakdown following a row with the nominal Egyptian ruler, the devious Khedive Abbas Hilmi. Cecil helped his chief recover his nerve but privately expressed concern over his "hopelessly weak" state of mind.

On leaving Cairo, Kitchener had been informed he was to be made an earl in the birthday honours. Once again he dreamed of ditching the hated plebeian handle by taking the title Earl of Broome; once again he was told the nation refused to part with the name that was its pride and joy, and in his letters patent he was designated Earl Kitchener of Khartoum and of Broome.

Over the remaining days of peace he watched helplessly as, in the words of his private secretary, Sir George Arthur, "events resulting from more than human cunning and wickedness unrolled themselves with apocalyptic majesty and inevitableness". As late as July 21 he was invited to lunch at the German embassy where his reception left him in no doubt that war was unavoidable.[xxxiv] In the final days he ran down to Broome to see the work in progress. Like Emily he was a great lover of flowers and one of his priorities had been the laying-out of a rose garden which was now coming to perfection.

Kitchener's original plan had been to stay in England until September but on the morning of bank holiday Monday, August 3, he astounded his aides by driving down to Dover on a sudden impulse and boarding the Channel steamer, intent on an immediate return to Egypt. Even before the summoned entourage arrived, he was striding up and down the deck, fuming at the delay in casting off. "Tell the captain to start," he kept saying. It was as if he was trying to outrun destiny. Shortly after noon the boat train arrived from London and a messenger came on board with a summons from the prime minister. It took the combined efforts of his aides to persuade him to leave the boat.

Kitchener had always resisted moves to put him in the War Office, saying he would rather sweep the streets. Even on August 4, with German troops in Belgium and Britain's ultimatum about to expire, he begged Asquith to let him go back to Egypt. The following morning he bowed to the inevitable and accepted the post of secretary of state for war. He was the first soldier to serve in a cabinet since General Monk. Once the burden was accepted, a monumental calm descended on Kitchener. At ten o'clock the next day he entered the War Office, for the first time as its chief.

The War Office he inherited was not the dank, cramped rabbit warren where Emily Hobhouse had bearded his predecessor of Boer War days, St John Brodrick. Kitchener ruled over the Edwardian baroque pile of 1906, a monument of Portland stone designed as a worthy symbol of a great empire. The new minister found it denuded of senior officers of the general staff as many had abandoned their desks for the chance of a spot of action in France before the fun was over.

"At least," murmured Kitchener as he settled behind his desk, "no one can say my colleagues in the cabinet are not courageous. They have no army and they declare war against the mightiest military nation in the world." An aide stepped forward to request a sample signature for the official stamp, and the new minister was handed a pen. It refused to work. Another pen was hastily produced, with the same result. "Not a scrap of army," mused Kitchener, "and not a pen that will write!"

*

Emily might have returned from Cape Town in the last months of peace in a state of physical and mental exhaustion, but her craving for a cause was as keen as ever. The prospect of Britain joining the European conflict left Emily horror-struck, and days before war was declared she fired off a letter to the *Manchester Guardian* demanding that the country stay neutral. "Few English people have seen war in its nakedness," she wrote, "hence the thoughtless cry for it. They know nothing of the poverty, destruction, disease, pain, misery and mortality which follow in its trail. I have seen all this and my experience adds force to my appeal to all lovers of humanity to avert the horror that is threatened."

Immediately hostilities broke out, Emily contradicted herself as to the public mood. "The world here did not want war and there is no fever as in the Boer War days,"

The enlistment of Oliver Hobhouse for the Front was a terrible blow to Emily. Her "almost son" later transferred from the infantry to the Royal Flying Corps.

she insisted in a letter to Smuts. Yet her friend Kate Courtney in her diary described huge crowds staying up to hear the declaration and sorrowfully noted: "About 2.30 am I heard parties passing our house in Chelsea singing patriotic songs, and all my hopes grew faint." Among the members of government who resigned over the declaration of war were two of Emily's oldest political friends – John Burns, the veteran radical she had laboured for during the Khaki Election, and Lord Morley, the man who had prevented Kitchener from becoming viceroy of India.

The Hobhouse family was split down the middle, half in favour of the war and half against. A great private agony which now overtook Emily was a breach with her brother, for Leonard broke with the anti-war camp once the scale of German atrocities in Belgium became clear. As his son Oliver wrote later: "Because he thought England was in the right in the Great War, he was as anxious that we should win as anybody." Leonard a jingoist! Truly, Emily's world was crashing round her ears.

Leonard Hobhouse's most powerful journalism dates from this time, directed against what he called "the mazes of German mysticism, militarism and megalomania" which had plunged the civilised world into war. From the untidy study in Wimbledon poured forth countless columns in which Leonard abominated Germany's mission to dominate Europe. The analyst in him sought the reason for the rise of German beastliness and discerned the baleful influence of the philosopher Hegel.

Leonard mortified Emily by advocating the retaliatory use of poison gas – to refuse to do so, he declared, might hand control of the world to the more barbarous and unscrupulous side. His son Oliver's decision to enlist was a source of immense pride to him, as it was of horror to Emily, and Leonard lamented that physical shortcomings and old age – he was fifty in 1914 – prevented his volunteering for the front himself. As it was, with his life continually plagued by insomnia, dyspepsia and the common cold, Leonard was forced to fight his war from an old wicker chair in South West London, wreathing himself with pipe smoke as he penned each new assault on an enemy lost to "gloomy arrogance and ice-bound pride of race and sex". All the same, the war dealt a shattering blow to the foundation of Leonard's philosophy, and Oliver would later blame the terrible moral dilemmas thrown up by the conflict for his father's final breakdown in health.

At the time of Leonard's *volte-face* on the war, Emily was busy with relief work for refugees from Belgium but she still clung stubbornly to her rose-tinted view of the Germans, insisting that the great catastrophe was the fault of the "wretched Imperialists" of her own nation. Though she admitted seeing "the same war-look" remembered from South Africa on the faces of the refugees, she struck a surprisingly complacent note in a letter to Smuts, remarking that the Belgians "have not suffered like your women of old, and already surrounded with care, freedom and kindness, are happy and flourishing". And she burst out with indignation that "we have allied ourselves against our good friends the highly civilised Germans", and sided instead with the Serbians – "said to be about the lowest set in Europe" – and the semi-barbarian Russians.

"For pity's sake," she begged Smuts, "don't let South Africa be dragged in. You have Germans, poor dears, on your flank and you have natives quite enough to deal with, and in any case the war is spread already wide enough." Emily signed off her first wartime letter "in broken-hearted grief" with the exasperated cry that Sir Edward Grey should be put in one battleship and the Kaiser in another, and the two left to sink each other.

The war left Emily's personal affairs in complete disarray. The flat in Rome was the nearest thing she had to a home, and in the early days of the conflict Italy seemed on the point of abandoning its neutrality and siding with the enemy. This meant most of her possessions and funds were inaccessible, and she wrote to friends of her dread of an enforced winter in England. But what she seems to have told none of her circle was that earlier in the year she had made an astonishing decision. With her debts accumulating, she asked to be readmitted to Chenies Street Chambers, from which she had been ejected as a troublemaker on the eve of the Boer War.

Fifteen years on, the key figures at Chenies Street were unchanged. The chairman of the board was still the clergyman friend of the Garrett ladies, and the Garrett ladies remained the principal shareholders; Miss Townshend, the secretary who had borne the brunt of Emily's anti-management campaign, was now a director. None had forgotten the unpleasantness of 1899 which ended with Emily receiving notice to quit; nor had memories faded of the vengeful article she wrote afterwards for *Nineteenth Century*, to say nothing of her public attacks on Millicent Garrett Fawcett during the Boer War. "Miss Hobhouse's application for a flat was reported and considered," reads the last item of the minutes of the February 24 meeting of the directors, "but as she was not a worker it was decided not to accept her as a tenant."

Emily must have been in dire straits to risk this refusal. Despite displays of indifference and bravado, snubs always wounded her deeply, and that she could have dreamt of being welcomed back to Chenies Street demonstrates either desperation or a remarkable level of obtuseness. Or was she unconsciously courting humiliation? Whatever was going on in her mind, it is no wonder she quickly drew a veil over the affair. As if to rub salt into the wound, not long after its terse rejection of Emily the management committee quietly changed the rules and admitted women without worker status.

The Chenies Street rebuff came at one of the lowest points of her life. Her elation at helping to resolve the Indian crisis in South Africa had faded and once more her bleak personal prospects dominated her thoughts. Again and again, in letters written during these months before the war, she spoke of being ready and willing to die. In April 1914, then at lodgings in Oxford, she was confined to a wheelchair and remained so two months later when her nephew Oliver invited her out on the river in his punt. "I begin more and more to regard death as a most desirable friend," she wrote to Smuts. "To us, whose freedom and independence was our all in all, and which we have lost either through sickness or old age, the feeling that death liberates – literally bursts our bonds – is very attractive." In June she was diagnosed with an advanced form of the gum disease pyorrhoea. Dentistry in those days struck fear into the bravest, and Emily recoiled in terror from the recommended solution of having all her teeth out. When at last she was persuaded that most had to go, the extraction of the first two brought a fortnight's agony.

Yet if she reached her lowest ebb just before the outbreak of war, predictably the great calamity itself saw a revival of her old fighting spirit. As ever, the worst of times were Emily's best of times, with the scent of battle breathing new life into her nostrils.

*

The enemy had started the war with a huge numerical superiority. Germany boasted a century-old system of conscription under which every fit male was called up at twenty and subjected to two years of rigorous training under the most professional officer class on earth, with regular recalls up to the age of forty. This meant that in 1914 almost every man in Germany was a highly disciplined soldier. On the first day of war over four million were ready for immediate action. The French too boasted a great standing army, with every Frenchman theoretically liable to conscription. But as Kitchener grimly remarked, this was not a war which would be won with mass charges of troops in red trousers led by sword-waving officers in white gloves. Alone, the French had no hope of resisting Germany's onslaught.

In contrast with the armies of other great powers, Britain's was little more than a colonial police force. The Royal Navy was seen as the guardian of the homeland, which left the generation of 1914 unarmed and untrained. Even the first lord of the admiralty, Winston Churchill, had for many years parroted Lloyd George's demands for cuts in expenditure, so the fact he could still count on the largest fleet in the world was little thanks to his own efforts. Only when the danger posed by the expanding German battle fleet became glaringly obvious had Churchill announced his conversion to spending on armaments. Even so, conscription on the continental model remained unthinkable.

At the first war cabinet Kitchener shocked his colleagues with a bald statement

That rare spectacle, a smiling Lord Kitchener – the antithesis of his stern image on the recruiting posters – became a best-selling postcard of the early war years.

of facts. To win, they must put armies of millions in the field and maintain them for several years. Britain must have a continental army not of the present six divisions – the same strength as tiny Belgium – but of seventy. Such an army could not come to strength until the third year of fighting, by which time the enemy's power would be in decline. In the same fashion he predicted the where and when of the coming German offensive, against the prevailing wisdom of the British and French generals. According to Sir Edward Grey, the foreign secretary, Kitchener seemed to have reached his conclusions by some flash of instinct rather than by reasoning.

Today Kitchener's forecasts on the Great War – the time over which it would be fought, the rapid spread of hostilities to theatres worldwide, the unprecedented numbers of combatants involved, the outcome for Britain and other nations many years afterwards – read like clairvoyance. No other major figure on the British side, with the exception of the maverick admiral Lord Fisher, seemed to entertain the faintest idea of what the future held. As early as 1908 Kitchener had said a world war was certain because of the weakness and indecision of political leaders. He had envisaged the fighting as lasting a minimum of three years – early in 1914 he revised the figure to five – and said that whether Britain or Germany won in a technical sense, both were destined to lose hugely in influence over world affairs, the long-term winners being the United States and Japan.

These were among Kitchener's preoccupations as he sat at his desk after the first war cabinet. On the plus side the Empire's armies were in fighting trim. He himself had overhauled the military organisations of India, Egypt, Australia and New Zealand; also thanks to him, South Africa could be counted as an ally. But months would pass before help arrived in force from any of these quarters, and in the meantime he must begin to create the needed great army from scratch. The recruits had to be accommodated, fed, clothed, trained, armed and equipped; as war minister he would also bear personal responsibility for munitions and supplies as well as for supervising military strategy worldwide.

Within days Kitchener issued his first call to arms for an initial one hundred thousand volunteers. As his supreme asset was the prestige and trust he enjoyed among the general public, the key to the immense recruitment effort was the poster bearing his own face, which was soon to appear the length and the breadth of the land. With its hypnotic eyes, gigantic moustache and pointing finger, it prompted the catty remark of Asquith's wife Margot that if Kitchener was not a great man, he was at least a great poster. In all an astounding fifty-four million War Office recruiting posters were to be printed during the war, in a country then with a total population of forty-six million. The "King and Country" image of Kitchener, with its air of accusatory power, remains today probably the most successful advertisement of all time, if only for the numbers it enticed to their deaths.

*

Initially Emily planned to remain at her dingy lodgings in Oxford, hoping to be joined there by Olive Schreiner. Some weeks previously Olive had abandoned the course of treatment in Florence urged on her by Emily, her initial enthusiasm for Dr Carloni giving way to loud complaints that his regime was too exhausting and too expensive. She became depressed and unable to write, which in turn made her indignant and angry. "That cure nearly made an end of me," declared Olive after a month under Carloni. Probably she was also suffering withdrawal symptoms, as the heavy doses of opium prescribed by her Cape Town doctor were now denied her.

Ever on the move, ever in the wrong place at the wrong time, Olive happened to have been in Germany on the eve of war, a guest at the castle of Count and Countess von Moltke. To contemporaries Moltke was an ill-omened name. The previous count had been the architect of Prussia's shattering victory over France in 1870, while Olive's host was the uncle of the present chief of the German general staff. As the international crisis deepened, the count became alarmed over Olive's precarious position and telegraphed Berlin for advice from his nephew the general.

The telegram came as an unwelcome distraction for Helmuth von Moltke, a taciturn, highly-strung perfectionist who had devoted the past ten years to honing Germany's secret war plan. That day his attention was divided between overseeing the immensely complicated interlocking schedules of troop movements involved in launching the greatest military strike in history, and calming the Kaiser's last-minute jitters. However, time was found to signal the necessary authorisation to his uncle's castle and Olive was allowed to cross the Dutch border in time to catch the last boat train for England. She landed exhausted at midnight on August 3 with the clothes she stood in. Almost the first thing she did was contact her old friend Emily.

In the event Emily found herself unable to offer Olive an immediate refuge in Oxford. Distressed by the sight of the beautiful colleges overrun by odious khaki uniforms, she had decided to return to her native county. She left Oxford at the end of August having arranged to rent a spacious house at Bude on Cornwall's north coast, not far from her birthplace and within visiting distance of her only living sister, Maud. The Bude villa, called Maer Lake, was to remain Emily's principal domicile in England for the duration of the war, its six bedrooms offering a temporary bolthole to those members of her family still on speaking terms with her and to a dwindling band of intimates like Olive.

*

Olive Schreiner was no longer the glamorous young novelist lionised by the great and good. Tempestuous old women attract fewer admirers than tempestuous young ones, and at sixty the South African had ballooned horribly. Never noted as a figure of fashion, she now dressed with striking eccentricity and had taken to wearing ludicrous hats decked with flowers. The infant ward of one of Olive's handful of remaining friends in England would later remember her terror of "the strong fierce face of a woman who seemed at least a hundred years old", and tell how this alarming apparition would shout against the war and thump the table until silenced by an attack of asthma.

As a pacifist with a German name, Olive met constantly with suspicion or outright hostility. Soon after arriving in England, writing to Emily in her flamboyant scrawl, she described a traumatic search for temporary accommodation in London. Finding nice cheap rooms in Chelsea kept by "a sweet refined-looking little woman", Olive agreed to rent them and gave her name, at which the landlady asked if it was German: "I said it was, but I was a British subject born in South Africa, that my husband was a British subject of pure British descent, and my mother was English, that my father who left Germany eighty years ago was a naturalised British subject." The landlady then "turned round and stormed at me, all her seemingly gentle face contorted with rage and hate, and poured forth a stream of abuse that was almost inconceivable".

To her shame, Olive dropped into a chair and burst out crying: "It's the only time I've cried in two years. It seemed so contemptibly weak of me; but you know how you feel when you are utterly worn out mentally and physically! I could only say, 'It isn't because you are so unkind to me, it's because all the world's so wicked.' Oh Emily, the worst of war is not the death on the battlefields; it is the meanness, the cowardice, the hatred it awakens."

As ever, Olive's life was in chaos. She remained as hard-pressed as Emily for money and even more obsessed with her ill-health. Over the years, Olive's correspondents learned rather more of her innards than they might have wished. Letter after letter would itemise her complaints at length, as in one typical missive to her veteran lover Havelock Ellis, opening with the ominous words "I've been very ill", which proceeded to list "big holes in the lungs" caused by childhood tuberculosis, the displacement of every organ in her body, a floating kidney pressing against the colon, arterial sclerosis of the blood vessels, a stone in the kidney, a much enlarged stomach "because the diaphragm has broken down", and continuous attacks of angina. These ills came on top of her worst insomnia in twenty years and, so she insisted, a third bout of measles. Nor was this all, she added, as "the specialist I went to last says the most serious thing is the enlargement of a gland in the middle of the chest", a condition which prevented her from eating. Like Emily, Olive was also a martyr to dental ills. The letter to Havelock Ellis announcing her departure for Emily's house at Bude informed him she had just had the root of a tooth removed and the abscess made her "not good for much". Convalescing at Maer Lake, Olive could at least write appreciatively of the comforts of her friend's seaside villa.

That much animus would continue to be directed at Olive is hardly surprising since she never disguised her contempt for "the cant and humbug" employed by England to justify fighting the war, and would loudly declare it was no more wicked for the Germans to kill Belgians than it had been for the British to kill Afrikaners. Nor was her description of the Belgian refugees – "the ugliest mongrel-looking folk I've ever seen" – likely to endear her to the average patriot of the day. Once again, the experiences of Olive Schreiner, mostly brought on her own head, might have been Emily's as reflected in a fairground distorting mirror.

And like Emily, Olive felt more than ever doomed to be an outcast. "It is funny why I have always to be out of everything," she wrote to her estranged husband in South Africa. "The day will never come when I can be in the stream. Something in my nature prevents it, I suppose. I have never before in my life been so lonely. Sometimes I don't seem to be alive at all, but only creeping about in a ghastly dream. No one wants me. I'm in no relation with life or thought in England or Africa or anywhere else."

Like countless others, Leonard Hobhouse among them, Olive would spend the war reading Jane Austen over and over, seeking solace from present horrors in that long-lost genteel world.

*

Also in England in those first months of war was Gandhi, who arrived from South Africa on August 6. He, Emily and Olive had long formed a mutual admiration society, so both women were aghast when the world's most famous advocate of non-violence not only openly supported the British side, but lent his name to a recruiting drive for soldiers in India. A similar impulse had moved him to organise Indian stretcher-bearers for the British during the Boer War.

It was given to few to take a high moral tone with Gandhi, but Olive Schreiner did. She fired off a furious letter declaring she was struck to the heart by news of his service to the English in an evil war. Spurning Gandhi's invitation to meet in London, she reworked her old line about Germans killing Belgians and said it was equally hateful to see Englishmen travelling thousands of miles to kill Indians in India, or Indians travelling thousands of miles to kill white men in Europe.

Emily had lost enough friends already and was determined not to break with Gandhi. She saw him on at least one occasion in London in 1914, and they were to maintain a regular correspondence for the rest of her life. As with Smuts, this was a friendship too precious to renounce, even after Gandhi voiced the paradox that his people had to learn to fight before they could truly embrace non-violence. This curious ambivalence on Gandhi's part had surfaced some months earlier in one of his letters to Emily when, ruminating on the deeds of "the great Mrs Pankhurst", he wrote: "At no stage do we believe in the use of physical force, but I am free to confess that we have certainly been encouraged, in the hour of our weakness, by the noble example of devotion to duty and self-sacrifice that the militants have set, though we condemn their methods and tactics as suicidal and beneath the dignity of women."

On this at least he and Emily could agree.

28 "JUST THE MAN TO BOSS THE POLITICIANS"

Kitchener chose as his War Office sanctum a huge panelled room with twin marble fireplaces. Because of his detestation of the English weather it was kept permanently overheated, with both fires ablaze even that first sultry August. In days to come, many a perspiring visitor must have made a wry connection with the hit song of 1914, *Keep the Home Fires Burning*.

From the outset he was showered with unwanted advice. Quick off the mark was the Archbishop of Canterbury, Randall Davidson – no favourite of Emily's – who sent a letter deploring the problem of drunkenness among new recruits and pledging the Church's support for any anti-drink initiative. And Dr Davidson thought Kitchener was paying his soldiers too much. "It sounds horrid to say it," he wrote, "but the fact is that the women dependents of our soldiers are getting more money than they can wisely handle, accustomed as they are to dealing with shillings where they now have in some cases pounds at a time."

In the first phase of fighting in France the German army made huge advances against the defending Allies but failed to achieve the knock-out blow demanded by General von Moltke's master plan. Paris, the primary objective, remained safe following the Battle of the Marne, in the course of which six hundred taxis ferried French troops from the capital to the front line less than forty miles away. His great design in ruins, Moltke's nerves gave way and he was replaced on September 14 – the date on which he had expected to turn his conquering armies on the third of the great allies, Russia. The Allies' position on the western front might still be desperate but the feared collapse had been averted. The British Expeditionary Force, dismissed by the Kaiser as "a contemptible little army", had played its full part.

Kitchener's first visit to France upset the insecure General Sir John French, British commander at the front, who felt undermined by the minister's appearance in field marshal's uniform. After the war he was to write a spiteful book, the first posthumous attack on Kitchener's military reputation. But in the meantime requests for jobs at the front poured in from retired officers, and among the few applicants Kitchener agreed to see was a frail, white-whiskered veteran of eighty-two who had fought in the Indian Mutiny and won a VC. He was the minister's old chief, mentor and friend, Earl Roberts. Kitchener let him down as gently as he could. In November, however, when the first Indian troops arrived at the front, Lord Bobs was allowed to visit Flanders, and was overjoyed to find the sons and grandsons of men who had served under him in the old days. On his third day in France he caught a chill which turned to pneumonia, and died within sound of the guns.

One request for active service Kitchener flatly refused. Edward, Prince of Wales, a twenty-year-old ensign in the Grenadier Guards, called at the War Office as his battalion was leaving for France, and asked the minister to overrule his orders to stay behind. As he had brothers to spare, argued Edward, his death in action would not matter. Kitchener amiably agreed the point but said he would not risk the heir to the throne being captured. Swallowing his disappointment, the future Duke of Windsor noted in his diary that Kitchener was "a rough customer but mighty strong and just the man to boss the politicians".

This was far from what was actually happening. Kitchener already knew some of his cabinet colleagues – Churchill and Lloyd George among them – but their way of doing things was proving entirely alien to his nature. They in turn found Kitchener's manner stiff and uncompromising, his utterances terse, formal, and totally devoid of any kind of oratorical appeal. When forced to speak, he would create confusion over who he was addressing because of the cast in his eye, and would frequently forget his colleagues' names. Before long he saw himself as a fish out of water and talked of resigning, especially when his military counsel was overruled.

Above all he loathed sharing information. As he was soon informing Asquith, "my colleagues tell military secrets to their wives, all except Lloyd George, who tells them to other people's wives". As a rule Kitchener refrained from repeating gossip, so the incident reveals the depth of his dislike for Lloyd George, now chancellor of the exchequer. The one man he willingly confided in was Asquith. Alone among the cabinet, Kitchener was blissfully ignorant of the fact that the prime minister routinely passed on war secrets to the indiscreet young woman he was in love with, Venetia Stanley.

*

Meanwhile, Emily's passionate entreaties to Jan Smuts to stay out of the war had been ignored. Even as she was pleading on behalf of "the Germans, poor dears", South African troops were in action in the desert of German South West Africa. Botha and Smuts attacked the neighbouring colony without consulting their own parliament – a highly provocative step in a country still nursing wounds from its own war with Britain. Too wary to argue politics with Emily, Smuts expressed his views unreservedly to trusted friends. "Botha and I are not the men to desert England in this dark hour," he wrote to Margaret Gillett's husband, but admitted that many Boers fiercely disapproved.

By October 1914 a pro-German army commander had mutinied. The most formidable figures to join the revolt were two of Emily's great friends, De Wet and Christian Beyers, the commandant-general; even one of Smuts's most trusted brothers-in-arms, Jan Kemp, declared against Britain. So now Smuts found himself fighting a dual war – one against the Germans, one against fellow Boers.

Emily wrote again to remonstrate. What had possessed her dear Oom to invade a country against which he had no quarrel in support of the country which only fourteen years ago was treating *his* country as Germany was now treating Belgium? "I cannot *bear* to think that dear de Wet and Beyers and Kemp will meet a rebel's death," she went on. "I write in a hurry to implore you if these men are captured to ask General Botha to consider these facts and *not* to shoot them unless in open fight. The issue might be awful – an internecine struggle – an enmity never forgiven. They are good, brave men. Keep them in prison if you will till the end but do not execute them, *do not, do not, do not.*"

In the event the rebellion was broken swiftly with an old favourite of Emily's, the aged General De La Rey, as its most prominent fatality. By the time the last rebel officer was captured on that most fateful date in the South African calendar, December 16 or Dingaan's Day, over five thousand mutineers including De Wet were languishing in gaol. The rising had been crushed by Boer commandos under Boer officers, and true to Emily's prediction was to leave Smuts with a legacy of undying hatred in his own land.

*

Emily had no intention of rusticating in Bude and undertook regular forays to London where, with the aid of the Courtneys, she busied herself in the pacifist cause. But even before war was declared, she had resumed hostilities with a daunting adversary.

Millicent Garrett Fawcett, as head of the British suffrage movement, was also vice president of the worldwide body, the International Woman Suffrage Alliance. As the European crisis worsened in late July Mrs Fawcett had found herself under intense pressure to call a peace rally and reluctantly agreed to chair a meeting in London, choosing the fateful date of August 4. The Kingsway Hall was booked and thousands of leaflets printed when, to Mrs Fawcett's horrified objections, the names of Emily Hobhouse and Olive Schreiner were proposed for the platform party. For once the normally submissive committee members outvoted their leader and the invitations went out.

The purpose of the rally was overtaken with bewildering speed. As delegates assembled on that oppressively hot Tuesday evening, German troops were already in Belgium. Emily was unable to be present at the rally, probably because of her state of health; there is one anecdotal report of Olive attending after her hair's-breadth escape from Germany, but no record of her speaking. Long before 1914 she had lost her faith in "those infernal gatherings of women". In any case, it is unlikely that either of them would have been a match that night for the determined Mrs Fawcett, who with consummate skill used the chair to silence every pacifist voice. She then hurried home to set pen to paper, composing a rousing message to her national membership containing the words "Women, your country needs you", thus anticipating the famous Kitchener poster.

But calls for an international peace conference at The Hague could not be silenced, and when the question was put to the vote at her own executive Mrs Fawcett found she had a terrific fight on her hands. Almost all the senior officers and a majority of the committee voted against her. At the next full council meeting, she used her presidential address to appeal to the rank-and-file over the heads of the executive, telling the packed hall that it was the nation's duty to drive the Germans from France and Belgium. "Until that is done," she declared, "I believe it is akin to *treason* to talk of peace." The diminutive, immaculate figure sat down to thunderous applause, but ten of the executive committee resigned immediately, along with every officer of the organisation except one. It was the greatest crisis of Mrs Fawcett's seventeen years as president of the national suffrage movement, ending with her roundly beating off the pacifist challenge. But the threat to her authority was not over.

*

When the great German offensive at Ypres failed to break the Allies in the spring of 1915, the invaders were the first to grasp the inevitability of protracted trench warfare. Digging in along a front stretching from the Belgian coast to neutral Switzerland, almost everywhere at an advantageous position, they were thus able to wage an essentially defensive war which inflicted far higher casualties on the opposing side. The appalling death-toll inspired the peace campaigners to new efforts.

Mrs Fawcett might have blocked an officially-backed international conference, but she was unable to prevent a private gathering of women activists from the warring countries in neutral Holland. Plans were laid for a massive peace meeting at The Hague on April 29, and Emily was one of nearly two hundred British women to enrol as delegates. She was immediately elected to the organising committee along with Kate Courtney and – temporarily overcoming her antipathy to women's meetings – Olive Schreiner. Asquith dismissed them as sparrows twittering in a storm.

Despite her poor health, Emily was bursting with plans, and when Italians entered the war on the Allied side she set off the next day for Rome. In a letter to Smuts she described travelling via Dieppe in the company of Quaker relief workers who were trying to heal "the gaping wounds which you men in your misgovernment of our beautiful world have brought upon it", while she herself meant to campaign against the war in Italy and Switzerland. A melodramatic flourish was now rarely absent from Emily's correspondence, and she went on: "I am bodily weak and snow is falling as I write, but I must go, and though my body must be carried my spirit is strong as ever." She declared that Smuts had no idea of "the wide, deep, ever growing indignation of Womanhood as it sees this destruction of life – the bodies of those it has created and cherished blown to pieces by murderous engines of war, and all for nothing at all". And she could not bear to think of all the money England was spending on "this wicked foolery against our good friends the German people". It was because of outbursts of this kind that many sorely-tried friends were finally washing their hands of her.

Emily got out of the country in time, but the wartime introduction of passports proved a useful government tool against the peace women. One week before the main body of delegates was due to sail for The Hague, the Home Office withdrew their passports. Arm-twisting in high places by Lady Courtney won a reprieve for twenty, only for the Admiralty to close the North Sea to all shipping. In the end just two of the two hundred British delegates made it to Holland. To great hostility and ridicule in the European press, the Peace Congress finally opened in the largest public hall at The Hague, an ornate Moorish-style building in the Zoological Gardens, with the platform party assembling against a surreal backdrop of gigantic potted palms. The location allowed the *Daily Express* to snigger over "Peacettes at the Zoo".

As in Britain, officialdom in other warring states obstructed attempts to reach The Hague. Not a single French or Russian delegate got through, but the women who did included five Belgians, six Austrians and twenty-eight Germans, and an unsanctioned United States delegation of forty-seven. Embarrassingly, Dutch delegates outnumbered all other nationals by a hundred to one.

*

A month after Emily left for Rome the British ambassador there, Sir Rennell Rodd, reported to the Foreign Office that a group of English pacifists were agitating for terms with Germany, among them a Miss Hobhouse. Sir Rennell recollected her name from the Boer War, and was of the opinion that nuisances of her sort ought to be kept at home. As a result the Foreign Office sent a note to the Home Office recommending that, in the event of Emily's return to England, further jaunts abroad should be barred.

By this time Emily had actually slipped out of Italy. Though she missed the Congress because of another bout of illness, as one of the handful of British activists holding a passport which predated the war she was later able to make her way to Holland, and was to spend the next five months there working for the cause. The Congress had set up an organisation based in Amsterdam called the International Committee of Women for Permanent Peace – women's groups of the time were addicted to clumsy and unmemorable names – and Emily was offered the appointment of acting international secretary. It was the kind of work familiar to her from her campaigning days during the Boer War, and despite her frail condition she accepted at once.

One of her first jobs was to pen an introduction to the official report of the Congress, a turgid document of over three hundred pages, and like much of Emily's polemical prose the style was purple-hued, breathless, and shot through with mixed metaphors. From the outset of the war, she wrote, "the hearts of women leapt to their sister women, the germ of the idea, nameless and unformed, that the women of the world must come to that world's aid, was silently and spontaneously conceived and lay in embryo in the hearts of many... The Women's Congress unfurled the white flag of Peace and – despite ridicule, disdain, opposition and disbelief – held it aloft before a bloodstained world."

With the other leading lights out of the country, the whole responsibility for running the International Committee fell on Emily. From the cramped office, with a skeleton staff of three or four, she ran off newsletters and pamphlets, raised money, and coordinated the work of a dozen national sections. "The Dutch ladies are all very kind to me," she wrote to Leonard Hobhouse in August, "and though I have to work in the office from 9-5 pm make it easy with long chairs and cushions and various amenities. The work is of exceeding interest and value and one day I think the world will own the fact."

Emily found official repression of the national sections greatest in France and Germany, where offices were raided by the police, activists harassed, and leaders exiled, gaoled or banned from public speaking. In Britain the national section called itself the Women's International League, the name soon to be adopted by the movement worldwide, and was officered chiefly by pacifist refugees from Mrs Fawcett's organisation. From the outset the British executive acted with far greater caution than their continental counterparts, and the appointment of the controversial Emily Hobhouse as international secretary was greeted with groans of dismay.

Despite the Foreign Office edict, Emily continued to flit unhindered between England and the Continent. On her next visit to London from Amsterdam, exhausted but glowing with the sense of a job well done, Emily was upset by the frosty reception she received from the British executive. "Women's International League held two meetings to discuss rather difficult question relating to E.H.," Kate Courtney noted in her diary, adding the terse observation, "her personality always excites extremes of feeling." Smarting at the committee's lack of appreciation, Emily resigned from the League. Sylvia Pankhurst was one of the few activists to offer her commiserations.

*

Emily's freedom to roam unmolested, already a bone of contention between the Foreign Office and the Home Office, was about to lead to serious conflict between the two departments. The Foreign Office now kept tabs on her movements and had received telegraphed warning of her departure from Holland for Tilbury on October 23. Around the time of her acrimonious confrontation with the Women's International League, the Foreign Office decreed that Emily should be barred from leaving England again and several applications she made for a new visa for Italy were refused. Unexpectedly, the newly appointed home secretary, Sir John Simon, took a very different line, saying it was up to the Italian authorities to act if they considered her presence obnoxious.

From the Foreign Office the under-secretary of state made plain his displeasure. This was Lord Robert Cecil, another of the old prime minister's sons, a man of priggish temperament and unfortunate vulture-like appearance, who was a personal friend of Millicent Fawcett. This was a remarkable honour considering Mrs Fawcett's modest roots in trade. The most snobbish of the Cecils, Lord Robert regularly expressed his unconquerable distaste for the middle classes. As he once observed: "They are squalid somehow and I'm never at my ease with them. And then they have such uncomfortable furniture."

It was not a question of Miss Hobhouse's presence being obnoxious to the Italians, Cecil replied sharply to Simon on November 8, but of a woman known to be guilty of "absurd and undesirable conduct" having liberty to repeat acts which prejudiced British interests.

Days and weeks passed with no answer to the Foreign Office memo. Then, to his astonishment, Cecil discovered his bird had flown. A new visa application by Emily had been approved and she was already out of the country. Clearly some powerful influence had been at work behind the scenes, and the finger pointed at Sir John Simon. Then on December 8 a telegram arrived at the Foreign Office from Britain's minister plenipotentiary in Berne, Evelyn Grant Duff, announcing that Miss Hobhouse had turned up at the British legation there. Was she to be allowed to go on to Italy? It was an embarrassing situation for Grant Duff as he happened to be related to her.

The next day witnessed a classic manoeuvre by Emily. An influential Liberal MP presented himself at the Foreign Office waving a telegram from the detained lady and demanding the personal intervention of Sir Edward Grey. "In weak health, must wind up affairs in Rome, cannot afford to keep flat there longer nor stay here," rambled the telegram from Berne. Letters then rained in on the Foreign Office from Emily allies like

Lord Robert Cecil, "the strangest-looking creature". As number two at the Foreign Office, he kept tabs on Emily's wanderings and ordered the seizure of her passport.

Courtney, each stressing the threat that the Swiss climate posed to Emily's delicate health. Unlike Kitchener and Milner in similar circumstances, Cecil caved in. Authorisation was grudgingly given for Emily to enter Italy provided she gave her word to refrain from making propaganda for peace. This she solemnly agreed to do.

It later transpired that Emily was indeed able to leave England because of direct intervention by Sir John Simon, in the teeth of opposition from the Foreign Office and Scotland Yard. In response to strong representations from the police, Simon ruled she might be detained only if evidence were found of past propaganda-making in Italy, but failed to disclose that Whitehall's files were bulging with the required proof. Simon avoided answering Cecil's note of November 8 until Christmas Eve, thus allowing no time for a rejoinder. Simon now coolly suggested it was up to Lord Robert rather than himself to cancel the lady's passport. "You of course know who she is," he added, "and will be able to estimate whether the circumstances justify this."

Sir John Simon, for all his eminence, appeared a strangely elusive, unattractive figure to many contemporaries. In a long political career he was to occupy almost every high office of state except the premiership itself, but fail to make a lasting mark in any. An Oxford-educated lawyer, unctuous yet pedantic, stubborn yet indecisive, the author of *Simon's Income Tax*, in five volumes, he seems to have owed each promotion to successive prime ministers' reluctance to choose a better man who might prove a rival.

Simon had form as a pacifist sympathiser. During the Boer War he had part-owned *The Speaker*, a pro-Boer journal noted for its extravagant praise of Emily. Before his election to parliament he worked briefly as leader-writer for the *Manchester Guardian*, welcoming Leonard Hobhouse as his successor. He had opposed the increase in naval expenditure and plotted ineffectually against Churchill, whose reckless courage and charisma made him everything Simon was not. On the declaration of war he resigned along with Burns and Morley, then quietly withdrew his letter of resignation.

The man's off-putting manner was notorious. The diplomat and critic Sir Harold Nicolson, who as a junior Foreign Office official found himself embroiled in the controversy over Emily's visa, was one of several diarists of the time to leave unflattering impressions of the man, scribbling in his diary: "God, what a toad and a worm Simon is!" Another shrewd observer of the political scene, Sir Henry "Chips" Channon, described Simon's smile as "like a brass knocker on a coffin".

Simon's tenure as home secretary did not long survive the granting of the visa. But if he thought his role in allowing Emily to leave the country would stay out of the limelight, he was due for a rude awakening.

*

The Courtneys too were busy in the pacifist cause throughout 1915, never more so than in June when Jane Addams, the American envoy appointed by the Peace Congress, arrived in England. Born the same year as Emily, Miss Addams was to become the first American woman awarded the Nobel Peace Prize. Kate Courtney introduced her visitor to many influential figures, and when it occurred to her that she ought to see the Archbishop of Canterbury, set off boldly for Lambeth Palace. Informed that His Grace was ill in bed, Lady Courtney announced she was staying put until His Grace got up. And that was what he did.

Emily had a low opinion of Archbishop Davidson. His term in office lasted a remarkable twenty-five years, though his only achievement as listed in *Chambers Biographical Dictionary* was to write the biography of his father-in-law, an earlier archbishop of Canterbury. Before the war Emily had deplored as "too disgusting" Davidson's decision to launch and bless one of Churchill's new warships, and he had recently compounded his sins by publishing his jingoist *Sermons in Time of War*. Taking as his text for Intercession Day "the peace of God, which passeth all understanding", he preached that defeatism about the war was "flatly disloyal to conscience and to God", and at Easter he had led prayers for more men and munitions. From the pulpit at St Paul's Cathedral he reminded the congregation that 1915 was the centenary of Waterloo, and cried out: "We are kneeling upon holy ground. The graves of Nelson, Wellington and Roberts are beneath our feet." In Emily's eyes he cut a sorry figure as successor to the great Archbishop Benson.

Kate Courtney was also doing her bit for the refugees, despite the Cheyne Walk servants' strong aversion to the Belgians she brought into the house. The servants were further disgruntled with their mistress when she refused them permission to go out to watch Zeppelin raiders passing over the neighbourhood. Kate insisted on maintaining proper standards despite the war, and recorded with evident satisfaction an overheard remark: "She is the only person who keeps up the social life of Chelsea, and yet she is a horrid pacifist!"

As Emily sometimes stayed with the Courtneys, so the Courtneys sometimes escaped London, where the guns of Flanders could be heard, and stayed at Emily's house in Bude. Leonard Courtney, branded a "peace crank" by the popular press after his first wartime speech in the Lords, rejoiced in these pilgrimages to his native Cornwall. Although in his eighties, and giving continual anxiety over his health, he could still walk a good nine miles a day, rambling the coastal paths or striking out across the downs. He greatly enjoyed trips in a hired motor car with Emily and liked to potter round country churchyards looking for his ancestors' graves. Other wartime visitors to Bude included Sidney and Beatrice Webb, though their political rift with Emily and the Courtneys was wider than ever. Kate wrote of her relief when the peace and beauty of the place temporarily charmed Sidney out of his "emphatic and coldly reasonable state of mind".

That summer Kate took a sentimental journey to the old Potter country home in the Cotswolds, now requisitioned as a military hospital. "Beds and soldiers in our best drawing-room," she marvelled, and tried to imagine the astonishment of the privileged sisters fifty years ago – "at Lallie's coming-out ball say" – had they been vouchsafed a glimpse into the future. In September, with the war continuing to go badly, she confided in her diary "a recognition that we are not winning and may be defeated", and worried over her sister Beatrice's prediction that a bill to introduce conscription would spark a revolution among the working classes.

Kate had noted a gathering anti-Kitchener feeling in her diary as early as May, 1915, when the *Daily Mail* ran an article critical of the war secretary. "Is it all hollow, the national belief in him?" she wondered. "I have never known how much it was justified, but supposed there was some great quality or capacity in spite of apparent stupidity of speech and look. At any rate, one remembers his conduct about the Fashoda difficulty, and at the Peace of Vereeniging when he shone in generosity and wisdom as compared with Lord Milner."

The *Daily Mail* and *The Times*, persecutors of Emily Hobhouse during the Boer War, were now turning their sights on her old adversary. Secretly encouraged by Lloyd George, who had designs on Kitchener's job, both newspapers blamed government incompetence for a shortage of high-explosive shells which had halted British initiatives at the front. The *Daily Mail* went further with a personal attack on the war minister under the headline "Lord Kitchener's Tragic Blunder". This time the *Mail* badly misjudged the public mood and overnight its circulation plunged by over a million. At the time Kitchener could only fume in private. "Did they remember," he cried, "when they went headlong into a war like this, that they were without an army, and without any preparation to equip one?"

Kitchener was losing many personal friends in action. Among the first killed was eighteen-year-old George Cecil, only son of Lord and Lady Edward, whose detached marriage was further strained by grief, pushing Lady Edward ever closer to Alfred Milner. Only once did Kitchener's staff see him overwhelmed by news from the front, when the loss of the young poet Julian Grenfell affected him so deeply that he abandoned his desk for an hour. In a letter of condolence to Grenfell's father he wrote: "We all wish sometimes that the trumpet would sound for us, but we have to stick it out and do our very best until the release comes." Kitchener would not himself survive to learn of the death of his dearest friend from Boer War days, charming, amusing Frank Maxwell, VC.

While public faith in Kitchener remained firm, disquiet over the war led to the replacement of the Liberal administration by a coalition. Kitchener's disillusion with politicians deepened when Asquith was forced to make the cabinet larger and more cumbersome as a result. Though Asquith continued to head the new government, Lloyd George secured the newly created post of minister of munitions, reaping the credit for foundations laid by Kitchener. Again he talked glumly of resignation.

Lloyd George was recognised as a shameless schemer even by his political allies. Asquith's wife Margot remarked that he could not see a belt without hitting below it. Kitchener was constantly arguing with him, but acknowledged his mettle. "The little Welshman is peppery, but he means to win the war, which is what matters," he said, even after a characteristically devious move by Lloyd George had deprived him of one of his comforts. In a bid to combat drunkenness among workers, the new munitions minister persuaded the King to set an example by taking the pledge for the duration of the war. Kitchener felt duty bound to follow his sovereign's lead, but sorely missed his glass of wine and bedtime brandy. At some cost to his temper he stuck to his word, even after discovering that Lloyd George did not.

The only good news of the year 1915 was from South West Africa, where Smuts and Botha accepted the surrender of all German forces. It was the Allies' first comprehensive victory of the war. The two former enemies were hailed as military geniuses, though it had helped that their soldiers outnumbered the Germans by six to one.

Kate Courtney's diary entry for Christmas that year reflected her growing anxiety that government and press were bracing the public for a fight to the finish. "It is no consolation that the German rulers may be doing the same thing," she added, "and I have a horrid fear that they have more grounds for confidence, for where are the war brains any more than the peace brains in England now?"

Conscription was now the greatest single issue. Kitchener doggedly resisted its introduction, preferring an army of the willing, and like Beatrice Webb fearing a working-class backlash against compulsion. Kitchener continued to insist that volunteers made better soldiers, and by this time he had raised nearly three million of them. But by October 1915 the colossal losses at the front had turned the majority of the cabinet against him, and his last effort to avert conscription was a scheme under which men between eighteen and forty-one could "attest" their willingness to serve if called upon. Within weeks, two and a quarter million attested, but it was still not enough. Universal military service came in the first month of 1916 with only muted opposition.

*

The new year opened with high hopes of victory. After the huge German advances early in the war, followed by stalemate in the trenches, the initiative seemed finally to be swinging the Allies' way. Kitchener's new army was at last coming to full strength, offering the first opportunity for a great counter-offensive. At sea too prospects were brighter, not least because the Kaiser pulled back from waging unrestricted submarine warfare.

The idea that Britain might lose never have entered Mrs Fawcett's head, but years later she confessed to a major miscalculation over the war's effect. "So ill did I read the future," she wrote, "that I thought the hope of women's freedom was indefinitely postponed, and that this was the supreme sacrifice asked of us at this stupendous moment." Though the call of duty was clear, she believed the war had destroyed her life's work. In fact it was the turning point in the struggle for women's rights, though in the event it was not Mrs Pankhurst or Mrs Fawcett, or any of their sex, who gave the crucial push to the historical process which finally guaranteed votes for women. The catalyst was Lord Kitchener. As men in their millions answered his call to arms, women stepped forward to make munitions, drive buses, deliver the mail, and till the land, while a hundred thousand of them volunteered for the auxiliary forces. This was the social revolution that would secure female suffrage.

Kitchener made a speech in praise of women's support for the war effort as gratifying to Millicent Fawcett as it was distasteful to Emily. "I cannot refrain," he said, "from a tribute of recognition to the large number of women, drawn from every class and phase of life, who have come forward and placed their services unreservedly at their country's disposal." Mrs Fawcett would also have strongly approved of Kitchener's position during a cabinet discussion over the wartime employment of women. When even Lloyd George accepted it was natural that trades like mining were barred to females, the war minister objected, pointing out that women did such work in Zanzibar. He was surprised and hurt when the rest of the cabinet burst out laughing.

*

A cousin of Emily's was about to become embroiled in the controversy over conscription. Born in 1881, Stephen Hobhouse was heir to the broad acres of Hadspen and heir-presumptive to the fortune of Lord Hobhouse. By a quirk of fate, Stephen was linked from infancy with a man who loomed large in Emily's life. On the day of his christening, the stand-in at the font for an absent Hobhouse godfather was an Oxford contemporary of the squire who happened to be visiting Hadspen at the time. He was an ambitious young fellow of Balliol named Alfred Milner.

Stephen grew up a skinny weakling, viewed by many in the family as a beastly little prig. But for all that he was the heir, ordained to tread the familiar path from Eton to Oxford, followed by a lucrative career in the civil service secured through family influence. Then at the age of twenty-one, at the bookstall on Oxford station, Stephen fatefully browsed through a sixpenny pamphlet by Leo Tolstoy. His conversion to the Russian novelist's idiosyncratic brand of Christian socialist pacifism led Stephen to a dramatic renunciation of the Hobhouses' sinful inheritance from slavery and, as a conscientious objector in the Great War, to a spell of hard labour in Wormwood Scrubs.

Poor Stephen turned out to be a chronic hypochondriac and depressive even by Hobhouse standards, constitutionally weakened by nervous breakdowns, extreme forms of vegetarianism and bizarre nature cures. Trust funds set up by the family to save Stephen from destitution were diverted to assorted socialist and pacifist causes, while he and his wife inhabited a bug-infested tenement block in Hoxton as a gesture of solidarity with the oppressed poor. Stephen's wife Rosa seemed a perfect partner for him. A daughter of the founder of the National Society for the Prevention of Cruelty to Children, Rosa Hobhouse was a champion of adult and child offenders, a self-taught homeopath, poet, failed Labour candidate, and prolific anti-war pamphleteer. In 1916, in a pitiful effort to launch a "pilgrimage of peace", she was arrested on a charge of prejudicing recruiting and spent three months in Northampton Gaol.

Emily seems to have disapproved of the extravagant excesses of Stephen's self-denial. She never lost pride in the family's social standing, though her frequent talk of her ancestors left out the slave-dealing founder of the Hobhouse fortune. Certainly her own vicissitudes had left her with a healthy respect for money. As her legacy drained away, she grieved over the enforced sale of her treasures, and evidently considered that Christ's injunction to the rich young man could be taken too literally. In her will she was to leave nothing to her fellow vegetarian-socialist-pacifist cousin – sensibly enough, since any money he came by was instantly given away – favouring instead the war veteran nephew Oliver. Stephen, on the other hand, was intensely proud of his controversial cousin, and in adult life would marvel at the memory of himself as an unenlightened schoolboy, earnestly haranguing Emily on the wickedness of the Boers. He always prophesied that Emily would be the most famous Hobhouse.

Stephen first set eyes on his future wife at a Hampstead supper party attended by Hobhouse relations. Instantly recognising one another as soul mates, he and Rosa left the house together – he recorded "the look of eager and affectionate curiosity on the face of my cousin Emily as she saw us depart" – and within weeks the couple were married. Immediately after the outbreak of war Stephen offered himself as chairman of a hastily-formed charitable group operating under the name of "Emergency Committee for the Assistance of Germans in Distress". This did not go down well in Hoxton. Branded as spies, Stephen and Rosa only narrowly escaped a mob intent on throwing them in the canal.

Once conscription was introduced, strings were frantically pulled to have Stephen exempted, but he was bent on martyrdom. Spurning all help, he not only refused to be inducted as a soldier, but refused the option of non-combatant service, refused to take his case to appeal, and repeatedly refused the medical examination that would have found him unfit to serve anyway.

Within the family, divisions deepened. Stephen had staunch support from his uncles Leonard Courtney and Alfred Cripps, but while confined in the guardroom before his trial received a robust letter from his aunt Beatrice Webb which declared him "guilty of the sin of rebellion" against a government that was defending his way of life. Nor was there any comfort from the other great intellectual of the family, Emily's brother Leonard, who refuted Stephen's moral right to duck out of a just war. Curiously enough, Emily herself seems to have kept out of the row. Cruelly torn both ways by the conflict was Stephen's mother Margaret Hobhouse, who had two other sons fighting at the front.

An old acquaintance now reappears in the story. Wyndham Childs, last encountered as one of the young rowdies storming the platform at Emily's peace meeting at Liskeard during the Boer War, was by 1916 a staff officer at the War Office under Lord Kitchener. Early in June Childs was called to the chief's sweltering office for special orders. With perspiration trickling down his face, he heard he was being entrusted with a special job. To his consternation, Kitchener had chosen him to stamp out the ill-treatment of conscientious objectors in the army. In this manner Childs became the protector of Emily's cousin Stephen, who was sentenced to hard labour not long after for refusing to be inducted in the Hackney Rifles.

Kitchener was remarkably sympathetic to those with genuine moral objections to war. Childs's private view of "conchies" differed radically from his chief's, but that he carried out his orders conscientiously would be borne out by Stephen Hobhouse's admission that, in stark contrast to his experiences at the hands of a hostile civilian authority, he was treated "almost uniformly with courtesy and in some cases with real kindness" while in military custody. Childs, later a major-general, seems to have resigned himself to his country's inexplicably liberal ways. "If ever there is another war," he would write in 1930, "I suppose we shall get the conscientious objector and his highbrow protagonists, as well as the cranks who believe and insist that war shall be conducted with humanity."

The issue was very much on Kitchener's mind in early June 1916, the last days of his life. Almost the last interview he granted at the War Office was to a deputation from the free churches who wished to press the case for conscientious objectors, and the personal orders to Childs were among the last he ever gave.

29 A PRIVATE INVASION OF GERMANY

I n June 1916 both Emily Hobhouse and Lord Kitchener embarked on secret missions abroad. Emily's was the boldest, or maddest, adventure of her life, proving vastly damaging to what reputation she still possessed, and leading to her denunciation in parliament as a traitor to her country. Kitchener's mission was his last and would end in his death.

By this stage of the war Emily was an embarrassment to all but the most resolute of her pacifist comrades. Her desperate determination to expose the war as a wicked nonsense only served to make her more dogmatic and incoherent, and her letters sorely tried the patience of Smuts and others. But a second winter in Rome had worked wonders for her health, and she now determined on an astonishing course of action. On her own, Emily would try to stop the war. Knowing no responsible friend would approve the escapade she had dreamed up, she kept her counsel. Unlike the secretary for war, she managed to keep everyone in the dark over her plans.

Kitchener, sick of the intrigues of the cabinet room, was by this time seizing any excuse to get away from London. He knew that many of his colleagues wanted rid of him. Lloyd George coveted his job; Churchill, who had bulldozed his colleagues into the disastrous joint navy and army campaign at Gallipoli, was scheming to shift the principal responsibility onto Kitchener. A suggestion by the Russian ambassador that the war minister should visit Russia early in June was eagerly accepted.

*

Days before the date of Kitchener's departure, the British and German fleets fought the battle of Jutland, the major naval engagement of the war. Of the British admiral, Sir John Jellicoe, it was said he was the only man who could have lost the war in an afternoon. Both sides suffered heavy losses at Jutland, but the Kaiser's fleet never again ventured out of port. The Royal Navy remained intact to enforce the blockade, tightening the grip around Germany's neck.

Kitchener's last free day was spent at Broome, where he observed that the roses in the sunken garden should be at their best on his return from Russia. The last private business he undertook was a trip to the studio of a sculptor he had commissioned to make a clay model of an elaborate stone fountain, based on Kitchener's own design, as a centrepiece for his garden. As they inspected the model, with its swarms of nymphs, cherubs and dolphins, the sculptor named his price, and Kitchener shook his head. "After the war," he said, "if the nation want to give me anything, it will be nice to have this scheme to put before them."

Kitchener left the War Office for the last time on June 4. His private secretary, Sir George Arthur, who saw him off from Kings Cross, recorded how Kitchener boarded the Scottish Express at once to avoid being recognised but then, most unusually, stepped back onto the platform and in a quiet sad voice asked Arthur to look after things while he was away. As if unable to understand the impulse which prompted him to speak a last word to his old friend, Kitchener again entered his private carriage and stared silently out of the window until the train started.

The supposedly hush-hush mission to Russia was an open secret in London. Within hours of Kitchener leaving Kings Cross, the United States ambassador informed Washington that he detected "a hope and feeling" in certain quarters that the war minister would not come back – a remarkable observation coming from a representative of a still neutral power, stemming from the kind of loose talk that Kitchener deplored.

The party slept on the express overnight, arriving at Thurso on Monday, June 5. There Kitchener embarked in gale-force conditions on the destroyer HMS *Oak*, having arranged a rendezvous with Admiral Jellicoe at Scapa Flow. By coincidence, Kitchener left British soil for the last time on the same day that the last division of Kitchener's new army, the fortieth, sailed for France.

Hours later Jellicoe welcomed the war minister on board his flagship, *Iron Duke*. The visitor was given ovations wherever he went on the huge ship. One rating later recalled his impression of Kitchener as "a gentle man in uniform with not a care in the world, whose humorous grey eyes looked at each one of us in passing as one might look on a child one has been pleased to meet, he so old in war, we so young".

The worsening weather faced Jellicoe with a dilemma. The armoured cruiser HMS *Hampshire* had been chosen to take Kitchener to Archangel, but the ferocity of the gale ruled out the preferred route sailing north-east into the open sea. A second regular route was rejected because of a report, later found to be false, of a submarine presence. But Kitchener refused to wait. Fatally, the admiral ordered a third course through the Pentland Forth, hugging the western coastline of Orkney. It was a route rarely used by warships though in constant use by merchant shipping. What naval intelligence had failed to detect was that one week earlier the German submarine U75 had slipped into the waters off the Orkneys and sown twenty-two mines.

At four in the afternoon Kitchener's party transferred to the *Hampshire* and steamed out of Scapa Flow. One of the few survivors was to say the ship was immediately in the teeth of the most terrific gale of his experience. Two escorting destroyers were unable to keep in contact, but the risk of submarine attack was regarded as negligible.

Shortly before eight o'clock those on board heard an explosion. All the lights went out, the *Hampshire* lurched to starboard, and in the darkness floods of water entered. The captain gave an immediate order to abandon ship. Kitchener, who had been resting in his cabin, came out onto the quarterdeck, where he was joined by others of his party. He was in uniform but without the khaki greatcoat he had pulled on earlier against the unseasonable cold. A survivor would describe Kitchener's demeanour as impassive. Either he did not hear the captain's shout to make for the lifeboats, or he ignored it as futile and undignified. He was last seen pacing the deck, talking with his aides, giving no sign of nervousness.

As daylight remained, a handful of islanders witnessed the disaster from nearby Marwick Head. Flame and smoke were seen clearly as the mine went off but no sound was heard above the storm. Ten minutes after the explosion the stern suddenly lifted and the *Hampshire* went down in forty fathoms about a mile and a half out from shore. Of the crew of six hundred and fifty, twelve reached land alive. All others who did not drown, die in the explosion or go down with the ship were killed by the intense cold of the water or smashed on the rocks. Of Kitchener the searchers found no trace.

News of his death came as a thunderbolt. People afterwards recalled what they were doing the moment they heard the newsboys' cry of "Kitchener is drowned" in the way later generations would remember the assassination of President Kennedy or the attack on the Twin Towers. Everywhere shops closed, blinds were drawn, flags flew at half-mast. No death since Queen Victoria's had inspired such national mourning; none since Nelson's had seemed so calamitous, and without the consolation of a Trafalgar. To most people today, Kitchener personifies a type of rigid, unimaginative and callous military mind that could throw away countless lives to gain a few yards of mud, but to the public of his own day he embodied Britain's power of endurance and unbreakable will. For millions, it was as if they had suffered a personal loss.

The grief-stricken George V consoled himself with the thought that he had never been swayed by what he called "the jealousies and ineptitudes of K's colleagues". The King's mother, Queen Alexandra, was distraught. "My beloved Georgie boy," she wrote from Marlborough House, "I feel quite stunned and collapsed at these *dreadful* and *awful* news of our beloved Kitchener's untimely loss – at *sea* too!" In a letter to his uncle, the Duke of Connaught, the King called Kitchener a personal friend of thirty years' standing and added: "I had the greatest admiration for him and absolute confidence in his judgment. I shall miss him terribly and his guiding hand." Connaught replied that the raising of Kitchener's volunteer army was an achievement "unique in the history of the world". By royal command the armies of the Empire went into mourning, with every officer instructed to wear a black armband for a week. No other subject, not even the Duke of Wellington, had been accorded this distinction.

Lady Salisbury, Kitchener's friend and correspondent of many years, wrote to commiserate with her brother-in-law Lord Edward Cecil, then serving in Egypt: "There are few heavier blows that could have fallen on you than this. One of the great loves of your life has gone." Hearing that the dead man's post was to go to his chief detractor, Lloyd George, she was moved to quote from the Psalms: "I have seen the wicked in great power, and spreading himself like a green bay tree." Asquith himself was shocked by the Welshman's blatant opportunism. "All this canvassing and wire-pulling about the succession," he wrote to the King's private secretary, "while poor K's body is still tossing about in the North Sea, seems to me to be in the highest degree indecent."

So the figure of Lloyd George provides another curious symmetry to the stories of Emily Hobhouse and Herbert Kitchener. Emily, at the start of her campaigning career, had shared an anti-war platform with Lloyd George; now the same man was replacing Kitchener as minister for war.

Kate Courtney recorded the drowning of Kitchener in her diary on the same day she wrote of the gaoling of Rosa Hobhouse for peace agitation. "There were some good points about K of K," she wrote, "apart from whatever his military qualities may have been or his present military value, and I do not think he ever made a war, or caused one, and he certainly helped to save us from one over Fashoda, and brought another to an end with some commonsense and generosity in South Africa. He recognised the Boers

as men and equal opponents, while Milner would have treated them as a subject race."
From a lifelong political opponent, it was not a bad obituary.

While much of the world mourned, Germany exulted. At his headquarters in France, Sir Douglas Haig was dismayed at the news, not least because he heard it first from an intercepted German wireless message. All along the front British soldiers heard shouted taunts from the trenches opposite that Kitchener was roasting in hell. Yet his hold on the public imagination was so powerful that many refused to believe the news. The absence of a body led to an outbreak of wild stories that Kitchener was not dead but mysteriously in hiding. He had been picked up by a submarine, or was a prisoner; some even said that, King Arthur-like, he was living in a cave to reappear to save the nation at its moment of supreme danger.

Extraordinary rumours spread also of who had betrayed the secret of Kitchener's last journey, the candidates including Asquith, Churchill, Lord Haldane – fantastically rumoured to be the Kaiser's illegitimate brother – and Lloyd George. Most exotic of the suspects was Rasputin. Prince Felix Yusupov, who was later to murder the monk because of his malign influence over the Czar's family, claimed the Czarina confided in Rasputin that Kitchener was coming, and he drunkenly betrayed the secret to German spies.

*

Emily had kept a low profile while recuperating in Rome during the early months of 1916. Unfortunately as her heart grew stronger, her finances plunged to new depths, as wartime inflation was worse in Italy than anywhere else in Europe. Then in May the Foreign Office received a new report from Grant Duff in Berne. Despite her promise, Emily was agitating for peace again – not in Italy, however, but back in Switzerland, under the very nose of the British plenipotentiary.

The Foreign Office had had enough. Grant Duff was instructed to seize Emily's passport and replace it with a document valid for a one-way journey to Britain only. The problem was that the woman was making herself scarce, and the police of neutral Switzerland refused to locate an "undesirable" for a foreign legation. It was not until June 5, the day Kitchener boarded the *Hampshire*, that Grant Duff managed to discover her new address and wrote immediately commanding her presence at his office. A scribbled note came from Emily in reply stating she was just leaving on a trip but would be sure to look him up on her return. Unknown to the Foreign Office, Emily no longer depended only on the passport it wished to confiscate. She now had papers from her good friends the Germans.

Even as she was being hunted by the British authorities, Emily had made contact with Grant Duff's German counterpart in Berne, a Baron von Romberg, and laid before him a secret scheme, or at least a part of it – for during the bitter controversy to come, she would stick doggedly to her story that a peace mission to the enemy was not in her mind at the moment she spoke to Romberg. As in the aftermath of her deportation from Cape Town, both Emily and the British government would seek to establish a legal point over the precise nature of her intention and the time at which it was formed.

What Emily later claimed to have discussed with the Germans was her desire to investigate the state of things in occupied Belgium, and to see for herself the conditions in a German camp for British internees. Impressed by her claim of personal acquaintance with his foreign minister, Romberg contacted Berlin and awaited instructions, telling Emily to wait patiently for news. Day followed day without a word. Night after night Emily lay sleepless in her bed, terrified by the thought of what she was doing. Knowing she was being actively sought by the British kept her in a state of feverish anxiety. Finally, after nearly a month, just as Grant Duff's agents picked up her scent, a message came from Romberg. Berlin said yes.

It was cloak-and-dagger from the start. The day after hearing from Romberg, Emily collected German papers from the legation. Written conditions from Berlin were attached to the permit to enter enemy territory, but in the excitement of the moment she forgot to read them, or so she would claim. Seizing her German phrase book, she dashed off the note to Grant Duff before catching a train to Basel on the German border. The secret rendezvous was a temperance inn chosen for its quiet situation. A courier appeared with Teutonic punctuality, placed Emily and her bags in a diplomatic car, and whisked her unchallenged past the Swiss customs post. "Who but Emily would have conceived such a scheme?" Leonard Hobhouse would later cry, aghast at his sister's "private invasion of Germany". Who but Emily could have actually carried it through despite all its "glaring absurdities and impossibilities"?

It was now June 6, the day Kitchener died, though no one knew it yet. "It was a wonderful moment, and I felt as if in a dream," she wrote. The car took her first to Cologne and next day across the border into Belgium where a new escort, a smiling Baron Falkenhausen von Friedensthal, was waiting.

Only now did it dawn on Emily what strict conditions applied to the visit. She was to be accompanied by a German officer at all times; in Brussels she was to stay at the hotel assigned to her; she was to speak to no Belgians. When Emily objected, the baron immediately reverted to stereotype, saying there could be no relaxation of the rules. "Your refusal to let me speak to Belgians is your greatest condemnation," she scolded.

The impressions Emily later published of the visit were widely condemned as pro-German propaganda. She decided the war damage had been greatly exaggerated, and the people struck her as "generally happy and cheerful". The martial law in force was no stricter than she had experienced in South Africa. As to the infamous burning of the great library at Louvain – condemned throughout the world as Hunnish vandalism – Emily parroted the German line that fighting in the city's ancient square was started by partisans, with the library fire an unfortunate but accidental consequence, and added that only prompt action by a brave German officer saved the cathedral too from destruction. Altogether, it is difficult to avoid the conclusion that Emily saw pretty much what the limpet-like escort wished her to see, and he would have been delighted with her conclusion that the heavy infant mortality rates in Belgium were caused by the British blockade.[xxxv]

In Brussels Emily was amazed to discover that the Germans possessed copies of all the English newspapers only two days old, and was able to read of Kitchener's drowning. When she was first told the news, a host of memories crowded into Emily's mind. From the day she left St Ive, free of the father who had ruled her for thirty-five years, Emily had learned to work her will upon the high and mighty. Only Kitchener had remained proof against her wiles from first to last.

Yet since the trauma of her deportation, Emily's heart had softened, and her view of the man had undergone a remarkable alteration. She now recognised the sinking of the *Hampshire* as a catastrophic blow to hopes of world peace and, more immediately, to the scheme on which she was gambling her future. The former great adversary, she had come to believe, was "probably the only man in England who was impervious to public opinion and with shoulders broad enough to bear that hostile opinion if he thought we could gain no military decision and *must* make peace by negotiation". Perhaps, at the thrilling moment of first crossing into Germany, she had pictured a triumphant return to England clutching a peace plan to place before Kitchener himself. If so, such day-dreams were gone forever.

*

On June 17 Emily travelled on to Berlin. The baron settled her into her hotel and then rushed home to see his wife instead of keeping tabs on his elderly English charge. This was a bonus for Emily, who used her unexpected freedom to contact women's groups in the capital, a cause of great alarm to Falkenhausen when he found out.

Later, to inquisitors in England, Emily insisted that only after reaching Berlin had she conceived the idea of a personal meeting with the German foreign minister, Gottlieb von Jagow, dashing off a letter announcing her presence on an impulse. Whatever the case, an invitation to the Foreign Ministry came by return post. On the evening of June 19 she was escorted to the Wilhelmstrasse, the administrative power centre of the German state, by Baron Falkenhausen, now in a state of panic over a possible charge of dereliction of duty. The foreign minister was notorious for his short fuse and fits of bullying rage.

Perhaps it was in the blood. Jagow's cousin was Berlin's chief of police, a man whose virulent hatred of Britain inspired a campaign to expunge all trace of English words from the capital. Thus famous hotels like the Bristol and the Westminster were made to adopt Teutonic names. The re-naming programme was of a piece with the frenzied anti-British feeling of the time, when the traditional form of greeting in the street was replaced by the cry "Gott strafe England" – God punish England – though Emily experienced nothing of this particular unpleasantness when she roamed Berlin.

To Frankenhausen's relief, Jagow was in expansive mood that evening. Emily found him very simple, unaffected and thoughtful, and the two were closeted together for nearly an hour, reminiscing about old times – she had known Jagow when he was ambassador in Italy – before getting down to business. In a telling passage in Ruth Fry's account of the meeting, Emily said she felt there was nothing strange about the experience because "she had so long determined on her journey to Germany".

Jagow said Emily could take the message to England that Germany was willing to negotiate a peace "if advances were made". Emily wrote down details of his offer immediately afterwards, but somehow managed to mislay the document. What she did preserve were brief notes on various bits of paper, and these included Jagow's observation that Germany had had victories but also great defeats, while England had had no great victories but no defeats. However, he stressed that Germany's peace offer was made in humanity and not out of weakness.

Emily was not the first woman pacifist to meet the German leader. Following the Peace Congress at The Hague in 1915, the American envoy Jane Addams had seen Jagow, though he happened to be in one of his fouler moods that day and put on a show of noisy belligerence. Two months after the American, the Hungarian activist Rosika Schwimmer, a great admirer of Emily, turned up at the Wilhelmstrasse, and she too secured an interview with Jagow. What made Emily's adventure unique was that she went to Berlin as a national of an enemy state, rather than as a neutral like Addams or, like Schwimmer, a national of a country allied to Germany.

*

Emily was about to intrude upon an area of responsibility entrusted personally to Lord Robert Cecil, which was the treatment of British prisoners of war in Germany. On June 22 she was escorted to the camp at Ruhleben, five miles outside Berlin, where the largest number of British captives was held. In peacetime Ruhleben had been a racetrack, and prisoners were shut up in the stables and haylofts with as many as six packed into each box-stall. The first internees were civilians who had failed to leave German soil in time, and were later joined by captured servicemen. Significantly, these included a number of Irish soldiers. Also at Ruhleben was a makeshift sanatorium for prisoners who had fallen mentally ill.

Emily found it curiously stirring to be in a camp again, instantly recognising the sordidness and artificiality, neatness, squalor and monotony, the forlorn efforts of the prisoners to keep themselves busy. But there were great differences too: "In this camp there were no children, no raging sicknesses, no starvation, no skeletons, no deaths." Her verdict, later offered to newspapers in Britain, provided more music for German ears: "I can and most truthfully say that Ruhleben Camp was not a bad one – that much was done for the amusement and occupation and instruction of the inmates, that the food was good (the bread was coarse but wholesome) and kindness shown by the enemy authorities."

But Emily's findings did not chime with the experience of the man most active on behalf of the prisoners at the time. This was the United States ambassador to Germany, James Gerard, who as a neutral had assumed responsibility for the interests of British subjects on the outbreak of war, and in his fashion performed a role similar to Emily's in the South African camps.

Like Emily, Gerard had ceaselessly badgered the authorities over their failings, and exposed instances of German civilians being fined or gaoled for showing kindness to prisoners. As the captives lacked clothing and blankets, he had toured the department stores of Berlin, buying up supplies for the camps where the British were confined, along with articles like crutches for the wounded. In some camps he recorded frightful conditions – savage beatings, attacks by guard dogs, and widespread reprisals for the alleged abuse of Germans in England. Worst of all, he documented a case of British and French officers being deliberately exposed to an outbreak of typhus.

By 1916, thanks to Gerard's vehement protests, Ruhleben was the best camp by far, which may explain the Germans' willingness to let Emily inside. Yet it was Gerard who had established the camp canteen, run by the inmates themselves; he also paid poorer prisoners a weekly allowance to cover necessities and little comforts. Food remained the paramount concern, and an American nutritionist who investigated Ruhleben earlier that year reported the prisoners were on a starvation diet.

*

Emily's time in Germany was at an end. She was now desperate to get back to London to unveil the peace plan, but filled with foreboding that she would be thwarted. As ever, her agitated state painfully affected her heart. At the Swiss border she was refused entry on her German papers, but waved through on production of her British passport. Back in Berne, she braced herself for the reckoning with Evelyn Grant Duff but decided the Germans should take priority, giving the first account of her visit to Baron von Romberg. Only then did she present herself at the British legation where her passport, with its incriminating stamp for re-entry to Switzerland, was confiscated immediately.

Grant Duff was a scion of an old diplomatic family. The traveller Gertrude Bell, who knew him during his previous posting in Persia, had thought him deadly dull even as a young man. At the time of his confrontation with Emily he was still in his early fifties, but far from hale; indeed almost immediately afterwards he would take early retirement on the grounds of ill health, with a knighthood as consolation. The stormy scene with Emily can hardly have improved his blood pressure.

"When she appeared," he wrote to Lord Robert Cecil, "I first taxed her with breaking her declaration of December 11 that 'if I receive the British visa to proceed to Italy, I undertake not to engage in propaganda of any sort, especially propaganda in favour of peace'." Emily boldly declared that her peace meeting in Berne was not a breach of the undertaking since that applied specifically to Italy. This argument Grant Duff dismissed as pure sophistry, but a hesitant note crept into his report to London. "I do not know whether by a quibble the declaration can be construed as applying only to Italy," he wrote, "but it was intended to cover her proceedings in Switzerland as well. Even if her contention is legally valid, it is a piece of sharp practice showing clearly the kind of woman with whom we have to deal."

Asked where she had been between June 6 and 24, Emily owned up at once. She had been given a safe conduct for Germany by her old acquaintance, the foreign minister. Grant Duff retorted that entering an enemy country without official sanction was most improper and very possibly an indictable offence. Emily countered that her business in Germany was so pressing it was her duty to go. "She then stated she had important information to lay before His Majesty's Government," he wrote, "but what it was she declined to divulge."

In Whitehall, Lord Robert read Grant Duff's report with mounting anger. Perhaps he was not in the best of humours that morning, since his domestic life at the time was far from tranquil. Dutifully, he and his wife Nelly had taken into their London home not only a refugee Belgian couple, but a displaced French couple as well. Unfortunately the French pair despised the Belgians, who detested the French, so at meals all communications had to pass through the Cecils. That Lady Nelly was totally deaf only added to the strain.

Then aged fifty, Robert Cecil was the high achiever among the old prime minister's brood, destined to become a viscount in his own right and a Nobel peace laureate. High-minded and austere, a devoted churchman, he was a worthy descendant of the founder of the Cecil line, the faithful servant of Elizabeth I. The high point of his life, and ultimately most crushing disappointment, would be his leading part in founding the ill-fated League of Nations, the first international body set up to secure world peace – a fact which contributes a certain irony to the imminent clash over Emily's mission.

Unsurprisingly, Cecil had little time for the demanding, capricious, fun-loving wife of his younger brother Lord Edward – "the most tiresome woman I know," as he called her. The atmosphere could be cut with a knife when both were staying at Hatfield, the Cecil mansion, where the religion-dominated formality was not at all to Lady Edward's taste. She in turn looked down on her disapproving relation, "the strangest-looking creature, with a head like Savonarola on a body almost deformed by a round back".

Robert Cecil disliked everything about his sister-in-law. He disliked her frivolity, her love of smart society, her manners, her moodiness, her artistic pretensions, her "childish worldliness and materialism". The drawn-out liaison with Milner must have pained him as a blot on the family escutcheon. He even nursed an obsession over the extravagant number of baths she took and would lie fuming in bed as he listened to her bathwater gurgling. To Lady Edward, he believed, life was nothing more than a game in which she intended to shine and attract as much attention as possible. Lord Robert's ideal woman was probably his great friend Mrs Fawcett or his own forthright, tireless, High Anglican mother. Yet now and then he would recall his Christian duty and admonish himself for brooding on his sister-in-law's imperfections.

In his humdrum autobiography Cecil draws a veil over the Emily controversy and the embarrassments it brought him throughout 1916. But then, neither can he once bring himself to acknowledge the existence of Lady Edward. He does however take a number of swipes at Sir John Simon, who had played such a devious role in the affair of Emily's visa.[xxvi]

As he read Grant Duff's report, Lord Robert came to a passage which must have brought on one of his alarming smiles, which the French premier Georges Clemenceau used to say made him look like a Chinese dragon. Poor Emily, in a muddle during her visit to the legation, had spread a mass of papers over the desk, and on her departure a highly compromising document was somehow left behind. This was a letter Emily had written ready for posting to the Dutch peace activist Dr Aletta Jacobs, the prime mover of the Hague Congress the previous year. Grant Duff did not volunteer whether the envelope was unsealed or had to be steamed open. Incredibly, the letter revealed Emily's intention to outwit the British authorities by opening a secret line of communication with Jagow in Berlin, using Jacobs as a go-between. It was clearly a scheme cooked up with German connivance.

That this of all her documents was overlooked by Emily is further evidence of the mental turmoil or sheer exhaustion that had already caused her to mislay the details of Jagow's proposal, or else indicates an unconscious wish to be caught out. As an example of her addiction to intrigue, and spectacular want of proficiency at it, the Jacobs letter is hard to beat, easily surpassing the bungled message in code about her deportation from South Africa. When the letter was returned to her, Emily grasped it must have been copied and flew into a comical fury against Grant Duff. "The man was a cad!" she exploded.

In place of the confiscated passport Emily was handed a new one endorsed "for one direct journey to England, to be given up on arrival, not valid for residence in Switzerland", and at a stiff final interview Grant Duff warned of the difficulties she could expect passing through France. In those desperate days of June 1916 the French were buckling under the great German offensive at Verdun, and would not be well disposed towards a notorious peace agitator travelling close behind the front line.

Emily left Switzerland on the night train accompanied by her maid. At the French border the officials were irritable and suspicious and both women were subjected to a strip search, an indignity Emily was getting used to. Her friend Rosika Schwimmer, who regularly suffered the same ordeal, told how she would have to undress, take down her hair to show nothing was hidden in it, and hand over her shoes for examination. Emily's passport was stamped "sans arête", though this did not prevent her from setting up a hurried meeting with a French pacifist group when she changed trains at Paris. Difficulties followed with the port authorities at Le Havre, where she glimpsed a bulging file being passed from hand to hand – no doubt "the wicked history of a pacifist" – before a British official stepped forward to claim her. As Emily described the scene, she alone stood "unperturbable and unconcerned" as everyone else flapped about her.

It was not in Emily's nature to act as if she was under a cloud. Immediately on arrival at Southampton on June 28 she sent a telegram addressed personally to Sir Edward Grey. "Arrive London about midday," it read. "Await kind instructions Westminster Palace Hotel."

30 "I NEVER TELL A LIE"

E mily's escapade was now engaging not only the attention of figures of cabinet rank like Grey and Cecil, but of a host of lesser lights at the Foreign Office and Home Office. Opinions divided sharply over what to do about the woman. The Special Branch wanted her arrested immediately. An adviser to Lord Robert said she should be ignored but watched by the police. Grey decided to reply by return to Emily's telegram via his private secretary, declining to see her but asking for a written account of the information she had to give. Emily put pen to paper again, though curiously in this second letter to Grey she positively denied carrying a message from Jagow or being any kind of emissary – "a thing which I am sure would not be acceptable to you". She could however offer "vivid and deep glimpses" into German thinking at the highest level.

During those final days of June the fretful Emily busied herself rallying sympathisers to exert their influence – a list headed by the ailing Leonard Courtney – and kept a promise to the prisoners at Ruhleben by contacting a government-backed Red Cross mission to aid British detainees. Ominously, on June 30 she was summoned to New Scotland Yard to be interviewed by Basil Thomson, head of the Criminal Investigation Department. That the chief himself should be personally involved showed she was in real trouble.

Arriving at Thomson's office, Emily was invited to sit in a particular low armchair. This was a chair with a sinister history. Every wartime spy, real or fancied, was seated there for interrogation; depending on the answers given, some would be exonerated, and not a few would face the firing squad or the hangman. Thomson had made the interesting observation – an article of faith for criminal investigators ever since – that by seating himself higher than the suspect an interrogator gained a psychological advantage, and that whenever a potentially incriminating question was posed, the occupant of the low chair felt an irresistible impulse to press down on its arms and rise slightly before replying.

Basil Thomson was not a man to trifle with. Eton and Oxford-educated, the son of an archbishop of York, he was the force's most senior investigator, and his deceptively mild manner proved the undoing of many. Thanks to the intelligence service he controlled from Scotland Yard, he had been able to round up the entire German spy network in Britain on the first day of war. One recent occupant of the notorious chair was Sir Roger Casement, who the day previous to Emily's interrogation had been sentenced to death for high treason.[xxxvii] One of the few enemy agents to walk free after being questioned in Thomson's armchair was the notorious spy-cum-exotic dancer Mata Hari, who had been detained briefly in England earlier in 1916 but released for want of evidence. She was later executed by the French.

After a gentle grilling, Emily was allowed to leave. Thomson reported to the Foreign Office that the Germans clearly regarded her as an unofficial peace emissary and expected results from her visit to Berlin, but said he had not pressed her on the subject of her conversation with Jagow because she preferred to communicate this to Sir Edward Grey himself, or to someone delegated by him.

As usual, Emily's haughty demeanour betrayed nothing of her acute inner anxiety. Thomson cautiously concluded she was speaking the truth "up to a point", but reserved final judgment until he had sight of a document which had just fallen into the hands of one of his agents abroad and was expected to reach Scotland Yard within twenty-four hours. This was a copy of a letter that she wrote to Jagow from Switzerland, in her own handwriting. Discovery of the letter was no light matter for Emily as throughout the interrogation she concealed the fact she was in secret communication with the Wilhelmstrasse. "Probably it will be possible to intercept the letter, but one cannot be sure, and therefore she ought to be treated with great reserve," advised the CID chief, adding that on balance he thought it sensible for the Foreign Office to talk to her.

Thomson took a far graver view once the copied letter landed on his desk. He phoned the Foreign Office and recommended that she be interned immediately for contact with the enemy. What changed his mind was that Emily's letter to Jagow mentioned an imminent British offensive.

It was now July 1, 1916. No other words, in a letter to a highly-placed enemy, could have rung louder alarm bells. The sound of an incessant bombardment in France, prelude to the long-awaited Big Push by Kitchener's armies, had been heard in London for the past week, and at 7.30 that morning in glorious sunshine a continuous line of men, eighteen miles long, had risen from the British trenches and advanced slowly towards the German lines. It was the first day of the battle of the Somme, the worst day in the history of the British Army. Within one hour thirty thousand would be dead or wounded, more than double the casualties suffered by combatants on both sides in the Boer War; by nightfall the figure would reach sixty-six thousand.

Emily's position was grim. Not only did the country's chief spy-catcher want her locked up immediately, but that same day the Foreign Office dossier on her was endorsed with a note suggesting darkly that "even more drastic action" than internment could be justified.

Meanwhile Emily had no response to a new appeal to Sir Edward Grey. Like the rest of the country, she was unaware that the foreign secretary was fighting a losing battle against blindness, and that his health was about to give way under the strain of war. It was on Lord Robert Cecil, as Grey's number two, that she next turned her attention. A first attempt to gain an interview was repulsed, but Emily persisted. Once again her letter was intercepted by a lower official who wrote on it: "Miss Hobhouse is a mischievous pacifist and I suspect you should not see her." Cecil happily bowed to this advice.

Thwarted again, Emily trained her sights on a newly-appointed assistant of Lord Robert's, the elderly career diplomat Lord Newton, and at last wangled an invitation to the Foreign Office. Newton struck her as very nice, and he even proposed that she write to Jagow to arrange an exchange of prisoners, suggesting that a letter could be forwarded via the United States ambassador, Gerard. Again Emily seems to have failed to mention she had her direct line of communication; possibly Newton set a trap to see if she would own up.

Next, despite having little faith in the man, Emily set off to Lambeth to tackle the Archbishop of Canterbury. By now it was August 2; for a month the casualties on the Somme had been mounting inexorably. Dr Davidson she found friendly, simple, kind-eyed, well-meaning, powerless. "A small man rattling about in a big palace" was her verdict. Even so, she begged for a strong plea for peace from the Church, and followed up with a letter to Davidson vainly dangling the prospect that multitudes would rise up and call him blessed if he spoke out.

Unknown to Emily, on the day of their meeting the primate was wrestling with his conscience. He had just refused to sign a petition calling for the reprieve of Roger Casement, who was due to be hanged at Pentonville at nine the following morning. The archbishop was one of a number of influential figures who had been sent extracts from the so-called "black diaries" discovered by Basil Thomson after Casement's arrest, which exposed him as a predatory homosexual. The lurid details persuaded many to withhold their signatures from the petition, though the reason later cited by Davidson was Casement's "treasonable blandishments" to the Irish prisoners in Germany.[xxxviii]

*

By this time Emily seemed to be off the hook. Days before, Thomson and Lord Newton had met to thrash out a conclusion on Emily's case and between them decided she presented no significant danger. "Lord Newton thought it would be wise not to lock her up," recorded Thomson in his journal. "She was a silly, mischievous old woman, but not disloyal to the country." But as August wore on, news of Emily's German adventure began to leak beyond government circles. Details of her travels inside enemy territory surfaced in the press, and everything changed. What had begun as a spat between two departments of state over an elderly spinster's visa quickly threatened to blow up into a repeat of the national furore over the Boer war camps.

Among the Hobhouse family members acutely embarrassed by the revelations were her brother Leonard, who believed a cherished plan to visit the trenches had been scotched by his sister, and favourite nephew Oliver, now a serving soldier, who was ribbed mercilessly over the antics of his madcap aunt. Margaret Hobhouse roundly declared that Emily had gone mad. Tricky questions were asked in parliament, with Lord Robert Cecil under fire as MPs, including serving officers, queued up to express outrage over Emily's ability to go in and out of an enemy country. "Are we to infer from the noble lord's replies," demanded one, "that if Miss Hobhouse obtained a passport to leave this country, she must have done so under false pretences?"

Lord Robert was forced into a number of embarrassing admissions over the issue of the visa which he blamed on "the military permit office". Pressed repeatedly on whether Emily obtained her passport under false pretences, he replied feebly that "everyone must draw his own conclusions from the answer I have given". But by pointing the finger at the military permit office, Cecil enraged the general in charge, who had consistently turned down Emily's applications. He now seized the opportunity to clear his name and at the same time to settle scores with the departed and much disliked home secretary. Caught on the back foot, the government caved in. An obliging MP was primed to raise the question again and Cecil made clear that neither the military nor the Foreign Office had approved the visa. It had been issued on the direct intervention of Sir John Simon.

The nastiest moment for Emily came when the Conservative MP for York, John Butcher, demanded: "Is there no means of bringing to justice a lady who goes abroad for the purpose of betraying her country?" This brought another member to his feet in Emily's defence. Was it not the case, he asked, that immediately on returning from Germany Miss Hobhouse had offered to give all possible information to the government? "I do not know anything about that," Lord Robert replied, "but I know that the general opinion of the House – and I believe of the country – is that Miss Hobhouse's activities have not been in the interests of this country." As to whether Emily should face justice, the question was one for the legal advisers to the Crown.

Legal hair-splitting followed. The renowned F.E. Smith, later Lord Birkenhead, said that if Miss Hobhouse had conceived the *idea* of entering Germany at the time she applied for the visa, her failure to inform the government might be punishable. Smith took the view that contacting the enemy from neutral territory was not a criminal offence as the law stood, unless aggravated by a false declaration. He announced the government's intention to close the loophole immediately by an alteration to the Defence of the Realm Act. Whatever Miss Hobhouse might or might not have done, he added, she would not be allowed to leave the country again as long as the war lasted, so would enjoy no further opportunity to disparage the Allied cause.

Angry MPs refused to let the matter rest, and one seized on the fact that Emily's stated reason for needing a passport was her health. "In view of the fact that her statement was not correct," he asked, "can the right honourable gentleman say whether she is going to be prosecuted like an ordinary woman, or is she going to be protected by high personages?"

The controversy raged not only in the Commons but in the Lords, where Leonard Courtney rose shakily to his feet as Emily's champion. He addressed the vexing legal issue by saying that "the intention of going to Germany did not exist in her mind at all when she started for Italy", but rather weakened his defence by adding: "If it did exist it lay there very dormant all the winter and through the early spring months." This line of argument is difficult to reconcile with Leonard Hobhouse's account of his sister's "invasion of Germany" and is flatly contradicted by Ruth Fry, who described Emily's journey as "long determined".

As the controversy rumbled on, Emily's case was not helped by the emergence of two eye-witness accounts of her visit to Ruhleben, one from an inmate of the camp, one from a repatriated patient of the sanatorium. The first came in a letter home from a prisoner who was present when Emily entered camp with the commandant and other officers. The lady was tired and sat down, he wrote, and as soon as she spoke he knew she was English: "She was very nice to me. She said I looked very well and asked if she could do anything for me... She did not explain what she was doing in the middle of Germany." The writer happened to be reading *Paradise Lost* when she walked in, "and curiously enough had just reached the Curse of Eve". The prisoners later speculated she was some kind of spy or a traitor like Sir Roger Casement, though he did not believe it himself. "I had not spoken to a lady for twenty months," he added wistfully.

The other letter appeared in *The Times* and was an angry tirade against "that ardent propagandist Miss Emily Hobhouse". The writer declared she had travelled "under the auspices of the Berlin War Office, who made every effort to suppress her identity". She praised the terrible food and made other fatuous and disingenuous remarks, blaming the British government for the small number of prisoner exchanges. The grim building, "where we were packed like sardines in a tin, and which made a mockery of the word sanatorium", she described as delightful, saying "it almost made her wish to be ill that she might dwell in such a place".

Once the press attacks began, there was no chance of the Foreign Office listening to Emily again. The Somme offensive ground on into the autumn, and the staggering cost in blood and prestige seemed to strengthen the nation's determination to fight on to total victory. No one then imagined that the battle of the Somme was only the midpoint of the war, or that eighty per cent of Britain's total casualties were still to be suffered.

Distraught by her failure, Emily left London for Maer Lake. Any faint remaining hope for her initiative seemed to disappear in November with the news of Jagow's dismissal by the Kaiser. Yet once again she decided to appeal to Cecil, her letter part *cri de coeur*, part carefully crafted self-justification. "I am anxious to inform you of the truth of the matter," she wrote. "I am not a diplomatist but a very simple direct person. I never tell a lie and have never made a false statement in my life. Neither do I go back on my word when given."

Of her sally into enemy territory she went on: "I hoped that the act of going there voluntarily in the midst of a great war would have a softening influence and be a link to draw our two countries together. I believe it has helped towards this." Jagow as an old acquaintance had smoothed the way, and once the Germans were convinced her quest was "in the interests of truth, peace and humanity" they had given her papers bearing the words "with humanitarian object". She concluded: "From the first your Government has at my desire been made aware of my visit and much information was (had you wished it) at your service. I shall always be glad I went and grateful to our opponents for their noble comprehension of my aims."

It is not difficult to imagine Cecil's reaction as he read this and brooded on Emily's doings in Switzerland – the promise to abstain from propagandising, the evasive tactics on departing for Germany, the eagerness to report the completed mission to the German legation before the British. And here was the woman claiming to have kept the government informed from the outset! Nor would her parting shot about the nobility of the enemy have gone down well at a time when the resumption of mass sinking of British shipping by submarine was threatening to starve the country into submission. On his instructions Emily's letter went unacknowledged.

In general, however, the Establishment's reaction to the Emily affair was curiously ambivalent, and it is by no means clear that she ran a genuine risk of being interned or tried for treason. Certainly the timing of her return from Germany was unfortunate, coinciding with intense anxiety over Verdun. For weeks the Germans had known an Allied counter-offensive was coming, but not where or when. Their agents had been frantically busy everywhere, striving to sift hard information from gossip and rumour. Emily's secret correspondence with Jagow was never known outside a tiny inner circle; had it been made public, the call for her to be charged with treason would have been deafening.

Yet despite the angry denunciations of Emily in parliament, there is no hint that the real decision-makers – figures of the old school like Grey, Cecil and Newton – ever seriously considered interning this woman of their own class, still less dreamt of exposing her to the possibility of the supreme penalty. Germany had committed one of the great blunders of the war the previous year by executing the English nurse Edith Cavell in occupied Belgium. British ministers were only too conscious of the risk of creating martyrs, as had happened in Ireland following the Easter Rising. A number of female spies were convicted in Britain during the war, though none was executed. Earlier in 1916 a Swedish-born woman had been found guilty of espionage and sentenced to death at the Old Bailey but reprieved by the King. The case was very different in France, where Mata Hari was one of a number of women to be executed.

Basil Thomson himself was contemptuous of female agents, believing an inherent inability to grasp technical detail made them unreliable, though this did not stop him from recruiting his own. Only the day before questioning Emily at Scotland Yard, he had sent two "lady police spies" along to an anti-war meeting and thought it hilarious when both were elected members of the committee. On the other hand, he would later say that all the spies, anarchists and terrorists caused him less trouble than Mrs Pankhurst's suffragettes.

So it seems likely that, as argued by critics in parliament, Emily's name still exerted influence at the highest levels. "You of course know who she is," as Sir John Simon remarked to Cecil, and everybody who mattered did, from the Archbishop of Canterbury to the man who in December that year finally succeeded as prime minister. Lloyd George, much as he might like to forget it, owed Emily that old debt of gratitude from Liskeard. Then again, this was a woman revered as all but a saint in South Africa, a highly valued fighting ally. Little wonder the wise heads decided to leave Emily to stew in her own juice in Cornwall.

Yet at the same time it is clear that her stock of goodwill was exhausted. For the majority of old friends who turned implacably against Emily, it was the German escapade that ensured the fall from grace which blights her memory to the present day.

*

Kitchener's death had hastened the collapse of Asquith's administration and his replacement by Lloyd George was grimly welcomed by Leonard Hobhouse as kill-or-cure. One of the new premier's first acts was to abolish the old war cabinet, the ponderous talking shop that Kitchener had so despised, and establish an all-powerful committee of five. Speculation mounted over who would be its members. Churchill, hated by Conservatives as a turncoat, waited in vain for the call, and so too did Admiral Fisher. Even Balfour, now foreign secretary, found himself excluded from the war council that would become Lloyd George's innermost circle of power.

The first name to emerge astounded everyone. After twenty-one years in the political wilderness, Lord Milner was back at the centre of power as minister without portfolio, appointed by the very man who had been his most merciless critic during the Boer War. One of the first to hear the exciting news was Lady Edward Cecil. At sixty-four, Alfred Milner seemed as energetic and decisive as ever, and quickly impressed

Sir Douglas Haig as the cabinet's strongest member. Nor was this to be the crowning glory of his career. In the game of musical chairs that was Britain's government in these coalition years, he would soon be named secretary for war in succession to Kitchener and Lloyd George.

There was another curious twist to the story. On the eve of the war, the job as Milner's private secretary had been landed by Emily's nephew Hugh Thornton – son of that sister Carrie who fell down dead in church. Leonard Hobhouse observed dryly that Hugh, like his clerical father before him, would no doubt succeed in maintaining a "detached philosophical attitude" to his job. In fact Hugh found his new employer highly congenial, moving with Milner on his return to power to a fine new office in Whitehall Gardens, and staying on as his secretary long after the war.

*

At Christmas 1916 Emily grieved over the death of old President Steyn. The Courtneys were in Cornwall when a letter arrived from South Africa telling of Steyn's sudden collapse while addressing a women's conference at Bloemfontein, and Kate copied the account into her diary: "In the middle of a sentence he hesitated, put his hand to his head, and dropped dead." The endless slaughter of the war had deeply affected the invalid, and almost his last words were: "The people seem bent on committing suicide. Can we not send up a prayer for peace and for a renewal of brotherly love?"

Despite his repeated wish to be laid in an unmarked grave on his own farm – "without stone or sign, like Moses" – Marthinus Steyn was buried at the foot of the Women's Memorial that had been his brainchild. Six thousand miles away, reading of the state funeral, Emily was reminded of that other ceremony she had been unable to attend, on what was now sacred soil for South Africans. Perhaps it entered her mind that here would be a fitting resting place for her.

31 "SWEET BUT A LITTLE MAD"

By the end of 1916 all sense of optimism about the war had vanished. The battle of the Somme ended with nearly half a million British losses for no obvious gain, but neither side had any better idea than bleeding the enemy white. The beginning of 1917 witnessed even greater trials, with turmoil in Russia leading to the Czar's abdication. Winning the war was now down to the little Welshman Emily had once guarded against a mob, and he brought a fierce new energy to its prosecution. But it was not until April, with America's entry into the war, that the Allies found genuine cause for celebration.

Jan Smuts had arrived in London a month earlier. He was to remain for over two years and take on numerous powerful and high-profile positions, the most important a place in the war cabinet – a unique achievement for a man who had borne arms against Britain. He was ushered to his seat next to his old enemy, Milner.

Emily wrote from Cornwall teasing Smuts over what a great panjandrum he had become and wondering when he would be made an earl. But perhaps he could find time to read a line or two from someone as "old and insignificant" as herself; perhaps some remnant of the old Oom Jannie survived who would put up with "the pacifist and anti-imperialist I am prouder than ever to be". A lost reply was conciliatory enough for Emily to issue a summons to Bude – her letter indicates that she will find room for him somehow in her frantically busy diary – but days later she materialised in London, swept into the Savoy, and demanded to be shown up to Smuts's suite.

As he grumbled in a letter home to Isie: "Miss Hobhouse is all for making peace ('by negotiation') and is a little troublesome and, of course, as always, tactless, so that her whole family, even her brother, is against her." A few days later he reports that Emily has descended on him again: "She is quite sweet and her letters are much exaggerated, but she is, of course, as always, a little mad." A couple of weeks on, he notes stoically: "Miss Hobhouse has now moved into town in order the more effectively to labour for the salvation of my soul."

Smuts was feted by the nation that had once placed a price on his head. Huge crowds cheered his speeches; he was showered with the freedom of great cities and the honorary doctorates of great universities. As the only cabinet member with military experience, he exercised considerable personal influence over Lloyd George. Praise for Smuts was so overwhelming that one friend in South Africa wrote to him: "Heartiest congratulations, but I beg you, Jannie, come back before they find you out."

Despite the demands on him, Smuts found time to see old friends such as Olive Schreiner – he found her a dear old girl, bewildered at the state of the world and constantly bursting into tears. Above all, being in England allowed him to pursue the intense relationship with Margaret Gillett. They met regularly in London or at her home in Oxford, and exchanged soulful letters in between. And a new intimate friendship blossomed between Smuts and wealthy widow Alice Stopford Green, an Irish nationalist who had funded the defence of Roger Casement. In earlier days, as an ardent pro-Boer, Mrs Green had advised Emily on setting up her spinning schools and talked her out of her original plan to promote lace-making. Now, as Emily was effectively frozen out, Mrs Green took a place at the heart of Smuts's circle.[xxxix]

Smuts affected to be indifferent to the favours of the great. As a guest of the royal family, he wrote to the Gilletts complaining of being stuck at Windsor Castle when he longed to be sharing their favourite country walk near Oxford, "through the magic circles traced by the mushrooms, and by the grass knots which symbolise the blending of spirits". It was in such language that their correspondence was conducted. On the same day he wrote to his wife: "I feel lonely and alone here in England and would much rather be with you in beloved South Africa."

Whether in London or Cornwall, Emily continued to bombard Oom Jannie by post, but the letters once graced by wit and charm were now crammed with impractical demands and strident complaints. Smuts must have opened each one with a heavy sigh. Emily clung to the conviction that her personal contact with the Germans could be the basis of a peace initiative, and penned an emotional appeal to her friend at the seat of power. "A bridge is needed – let me be that bridge," she pleaded. "I have begun to build it – and am not afraid to cross it alone to begin with. Each side is sensitive – the greatest tact and gentleness is needed. Lloyd George would trust me I know and the Germans will. It need never be known – I ask nothing better of life than to make a bridge across the gaping chasm that divides two countries I love. And you *must love both* to be able to do it."

Later, when Smuts shouldered the responsibility for protecting the public against air raids, she wrote waspishly: "As to your defence of London by this infernal barrage, I do trust you will stop it, as it is a remedy worse than the disease. We have lived under showers of this odious shrapnel (purely home-made) and it is costly in life and property. A woman close to me was killed in bed thereby! The German bombs will be fewer and more local, and if you must shoot at them pray do so *only* as they cross the coast line."

Despite constant provocation, Smuts remained a model of tolerance, never forgetting Emily's past deeds for his people or the strains caused by her state of health. These, as he later told her brother, "excused many things to which otherwise one would have taken serious exception." Yet he largely avoided her during his time in England. Emily was "a pacifist of a very troublesome kind", and he invariably found excuses not to visit the *pied-a-terre* Emily rented in Hammersmith, only minutes from the Savoy. At long intervals he would invite her up to his luxurious suite, though only when Margaret Gillett was present. This was hurtful enough, but worse was to come from another great friend of South African days. Louis Botha, in London with his wife, flatly refused to see her. For once Emily made no effort to hide her vulnerable side and to the faithful Mrs Steyn wrote: "I called on their arrival and just saw *her* a few minutes but never again and General Botha not at all. They dropped me entirely."

Oddly enough, as old friends snubbed her one former adversary treated her with unexpected civility. Lord Milner agreed to see her and hear her out, perhaps intending a kindness to his secretary, her nephew Hugh. Like Kitchener, Milner was now at least partially rehabilitated in Emily's eyes, since he appeared more inclined to peace than those around him. "Life is a curious jumble, dear Mrs Steyn," she remarked of this strange turn of events.

The latter days of 1917 witnessed an outcry in the press when the ancient Marquis of Lansdowne, who had been war secretary at the start of the Boer War, openly advocated a negotiated peace. After three years of slaughter he believed the alternative was the ruin of the civilised world. Emily was cock-a-hoop, but the resultant storm of protest had other politicians running for cover. Lansdowne was dismissed as "ga-ga" by Rudyard Kipling, who in a private letter put forward the interesting suggestion that an unnamed female "in the Liberal interest" had influenced the "old imbecile". For Emily one encouraging outcome of the controversy was a limited reconciliation with her brother Leonard, who had himself come round to the idea of a negotiated settlement, if only because he no longer had faith in an Allied victory.

*

In the meantime Smuts was being petitioned by another of Emily's family. Margaret Hobhouse, in her unceasing campaign to get Stephen out of gaol, wrote asking Smuts to condemn government policy on conscientious objectors. The South African replied warily: "I can be of better service in other ways to the cause which you have at heart and hope to be of some service in those ways".

Not until five months later, in December 1917, was Stephen finally set free, but Emily immediately jumped to the conclusion that Smuts had engineered the release; perhaps she also saw a chance of making peace with the prickly Margaret, who had declared her mad. "Dear Angel that openeth Prison Doors," Emily gushed in a letter to the general, "I fled to Stephen's mother with that news which she had but just heard and with the sudden relaxation of the great strain was shaken to her foundations. She looked twenty years older than when I saw her two months ago. Poor Maggie!" However, there seems to be no evidence that the encounter restored intimacy between the two women, if that was Emily's hope.

Stephen himself believed his deliverer was not Smuts but his godfather-by-proxy, Lord Milner. If this was the case, Milner had been worked upon by an unexpected lobbyist. The Archbishop of Canterbury had penned a private appeal to him begging "a little arbitrarily exercised commonsense" in the handling of conscientious objectors, singling out Emily's cousin: "Stephen Hobhouse is of course the most conspicuous instance of a really fine fellow who is, or has been, suffering in mind and body on account of 'crankiness' which is in no sense mischievous in itself," he wrote. On the other hand, at that stage of the war cabinet members might have felt there were more pressing matters than Stephen Hobhouse, and it seems just as likely that his release – one of many ordered around that date – was an event following its natural course. Certainly neither Smuts nor Milner ever admitted pulling strings.

*

According to the perennial insider C.P. Scott, by the end of 1917 the war cabinet was so sickened by the butchery in France that any overture for ending the war would have been welcomed. But now Germany saw a chance of breaking the deadlock before the Americans could reach full strength. The collapse of Russia released reinforcements for the western front and at the beginning of 1918 the Allies braced themselves for a terrible new onslaught.

Massive German attacks beginning in March once again brought the British Army to the edge of destruction, with the heaviest losses since the murderous early days of the Somme. On April 13 Haig issued a chilling order of the day: "With our backs to the wall and believing in the justice of our cause each one of us must fight to the end." It was during these desperate hours that Milner was sworn in as secretary of state for war, "chucked in," as he said, "at the most critical moment of all our history".

Days before, on the eve of her seventy-first birthday, Kate Courtney heard that her nephew and Emily's cousin, Paul Hobhouse, younger brother of Stephen, had almost certainly been killed at the battle of St Quentin. He was last seen fighting frantically and falling surrounded by Germans. Only his mother Margaret refused to abandon hope, insisting that he must either have been taken prisoner or moved elsewhere wounded and unrecognised.

Soon after Easter came another loss long dreaded. Leonard Courtney, returning home after one of his vigorous walks, suffered a haemorrhage that would prove fatal. Almost his last conversation was with Emily. Even in his stricken state he remained mentally alert and exercised over current affairs, and begged her intercession with Jan Smuts in a political case that interested him. Emily did as he asked but, failing to grasp the seriousness of Courtney's condition, thought she would wait until her next visit to Cheyne Walk to report the successful outcome. For the rest of her life she blamed herself for not writing immediately to give him the good news.

Just as Emily's great friend and mentor lay dying, in France the last enemy offensive of the war had begun to falter. Ironically Courtney's final act was to dictate a letter to *The Times*, insisting that the Germans could not be defeated and calling for "the wise, the chosen, the men of intellect, and of conscience of all classes" to rise up and stop the carnage. *The Times* refused to print the deathbed letter, but it was accepted by the *Manchester Guardian*.

Kate recorded her husband's last hours in her diary. He suffered a sudden relapse at midnight, she wrote, "and after that I felt he must go, and I am sure he did too, for he whispered several times 'poor Kitty'; and when I said something about a happy life he added 'and such a wife'." For two months the distraught widow could not touch the diary again, and when it was later printed for private circulation among her nephews and nieces a page was left blank to mark the hiatus.

Beatrice Webb noted the passing of her brother-in-law in her diary and described her last sight of "a noble old man", still vigorous in mind and emotion, his eyes flashing and his clenched fist beating on the bed as he dictated his final letter. Beatrice being Beatrice, what begins as a warm tribute turns into a chilly analysis of the dead man's faults, singling out the "mediocrity of intellect" of a figure almost universally praised for his towering mind.

*

As late as June it was touch and go whether the British would be driven from France and forced to acknowledge the war as lost. But the Germans had thrown their last dice. Thereafter the Allies went onto the offensive and the battle of Amiens on August 8 proved the breakthrough long dreamed of by the generals – "the black day of the German army," in the words of its commander, Erich von Ludendorff. The next few weeks saw the greatest Allied advance of the war, with the invaders hurled back in one continuous line from the Meuse to the sea.

Throughout the summer of 1918 Emily had been plagued by an intermittent paralysis of both arms which interrupted the flow of her correspondence but failed to halt it. Even in August she clung to the idea of a negotiated peace on the Lansdowne model, and from Bude posted a letter to Smuts more than usually scattered with capitals and furious underlining, urging him to make common cause with the aged peer. Were Kitchener alive, she insisted, he would be doing exactly that.

"A strong Man who will snap his fingers at the Press and who had a Policy of Peace could be Prime Minister of England before Xmas!" she declared. "I hope I have made it clear. It is useless Statesmen fearing the Press and cowering before the nicknames it hurls at them. Some one Man among them *must* be found who will challenge it, defy it, laugh at it, and that MAN will win the confidence of our people and their admiration. It is a *mistake* to think Lloyd George safe in the saddle. The feeling against him is intense; but *if* he sticks on it will only be because *none other stronger* shews himself – *faute de mieux*. Shew yourself that stronger man and I dare prophesy you a sweeping success."

That Emily could seriously envisage Smuts seizing the premiership, at the very time when victory seemed at last within reach, gives weight to the South African's remark that "poor Auntie" was a little mad. Yet she was not the only one to urge him to aim for supreme power. His fervent devotee Alice Clark was at the same time assuring him that "the English would almost require you to enter Parliament and be prepared to accept the Premiership". At least Miss Clark remembered that a prime minister must first be an MP, which seemed to have slipped Emily's mind.

*

The end of the war came with thrilling speed. Late in September Bulgaria was the first enemy state to sue for peace, followed by Turkey. The defection of Austria-Hungary, whose move against Serbia had sparked the whole catastrophe, left Germany to stand alone and rumours spread of imminent revolution in Berlin. On November 4 the German fleet, which had been bottled up in Kiel since the battle of Jutland, was ordered to sea for a do-or-die showdown with the Royal Navy, prompting a mutiny by the sailors. Soldiers sent to suppress the rising fraternised with the mutineers instead. The Kaiser abdicated on November 9, slipping away to exile in Holland. Over the previous few days all the generals of Germany's high command had melted away across their own border, leaving a delegation of civilians to face the Allied armies.

The Armistice was signed on the hundredth day of the fifth year of war with the final death toll for the Empire standing at almost one million, three-quarters of them British. Twelve thousand South Africans had been killed, twice as many as in the Boer War.

Few were untouched by the slaughter. Beatrice Webb in her diary recorded the toll for the family as three dead and four wounded, two of them seriously. Both Asquith and Kipling lost a son, and the Cecils of Hatfield lost four more after young George. Mrs Fawcett's personal toll was even more remarkable with no fewer than twenty-nine "splendid young men" of her extended family killed.

*

Emily had spent the last month of the war with Lady Courtney in Chelsea. The country was agog to think that the end might be in sight, and on October 14 Kate began embroidering a banner to hang up when peace was declared. After so many dashed hopes, Emily was suddenly seized by a superstitious fear of tempting fate, and tried to persuade her to wait – "a caution so unlike her adventurous spirit," Kate mused in her diary.

On October 29 Kate wrote that for a full fortnight she and Emily had been "living day to day on the wonderful developments" while deploring the headlines screaming of great Allied victories. She noted that Lord Milner had roused a storm by speaking a few "kindish" words about Germany, adding: "The press is filled with sneers, brutal threats and every possible old atrocity to prevent any forgiving." On the eve of the Armistice Kate threw a small party at which Emily enjoyed the company of the future Labour premier, Ramsay MacDonald, whose book on the aftermath of the Boer War gave them something in common besides their politics. Animated talk went on till nearly eleven o'clock with MacDonald "interesting and attentive".

Emily seems to have left no record of her thoughts on the day the war ended, Monday, November 11, but Kate Courtney did. She was on top of a No 11 bus to Whitehall when she was startled by impromptu celebrations greeting the peace, and observed with disapproval the scenes of jubilation – frantic flag-waving, shouting, singing and cheering. "I do hope the public houses will be ordered to shut," she wrote, "or we shall have some less harmless jollity later." No doubt the Cheyne Walk servants were reminded how they should behave. The terms of the surrender Kate believed to be "cruel enough to satisfy any desire to humiliate Germany".

Also in London on November 11 was Kate's sister Beatrice Webb, who recorded "a pandemonium of noise and revelry" in spite of fog and steady rain, with the streets full of "discords of sound and struggling, rushing beings and vehicles". Thrones were crashing everywhere in Europe, and she wondered how long it would take for the tide of revolution to reach England. She guessed between six months and a year.

Lady Edward Cecil had the benefit of inside information from Milner some hours before the Armistice was signed, and set off to enjoy the scenes of rejoicing outside Buckingham Palace. Later she and Milner went out to dinner together and speculated on his likely role at the peace conference that would follow to impose terms on vanquished Germany.

And so at last the little peace banner went up outside the Courtney house in Cheyne Walk, and later that day Kate offered a larger version she had made to Chelsea Town Hall. The scene was indignantly described in her diary entry for November 12:

"Yesterday I took up the banner I had been embroidering – a large blue silk one

266

with a dove in the centre and olive branch – to ask if they would like to put it among their many flags on the Town Hall. I went today and was told by the Town Clerk they thought it wholly unsuitable. 'You have put an olive branch in,' he said, 'and we are not ready to offer Germany the olive branch,' and added with a nasty sneer: 'We are not pro-Germans here.'"

"Nor Christians either apparently," retorted Kate as she flounced out.

*

The Armistice brought no peace for the other Potter sister, Margaret Hobhouse. Grief had turned that once robust mind, worn out by the long battles over the conscientious objector Stephen and eight months of intense anxiety over her favourite Paul, still officially listed as missing. After her death the family would discover a sheaf of her letters to Paul, filled with the minutiae of life at Hadspen, sent back to her after making the round of German prison camps. Not until two years after the war did Margaret accept he was dead, and then sought to communicate with him through spiritualists.

32 "THAT DEN OF THIEVES"

The war ended as Kitchener predicted, with the United States and Japan the big winners. Booming America, fatted on the insatiable demand for wartime commodities, was banker to the world, owed over ten billion dollars by the European allies. Japan, despite making a negligible effort on behalf of the Allies, had benefited from an unprecedented economic surge, and mopped up valuable German possessions in the Pacific; the Japanese navy was now the world's third largest, with the American rivalling the British.

As soon as the Armistice was signed Emily's paramount concern became the conditions in Germany. Her letters to Smuts harped on the need for the victors to show magnanimity – to start with, by lifting the blockade and allowing the Germans to fish the North Sea. No one had a right to celebrate Christmas, she wrote on December 19, while German women and children were being kept hungry. In contrast, Mrs Fawcett showed herself at her most implacable, firmly opposing an end to the blockade. She wrote to *The Times* blaming the worldwide food shortage on Germany's submarine warfare, which ordinary Germans had done nothing to impede, so the claims of Allied, liberated and neutral countries must be given priority. "The British people are not vindictive," she remarked, "but they have a strong sense of justice."

Mrs Fawcett's views prevailed with the British public and the post-war election resulted in a sweeping victory for a coalition of Lloyd George supporters and Tories pledged to squeeze Germany "until the pips squeaked". Many left-leaning Liberals lost their seats, along with Labour members like Ramsay MacDonald. This was the first election in which Emily could have voted, though she seems to have allowed the occasion to pass without comment.

*

The first great triumph of female suffrage had come early in 1918. The contribution women were making to the war had overwhelmed opposition in the Commons, and a bill giving the vote to all over thirty was accepted by the Lords after a last-ditch stand by diehards led by Lord Curzon. Over eight million women were enfranchised at a stroke. Kate Courtney, watching the dramatic proceedings from the packed peeresses' gallery, noted the presence of Mrs Fawcett, and gracefully handed her long-time political adversary the greater part of the credit. Few contemporaries doubted that it was the veteran campaigner's painstaking work over many decades, rather than the militant tactics of the Pankhursts, that finally won justice for the cause.

Soon afterwards, women's organisations joined together to hold a rally of public thanksgiving in a banner-festooned Queen's Hall. Wanting a musical highlight for the evening, Mrs Fawcett turned to her friend Sir Hubert Parry, a supporter of women's suffrage, who responded with his setting to Blake's *Jerusalem*. The Queen's Hall audience heard the first ever performance, conducted by Parry himself.

Despite her work for universal suffrage, the vote was never really one of Emily's overriding preoccupations. Leonard Courtney might have been one of the earliest campaigners for emancipation, but she herself had worked tirelessly for the election of John Burns, who opposed the women's cause, and she had constantly vilified politicians who were firm supporters, like Sir Edward Grey. In this Emily showed something of the irrational character of much of the suffrage leadership; or perhaps she had already grasped that the great Liberal dream was about to vanish into thin air, with female suffrage delivering a preponderance of Conservative voters.

Like most of the Potter sisters, Kate Courtney paid no particular attention to female suffrage, but rather indulged a hobbyhorse of her dead husband's. Confessing to minimal concern in Chelsea's postwar parliamentary contest, she dismissed the feminist candidate as useless and bemoaned the general lack of interest in politics locally. There would be thousands of absent voters yet the result would be called "the Will of the People", she wrote in her diary, adding rather inconsistently: "It is a huge farce. I shall have no Will here, and shall not pretend to one by voting." One wonders whether the servants were allowed out to vote. Sister Beatrice too noted the coming of the vote with her habitual detachment. "I have never exerted myself to get it," she wrote. "It has no glamour for me." In earlier days Beatrice had positively opposed suffrage for women, though had eventually recanted at the urging of Mrs Fawcett; her sisters Margaret Hobhouse and Theresa Cripps confined their politics to canvassing for their spouses.[xl] The first woman elected to parliament was a shock to them all. The renegade aristocrat Countess Markievicz, formerly Constance Gore-Booth, won a Dublin constituency for Sinn Fein but failed to take her seat as she was sewing mailbags in Holloway Gaol at the time, on account of her gun-toting participation in the Easter Rising. No other female candidate was successful in the postwar election, and when a woman finally entered the Commons it was a Conservative, Lady Astor.

A sense of anti-climax over the vote was not confined to Emily's circle. Within a couple of years of the triumph, even Mrs Fawcett's comrade-in-arms Ray Strachey would be pining for the old days when everything had seemed so simple and straightforward: "How picturesque it was! The Pilgrimage: the Banners: the Processions: Hyde Park on a Sunday, and the rotten eggs at street corners! Gone are all these pleasures, and in their place – the vote."

The peace saw honours rained upon Millicent Fawcett. The day after the Armistice she received another honorary doctorate, this time from the chancellor of Birmingham University, Lord Robert Cecil; she was named among the first batch of women magistrates; she was awarded a medal by the Queen of Belgium; she was the only woman delegate at the newly-formed League of Nations Unions, and elected its vice-president. Yet soon afterwards she resigned the presidency of the national suffrage movement, giving age as the reason. A likelier motive was the growing agitation within its ranks for voting rights for women under thirty, of which she firmly disapproved.

*

When the Versailles Peace Conference convened in January 1919, Mrs Fawcett headed the only women's group allowed to take part. She secured personal interviews with all the world leaders, starting with President Woodrow Wilson, and won an agreement that women should be eligible for all posts within the newly-formed League of Nations. It was the only solid achievement for women agreed at Versailles. Even so, Mrs Fawcett did not enjoy her trip to Paris, strongly disliking, in the words of Mrs Strachey, "the rather hectic gaiety to be seen".

The hectic gaiety of Paris was very much to the taste of the newly widowed Lady Edward Cecil, Lord Edward having succumbed to tuberculosis just before Christmas 1918. By the spring of 1919 she was keeping what one observer called "a very jolly house" in the Bois de Boulogne and throwing herself into a whirl of balls and parties that marked the return of peace in the revivified capital. Alfred Milner, now Britain's colonial secretary, figured as a key negotiator at the conference alongside her disapproving brother-in-law Lord Robert Cecil. Just as in Cape Town days, Milner and Lady Edward went everywhere together – dining, shopping, strolling in the woods, and going off on motor trips.

Lloyd George, one of the Big Three decision-makers, was also determined to indulge himself while settling the affairs of the world, and moved into a luxurious flat with his long-time mistress. He later recalled his six months in Paris as the happiest time of his life. Another figure intent on enjoyment was that jaunty ladies' man Admiral of the Fleet Lord Fisher, who turned up with a beautiful duchess in tow, declaring: "The saints were all sinners to begin with, so what I say is, sin like blazes."

At the outset the high-minded rested their hopes for a just peace on President Wilson, who urged moderation rather than the naked vengeance sought by the French, or the opportunistic seizure of German territory advocated by the Italians and Japanese. Emily and her like were quickly disillusioned. For all his high moral tone, Wilson wanted the Europeans to pay back everything America had lent them with interest, and for Lloyd George the issue was simple: "The war has to be paid for. If Germany does not pay, the British taxpayer has to pay." France proved even more intransigent. After all, the French had been forced to stump up when Napoleon was defeated, and again after the Franco-Prussian War. Germany reaped the benefit both times and had planned to squeeze France again if they won the Great War.

For those who fought in the South African war, the wheel of fortune had brought scenes once impossible to imagine. Already Smuts and Milner had sat together in the Downing Street war cabinet; now, as one of the victors at Versailles, General Botha clapped his hand on Milner's shoulder and declared the generous treaty after the Boer War a perfect model for the business in hand. Lord Milner, basking in the old enemy's praise, conveniently forgot it was Kitchener who had forced the pace at Vereeniging against his own opposition.

Yet Milner had changed since those days, and vainly joined with Cecil in urging Lloyd George to stand up to the French. This time there was no Kitchener to clinch an imaginative deal and the French got their way. Of Milner the French leader Clemenceau complained: "If he does not agree with you, he closes his eyes like a lizard, and you can do nothing with him." The British always seemed to remind him of reptiles.

Smuts too was in Paris, and partly redeemed himself in Emily's eyes by advocating a generous peace. The greatest experience of his life, he declared, had been to see how Britain's policy of conciliation had healed the wounds of the Boer War, and the same goodwill should be shown to the Germans. Smuts wrote daily to one or other of his devotees in England, usually to Margaret Gillett. It is a striking fact that the most vivid and revealing remarks by the leading male figures in this story – Smuts, Milner and Kitchener – were contained in letters to other men's wives. Kitchener's great confidant had been Lady Cranborne, while Milner had his Lady Edward.

On May 7, the day the harsh final terms were handed to the German delegation, Smuts wrote despairingly of having to dress up in a frockcoat and top hat for the ceremony. The gloom only lifted, he informed Margaret, when a nightingale had sung to him most fascinatingly in the Bois de Boulogne "with that same thrilling whistle at the end which we heard in Ashampstead Common". He complained constantly of their separation. "How I wish I were today loitering with you over the Downs," he wrote, "or by the wooded slopes of Evenlode, and over the great table lands of the Spirit." To Mrs Smuts meantime he wrote of dreaming of his farm, and on the treaty expressed himself in blunter Boer fashion: "Germany is being treated as we would not treat a Kaffir nation."

As news of the Versailles terms leaked out, Emily's indignation was boundless. She denounced the Allied representatives as "that den of thieves" and fiercely condemned her former hero Wilson. One proposal she declared particularly wicked was a demand that Germany, on the brink of anarchy and full of starving mothers and children, should surrender 140,000 milking cows to the victors.

It was now Emily seized on the last great cause of her life.

33 "UNDAUNTED BY ALL OPPOSITION"

I t was like the challenge of 1900 all over again. Emily was now nearly sixty and in continual bad health, but there was nothing like a humanitarian crisis to rouse her spirit. Once more she exercised herself over soap, disinfectant, medicines, and bedding. Once more she organised petitions and protest meetings. She began by raising funds for a Swiss charity set up to feed Austrian children, quickly extending the scheme to famine regions in Germany, Czechoslovakia and Hungary. By June 1919 she was also chairman of a Russian Babies Fund, and even roped in her brother Leonard to help her. But around this time she was hurt to discover that Smuts, needing a report on conditions in Vienna, had quietly chosen to send Hilda Clark – sister of Margaret Gillett – instead of herself.[xli] Two of the funds she organised were later merged and renamed the Save the Children Fund, making Emily one of the creators of the worldwide charity. Characteristically, she regretted the global aspirations of Save the Children, preferring to help, to quote Ruth Fry, "only ex-enemy children". Here again was that trait in Emily which most contemporaries found utterly perverse, while she herself insisted that a concentration of effort in former enemy lands would convey "a special message of peace".

Despite the differences with colleagues, she was initially able to carry out her work how and where she chose. In September, having prevailed on Smuts to help her reclaim her passport from the Foreign Office, she was off to Germany and Austria as Save the Children Fund organiser. The city of Leipzig she found in the worst state of all, the horses in the street walking skeletons, the children pale, emaciated and rickety. Here and elsewhere she introduced mass feeding programmes; to avoid competing for local food stocks, she bought her provisions in Denmark and Sweden.

Germany proved Emily had not lost her extraordinary flair for the detailed organisation of humanitarian projects, in absolute contrast to the shambles she made of her private life, and from April 1920, operating independently of Save the Children, she demonstrated once again her genius as a fundraiser. Using Mrs Steyn as her agent, she collected £12,000 from South Africa alone, to which the South African government was induced to add £5,000. Here Smuts helped more than ever, having become prime minister following the sudden death of Louis Botha.

Statistics painstakingly collected by Ruth Fry show what Emily managed to achieve without an office or paid helpers. In all she fed around eleven thousand children. In the year from January 1920 she distributed nearly three and a half million "portions of warm dinner", each containing seven hundred calories; between January 1921 and March 1922 she handed out nearly one and a half million litres of milk or cocoa. Nor did her efforts stop at food and drink as she also organised distributions of clothing and provided money to send the more sickly children to recuperate in the countryside or by the sea.

Emily also managed appeals in Switzerland, Scandinavia and even in Britain itself, for despite continuing anger against the defeated enemy, consciences at home were stirred by the reports of suffering coming out of Europe. Half the babies born in Berlin during the year following the war had died; throughout Germany the death rate was highest of all among teenagers whose weakened state made them easy victims of the influenza epidemic then sweeping the world. Conditions in Austria and Hungary were if anything worse. In London, following a rally by the Women's International League which drew twenty thousand, a "Million Teats" campaign was launched to send rubber teats to German mothers unable to nurse their babies because of malnutrition.

As in South Africa days, Emily's European mission attracted earnest, wellborn young volunteers. One of her helpers at this time, twenty-six-year old Lady Clare Annesley, left a pen-sketch of Emily in Germany to set beside the earlier descriptions of her in action by Margaret Clark and Marion Rowntree. "The thing which I admired most about Miss Hobhouse," wrote Lady Clare, "was her tireless energy, the domination of her mind over physical weakness. She was undaunted by all opposition... Her amazing power of organisation did not lessen her intense sympathy with individual cases of suffering, nor did it diminish her delight in moving among the children and teachers in the schools as their friend." On the other hand, admitted Lady Clare, "the self-discipline, which seemed to be part of her nature, must have appeared often to others as harshness. She had no tolerance with doing things 'rather more or less' and would accept no excuse for any inaccuracy."

In Leipzig Emily became a legend. She was decorated by the Red Cross and a marble bust of her was placed in the *Rathaus* among the city's worthies. As in South Africa, she received countless individual tokens of gratitude, and at one official ceremony of thanksgiving – the kind of thing Emily shrank from in embarrassment – a small child recited a lengthy poem declaring that the Lord had inscribed her deeds in the Book of Life. At her hotel everyone treated her like a queen.

As ever, her enormous postage bill and working expenses were met from her own purse, placing even greater strain on her personal finances. Her position had been further undermined by the postwar slump and it was over this period she was forced to sell off most of her remaining treasures in a buyer's market. The jewellery and furs went first, followed by paintings she had collected in South Africa; lost too was her most valuable possession, a Canaletto, the gift of an admirer in the old days. Hardest of all to part with was her piano.

*

Shortly before Christmas 1920 Emily was saddened by news of the lonely end, in a suburban boarding house near Cape Town, of Olive Schreiner. What Olive had called her "long life of dying" was finally over, at sixty-five. Despite her incessant tirades against the English all through the war she had returned to her native country only four months before, and within weeks was bitterly missing England. In a letter to Betty Molteno, Emily's old friend, she lamented: "Oh Betty, why did I come out? I have made many mistakes in my life but this is the greatest of all." She was found cold in bed with a pen in her hand and a gutted candle by her side. But Olive proved restless in death as in life, and Emily was later to hear the macabre story of her friend's last journey.

The long-estranged husband Samuel Cronwright-Schreiner had joined Olive in England the previous July. When she opened the door he had at first failed to recognise the obese decrepit hulk before him, and he had tarried in London when Olive travelled home in August. On his own return to Cape Town the following year he had Olive's coffin exhumed from the Schreiner plot in the city cemetery and taken by train to their old home at De Aar, nearly seven hundred miles distant. There he dug up the bodies of their unnamed baby daughter, who had died in 1895, and Olive's beloved dog Nita. All three coffins were then transported to a wild and remote spot on the Karoo called Buffels Kop and, in accordance with Olive's will, reburied at the two-thousand-feet summit.

*

Emily's health was constantly breaking down. Between stays in Leipzig, she returned either to Italy or England, where she would make disturbing remarks to people about "the abnormal size of the children". After collapsing in Leipzig she was ordered to go back to Cornwall to rest, as Bude was still the closest thing to home; then in the winter of 1920 one of her legs became temporarily paralysed and her brother had to put her up in Wimbledon. A serious illness followed in 1921 when she was nursed by French sisters at a hospital in Rome. Back in Leipzig, though confinement to a wheelchair failed to halt her labours, the realisation grew that Germany would be her "last bit of public work".

But what was she to do with herself? Where would she retire and how could she make ends meet? Italy, the refuge of pre-war days, was increasingly distasteful to Emily because of the rise of Mussolini's fascists – "largely ex-gaolbirds," she informed Smuts – who were making life dangerous for socialists like herself. Of course there was still the house Mara in Johannesburg, whose rents had kept her afloat for so long, and she fleetingly toyed with the idea of selling up and buying a South African farm for her nephew Oliver – this daydream came complete with a vision of herself as the young man's housekeeper and gardener. A madly impractical scheme, it was quietly dropped.

But if England as a whole no longer seemed like home, what of her birthplace in the far west, numinous Cornwall? Bude had been a haven in the war years, and during her convalescence there in 1920 she cast wistful eyes on a property for sale, low and red-roofed and boasting magnificent sea views. She mentioned this "dear little house" in passing in a letter to Mrs Steyn – "in normal times just the sort of thing I could have bought" – but alas, she no longer had the money.

Was there an element of calculation here? There were previous occasions when a seemingly casual remark had borne fruit with the open-handed likes of Mrs Steyn, Jan Smuts and the late Uncle Arthur. Emily would never have descended to an open appeal, but her confidants tended to be individuals with a history of exerting themselves on her behalf. It might be said unkindly that Emily had a way of nudging people into spontaneous gestures. Certainly Mrs Steyn had never forgotten how the generosity of Emily and her circle had purchased the best medical care for the stricken President. Now, as it became clear how wretchedly poor Emily was, her old friend quietly set to work to open a public subscription fund.

In May 1921, returning to London, Emily was staggered by a letter from Mrs Steyn announcing a gift of money from her South African admirers. If she had half-hoped for some form of assistance, she surely never dreamt of anything on this scale. The remarkable sum of £2,300 had been collected, mostly in half-crowns. Present-day monetary equivalents are difficult to calculate, and to say the sum was equivalent to around £77,000 today takes no account of the hugely disproportionate rise in property prices in recent years. Then, it was enough to buy a very substantial house outright.

Emily wrote to break the news to Smuts, though she surely guessed he had been not only a major contributor to the appeal but a sponsor. As she explained it, Mrs Steyn had announced the gift in such a way as to make refusal impossible. Emily may well have recalled her own efforts to raise money for Olive Schreiner ten years before, and her remark – "I fancy one can err by being *too* proud" – when Olive refused it. Even so, she confessed it was embarrassing to benefit from a public collection, a device usually reserved "for successful generals who have killed a lot of people and ruined property, the Kitcheners and Haigs". That said, she would be eternally grateful for the wonderful gift, "and certainly I could *not* otherwise have had a home again".

Finding nothing to her liking on the market at Bude, Emily fixed instead upon a house in St Ives, at the westernmost tip of Cornwall. The old fishing port had recently found a new role as artists' colony though the names now synonymous with St Ives, like Christopher Wood and Ben Nicholson, were only just then beginning to arrive. As Emily moved into town, a retired local mariner called Alfred Wallis was scraping a living as a rag-and-bone man but experimenting on the side with nautical subjects on odd bits of cardboard.

Emily's choice of Warren House, a recently built villa with a broad row of chimneypots, irregular windows and oddments of half-timbering, was clinched by its sunny sloping garden looking down on Porthminster Sands. She was ecstatic about the magnificent views over the bay and, westwards, over the picturesque harbour and ancient granite tower of the parish church of St Ia, of which Francis Kilvert noted in his diary: "The vicar says the smell of fish there is sometimes so terrific as to stop the church clock". Among neighbouring properties which still exist is the grander Talland House, childhood home of Virginia Woolf, which directly overlooks the roof of Warren House towards Godrevy, the inspiration of her novel *To The Lighthouse*.[xlii]

It was only to be expected that Emily should decide on a town and a house wholly unsuitable for an invalid, beginning with an awkwardly situated front door reached by half a dozen steps directly off a public road on a steep hill. St Ives claims the mildest weather in Britain, but the damp climate does no favours for sufferers of arthritis, and the St Ives of the Twenties was unequipped to provide the kind of medical care on which Emily depended. Judging from local newspapers of the time, there was a desperate shortage of servants, worse even than in London. Perhaps most significantly of all, St Ives was as remote as possible from her metropolitan friends.

Naturally, none of this weighed with Emily once she had set eyes on Warren House. As ever, when she fell in love with a beautiful view, every other consideration went out of the window. Enticingly, the sub-tropical garden was ideal for cultivating the kind of South African and Mediterranean plants which she had collected throughout her rootless years, wistfully despatching seeds and cuttings to friends and

The house in St Ives paid for by public subscription. Emily said she "felt hot all over" at the thought of all the half-crowns collected from an impoverished people.

relations. St Ives entranced her utterly. "It is Italy in England – foreign parts without travel!" she enthused to Smuts. Indeed, it might have been perfect for her younger, able-bodied self. The summer of 1921 was one of the most perfect in living memory and Emily was seeing St Ives at its best.

On July 31 she wrote to the organiser of the fund: "This is to tell you, dearest Mrs Steyn, that last night I lay to rest for the first time in your house and that the dream which you cherished is actually realised! I was alone – for my maid of former days cannot come for several weeks, and the charwoman goes home at night. And I think I was glad to be alone the better to enter into the spirit of you all which seemed pervading the place in the stillness of the short summer night, to summon you all in long procession to greet and thank.

"From my bed I can look across this lovely bay. Sea and sky mingled now in the blue summer haze – and watch the white-sailed fishing boats flit by like butterflies in the blue – and lying there my mind turned back over the many years and hosts of women and children I then knew came back to me in mind and thought followed by the many who have gone from us…"

A tinge of doubt soon crept into letters to others. "I shall do my best to try to occupy the house presented to me," she told Smuts, "but I have to recognise that any housekeeping may be beyond my means now." To one correspondent she stressed her determination "to make a gallant fight to live in this house" and to another spoke of "not giving up without a struggle". Then, hopelessly unrealistic, she talked of taking in lodgers.

Still, after all the years of wandering she had a home to call her own at last, somewhere to unpack the much-travelled trunks of papers, including the notes for her planned second book about the women of the camps. But first she dusted off the manuscript of a much deferred project, the translation of the Boer War diary entrusted to her by old Mrs Badenhorst, now long buried.

Emily takes tea in the garden of her gift-house at St Ives. On the table are preserves from a "wonder box" sent by South African admirers, probably for her sixty-second birthday.

"The work is very hard and at times I turn sick and faint," Emily wrote to Mrs Steyn in September, "but then I take a few minutes in the garden among my plants and so go back refreshed. I feel certain it will take a place in the history and literature of your own country and even amongst the diaries of the world." She worked on the manuscript for a year and saw it published in 1923 as *Tant' Alie of Transvaal*. The same year marked the appearance of the first Afrikaans edition of *The Brunt of the War* for which Olive Schreiner wrote a foreword, though she had died before completing a promised introduction to *Tant' Alie*.

The autobiography proved more troublesome. "A strange thing is memory," she wrote to Mrs Steyn, "and one that plays one many tricks. Moreover it gets tangled up with imagination till sometimes one can hardly tell which is which. I am finding out that, as I write my little memoir and am fortunate in having many documents and letters to keep me close to actual facts, often they show me how imagination playing upon memories is in danger of leading me astray. And I want to be *very* accurate." Soon afterwards the manuscript was laid aside "till I am stronger".

But Emily could look forward to what she called her "wonder box", a cornucopia of presents sent to her each birthday on April 9, when towns throughout South Africa took turns to offer tribute to the revered Miss Hobhouse. Typically, a wonder box would contain a huge iced cake, more than fifty pots of jam and forty pounds of dried fruit, each contribution bearing an affectionate note from its donor.

That first Christmas at St Ives she wrote to Mrs Steyn: "For all that surrounds me and gives me a feeling of comfort and rest and security, the warmth of my little room – the feeling of being at home – for all this I have you to thank. As I look back on the year I am more and more amazed at what you and your people have done for my happiness and well-being."

Yet Ruth Fry's statement that Emily was happy at St Ives, based on the Steyn correspondence, must be challenged. The evidence points to the contrary. Besides the inconvenience of the house itself, Emily evidently suffered considerable social isolation, yet she would have thought it ungrateful and ungracious to say this to Mrs Steyn, whose initiative had made the house possible, or to admit that the move to Cornwall was all a terrible mistake.

To begin with, she came with a notorious reputation for loving Boers and Germans. Her claim to be Cornish to the bone would have cut little ice among the common folk of the far west, many of whom lived their entire lives without venturing as far as Truro. Most were wary and suspicious of a new face, and anyone born all of sixty miles away, practically on the Devon border, would have seemed almost like a foreigner. Given her taste in painting, she would have had no interest in the *avant-garde* artists working in St Ives, even supposing she was aware of them. As she was unable to get about unaided in the maze of steep cobbled streets and passages, much of what was happening in town must have been a closed book. Unlike Bude, St Ives did not offer Emily the social circle of a long-established sister, and there seems no record of her seeking the society of the handful of middle class neighbours like the vicar, Canon Sidney Marsh. The kind of sophisticated *milieu* she had known in London, Oxford, Rome and Florence simply did not exist.

There was never any question of her being received in the best houses. The prominent aristocratic family in these parts were and are the St Aubyns, Lords St Levan, whose seat St Michael's Mount lies six miles from St Ives. This family would have known only too well who Emily Hobhouse was. No fewer than four St Aubyns had seen active service in South Africa and it was a St Aubyn who engineered Leonard Courtney's removal as MP before the Khaki Election. The Lord St Levan who headed the family during Emily's time at St Ives had seen two of his brothers killed in the Great War; he himself, with the rank of brigadier general, had been considered too old for an overseas command and had demoted himself to lieutenant in order to serve in France. St Levan was the son-in-law of that Earl of Mount Edgcumbe who had refused to shake hands with Courtney at the end of the Boer War, and would certainly have declined to meet Emily under any circumstances. No doubt the neighbouring gentry followed his lead.

All in all, her prospects of contented retirement at St Ives were non-existent. Starved of intellectual stimulus, cut off from the social pleasantries of her own class, viewed with suspicion if not open hostility by the few ordinary folk with whom she came into contact, Emily was an outsider even in her own county. Always touchy and sensitive, she would have felt the isolation keenly, and snubs by provincials must have been nigh insupportable. Yet as ever, she was too proud to admit an error of her own making.

*

Emily had contact with one prominent figure living locally, but he too was a social pariah. Havelock Ellis, rival of Sigmund Freud and long-time lover of Olive Schreiner, had spent much of his adult life in the far west of Cornwall. One year older than Emily, a tall, rake-like figure with a patriarchal white beard, Ellis had for many years maintained a cottage at Carbis Bay, a mile from Warren House, and it was there he had completed his monumental *Psychology of Sex*. At the time of Emily's arrival, Ellis had only recently returned to the county following a lengthy absence caused by the death of his unstable novelist wife Edith.

The years in Cornwall had been tumultuous ones for the Ellises. Edith had long scandalised St Ives with her lesbian affairs, bouts of drinking and sudden outbursts of rage, moving Havelock to describe life with her as "living in an earthquake". After the outbreak of the Great War her behaviour became more alarming than ever, and by 1915 she was obsessed with the idea that the neighbours were plotting against her at the instigation of her maid. Ellis himself, a recluse by nature, remained loftily unperturbed by what the locals might think; besides, he could count on regular escapes to his flat in London, where he enjoyed a circle of devoted female admirers.

Edith's insanity finally led to confinement in a nursing home at Hayle, a few miles east of St Ives, where she attempted suicide by throwing herself out of an upstairs lavatory window. Escaping to London, she went out one night in autumn to watch a zeppelin raid and on impulse handed her coat to a shivering woman bystander. The resulting chill turned to pleurisy and she died a few days later.[xliii]

For some years Havelock Ellis shunned Cornwall for its painful memories but returned shortly before Emily's move to Warren House, taking lodgings in the fishing village of Cadgwith. His stay in 1921 was not a long one. As Emily wrote her first Christmas letters from St Ives, Ellis was summoned back to London, curiously enough to help Samuel Cronwright-Schreiner to make a selection of the dead Olive's letters for publication.

Emily did not welcome the appearance of Olive's letters. "I think much had perhaps better have been left out," she wrote stiffly to Smuts. She did not enlarge on which letters she found distasteful, though the book astonished contemporaries because of the inclusion of Olive's passionate missives to Havelock Ellis. Emily, increasingly strait-laced in old age, would have deplored the public airing of her friend's rhapsodies on sex and the painful details of her thirty-year drug habit, and no feminist would have relished Olive's frequent moments of apostasy as when she wrote, "You know, it is possible that women are absolutely and altogether the inferiors of men", or declared that "the women's-rights women" were all mad.

Even some of Olive's casual asides may have struck Emily as unseemly. "It's one of the things I value most in my life," she wrote, "that all my men-friends' wives love me almost more than the men do." Then from her latter years there were anguished accounts of being laughed at in the streets, of being stoned by street urchins in Italy, of being snubbed by old friends, and of the constant struggle against her illnesses "sopping up money like water". As a chronicle of interminable wanderings, of emotional and physical distress, of crushing poverty and loneliness, Olive's story was too close for comfort.

Olive suffered deep anguish over the existence of the correspondence to her old lover Ellis, and Emily may well have been aware that not long before her death she had begged him to destroy or return her letters.

*

So within weeks of Emily moving to St Ives the idyll turned sour. Early in 1922 she was

Emily at Warren House.
Even in her sixties the face was
relatively unlined but her two years
at St Ives were "all downhill".

unsettled by the sudden prospect of buying a coveted property at Bude, and when the deal fell through she never again felt at home in Warren House. There would be no more talk of the joys of Italy in England. In February she wrote to her brother that cracks had appeared in the foundations of the house and that all desire to live in it had drained away. Then there was the servant problem. Emily was notoriously incapable of keeping domestic help for long, a difficulty exacerbated by the local shortage. She had engaged two servants but both left claiming illness. By summer she was struggling pitifully with three untrained young girls and every evening retired to bed exhausted at an early hour. By June she passed most of her days without getting up.

"I have been going downhill all the winter," she wrote to Smuts, "and the last two months very rapidly. I have not been able to go upstairs since Easter and have had to arrange a chair-bed in the little study. I have only been outside the gate twice since Xmas and now cannot even reach the gate."

Even with her spirits at rock-bottom, Emily continued to coordinate the international fund-raising effort for Leipzig by post, refusing to resign her stewardship until the summer. Later that year an invitation to attend a women's conference to protest against the Versailles treaty galvanised her long enough to travel to and from The Hague. One of the few practical advantages of Warren House was its proximity to the railway station. Now she dreamed only of moving back to London, but it was not until July 1, 1923 – two years to the day after the purchase – that she finally managed to sell the place. It went for exactly the sum raised by her South African friends. That her modest villa went for £2,300 speaks volumes of postwar inflation, considering that in 1911 Lord Kitchener had acquired the grandiose Broome Park and a large holding of land for just £1,400.

All that remained was to write tactfully to Mrs Steyn to explain her departure from the place where she had been expected to end her days. The house so kindly gifted to her had been an enjoyable home, she said, "marred only by servant difficulties and my own decaying health".

34 "TOO BRAVE"

E mily's final years followed the familiar pattern of ups and downs set against the constants of her existence – anxieties over money, ailments and mood swings, difficulties with servants. At least the move back to London brought some relief, and the last property she bought, a pretty house in Kensington, had all the appearance of being that rare thing in her domestic life, a sensible choice.

Tor Gardens is an early Victorian terrace of stucco-fronted houses, three stories over a basement, and today seems hardly changed since the Twenties. Emily's was No 7, at the end of the terrace, which has two magnificent magnolia trees in the front garden. The magnolia was always a great favourite of Emily's, and their present heights are consistent with planting during her tenure; certainly in the St Ives garden she planted specimens of the Orange River lily, the official flower of the old Free State, which bloom there still. However, she found herself £1,000 short of the asking price for Tor Gardens, forcing her to borrow from the bank on pledged securities.

Her new address was close to old haunts such as Kate Courtney's house in Cheyne Walk, and just round the corner from the grand London residence of her cousin Henry Hobhouse of Hadspen, one of the relations with whom she remained on tolerably cordial terms.[xliv] Once again she could immerse herself in the political and cultural life so desperately missed at St Ives, enjoying art galleries, museums and exhibitions, even the occasional lecture at the London School of Economics, the creation of Beatrice and Sidney Webb. Here she could conjure up her own *milieu* – social philosophers, radical parliamentarians, charity workers, writers – and receive a steady stream of reverent visitors from South Africa. She was even asked to stand as Labour candidate in deepest-blue Kensington, but this was one hopeless cause she declined to embrace.

Emily's heart continued to give trouble and at times she would confine herself to bed; at other times, galvanised by some new imperative, she would rise up full of the old vigour, reawakening suspicions as to the genuineness of her maladies. It was during one such period in October 1923 that she briefly resumed her humanitarian work in Germany. "It is a 'call' which I cannot, dare not, refuse," she wrote to Mrs Steyn. "It responds to something inside myself which was accusing me of not using my renewed vitality (I can hardly say strength) for the good of the sufferers of this world's tragedy." Emily's enduring influence in high circles there procured her a private sleeping car on the railway, and she was able to travel in comfort between Hamburg, Heidelberg and Leipzig, embarrassed by the contrast between her luxurious surroundings and the abject misery caused by Germany's raging inflation. One of her projects in Heidelberg was to feed starving university students at a subsidised price – a mere ten million marks a head – though the meal consisted of "eternal turnips and potatoes, never a bit of meat or fat". Emily directed everything from a bath chair pushed about by one of the students.

The trip was to be her swansong. By the Armistice anniversary on November 11 she was at the end of her tether. A nasty fall downstairs led to a prolonged stay in bed, after which she returned thankfully to cosy Tor Gardens.

But Emily was like Lucky Hans in the nursery tale, forever exchanging what she had for something of less worth. True to form, she threw away her last chance of arranging her domestic circumstances for convenience and comfort and in a moment of weakness consented to take in a lively young cousin, Ursula Hobhouse, a granddaughter of Bishop Edmund. Emily's financial plight had worsened with Britain's return to the gold standard abandoned during the war, and she probably hoped for a contribution to the household expenses. Ursula seems quickly to have colonised the whole house, moving in her own furniture and inviting round a constant procession of chain-smoking friends.

No longer mistress in her home, Emily retreated to her own room, where she had no space to work. Unable to spread out her papers, lacking even a table for her typewriter, she lost faith in her ability to complete her last great project, her autobiography. "Have you any conception how harrowing it is to wade through all the records of a lifetime?" she had asked Mrs Steyn while still at St Ives. "Often I felt inclined to cast it all to the flames and live for the present." Later she wrote: "It is so painful and so emotional to live again through the long buried years." As her mood darkened to melancholy and self-doubt, she wrote of "odd holes in memory" which brought her clearest recollections into conflict with documented facts.

Even so, nothing could halt her flood of letters in which she continued to lay down the law with customary verve: "History does not incline one to believe in empires and the sooner ours cracks up the better" – "No corner of the world is decent, unless it be with Gandhi" – "Heaven save us from Churchill". Writing letters, she once told Ruth Fry, compensated for a solitary life without mental or spiritual companionship, "often without even the relief of a servant to speak to".

Emily still followed world events avidly, those in Germany and Italy in particular. In April 1924 she shook her head over news of Mussolini coming to power and in the same month read about an Austrian former corporal called Adolf Hitler being gaoled after a failed beer-hall putsch in Munich. There was interesting news in London too, and Emily would have devoured reports of the court appearances of Lord Alfred Douglas, notorious for his role in the downfall of Oscar Wilde. Douglas was gaoled six months for slander after claiming that Winston Churchill had plotted the murder of Lord Kitchener during the World War.

Around the same time she would also have spotted a startling newspaper item that brought back vivid memories of her wartime interrogation at Scotland Yard. Basil Thomson, by now Sir Basil, had been arrested for what was described as "an offence in a London park", a euphemism for an illicit sexual encounter. At the magistrates' court the police chief was found guilty and fined £5, but always claimed he was the victim of a politically-motivated plot. The incident was not without a certain irony as, according to a widely believed conspiracy theory, Thomson had forged the infamous homosexual diaries of Sir Roger Casement. A second reminder of Emily's German escapade of 1916 was to come shortly before her last decline, when *The Times* carried an obituary of Sir Evelyn Grant Duff, the diplomat who had seized her passport.

*

Politically, all Emily's hopes had turned to dust. Lloyd George had fallen from power in 1922, tarnished by a sale-of-honours scandal which was rumoured to have netted the Welshman five million pounds. Following two fleeting Conservative administrations, Emily saw a long-cherished dream realised when the election of December 1923 allowed Ramsay MacDonald to form the first Labour government, though with Liberals holding the balance of power. Emily said she felt represented in parliament for the first time in her life. She had expected great things of the Labour leader since their encounter at Cheyne Walk on the eve of the Armistice, and MacDonald had further endeared himself by losing his seat at the 1918 election because of his unapologetic pacifist speeches.

Yet as with female suffrage, the reality of socialist rule brought disillusion. Labour dragged its feet on full voting rights for women, though the driving cause of Emily's growing animosity towards MacDonald was his failure to overturn the Versailles Treaty, which led to her denouncing the erstwhile hero as a weakling. But worse was to come. Hopeless divisions between Labour and Liberal, sparked by MacDonald's recognition of the Soviet regime in Russia, toppled the administration after only ten months in power, and the ensuing election of October 1924 delivered a landslide for Stanley Baldwin's Conservatives. After five changes of prime minister in two years, Britain yearned for stability and for the rest of her days Emily was condemned to live under Tory rule. Unlike Mrs Fawcett, she did not live to see Baldwin legislate in 1927 for equal voting rights at twenty-one; or to throw up her hands in horror at the once incredible spectacle of Mrs Pankhurst standing for parliament as a Conservative.

Nor was she consoled by developments in South Africa. In 1924, showing scant feeling for her old friend and benefactor, Emily openly welcomed the fall of Smuts's administration and its replacement by a nationalist government led by Barry Hertzog, yet another of her friends among the old Boer generals, who had opposed siding with Britain in the Great War. But she quickly grew alarmed over the direction the new regime was taking. Hertzog's harsher policies towards the blacks and Indians filled her with dismay, as she spelt out in letters to Mrs Steyn. "Personally I believe segregation of any or either race or colour or class the wrong policy and one which can only lead to discontent and ultimate disaster," she wrote. The races of the earth must gradually mingle, she declared in another letter, though not necessarily by marrying. Marriage between races would always be rare, she added in a typical Emily aside, "just as it is rare for us whites to wed our lower classes". The most disturbing news from South Africa in 1925, her last full year of life, was the introduction of a legalised colour bar.

*

Also in 1925 she heard of the death of Lord Milner. Five years before, telling only a handful of close friends, Milner and Lady Edward Cecil had finally married, more than two decades after the title-tattle of Cape Town first linked their names. He was nearly sixty-seven, the new Lady Milner forty-nine. After a honeymoon in Paris they divided their time between their manor in the country and a large new house in a fashionable

*Head of the Hadspen family,
Henry Hobhouse V remained on
visiting terms with Emily
during her last years.*

part of London. Late in 1924 the couple made a sentimental journey to South Africa and
were received hospitably at the Smuts farm, where they drank the best champagne. But
Milner looked aged and ailing on his return to England the following March, and within
a month was without the power of speech and partially paralysed. To the glee of Boer
irreconcilables, the doctors diagnosed sleeping sickness caused by a tsetse-fly bite during
the South African holiday. He died on May 13, the day after being elected chancellor of
Oxford University[xlv]

Milner's death saddened Emily, but then against all expectations she had outlived
so many old friends and foes – De La Rey in 1914; President Steyn and Kitchener in
1916; revered Dr Carloni of Florence, suddenly and at a shockingly young age, in 1917;
irreplaceable Leonard Courtney in 1918; Louis Botha, of a heart attack, in 1919; poor
Olive Schreiner in 1920; De Wet, worn out by imprisonment following his rebellion, in
1922.

Margaret Hobhouse of Hadspen too had met a distressing end. Having spent years
effectively separated from her husband Henry and exhibiting little interest in her living
children – she preferred communing with the dead Paul at séances – she lost a long
painful fight against lung cancer in 1921. Not long before she had visited the scarred

battlefield of St Quentin where, wandering among the old trenches and shell-holes, she felt drawn towards an unmarked grave and, with no evidence whatsoever, decided it was that of her son. At least the delusion brought her some comfort. But Henry Hobhouse remained on visiting terms with Emily, and these days there was a new spring in his step. Soon after becoming a widower he had taken the eyebrow-raising steps of first adopting, then marrying, Maggie's paid secretary-companion, a lady some thirty-two years his junior.

One old enemy still going strong was Millicent Fawcett, and the New Year honours of 1925 listed her appointment as Dame Grand Cross of the British Empire. It is not hard to imagine Emily's derisive snort, but what on earth did she make of the campaign launched in her beloved *Manchester Guardian*, demanding that Dame Millicent be awarded the Order of Merit and a peerage? Leonard must have faced one of his sister's great volcanic eruptions over that.

Another notable event of 1925, on the ninth anniversary of the sinking of the *Hampshire*, was the dedication in St Paul's Cathedral of a memorial chapel to Lord Kitchener, at its centre a life-sized recumbent figure of the field marshal in white marble, like one of the knights of old. Beneath the effigy, according to family tradition, the Dean of St Paul's placed Kitchener's treasured miniature of his lost fiancée Hermione Baker.[xlvi] It is tempting to picture Emily visiting the cathedral to view the monument and reflect on her old battles with Kitchener, but if she did so she left no record.

In the years since Kitchener's death, many conspiracy theories had grown up around the tragedy of HMS *Hampshire*. Claims that the truth had been suppressed by the Admiralty began to gain credence among many influential figures including Kitchener's family and his private secretary, Sir George Arthur, reaching their height during Emily's last year of life. A furore in press and parliament, leading to demands for a full enquiry from seventy-eight branches of the British Legion, was an unwelcome distraction for Baldwin's struggling government.

*

There was great pathos in Emily's final months. A shadow of her former decisive self, she seemed more than ever incapable of establishing order in her life and haunted by dread of some imminent disaster. The need to take a practical decision would throw her into a state of fluttering hesitancy, which in turn would precipitate some foolish resolution, which would then be defended stubbornly against all argument. She was almost continually in pain, querulous, and desperately lonely. It was like a repeat of her father's last days, with the difference that Emily had no dutiful and uncomplaining carer.

Photographs through the years show how Emily took care of her appearance. Even in her sixties the face is relatively unlined, though the years have sharpened the imperious nose and high cheek-bones. As ever, she confronts the camera with an expression that might be haughty or guarded, the eyes alert under their hooded lids; often one senses a scarcely contained impatience with the photographer, the latest specimen of dithering, unsatisfactory manhood to fall under her gaze. Only in the last picture of her have time, illness and worry made sudden inroads.

She talked of taking up invitations to visit South Africa one last time, perhaps having it in mind to die there, but by the end of 1925 the idea was abandoned. She knew she could not survive the journey. Restless as ever, she resolved to spend the winter on the south coast and took it into her head to rent a holiday cottage at East Wittering near Chichester in Sussex. It was another of her sudden unfathomable decisions, severing her from her friends in London. The Sussex property was not even weatherproof and she was soon bemoaning the absence of friendly faces and cultural stimulation. In a wistful Christmas letter to Jan Smuts she pictured the happy family circle at Doornkloof, his farm near Pretoria, which that year welcomed Margaret Gillett and her husband. What a merry time they must all be having, Emily wrote, while she suffered alone in her cold draughty bungalow, reading Schopenhauer. "In my limited and solitary life I need philosophy," she explained. It was not a letter calculated to add to the gaiety around the Christmas table at Doornkloof.

"Life is filled up with the mere effort to eat and sleep decently," she wrote to Mrs Steyn, and grieved over "the decay of the intellectual life, the impossibility of maintaining the life of mental activity under the grinding circumstances of present physical and financial difficulties".

Emily's chief complaints at this date were angina and asthma, and soon after New Year 1926 she contracted pleurisy for a second time. To her surprise, she recovered. As soon as she felt fit to travel she was on the move again, though not to such comforts as she might find back in London. One last time she exercised her talent for choosing the wrong place to live. Still insisting that the south coast climate was good for her, she travelled on to the Isle of Wight. Leonard and Maud visited her there in March and found her very ill.

She had always said there was no point in staying alive once the capacity for work was gone, and she now accepted that her active days were over. "I have all my life looked forward so greatly to death," she told Mrs Steyn, "the rest, the peace, the greatness of it." This was written shortly before her last birthday, her sixty-sixth. On May 2 she finally admitted in a letter to Smuts: "The uprooting from my cosy little home in Tor Gardens was too much for me and nearly killed me."

Her last month was marked by the worst social unrest of the age, for May 3 saw the start of the General Strike. In the Isle of Wight Emily must have been shielded from the worst of the disruption, though not immune from the nationwide disturbances to the distribution of food, fuel and other supplies, the loss of means of transport, or – perhaps most galling for her – the breakdown of newspaper production. Like other socialists from a privileged background, Emily was ambivalent over the General Strike. At heart she might remain "agin the government" but a threat to the social order was a threat to her income.

Ruth Fry witnessed the misfortunes of the close of her life: "In extreme weakness, and often great suffering, scarcely able to leave her bed, with only the care of a young girl, and surrounded by none of the comforts so necessary in illness, she could not avoid feeling sad and lonely. She was constantly worried by the difficulty of making arrangements in her weak condition for a permanent home which she still thought she might need, and how to meet the heavy expenses."

Still no one believed this was the end. Neither brother nor sister guessed Emily's condition was terminal and they left her bedside anticipating her umpteenth recovery. After all, there had been so many false alarms, and as ever they had pressing troubles of their own. Leonard especially was always inclined to self-absorption and irritability, and of late his life had been blasted by calamities. He had been diagnosed with phlebitis, a condition that was to keep him in pain for the rest of his days; the doctors talked of amputating his leg. But the most crushing blow to his spirit had come the previous year with the death of his adored wife Nora.

Then on June 1 a visitor finally grasped the seriousness of Emily's condition and made immediate arrangements to have her taken back to London by ambulance. A bed was found in a nursing home in Bedford Gardens, a stone's-throw from her house. Even in the nursing home, Emily was still summoning friends to discuss the urgent questions of the day. As ever, she had strong opinions on everything and everybody. But she was racked by a cough and in great pain, and doctors found a growth in her chest which had previously gone unnoticed. When Leonard arrived, he found her dying.

He described the final scene to Ruth Fry: "'You were always brave,' I said to her in the last sad hours of endurance, and she answered, 'Yes, too brave.' So in a way she spoke her epitaph."

Emily's ardours and sorrows ended on Tuesday, June 8, 1926. The death certificate listed the causes as pleurisy, cardiac degeneration and a form of cancer. Since she had been talking of dying as long as anybody could remember, the news came as a shock to all her friends. Smuts wrote to Leonard: "She had been moving up and down in her ailments for so long that one had come to believe the end was in the distant future." He added: "I loved her very tenderly and I reverenced her as one of the great women of my time."

Margaret Gillett, writing to Mrs Steyn, pictured with wonder an Emily now at rest: "All so strangely, poignantly peaceful after that vigorous, strenuous, passionate and even stormy life – how ardently loving, how much loved, how much admired, full of faults, full of great gifts, full of greatest devotion to duty." Those who like herself had experienced Emily's flaws at first hand always recognised them as the defects that went with great qualities, Margaret added, "and we do not admire or love the less – perhaps even more".

*

Emily's will had been drawn up soon after the move to Tor Gardens and witnessed by two lady neighbours. The estate totalled £5,621, largely composed of the value of her house on which the bank loan was outstanding. As executors she named Oliver, "my dear nephew and almost son", and her niece Dorothea Thornton, one of the six children of Carrie.

There were small bequests to South African friends including Smuts. Her sister Maud Hebblethwaite was left £50 in cash and a small annual income "for her exclusive use and comfort in declining years", along with all of Emily's clothing. Brother Leonard received £100 "for publication of his books or a good holiday".[xlvii] Keepsakes and oddments of table linen went to various friends and nieces, but none of the Hobhouses of Hadspen was mentioned. There was a bequest of two pounds for each year of service plus a month's wages for "any woman who has been over a year in my employ", wording which reflected Emily's lifelong difficulty in keeping servants. The lion's share of the estate went to Oliver with his aunt's warning not to risk it on speculations, a sign that Emily's rash doings in Mexico were haunting her to the last.

Emily apologised for failing to repay South Africa for the house at St Ives but set aside £500 for Gladys Steyn, daughter of her great friend, along with the manuscripts of her incomplete memoirs and her history of women's experiences in the Boer War. Emily expected the sum to cover the printing of both, though this proved too optimistic; she had in any case attached a note to the memoir stipulating it should not be published "if I do not get the strength for a second writing". Her copy of the rare *History of Trigg Minor*, the deanery of East Cornwall, was left to the Morrab Library in Penzance in memory of her late friend Lord Courtney. This massive three-volume work, prized by Emily for its detailed pedigree of the Trelawny family, had originally come from Courtney's library and was given to her by the widowed Kate.

Emily stated her wish to be cremated and asked for "South African wishes" to be sought over the disposal of her ashes. Cremations were still exceptional in Britain, with only three or four to every thousand burials. In choosing the method, Emily stifled any remnant of the prejudice of church traditionalists who abhorred cremation for its pagan connotations.[xlviii] Parliament had legalised the practice only in 1902, and a year later Kate Courtney attended one of the first cremations at Golders Green, that of the Potter sisters' crony Herbert Spencer. She found nothing repellent about it and the ceremony struck her as "simple and reverent".

Kate's judgment made a powerful impression on Emily, and in later years cremation suggested how she might realise the otherwise impractical ambition to be buried in South Africa. And there were family precedents: Lord Hobhouse was cremated at Golders Green in 1904 and Margaret Hobhouse in 1921. Edith Ellis had been cremated there in 1916, as had Olive Schreiner's brother Will in 1918. Like Emily, Will had wished to be buried in South Africa, and Olive went to Waterloo Station to see off the box of ashes.

It is likely that cremation was one of the topics philosophised over together by Emily and Lord Hobhouse. Much of Uncle Arthur's career had been spent in India, and the early British converts to cremation tended to be retired officials of the Raj who were familiar with Hindu customs.[xlix] Certainly her thoughts had turned firmly in this direction as early as 1914. "I like to think of cremation," she told Smuts, "and then the scattering of one's ashes to the four winds, the confined spirit free to join the universal spirit of life."

*

The funeral service took place on June 11 at her local church of St Mary Abbots. Low key to the point of invisibility, it passed off unreported even by the two Kensington papers. According to Ruth Fry, there was "a quiet gathering of her personal circle". Church records show that the service was at 11.45 am and was conducted not by the vicar but by one of the parish's assistant curates, the Rev Vere Hobart, a Canadian who had served as a chaplain in the Great War. The vicar, the Rev Ernest Marling Roberts, had presided at Holy Communion earlier that morning but absented himself before Emily's funeral.

Leonard Hobhouse signed the authorisation for the cremation which took place at Golders Green on June 14, three days after the funeral service. Separated from the service of committal, it seems to have been a simple incineration unaccompanied by mourners or clergy. Perhaps it is fitting if the end of Emily's lonely, dislocated life was marked by one last symbolic desertion. But in the meantime the South African government had been consulted, and a formal claim had been made for her remains.

Two days after the cremation the ashes were removed from Golders Green by someone signing the register as J. Barker, presumably a representative of the firm of undertakers. As the remains were to be shipped abroad, they were more likely to be in a wooden box than an urn. Mr Barker would have taken the box to Waterloo to place on a train for Southampton, and there it would have passed between porters from goods van to ship's hold. Leonard was too unwell to think of the long voyage to South Africa, even had he wished to go; in any case, his was the kind of mind that could maintain a philosophical detachment from a few pounds of skeletal ash.

*

There could hardly have been a greater contrast between Emily's death and that of Kitchener ten years before, when Britain was united in mourning. Hers passed unnoticed by most national newspapers, all of which recorded among the notable events of the day the unveiling of the statue of Lord Kitchener on Horse Guards Parade. An obituary appeared in *The Times*, however, which criticised her actions in South Africa and Germany and was regarded by Emily's friends as tasteless and vindictive. "In spite of her humanitarian zeal," it ran, "her judgment and discretion might be questioned." No Cornish newspaper reported her death.

Predictably, the one sympathetic obituary, over one and a half broadsheet columns, was in the *Manchester Guardian*, almost certainly written by her brother Leonard. Under the heading *Noble Work in South Africa*, it emphasised Emily's eminent ancestry and family connections, and after briefly alluding to missionary work in America devoted the remaining space to her crusade against the concentration camps. The wartime adventure in Germany was ignored. An editorial in the same edition compared Emily with Florence Nightingale and praised her courage and persistence "in the face of the foulest calumnies". Strangely enough, the leader column on Emily appeared side by side with one headed *Kitchener*, to mark the unveiling of his statue by the Prince of Wales. It reported the royal remark that, had Kitchener lived, he might have proved the great peacemaker at Versailles.

Abroad, Emily's death was greeted with expressions of deep respect, most feelingly in Germany and South Africa. In India, Gandhi wrote a lengthy obituary in which he called her "one of the noblest and bravest of women" and asked the women of India to treasure her memory: "She worked without ever thinking of any reward. Hers was service of humanity dedicated to God... Emily Hobhouse, frail as her body was, went again to South Africa at great personal risk to court insults and worse. She was imprisoned and sent back. She bore it all with the courage of a true heroine." He ended: "She never married. Her life was pure as crystal."

In Britain, after that almost hole-and-corner funeral, the forgetting of Emily

Hobhouse began. The final rite following a cremation is normally a private family affair, with the ashes scattered or interred at some quiet peaceful spot or, as in the case of Beatrice Webb, absentmindedly left on a mantelpiece. In death as in life, Emily was to be different. Her ashes were now on the high seas, and at the end of a six thousand mile voyage were to be received with the honours denied her in her own country. What followed in South Africa would be not merely the great public spectacle of a state funeral, but an apotheosis. Yet before that, there was to be one last interweaving of the stories of Emily and Lord Kitchener, and it would prove the oddest of all.

*

On April 7, 1926, soon after the sick Emily had moved to the Isle of Wight, the long-running controversy over the sinking of the *Hampshire* took an unexpected turn when a retired member of the Admiralty's law service, Mr A.C. Fox-Davies, told the press that the body of a British officer had been washed ashore in Norway and buried there, adding: "There are reasons for thinking that it may have been the body of Kitchener."

In her last days Emily would have read a sensational public announcement by the leader of the campaign to force an official enquiry into Kitchener's death, a former *Times* correspondent called Frank Power. The body in Norway had been exhumed, stated Power, and positively identified as the lost hero. The campaigner declared his intention to bring the remains home to England in the huge elm coffin which had been made especially for Lord Kitchener ten years before in case his body was recovered. It had lain forgotten in a mortuary on Orkney until now, and Power arranged for its shipment to Stavanger in Norway, where the corpse was to be placed inside and loaded onto a Norwegian ship bound for Southampton.

So it came to pass that around the time the little box containing Emily Hobhouse's ashes was being shipped out of Southampton, a heavy outsized coffin, supposedly containing the mortal remains of Field Marshal Earl Kitchener of Khartoum, was unloaded at the same dockside. Over the years the great port had witnessed momentous occasions in the lives of these two remarkable figures – Kitchener's ecstatic public welcome after his victories, Emily's hounding by the press after her deportation, the reception of the Boer generals at which both were present – but who could foresee one as strange as this?

From Southampton the Kitchener coffin went by rail to London where it was seized by order of the Westminster coroner and opened on August 16 by Sir Bernard Spilsbury, the celebrated pathologist. A terse Home Office statement was issued stating that the coffin had been found to be empty. Frank Power protested that a switch had been made and produced a receipt issued by the railway company at Southampton which showed that the coffin loaded on the train had tipped the scales at 407 lb, an impossibility had it been empty. The undertaker who collected the coffin from Waterloo Station confirmed paying a weight surcharge of £4.

The government branded the whole affair as a farrago of "ridiculous and wicked fabrications" and by the time of Emily's second funeral in South Africa it was generally accepted that some elaborate hoax had been perpetrated. But by then too many inconsistencies had been exposed in the official story on Kitchener's death. The

Admiralty was forced to issue a White Paper on the *Hampshire* tragedy which raised more questions than it answered, ensuring a spate of conspiracy theories lasting to the present day.

35 "SHE GAVE TO US ALL SHE HAD"

No other non-South African has ever been honoured by the kind of ceremony that took place in Bloemfontein, the capital of the old Orange Free State, on October 27, 1926. It was twenty-five years to the day since Emily's arrest by order of Lord Kitchener. Now in a handsome casket, her ashes lay in state at the city's twin-steepled Great Church, with the memorial service to be followed by burial at the national monument which she had so nearly unveiled. Only two people had been buried there before her, and they were not only national heroes but her close friends: President Steyn and General de Wet.

One of many accounts of the ceremony was left by an old friend of Emily's, her Cape Town hostess Caroline Murray: "At the church, which was overflowing, the way to the door was lined with students in capes and gowns – the girls on one side and the boys on the other; the scene in the church was very impressive – beneath the high pulpit and the wide space in front were banked masses of wreaths and flowers, and in the centre on a table covered with a purple velvet cloth rested the casket with the ashes, on

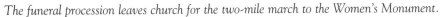

The funeral procession leaves church for the two-mile march to the Women's Monument.

293

A camera crew records the scene for the cinema as the platform party await the casket.

either side of which lay a sheath of Madonna lilies."

Six young girls entered, all dressed in pale mauve with veils of the same colour, and stood with heads bowed, three on each side of the casket. They had been chosen specially to bear the remains: two were granddaughters of Presidents Kruger and Steyn, two were pupils of the spinning schools, two had been christened Emily Hobhouse. With the heat and the overpowering smell of flowers, the strain of standing through the drawn-out service began to tell, and one of them was carried out in a dead faint.

As it took so long to clear the church after the service, Mrs Murray was unable to see the cortege forming in the street outside in brilliant sunshine for the two-mile march to the Women's Monument. The route went past the door of Emily's refuge of old, the Fichardts' beautiful house Kaya Lami. A mounted commando set off first, behind the flag of the old republic, then the band, then what the Afrikaans order of ceremonies called *Emily Hobhouse-meisies* – yet more young women who had been christened with her name, and who acted as the immediate escort to the ornate hearse which was drawn by mounted soldiers and adorned with six columns of nodding black plumes. Then came the students in their mortarboards, then several hundred schoolgirls in white with white veils, each carrying a palm branch, attribute of virginity and martyrdom, then a great procession of walking mourners who were to join the estimated twenty thousand already gathered in silence at the obelisk. The veils fluttered in hot gusts of wind.

Mrs Murray's car headed the seemingly endless, slow-moving motorcade, itself followed by a second formation of mounted commandos, and it seemed an age before she was able to catch sight of the isolated monument, impressively sited near two brush-covered *koppies*, or hillocks, with the vast veld stretching beyond: "It seemed to me that the lower koppie was occupied by natives and coloured people, but the higher one was massed with people to the very top, and made a really very wonderful picture with the choir all in white and the band a little lower. As the casket was placed in its niche the band played the Dead March and everyone stood."

Only Mrs Steyn's car was allowed up to the foot of the great obelisk with its

Emily's ashes are carried to the foot of the monument. Two of the girls were granddaughters of the wartime presidents, two were pupils at the spinning schools, two were christened Emily Hobhouse.

towering bronze figures based on Emily's wartime vision of broken-hearted womanhood by the cattle trucks at Springfontein station. Incongruously draped over the figures were the leads to huge loudspeakers which relayed the proceedings to the crowds, while a crew with a hand-cranked movie camera recorded the scene in jerky motion for the nation's cinema-goers. The girls in white filed by to place their palms at the foot of the monument and on top of these were laid the hundreds of wreaths. Accompanied by the band, the congregation sang verses from Psalms 118 and 146. The blessing of the ashes was conducted by the Rev John Kestell, President Steyn's pastor, then the commandos lined up to fire their Mausers in the air as a last salute.[1]

A telegram was read out from the premier General Hertzog, then in London: "Emily Hobhouse is henceforth one with us in all our tributes of honour and affection." Addresses followed from government ministers and from the Steyns' son-in-law, Nico van der Merwe, who as a boy had survived one of the concentration camps. For want of a suitable woman, Emily had chosen Van der Merwe to translate *The Brunt of the War* into Afrikaans; he was also her first biographer in that language, having rushed out a slim volume to coincide with the ceremony.

Emily's old friend and sparring partner, Jan Smuts, was there as leader of the opposition. His speech made the deepest impression that day, ranging over all Emily's services to humanity, but returning again and again to her role in the Boer War: "We stood alone in the world, almost friendless among the peoples, the smallest nation ranged against the mightiest empire on earth. And then one small hand, the hand of a woman, was stretched out to us. At that darkest hour, when our race almost seemed doomed to extinction, she appeared as an angel, as a heaven-sent messenger. Strangest of all, she was an Englishwoman."

He spoke of her coming to South Africa at the height of power and strength and leaving eight years later with her body shattered by an illness from which she never recovered: "During those eventful years she gave to us all she had; she gave her health and she poured out her soul." He told how Emily had sacrificed the last of her strength in succouring starving women and children in Europe. "It was her wish that her ashes should be buried in this land," he said, "should become part and parcel of the land where the best service of her life had been rendered. She now becomes one with us

295

everlastingly."

Thus far Smuts had spoken in Afrikaans, but for his closing words he changed to English – "the *taal* of Emily Hobhouse" – observing how often in history a woman appeared at the decisive moment, and in her weakness turned the tide of events. Emily's life was a striking instance of that profound influence and power wielded by women. "Let us not forget Emily Hobhouse," he said. "She wholeheartedly took our side against that of her own people, and in doing so rendered an imperishable service, not only to us, but also to her own England and to the world at large. For this loyalty to the higher and greater things of life she suffered deeply. Her action was not understood or appreciated by her own people. But to us her example makes a special appeal. Emily Hobhouse will stand out in our record as a trumpet call to the higher duty."

After the ceremony, Smuts wrote to Emily's nephew Oliver: "We buried her like a princess."

EPILOGUE

Fate might have been kinder to Emily Hobhouse had she died in 1916 instead of Kitchener, after the bitterness of the South African War had faded, but before her misinterpreted adventure to the heart of Germany. Other campaigners against the Boer conflict, roundly abused at the time, were not only forgiven by society but in retrospect admired and honoured for their lonely stand. General Sir Wyndham Childs, former Liskeard rioter, was one of many Establishment figures who later denounced the iniquity of the Boer War, and humbly acknowledged Emily's courage and foresight. Pro-Boers rehabilitated in the eyes of all included Morley, Simon and Lloyd George himself. The Great War was different because it was seen to threaten the very existence of the nation, and anyone perceived to side with the Germans could expect no forgiveness. Emily might have escaped arrest for treasonable communication with the enemy, but her last decade was inevitably the most blighted of her life.

Kitchener, had he survived the Great War – a war possibly shortened by further acts of his own – would surely have enjoyed his retirement, pottering around the country estate, arranging his splendid collections, and admiring the monumental new fountain in his rose garden, one of countless gifts he could expect from a grateful nation. His honours and rewards would have excelled those of any soldier since Wellington, for with the likes of Haig and French made up to earls, Kitchener would almost certainly have been promoted to a dukedom; as a duke he would have taken a territorial title and at last rid himself of the hated surname.

*

The night before her execution, Edith Cavell addressed a visitor to the condemned cell with the famous words "Patriotism is not enough." For Emily Hobhouse too, the patriotism of her very personal coinage was never enough to compensate for the deep stain of unhappiness in her life, nor was pacifism, nor feminism, nor any other -ism on which she seized through the years. Like that other uprooted soul, Olive Schreiner, she failed to reconcile the inner conflicts that arose once she had torn herself from the suffocating culture into which she was born. And though Emily had always appeared perfectly conscious of her importance in the scheme of things, towards the end she seemed to be deserted by a sense of her achievements, and a prey to countless regrets. "I do wish for justice," she wrote in her last letter to Mrs Steyn, "or at least for some wise strong words for the removal of injustice such as at present rests on my name."

In a private note forwarded to Mrs Steyn after her death, Emily said that in reading over her papers of sixty years the first thing that struck her was the many mistakes she had made in her life: "Viewing it all in the light of experience I see in a flash how much better I could have acted – or written – or spoken." The second thing was that all pain passed eventually, whether physical, mental or spiritual: "Gashes may be left, but they *do* heal." And the third thing to strike her: "How often I have been misunderstood – almost entirely from my inability to explain myself – through lack of ready words, or through lack of courage."

In reproaching herself for lack of courage, it is Emily who does herself an injustice.

Yet posterity has not dealt kindly with this woman, and the mark against her name remains today. An hour spent among the reference books of a public library will confirm that the animosity and embarrassment felt by eminent contemporaries, combined with a mishmash of indifference, misunderstanding and political correctness in modern times, have brought to pass what Lord Kitchener in his wrath could only dream of – the virtual disappearance of Emily Hobhouse.

Only two full-length biographies have previously appeared in Britain, the Ruth Fry memoir of 1929 and John Fisher's *That Miss Hobhouse* of 1971. Neither sold well, neither was reprinted. There is no entry for Emily in *Chambers Biographical Dictionary*, in which her brother Leonard is noted at length, nor has her name figured in any edition of *Who Was Who*. Incredibly, even *Chambers Biographical Dictionary of Women* overlooks her, despite the editorial claim to provide "concise biographies of the women commonly perceived to be famous, as well as hundreds who seem to have been marginalised". The one shaft of light is that the latest edition of the mammoth *Dictionary of National Biography*, which covers 55,000 British lives in sixty volumes, makes amends with a short entry after ignoring Emily in all previous editions. Reportedly the editors had no plans to include Emily, but succumbed to forceful representations from an admirer, the distinguished historian Lord Morgan.

The pattern was set long ago. The diaries and memoirs of contemporaries, including fellow campaigners, supposed friends, and family connections, show that the majority had reasons of their own to forget her existence. There is no mention of her, for instance, in Beatrice Webb's autobiography, or in the family gossip retailed in her voluminous diaries. Typical are the diary entries for June 1926, in which Beatrice studiously ignores Emily's death while agonising over whether to give money to a fund for striking miners' families, and recording her depression because George Bernard Shaw is feeling poorly.

After Lord Hobhouse's death, Emily's most influential relation was the long-serving Liberal MP Sir Charles Hobhouse, head of the senior line of the family, and another prize hypochondriac. A fierce opponent of the female vote – the suffragettes tried to burn his house down – Sir Charles became chancellor of the Duchy of Lancaster and kept an insider's record of Asquith's cabinet; his diaries published posthumously are full of family gossip as well as politics, but not once is Emily's name mentioned. Similarly, biographers of Lloyd George turned a blind eye to the part Emily played in his stormy pro-Boer years, and there are only scattered references to her even in the official *Life* of her mentor, Leonard Courtney. Nor does her name appear in the biography of her great friend Olive Schreiner by Cronwright-Schreiner, though he drew heavily on correspondence with Emily for the published *Letters*.

Adversaries were similarly reticent. The published version of Lord Milner's papers devotes almost 1,200 pages to his South African years but contains only one fleeting mention of Emily. Predictably, Millicent Garrett Fawcett refuses to sully her autobiography with Emily's name, and in the three-volume *Life of Kitchener* by Sir George Arthur the single disdainful reference to "a lady called Hobhouse" occurs in a footnote. At the other end of the spectrum, Emily's renown as a pacifist suffered from the repeated rancorous divisions within the peace movement, to the point where the official history of the Women's International League for Peace and Freedom fails even to mention her name, despite her role as international secretary for the body from which it was formed. Keir Hardie, the founder of the Labour Party, once remarked that there are no more hopelessly incompetent folk on the face of the earth than "peace people", or as he might have added, none more intolerant of one another once they fall out.

Between the Thirties and the Fifties it seemed Emily might receive something of her due. Sir Robert Ensor, author of the *Oxford History of England* volume covering the Boer War, began to reassess her work in sympathetic terms, while Winston Churchill, a bugbear of Emily's later years, repaid her invective with a generous compliment: in his epic four-volume *History of the English-Speaking Peoples*, the first Englishwoman named is Boadicea, the last is Emily Hobhouse.

White South Africa's heroine-worship proved her undoing. A town in the Eastern Free State was named after her; a postage stamp bearing her portrait was issued to commemorate the anniversary of her death; as a breathtakingly ham-fisted accolade, the South African Navy named one of its brace of French-built submarines the *Emily Hobhouse*. Biographies in Afrikaans poured from the presses, frequently running into several editions. And once the anti-apartheid campaign in the West reached its zenith, being admired in South Africa was the kiss of death. As well be admired in Hitler's Germany: but then Emily did herself no favours there either, since it was her Boer War exposures which allowed the Nazis to claim that concentration camps were a British invention. So here is a classic case of guilt by association, and one rich in irony. The woman who was the first to protest against the black camps, who publicly and persistently attacked segregation, who scandalised the Boers not only by befriending individual blacks but by feeding thousands of black refugees, herself fell victim to the outside world's moral outrage against apartheid.

Soon after the Boer War ended, a South African admirer wrote to the despondent Emily to assure her the day was coming when her true worth would be recognised at last: "History will, when the fever of the present is over, tell English girls of Emily Hobhouse, who went, for love of England, to soothe and make bearable, suffering which ought never to have been caused. Wait, my sister, for your due."

The prediction has yet to be borne out. By contrast to her ubiquity in South Africa, there is hardly any tangible evidence of the existence of Emily Hobhouse in her own country, even in Cornwall. Two years after her death, favourite nephew Oliver applied to the Truro diocesan authorities for a licence to erect a small brass tablet to Emily's memory in St Ive Church, which can be seen to this day as well as a small statuette of Emily with a camp child in her arms and others clinging to her skirts, left there years ago by visitors from Cape Town.

What else is there? A small plaque can be found on the wall of the birthplace opposite the church, and a second within the St Ives hotel which incorporates her last Cornish home; a small suite is named after her in the community centre at Pensilva.

Beyond the Tamar, there is nothing at all to commemorate this extraordinary Englishwoman who crammed an epic life into half a lifetime.

The National Women's Monument, Bloemfontein where Emily's ashes are buried; the only others to be interred there are General de Wet, President and Mrs Steyn and J.D. Kestell.

KEY FIGURES IN THE STORY

Names in *italics* have their own listings

BOTHA, General LOUIS (1862-1919) and **ANNIE** (1864-1937)
A sheep farmer with three years schooling, **Botha** became commander-in-chief of Boer forces from 1900. He parleyed with Lord Kitchener at Middelburg in an unsuccessful attempt to end the war early; with *De la Rey* and *De Wet*, he was one of the generals welcomed to England by Emily in 1902. He was prime minister of Transvaal in 1907 and first premier of the Union of South Africa from 1910 to 1919, when his sudden death carried the premiership to *Smuts*. His wife **Annie** was the daughter of an Irish-born auctioneer. Emily first stayed with the Bothas at Pretoria in 1903 but they dropped her because of her opposition to the Great War.

BRODRICK, ST JOHN (1856-1942), later **ninth VISCOUNT** and **first EARL of MIDLETON**
The owner of extensive Irish estates, he held minor posts in the War Office before becoming secretary of state during the Boer War. After blocking Emily's return to South Africa he appointed *Mrs Fawcett* to head the commission to investigate the concentration camps. Between 1903 and 1906 he was secretary of state for India and favoured Kitchener in his struggle with Lord Curzon for supreme power.

CAMPBELL-BANNERMAN, Sir HENRY (1836-1908)
A wealthy Scottish Liberal MP, he served in Gladstone's cabinet and became party leader in 1899. His fateful meeting with Emily, fresh from South Africa, inspired the famous "methods of barbarism" speech. He became premier in 1905 and soon afterwards granted the Boer ex-republics self-government. He resigned in April 1908 citing illness and died days later at 10 Downing Street.

CECIL FAMILY
Robert Gascoyne Cecil, third Marquis of Salisbury (1830-1903), three times Tory prime minister under Queen Victoria, was an early sponsor of Lord Kitchener, and three of his sons loomed large in the entangled histories of Kitchener and Emily Hobhouse:
Lord Edward Cecil (1867-1918) joined Kitchener's staff in the Sudan and became a lifelong friend. His wife **Lady Edward**, born Violet Maxse (1872-1958), accompanied him to South Africa at the outbreak of the Boer War and became the inseparable companion of *Milner*, later her second husband.
Lord Robert Cecil, later Viscount Cecil of Chelwood (1864-1958), was under-secretary for foreign affairs during the Great War and faced the parliamentary furore over Emily's secret journey to Berlin. An architect of the League of Nations, he was awarded the

Nobel peace prize. A hypochondriac of Hobhousian stature, he complained incessantly of a range of ailments till his death at ninety-four.

Lord Hugh Cecil, later Lord Quickswood (1869-1956) was MP for Greenwich during the Boer War and led the government counter-attack against *Campbell-Bannerman* after the "methods of barbarism" speech.

Alice, Lady Cranborne (1867-1955), who became Lady Salisbury on her husband James's succession as fourth marquis in 1903, conducted a revealing correspondence with Kitchener during the Boer War and later.

CHAMBERLAIN, JOSEPH (1836-1914)

After making a fortune in the family screw factory, he was Birmingham's mayor from 1873 to 1876, the year he entered parliament. He made his mark as a radical, became a cabinet member under Gladstone, but resigned to lead the opposition to Irish Home Rule. As colonial secretary in the coalition government of 1895, he sent *Milner* to South Africa and was effectively Britain's war leader during the Boer conflict. He resigned office in 1903 to champion tariff reform, an Empire-first scheme opposed by *Leonard Hobhouse*. Chamberlain was the lukewarm party in a love affair with *Beatrice Webb*; his scandal-prone sister-in-law, the curiously-named Rahmeh Theodora, embarrassed Milner by pursuing him to South Africa. The ill-starred premier Neville Chamberlain (1869-1940) was Joseph's son.

CLARK, MARGARET (1878-1962), later GILLETT

A member of the wealthy shoe-manufacturing Quaker family of Street, Somerset, she was a granddaughter of John Bright, the radical statesman, and educated at Newnham College, Cambridge, founded by *Mrs Fawcett*. Emily's lieutenant in the spinning schools, she became a lifelong friend. Her remarkable close relationship with *Smuts* was later echoed by a friendship between the Boer statesman and her husband, the banker Arthur Gillett. Margaret's first child, born in 1911, was christened Jan. Emily, writing to Smuts after her first sight of the boy, remarked tactlessly on his having "curly pale gold hair as fair as your own". All three of Margaret's sisters, Hilda, Esther and Alice, were very friendly with Smuts. Another of the family, Bancroft Clark, married one of Smuts's daughters.

COURTNEY, LEONARD (1832-1918) and KATE (1847-1929), later LORD and LADY COURTNEY of PENWITH

Son of a Penzance bank cashier, **Leonard Courtney** left school at thirteen to work as a clerk but after taking private lessons won a scholarship to Cambridge. He became a professor of politics and leader-writer for *The Times*. He represented Cornish constituencies as a Liberal between 1876 and 1900, twice losing his seat over an issue of principle. Gladstone, who made him financial secretary to the Treasury, described him to Queen Victoria as "a gentleman of great talent, great mental ability and assiduity, and I should add to complete my portrait, considerable self-assertion". Courtney went blind in 1896 but refused to retire from public life. His wife **Kate** was the eldest of the Potter sisters who included *Beatrice Webb* and *Margaret Hobhouse*.

DE LA REY, General KOOS (1847-1914)

Farmer son of a *Voortrekker*, he became the youngest-ever Boer field-cornet, fighting in native wars and the First Boer War. He was one of the soldiers who foiled the Jameson Raid. Among the boldest generals of the Great Boer War, he was noted for his chivalry, as when he freed the wounded captive General Lord Methuen, who had earlier burnt down the De la Rey farm. As one of the trio of Boer generals, with *Botha* and *De Wet*, he was welcomed to England by Emily. He was killed during the 1914 Afrikaner rebellion.

DE WET, General CHRISTIAN (1854-1922)

A former big-game hunter, the most charismatic of the Boer leaders became world-famous for his hit-and-run tactics. With *Botha* and *De la Rey*, he was one of the trio of generals who visited England and in 1907 became minister of agriculture for the Orange River Colony. His *Three Years War* was one of the best-selling books on the conflict. He joined the Afrikaner rebellion in 1914 and on surrendering was sentenced to six years in prison.

FAWCETT, Mrs MILLICENT GARRETT (1847-1929) later DAME MILLICENT

Born into a Suffolk merchant family, she was the younger sister of Elizabeth Garrett Anderson, the first English woman doctor, and Agnes Garrett, principal of the Chenies Street Chambers from which Emily was ejected. Millicent was the widow of Henry Fawcett, a Cambridge professor who despite blindness became a Liberal MP and postmaster general under Gladstone. A vigorous campaigner for women's rights and educational reform, she opposed the militancy of the Pankhursts and was arguably the single most important figure in the struggle for the female vote. She was a founder of Newnham College, Cambridge, and the Fawcett Society was named in her honour. Her daughter Philippa (1868-1948) accompanied her on the government-sponsored tour of the concentration camps and later returned to South Africa to carry out pioneering work in education.

FICHARDT FAMILY

Among the richest and most influential families of the Orange Free State, the Fichardts of Bloemfontein were close allies of *President Steyn*. **Mrs Caroline Fichardt** (d 1903) defied officialdom to offer her home as Emily's base. Her son **Charles Fichardt** (1870-1923), as a captured Boer captain, was the first family member to befriend Emily while serving parole in Cape Town; a second son, **Everard**, married Steyn's daughter Hanna. The daughters of the house, **Ella** and **Maude**, comforted Emily between her tours of the camps.

FRY, A. RUTH (1878-1962)

She was the first biographer of Emily in English. The two met through the friendship between the wealthy Fry chocolate family and *Lord and Lady Hobhouse*. A Quaker and lifelong peace activist, Ruth Fry became treasurer of the Boer Home Industries Commission. During the Great War she organised relief in war zones and became the first chairman of the Russian Famine Relief Fund.

GANDHI, MOHANDAS, known as **MAHATMA** (1869-1948)
The great Indian leader studied law in England. In 1893 he gave up a lucrative practice in Bombay to move to South Africa where he spent over twenty years opposing discrimination against the Indian population. During the Boer War he ran an ambulance service for the British. Emily wrote: "I have always felt Gandhi to be far and away the greatest man I have ever met." He treasured his friendships with Emily and *Olive Schreiner*. After the First World War he became head of the movement for Indian Home Rule and was gaoled repeatedly. In 1946 he negotiated with the British cabinet mission and the following year Britain decided to grant India independence. He was assassinated by a Hindu fanatic. In his autobiography Gandhi wrote of Emily warning him that he might have to die "for the sake of truth".

GILLETT, MARGARET: see **CLARK**

GREENE, ALICE (1858-1920)
From a distinguished Cambridge family, she overcame parental opposition to train as a teacher and moved to South Africa in 1887 to work at a girls' school in Port Elizabeth. There she formed a lifelong relationship with *Betty Molteno*, the headmistress. A passionate pro-Boer, she was an active supporter of Emily in her campaigns and sent Emily's sister-in-law *Nora Hobhouse* the muddled telegram about her deportation. Alice Greene and Betty Molteno left for England in 1913 and settled at Trevone in Cornwall. The two are buried in a double grave at St Merryn under a tombstone inscribed "They loved and served South Africa." The nature of their friendship became clear with the posthumous discovery of torrid love letters which had passed between them. Alice was the aunt of the novelist Graham Greene. She should not be confused with Alice Stopford Green (1847-1929), the Irish nationalist who persuaded Emily to sponsor spinning and weaving in South Africa rather than lace-making.

HOBHOUSE FAMILY
Emily Hobhouse descended from the Hadspen branch of Castle Cary, Somerset. Her father **Reginald** (1818-1895) was Rector of St Ive and Archdeacon of Bodmin. He and his wife **Caroline** (d 1880), of the famous Cornish clan of Trelawny, had five surviving children, two of them boys:
Alfred (1856-1918), Emily's elder brother, rebelled against his father and left home to become a schoolteacher in New Zealand.
Leonard (1864-1929), the celebrated social philosopher and journalist, was the sibling closest to Emily. By his wife **Nora**, nee Hadwen, Leonard had three daughters and a son **Oliver** (1892-1963), a solicitor who served in both world wars and inherited the bulk of Emily's estate. Oliver married a St Ives girl, Margaret Read.
Emily's three sisters were:
Carrie (1854-1913), who married **Augustus Thornton**, Rector of St Mellion, and whose son **Hugh** became private secretary to *Milner*.
Blanche (1857-1877), Emily's closest confidante in youth, who died in Toulouse of consumption.
Maud (1858-1929), who married **Ernest Hebblethwaite**, Vicar of Poundstock. Maud

and Leonard were the only siblings to survive Emily.

The brothers of Emily's father were:

Arthur, later **Lord Hobhouse** (1819-1904), distinguished judge and reformer, who spent his early career in India. His wife **Mary** (d 1905), nee Farrer, was an influential Mayfair hostess whose correspondence with Emily provides an invaluable record of her time in America and South Africa. The couple's house in Bruton Street was the closest thing to home for Emily following her father's death.

Edmund Hobhouse (1817-1904) was the unhappy Bishop of Nelson in New Zealand, later Assistant Bishop of Lichfield. His granddaughter **Ursula** (1899-1957) moved in with Emily at Tor Gardens, her last home; like her kinswoman, Ursula died unmarried.

Henry Hobhouse IV (1811-1862), eldest of Emily's paternal uncles, was succeeded as head of the Hadspen family by his son, **Henry V** (1854-1937), described in the *Dictionary of National Biography* as "the pattern of a public-spirited country gentleman". His wife **Margaret** (1854-1921), known as Maggie, was one of the Potter sisters who included *Kate Courtney* and *Beatrice Webb*. Among the sons of Henry and Maggie, the eldest **Stephen** (1881-1961) was the conscientious objector who served time in Wormwood Scrubs, and Maggie's favourite **Paul** (1894-1918) was killed fighting in France. Of the Hadspen daughters, the closest to Emily was **Eleanor** (1884-1960), who served as a Red Cross nurse in both world wars and never married.

The senior line of the family was that of Hobhouse of Broughton Giffard and Monkton Farleigh in Wiltshire. Its most famous member was the second baronet, Byron's crony **Sir John Cam Hobhouse**, later Lord Broughton (1786-1869). The fourth baronet, **Sir Charles** (1862-1941), was a Liberal MP notorious for his opposition to the female vote. Another hypochondriac, he resigned from Asquith's cabinet in 1915 forecasting he would die next day on the operating table, and lived on for twenty-six years. He lost his seat in the 1918 general election, suffering the indignity of being the first ex-cabinet minister ever to lose his deposit.

KESTELL, Rev JOHN DANIEL (1854-1941)

Son of a settler of 1820 originally from Devon, he was chief chaplain of the republican forces during the Boer War and personal minister of *Steyn* and *De Wet*. He translated the Bible into Afrikaans and published an account of his wartime adventures on the veld. He presided at the interment of Emily's ashes at the Women's Monument and was himself the last person buried there. The Free State town of Kestell is named after him.

KITCHENER FAMILY

Field Marshal Lord Kitchener (1850-1916) was one of five children of **Colonel Henry Horatio Kitchener** (1805-1895), a descendant of Hampshire yeomen, and his wife **Anne Frances**, nee Chevallier, from a family of minor gentry in Aspall, Suffolk.

The siblings of Lord Kitchener were:

Henry (1846-1937), the eldest brother who succeeded as second Earl Kitchener and was a lieutenant colonel in the Duke of Cornwall's Light Infantry.

General Sir Walter (1858-1912), the youngest, who served under his illustrious brother in Sudan, South Africa, and India, and whose wife **Caroline** (1856-1901) died in South Africa at the height of the deportation crisis.

Arthur (1852-1907), the only civilian among the brothers, who was excluded from succession in the peerage by Lord Kitchener's desire.
Emily (1848-1925), "a managing woman" known as Millie, was the only sister.

KRUGER, President PAUL (1825-1904)

Born in Cape Colony, he trekked through Natal and the Orange Free State to avoid British rule before finally settling in the Transvaal. "Oom Paul" won a reputation for courage and cunning in the First Boer War and was elected president of the Transvaal or South African Republic four times, between 1883 and 1898. *Smuts* first rose to prominence as his attorney general. Emily's sole meeting with Kruger was during his postwar exile in Europe, shortly before his death.

LLOYD GEORGE, DAVID (1863-1945) later EARL LLOYD-GEORGE of DWYFOR

A lawyer by training, he was elected Liberal MP for Carnarvon in 1890 and found notoriety as a vociferous pro-Boer and ally of *Leonard Courtney*. Charismatic and compelling, he was a reforming chancellor in the Asquith government yet as an arch intriguer was trusted by no one. Emily protected him from a Liskeard mob; he supported her during the concentration camp controversy but later distanced himself. He succeeded Kitchener as secretary for war before becoming premier. Though hailed as a great war leader, he fatally split the Liberal party and his reputation was permanently soiled by the sale of honours.

MILNER, Sir ALFRED (1854-1925), later VISCOUNT MILNER

Son of a university lecturer, he made his mark in the civil service in Egypt. Governor of Cape Colony from 1897 and of the Transvaal and Orange River Colony from 1901 to 1905, he vied with Kitchener for supreme power in South Africa. Initially sympathetic to Emily's campaign over the camps, he later sided with Kitchener to order her deportation. He served *Lloyd George* as secretary for war and colonial secretary. He remained a bachelor until his secretive marriage in 1921 to *Lady Edward Cecil*.

MOLTENO FAMILY

The Moltenos, staunch allies of Emily's, were among South Africa's most influential clans, descending from the thrice-married **Sir John Molteno**, first prime minister of Cape Colony. **Betty Molteno** (1852-1927), eldest of his eighteen children, was the eyewitness of Emily's deportation. She was one of the earliest white supporters of *Gandhi* and the inseparable friend until death of *Alice Greene*. One of Betty's sisters was *Mrs Caroline Murray*. Among the girls' brothers, **Percy Molteno** (1861-1937) married the daughter of the Union Castle shipping magnate and **Charles** (1860-1924) was one-time speaker of the South African parliament. Both were generous sponsors of Boer causes. **James Molteno** (1865-1935) was the last speaker of the Cape parliament and was knighted in 1911.

MURRAY, Mrs CAROLINE (nee *Molteno*)

She was one of Emily's first South African friends, her most frequent hostess in Cape

Town, and a regular correspondent. Her husband, a former naval surgeon, was Emily's doctor in Cape Town. She was a stalwart of the Cape Town relief committee criticised by *Mrs Fawcett*.

POTTER SISTERS: see *Kate Courtney, Margaret Hobhouse* and *Beatrice Webb*.

ROWNTREE FAMILY
A member of the philanthropic Quaker family, and owner of a chain of grocery stores based in Scarborough, **Joshua Rowntree** (1844-1915) organised a committee to provide clothing for needy Boer families, much of which was distributed by Emily. She met Joshua and his wife **Isabel** (1843-1929) during her first voyage to South Africa in 1900. Earlier that year, incensed by the Rowntrees' pro-Boer stance, a drunken mob broke £1,000 worth of glass at one of their properties. **Marion Rowntree** (1878-1963), who took over from *Margaret Clark* in the spinning schools, was another of the Scarborough clan. Joseph Rowntree (1836-1925), who left the family grocery business to set up as a chocolate-maker in York, was the founder of the charitable Rowntree Trust, still active in South Africa.

SCHREINER, OLIVE (1855-1920)
The ninth of twelve children of a German-born missionary and an English mother, she earned her living as a governess before finding fame as South Africa's first woman novelist. A visit to England led to her remarkable lifelong relationship with Havelock Ellis, Sigmund Freud's rival as the pioneer of sexual psychology. Olive married in 1884 an ostrich farmer-turned-politician, Samuel Cronwright, who adopted the name Cronwright-Schreiner. Her brother Will Schreiner (1857-1918) became Cape prime minister in 1898 and sparked outrage by advocating the vote for blacks. The friendship between Olive and Emily began in 1903 and was interrupted only by Emily's refusal to break with *Smuts*. Olive wrote the foreword to the Afrikaans version of *The Brunt of the War*. Like Emily, she befriended *Alice Greene* and *Gandhi*.

SIMON, Sir JOHN (1873-1954) later VISCOUNT SIMON
A Liberal MP and lawyer, he held a remarkable series of great government posts in the course of a marathon career. Beginning as solicitor-general in 1910, he was then attorney-general, home secretary, foreign secretary, chancellor of the exchequer, and finally lord chancellor in Churchill's war cabinet of 1940 – all this despite his anti-war reputation. He resigned as home secretary in 1916, soon after the scandal over Emily's visa.

SMUTS, Field Marshal JAN CHRISTIAN (1870-1950) and ISIE (1870-1954)
A Cape farmer's son, **Jan Smuts** shone at Cambridge before qualifying in law and becoming attorney general under *Kruger*. As a prominent Boer general he played a key role in persuading his side to make peace. Converted to imperialism by Lord Kitchener, he became a member of the British cabinet in the Great War and held various cabinet posts in South Africa before succeeding *Botha* as premier from 1919 to 1924. Prime minister again in 1939, he became a close friend of Winston Churchill and a field

marshal in the British Army. He was the only man to sign the peace treaties ending both world wars. His political career ended with defeat by the nationalists in 1948 which ushered in the era of apartheid. Despite his politics, Smuts was the Boer leader to whom Emily was closest, though she played second fiddle in his affections after introducing him to *Margaret Clark*. Smuts's wife **Isie** never forgave Emily for endangering his career by passing a private letter to *The Times*.

STEYN, President MARTHINUS (1857-1916) and ISABELLA (1865-1955)

A kinsman of *Kruger*, **Steyn** grew up on a farm but trained as a lawyer and became an admired orator. He was elected president of the Orange Free State at thirty-nine and spent much of the Boer War in the field with *De Wet*. An invalid from 1902, he was revered like no other Boer leader and out of office continued to wield great political influence. Emily was a regular guest at the Steyn farm near Bloemfontein. His wife **Isabella**, known as Tibbie, launched the public appeal that raised the money for Emily's house at St Ives and corresponded with her until her death; she was then instrumental in having Emily's ashes interred at the Women's Monument. Emily always addressed her formally as Mrs Steyn in acknowledgement of her former position as First Lady and her unfailingly regal manner. The Steyns' daughter Gladys arranged the posthumous publication of Emily's *War without Glamour*; their son-in-law Dr Nico van der Merwe translated *The Brunt of the War* and was Emily's first biographer in Afrikaans.

WEBB, BEATRICE (1858-1943) and SIDNEY (1859-1947), later LORD PASSFIELD

Younger sister of *Kate Courtney* and *Margaret Hobhouse*, and the most formidable intellect among the Potter heiresses, **Beatrice** as a young woman fell furiously in love with *Joseph Chamberlain*, then a highly eligible widower. He responded coolly and on the rebound she married the socially inferior **Sidney**, at the time a junior civil servant. The couple went on to form a famous partnership. Sidney became one of the earliest Labour MPs and, jointly with Beatrice, founded the London School of Economics; they became notorious for their enthusiasm for Soviet Russia. Sidney completed a circle in 1929 by becoming colonial secretary, the post formerly occupied by Chamberlain and *Milner*. On Sidney's elevation to the peerage Beatrice refused to use her husband's title.

NOTES

i Reginald's rectory is now a private house called The Chantry.

ii The Rev Kenneth St Aubyn Rogers was one of fourteen children of a highly-decorated naval officer.

iii Augustus was descended from the wealthy banker John Thornton, co-founder of the Clapham Sect which funded Wilberforce's anti-slavery campaign. The Sect bought up many church livings to present to "thoroughly evangelical clergymen". In 1885 the Thorntons moved further afield to Roche in the bleak clay mining country near St Austell.

iv This is not exceptional in Cornwall, where many striking examples are recorded of longevity among the clergy. The palm in modern times goes to the Reverend William Wriothesley Wingfield, who died in harness in 1913 after serving as Vicar of Gulval, near Penzance, for seventy-three years.

v Emily's kinsman John Cam Hobhouse is notorious for destroying the manuscript of Byron's memoirs.

vi Field Marshal Lord Roberts and Lieutenant Frederick Roberts remain today among only three instances of father-and-son VCs.

vii After Wilberforce, Clarkson was the leading figure in the campaign to abolish the slave trade. He died in 1846, four years before Kitchener's birth.

viii The game of croquet is said to have been introduced into England from Ireland in the year of Kitchener's birth.

ix Over a century later, the Cyprus government acknowledged the superiority of Kitchener's charts over all later official maps of the country.

x By coincidence, the biographers of Emily's brother Leonard Hobhouse record a snobbish early remark of his on "how unpleasant it must be to have a surname like Chandler or Butcher, which showed the low origin of one's family".

xi The one instance known to the writer of contemporary gossip occurs in a letter by, of all people, the French novelist Proust, who in 1911 claimed to have it on good authority that Kitchener was a homosexual "like Caesar". See *Marcel Proust*, by William C. Carter, Yale University Press, 2000.

xii It was after nursing Boer prisoners-of-war taken with Cronje that the celebrated explorer Mary Kingsley died of enteric fever.

xiii Invalided home one year later, Major Pine-Coffin was welcomed back to his Devonshire estate with a triumphal arch and flag-decked drive to the manor house, followed by a presentation of commemorative silver from the tenantry.

xiv The first concentration camps for non-combatants were set up by a Spanish general during the Cuban insurrection of 1896. Contemporary American estimates put the civilian death toll in Cuba as high as half a million.

xv When Emily arrived in South Africa around 15,000 were concentrated into camps. At the height of Kitchener's sweeps, the total swelled to between 100,000 and 120,000.

xvi Unknown to Emily, Brodrick's wife was desperately ill at the time and indeed would die within days of this exchange of letters. London society was to be shocked and titillated when Brodrick remarried a year later, the woman being twenty years his junior.

xvii In his biography of Millicent Fawcett, the academic David Rubinstein compares his subject to her contemporary Lenin in her utter lack of sentimentality and determination to get her own way.

xviii In the stirring lines of R.S. Hawker: *And shall Trelawny live? And shall Trelawny die? Here's twenty thousand Cornishmen will know the reason why!*

xix The *Daily News* had shifted to an anti-war stance owing to a change of editor, whereupon the circulation plummeted and advertising sales collapsed. Eventually the paper had to be rescued by the Quaker chocolate millionaire George Cadbury, who was already financing special trains to deliver anti-war publications throughout the Midlands.

xx The portraits of Emily and the generals are now in the national war museum at Bloemfontein.

xxi Private communication from Mr Peter Tummons, managing director of Methuen.

xxii The future Labour leader Ramsay MacDonald, who wrote a well-received book about his post-war travels in South Africa, scathingly described the immigration policy as a jingoist plot to apply the methods of the stud to a political problem.

xxiii Richardson himself went cool on the idea once he was on the spot, noting in his journal that the blacks seemed to have been well compensated for their suffering by the government. Though some had had a hard time, he wrote, "altogether they have not done badly and will not need help".

xxiv Those who cherish the persistence of character in families should compare the newspaper obituaries of Arthur Hobhouse with those of his great-great-nephew John Hobhouse, born in 1932. Likewise educated at Eton and Oxford, likewise ending a distinguished legal career as a privy councillor and law lord, John was raised to the peerage as Lord Hobhouse of Woodborough. Much of John's *Daily Telegraph* obituary in 2004 might have been saved in type from the obituary of the first Lord Hobhouse in 1904, with passages describing his judicial reputation for fierce independence, his infinite capacity for painstaking work, his striking old-world courtesy, and his retirement pastime of hill walking.

xxv The bulk of the fortune was willed to his widow for life and on her death to Henry Hobhouse of Hadspen.

xxvi Emily left the Naude picture in South Africa intending it to be exhibited in the planned National Portrait Gallery but forbade the sale of any reproductions in her lifetime "as that kind of publicity is repugnant to me". The portrait, now hanging in the National Cultural History Museum, Pretoria, was used on the South African stamp of 1976 commemorating the fiftieth anniversary of her death.

xxvii Emily was prescient. Seven years later, when driving near Oxford, Smuts hit and killed a seventeen-year-old girl from a poor family. He wrote to Mrs Smuts describing how he had condoled with the mother, adding: "I gave her £100, although I do not admit responsibility."

xxviii General Botha ordered his release soon after becoming premier.

xxix Modern medical thought sides with Smuts over Carloni, one eminent consultant describing Emily's treatment at his hands as "rubbish". Iodine does not reduce heart size or liquefy viscous blood.

xxx To Botticelli's contemporaries the picture also carried a political message alluding to the victory of peace over discord which was claimed as their legacy by the Medici, whose heraldic device adorns the goddess's white robe.

xxxi Van Wouw is regarded as the father of South African sculpture, though the most prized of his works today are sculptural portraits of indigenous blacks.

xxxii During the apartheid era the text of Emily's speech was censored routinely, as in a souvenir copy published to mark the fiftieth anniversary of the unveiling from which all references to the blacks and criticism of the Boers were removed.

xxxiii The precise number of 26,370 fatalities inscribed on the monument still sparks controversy among historians. Andrew Roberts denounces "Afrikaner propaganda" and says the total was around 20,000. Professor Stanley suggests the total could have been even higher because categories such as black domestics and illegitimate or unbaptised infants went uncounted. Significantly, there is no mention on the monument of the 1,670 men who died in the camps, but then these were overwhelmingly "hands-uppers".

xxxiv Kitchener met the Kaiser twice. On the second occasion, a private lunch at the London home of Lord Haldane in 1911, the Kaiser teased Kitchener over his bachelor status and facetiously offered him a Hohenzollern princess as bride. How Kitchener responded to the imperial jest is not recorded.

xxxv After the first Gulf War an almost identical propaganda battle was waged over children's deaths linked to sanctions against Iraq.

xxxvi In the interwar years Simon was to become foreign secretary and a noted appeaser. The defining moment of his career came when he interrupted a prime ministerial speech during the international crisis of September, 1938. Watched by a tense House of Commons, Simon tugged excitedly on the sleeve of Neville Chamberlain and passed him Hitler's invitation to Munich.

xxxvii In a bungled operation, the Irish rebel had been captured in County Kerry after slipping ashore from a German submarine. A key accusation at Casement's trial was that he tried to persuade Irish internees at Ruhleben to fight against Britain.

xxxviii Before the execution the Archbishop wrote to the home secretary suggesting Casement's immorality was evidence that he was mentally unhinged. However, he added, "I certainly do not attempt to deny that he *deserves* hanging."

xxxix An old friend of Sir John Simon, Mrs Green had tried to persuade him to defend Casement in court. The former home secretary declined the brief but hinted that his influence might be exerted quietly "in high quarters".

xl The one genuine enthusiast among the nine-strong sisterhood was Georgina, born the same year as Emily, who campaigned for Mrs Fawcett.

xli Hilda was another of the doting coterie constantly deluging Smuts with letters, though a third Clark sister, Alice, took the palm for flowery prose, writing to him ecstatically to share her mystical experiences under the stars on a hill in Somerset. The general wrote back to Alice praising "the garden of your soul".

xlii The fabric of Warren House is now incorporated into the neighbouring family hotel called the Porthminster, but remains essentially as it was in Emily's day.

xliii The Ellises were not the only outsiders who were viewed with deep suspicion by the locals. D.H. Lawrence, seeking quiet and solitude with his German wife Frieda, moved in 1916 to an isolated cottage at Zennor, a few miles west of St Ives. Their walks on the sea cliffs were interpreted as a cover for signalling to enemy submarines and the villagers forced them out.

xliv Henry sold the Bruton Street property inherited from Lord Hobhouse to buy an "airier and more capacious residence" on Campden Hill.

xlv Lady Milner survived until 1958, deaf and infirm, but still relishing her double Martini in her eighty-seventh year.

xlvi A service of remembrance is still held in the Kitchener chapel on the Sunday closest to the anniversary on June 5.

xlvii Neither of the siblings had long to live. Maud died in May 1929 and Leonard a month later.

xlviii The Church of England did not formally accept cremation until the Second World War.

xlix Dame Millicent Fawcett would follow Emily to Golders Green in 1929, while other famous contemporaries cremated there would include Rudyard Kipling in 1936, and Havelock Ellis and his rival Sigmund Freud in 1939. Another was Beatrice Webb, who died in 1943. Sidney kept her ashes at home and used to point the urn out to visitors with the words, "That's Beatrice, you know." The couple were later buried in Westminster Abbey.

l Only two burials have taken place at the monument since Emily's, those of Dr Kestell in 1941 and Isabella Steyn in 1955. Like her husband, Mrs Steyn asked to be buried on the family farm but her wish was ignored. She was last surviving symbol of the Boer republics.

ORIGINAL SOURCES

Emily Hobhouse's private papers are in the collection of Jennifer Hobhouse Balme at Cobble Hill, British Columbia.

Research into official government papers such as the correspondence of Lord Kitchener with the War Office and Colonial Office is easier nowadays thanks to on-line access to the National Archives at Kew. The papers of Lord and Lady Courtney and the Sidney Webbs are at the London School of Economics. Lord Milner's papers are at the Bodleian Library, Oxford. The main source on the Quakers' relief work during the Boer War is the Friends' Library, London. The minutes of Chenies Street Chambers are in the Westminster Archives. The letters of Alice Greene are the property of of John E. Barham. Maud Hobhouse's exercise book is in the Cornwall Record Office.

The key archival sources in South Africa are the papers of Isabella Steyn at Bloemfontein, of Jan Smuts at Pretoria, and of the Schreiner family at Cape Town. The Molteno-Murray archive is held by the University of Cape Town Library.

FURTHER READING

Original editions of books by Emily Hobhouse are virtually unobtainable, though like other antiquarian rarities may now be obtained as print-to-order facsimiles. *The Brunt of the War* went through several editions in Afrikaans but only the single edition of 1902 appeared in English. The posthumous *War without Glamour* printed in South Africa, the translation of Alida Badenhorst's diary, and the first English biography of Emily by her Quaker friend Ruth Fry are all collector's items. Easier to find is John Fisher's *That Miss Hobhouse* of 1971, but it was written without access to much important material and there are significant omissions and errors. A short homage in large print, *The Angel of Love*, was privately printed by Frank H. Beer, town crier of Liskeard and an ardent admirer of Emily. Numerous biographies published in South Africa are all in Afrikaans.

To Love One's Enemies, a 700-page compilation privately published in Canada by Emily's great-niece Jennifer Hobhouse Balme, is a treasure-trove of information – family letters, excerpts from memoirs, newspaper clippings and official documents – and as such is indispensable to the serious student of Emily's life and work. As the print run was so small copies are hard to come by and expensive. An excellent work published in South Africa in English is *Boer War Letters*, a selection of correspondence from the Steyn family collection in the state archives at Bloemfontein, edited by the late Rykie van Reenen.

Emily Hobhouse has figured as a character in two novels set in the Boer War, *The Stricken Land* by E.V. Thompson and *No Place for a Lady* by the South African writer Anne Harries.

The best-sellers on the Anglo-Boer conflict are Thomas Pakenham's *The Boer War* and Rayne Kruger's *Goodbye Dolly Gray*, with more recent works listed below. Yet even today, historians of the war continue to repeat errors of fact about Emily, giving her place of birth as St Ives, stating she was a Quaker, or following the lead of Pakenham, describing her as "dumpy" – an affront that would have cut Emily to the quick. The letters of her friend Alice Greene, privately published by her great nephew, vividly picture the ferment in South Africa through the 1890s, the war, and its aftermath.

The outstanding modern biographer of Kitchener is John Pollock, whose *Saviour of the Nation* and *The Road to Omdurman* were combined in a single volume in 2001 to form a comprehensive life study. Countless early biographies can be found in secondhand bookshops, the most important Sir George Arthur's three-volume *Life*.

The authoritative work on the concentration camps is by Professor Spies; the pioneering study on the war's impact on the majority population is Peter Warwick's *Black People and the South African War*, though the black experience is dealt with extensively in recent academic books such as that of Professor Stanley, which also examines nationalist mythologies stemming from the concentration camps.

A superb overview of the period in which the Boer War fell is Andrew Roberts's biography of Lord Salisbury, which controversially revives the argument that Boer women in the camps brought much of their suffering on their own heads. Also recommended are the two listed books by A.N. Wilson which span the Victorian and Edwardian ages.

BIBLIOGRAPHY

Amery, Julian, *The Life of Joseph Chamberlain*, Volume 4, Macmillan, 1951. (See also Garvin, J.L.)

Amery, L.S. (ed.), *The Times History of the War in South Africa*, Sampson Low, Marston, in ten volumes, 1905-1909.

Arthur, Sir George, *Life of Lord Kitchener*, in three volumes, Macmillan, 1920.

Baedeker Guide to South Africa, English edition published by the Automobile Association, 1996.

Balme, Jennifer Hobhouse, *To Love One's Enemies*, The Hobhouse Trust, British Colombia, 1994.

Barton, D.B., *A History of Tin Mining and Smelting in Cornwall*, Cornwall Books, 1989.

Beer, Frank H., *The Angel of Love*, Charaton Books, Liskeard, 2002.

Bell, G.K.A., *Randall Davidson*, Oxford University Press, 1935.

Bonham Carter, Violet, *Winston Churchill as I Knew Him*, Eyre & Spottiswoode and Collins, 1965.

Boyden, Peter B., Guy, Alan J., and Harding, Marion (ed.), *"Ashes and Blood": The British Army in South Africa, 1795-1914*, National Army Museum, 1999.

Bradley, Katherine, *"If the vote is good for Jack, why not for Jill?" The Women's Suffrage Movement in Cornwall, 1870-1914*, in Cornish Studies 8, University of Exeter Press, 2000.

Burke's Peerage, 1914 and later editions (for Hobhouse and Kitchener pedigrees).

Bussey, Gertrude, and Tims, Margaret, *Women's International League for Peace and Freedom 1915-1965: a record of fifty years' work*, George Allen and Unwin, 1965.

Butler, David, and Freeman, Jennie, *British Political Facts 1900-1967*, Macmillan, second edition 1968.

Caine, Barbara, *Destined to be Wives: the Sisters of Beatrice Webb*, Oxford University Press, 1986;

Victorian Feminists, Oxford, 1992.

Calder-Marshall, Arthur, *Havelock Ellis*, Rupert Hart-Davis, 1959.

Carl, Ernst, *One against England*, Dutton, New York, 1935.

Carver, Field Marshal Lord, *The National Army Museum Book of The Boer War*, Pan Books, 2000.

Cecil, Hugh and Mirabel, *Imperial Marriage*, John Murray, 2002.

Cecil of Chelwood, Viscount, *All The Way*, Hodder and Stoughton, 1949.

Churchill, Lt Col. Seton, *General Gordon: A Christian Hero*, Nisbet, 1907.

Churchill, Winston S., *My Early Life*, Odhams, 1930;

A History of the English-Speaking Peoples, in four volumes, The Educational Book Company, Chartwell edition, 1956.

Clifford, Colin, *The Asquiths*, John Murray, 2002.

Coetzer, Owen, *Fire in the Sky: The Destruction of the Orange Free State*, Covos Day, Johannesburg, 2000.

Courtney, Kate, *Extracts from a Diary during the War*, privately printed for her family, 1927.

Crafford, F.S., *Jan Smuts*, George Allen and Unwin, 1945.

Crawford, Elizabeth, *Enterprising Women: The Garretts and their Circle*, Francis Boutle, 2002.

Cronwright-Schreiner, S.C, *The Life of Olive Schreiner*;
(ed.), *The Letters of Olive Schreiner*, both Fisher Unwin, 1924.

Cutherbertson, G., Grundlingh, A., Suttie, M-L, *Writing a Wider War: Rethinking Gender, Race and Identity in the South African War*, Ohio University Press, 2002.

Davey, Arthur, *The British Pro-Boers, 1877-1902*, Tafelburg, Cape Town, 1978;
(ed.), *Lawrence Richardson: Selected Correspondence (1902-1903)*, Van Riebeeck Society, Cape Town, 1977.

Davidson, Dr Randall, *Quit You Like Men: Sermons in Time of War*, SPCK, 1915.

Demoor, Marysa, *Their Fair Share: Women, Power and Criticism, 1870-1920*, Ashgate, 2000.

De Wet, C.R., *Three Years War*, Constable, 1902.

Donaldson, the Rev A.B., *The Bishopric of Truro: 1877-1902*, Rivingtons, 1902.

Draznin, Y.C. (ed.), *My Other Self: The Letters of Olive Schreiner and Havelock Ellis, 1884-1920*, Peter Lang, 1992.

Elletson, D.H., *The Chamberlains*, Murray, 1966.

Ensor, Sir Robert, *England, 1870-1914*, Oxford History of England series, 1936.

Farwell, Byron, *The Great Boer War*, Wordsworth Military Library, revised edition 1999.

Fawcett, Millicent Garrett, *What I Remember*, Thoemmes Press, 1995 (reprint of 1925 edition).

First, Ruth, and Scott, Ann, *Olive Schreiner*, Andre Deutch, 1980.

Fisher, John, *That Miss Hobhouse*, Secker and Warburg, 1971.

Fry, A. Ruth, *Emily Hobhouse: A Memoir*, Cape, 1929.

Garrett, Richard, *General Gordon*, Book Club Associates, 1974.

Garvin, J.L., *The Life of Joseph Chamberlain*, Volumes 1-3, Macmillan,1932-4. (See also Amery, Julian.)

Gaskell, H.S., *With Lord Methuen in South Africa*, Henry Drane, 1906.

Gerard, James W., *My Four Years in Germany*, Hodder and Stoughton, 1917.

Geyser, Ockert, *Jan Smuts and his International Contemporaries*, Covos Day, Johannesburg, 2001.

Gilmour, David, *The Long Recessional: The Imperial Life of Rudyard Kipling*, Murray, 2002.

Gooch, G.P., *Life of Lord Courtney*, Macmillan, 1920.

Greene, Alice (Barham, John E. ed.), *Alice Greene, Teacher and Campaigner: South African Correspondence 1887-1902*, Troubador, 2007.

Grey of Fallodon, Viscount, *Twenty-Five Years*, in two volumes, Hodder and Stoughton, 1925.

Grosskurth, Phyllis, *Havelock Ellis*, New York University Press, 1985.

Hancock, W.K., *Smuts*, in two volumes: *The Sanguine Years*, 1962, and *The Fields of Force*,

Cambridge University Press, 1968;

(with van der Poel, Jean), *Selections from the Smuts Papers*, Cambridge, in four volumes, 1966.

Hanekom, L., and Wessels, E., *Woman, Thy Name is Valour: An overview of the role of Afrikaner and Uitlander-women and children inside and outside Anglo-Boer War concentration camps, 1899-1902*, the Anglo-Boer War Museum, Bloemfontein, 2000.

Hannah, W.H., *Bobs, Kipling's General: The Life of Field-Marshal Earl Roberts of Kandahar, VC*, Leo Cooper, 1972.

Hay, Ian, *One Hundred Years of Army Nursing*, Cassell, 1953.

Headlam, Cecil (ed.), *The Milner Papers*, in two volumes, Cassell, 1931 and 1933.

Hewison, Hope Hay, *Hedge of Wild Almonds: South Africa, the "Pro-Boers" and the Quaker Conscience*, James Currey and Heinemann, London and Portsmouth, New Hampshire, 1989.

Hobhouse, Sir Charles (David, Edward, ed.), *Inside Asquith's Cabinet*, John Murray, 1977.

Hobhouse, Emily, *Report to the Committee of the Distress Fund for South African Women and Children*, Friars Printing Association, 1901;

The Brunt of The War and Where It Fell, Methuen, 1902;

War Without Glamour, Nasionale Pers Beperk, Bloemfontein, 1927;

(trans.) *Tant' Alie of the Transvaal*, George Allen and Unwin, 1923;

(van Reenen, Rykie, ed.) *Boer War Letters*, Human and Rousseau, Cape Town, 1984.

Hobhouse, L.T., *Memoir of Lord Hobhouse*, Arnold, 1905.

Hobhouse, Mrs Henry, *I Appeal unto Caesar*, George Allen and Unwin, 1917.

Hobhouse, Stephen, *Margaret Hobhouse and Her Family*, Stanhope Press, 1934;

Forty Years and an Epilogue: An Autobiography (1881-1951), James Clarke, 1951.

Hobman, D.L., *Olive Schreiner: Her Friends and Times*, Watts, 1955.

Hobson, J.A. and Ginsberg, M., *L.T. Hobhouse: His Life and Work*, George Allen and Unwin, 1931.

Hunter, Archie, *Kitchener's Sword-Arm: The Life and Campaigns of General Sir Archibald Hunter*, Spellmount, 1996.

Hyde, H. Montgomery, *Famous Trials: Roger Casement*, Penguin, 1960.

Jackson, Tabitha, *The Boer War*, Channel 4 Books, 1999.

Jacobs, Alettea (ed. Harriet Feinberg), *Memories: My Life as an International Leader in Health, Suffrage and Peace*, The Feminist Press at the City University of New York, 1996.

Journal for Contemporary History, The Anglo-Boer War, 1899-1902: A Reappraisal, University of the Orange Free State, 2000.

Jenkins, Roy, *Gladstone*, Macmillan, 1995.

Judd, Denis, *The Boer War*, Granada, 1977.

Kilvert, the Rev Francis (Plomer, W., ed.), *Kilvert's Diary, 1870-1879*, in three volumes, Jonathan Cape, 1969;

(Maber, R. and Tregoning, A., ed.) *Kilvert's Cornish Diary*, Alison Hodge, 1989.

Koss, Stephen, *The Anatomy of an Anti-War Movement: The Pro-Boers*, University of Chicago Press, 1973.

Kruger, Paul, *The Memoirs of Paul Kruger*, Fisher Unwin, undated.

Kruger, Rayne, *Goodbye Dolly Gray*, Cassell, 1959.

Le Bas, Sir Hedley (ed.), *The Lord Kitchener Memorial Book*, Hodder and Stoughton, 1916.

Lee, Sir Sidney, *King Edward VII*, Volume 2: *The Reign*, Macmillan, 1927.

Longford, Elizabeth, *Victoria R.I.*, Weidenfeld and Nicolson, 1964;
   Jameson's Raid, Weidenfeld and Nicolson, revised edition 1982.

McCormick, Donald, *The Mystery of Lord Kitchener's Death*, Putnam, 1959.

MacKenzie, Jeanne, *A Victorian Courtship: The Story of Beatrice Potter and Sidney Webb*, Weidenfeld and Nicolson, 1979.

MacMillan, Margaret, *Peacemakers*, John Murray, 2001.

Magnus, Philip, *Kitchener: Portrait of an Imperialist*, John Murray, 1958.

Meintjes, Johannes, *President Steyn*, Nasionale Boekhandel, Cape Town, 1969.

Meredith, John, *Omdurman Diaries 1898*, Leo Cooper, 1998.

Mitchell, David, *Women on the Warpath*, Cape, 1966.

Morgan, Ted, *Churchill: 1874-1915*, Cape, 1982.

Morris, James, *Farewell the Trumpets: An Imperial Retreat*, Penguin edition, 1979.

O'Brien, Terence H., *Milner*, Constable, 1979.

Orme, Nicholas (ed.), *Unity and Variety: A History of the Church in Devon and Cornwall*, University of Exeter Press, 1991.

Owen, Frank, *Tempestuous Journey: Lloyd George, His Life and Times*, Hutchinson, 1954.

Pakenham, Thomas, *The Boer War*, Weidenfeld and Nicolson, 1979.

Pemberton, W. Baring, *Battles of the Boer War*, Batsford, 1964.

Phillips, Melanie, *The Ascent of Women*, Little, Brown, 2003.

Pine-Coffin, Susan (ed.), *One Man's Boer War, 1900: The Diary of John Edward Pine-Coffin*, Edward Gaskell, 1999.

Pollock, John, *Kitchener*, Constable, 2001.

Pretorius, Franzjohan, *The Anglo-Boer War 1899-1902*, Struik, Cape Town, 1998;
   (ed.), *Scorched Earth*, Human and Rousseau, Cape Town, 2001.

Ransford, Oliver, *The Great Trek*, John Murray, 1972.

Reitz, Deneys, *Commando*, Faber and Faber, 1929;
   Trekking On, Faber and Faber, 1933.

Richter, Donald C., *Riotous Victorians*, Ohio University Press, 1981.

Roberts, Andrew, *Salisbury: Victorian Titan*, Weidenfeld and Nicolson, 1999.

Roberts, Brian, *Those Bloody Women: Three Heroines of the Boer War*, John Murray, 1991.

Rose, Kenneth, *The Later Cecils*, Weidenfeld and Nicolson, 1975.

Rubinstein, David, *A Different World for Women*, Ohio State University Press, 1991.

Sibbald, Raymond, *The War Correspondents: the Boer War*, Jonathan Ball, Johannesburg, 1993.

Simon, Viscount, *Retrospect*, Hutchinson, 1952.

Smithers, A.J., *The Fighting Nation: Lord Kitchener and his Armies*, Leo Cooper, 1994.

Smuts, J. C., Jr, *Jan Christian Smuts*, Cassell, 1952.

Sparks, Allister, *The Mind of South Africa*, Mandarin, 1991.

Spender, J.A., *The Life of the Right Hon. Sir Henry Campbell-Bannerman, GCB*, Hodder and Stoughton, 1923.

Spies, S.B., *Methods of Barbarism? Roberts, Kitchener and Civilians in the Boer Republics, January 1900 – May 1902*, new edition by Jonathan Ball, Johannesburg and Cape Town, 2001.

Stanley, Liz, *Mourning Becomes… post/memory, commemoration and the concentration camps of the South African War,* Manchester University Press, 2006.

Starritt, S. Stuart, *Kitchener: Soldier and Statesman,* Religious Tract Society, no date.

Steevens, G.W., *With Kitchener to Khartoum,* Blackwood, 1898;
From Capetown to Ladysmith, Blackwood, 1900.

Storrs, Sir Ronald, *Orientations,* Ivor Nicholson and Watson, 1937.

Strachey, Ray, *Millicent Garrett Fawcett,* John Murray, 1931.

Thomson, Sir Basil, *My Experiences at Scotland Yard,* Doubleday, Page, 1923;
The Scene Changes, Collins, 1939.

Trevelyan, G.M., *Grey of Fallodon,* Longmans, Green, London, 1937.

Trollope, Anthony, *Clergymen of the Church of England,* Chapman and Hall, 1866 (reprinted by The Trollope Society).

Tuchman, Barbara W., *The Guns of August,* Dell, 1962.

Van der Merwe, Dr N.J., *Tot Nagedagtenis van Emily Hobhouse,* Nasionale Pers Berperk, Bloemfontein, 1926.

Wagner, Sir Anthony, *Historic Heraldry of Britain,* reprinted by Phillimore, 1972 (covering armorial grants to Lord Kitchener).

Warner, Philip, *Kitchener: The Man Behind The Legend,* Hamish Hamilton, 1985;
Dervish: The Rise and Fall of an African Empire, Wordsworth Military Library, 2000.

Warwick, Peter, *Black People and the South African War, 1899-1902,* Cambridge University Press, 1983.

Webb, Beatrice, *Our Partnership,* Longmans, Green, 1948;
(Cole, M. ed.) *Diaries, 1912-1924,* Longmans, Green;
(Cole, M. ed.) *Diaries, 1924-1932,* Longmans, Green, 1952.

Wessels, Andre (ed.), *Lord Roberts and the War in South Africa, 1899-1902,* Army Records Society, 2000.

Williams, Basil, *Botha, Smuts and South Africa,* Hodder and Stoughton, 1946.

Wills, W. David, *Stephen H. Hobhouse: A Twentieth Century Saint,* Friends Home Service Committee, 1972.

Wilson, A.N., *The Victorians,* Arrow, 2003;
After the Victorians, Arrow, 2006.

Wilson, Keith (ed.), *The International Impact of The Boer War,* Acumen, 2001.

Wilson, Trevor (ed.), *The Political Diaries of C.P. Scott,* Collins, 1970.

Wiltsher, Anne, *Most Dangerous Women: Feminist Peace Campaigners of The Great War,* Pandora, 1985.

Woodham Smith, Cecil, *Florence Nightingale,* Constable, 1950.

ACKNOWLEDGEMENTS

My thanks first and foremost to Jennifer Hobhouse Balme, not only for permission to quote from the unrivalled private collection of her great aunt's papers now in British Columbia, but for her patience in answering endless questions and for a generous flow of memories of the Hobhouse clan. It is Jenny I must also thank for the family photographs in this book, many published for the first time.

I am indebted to the staffs of many museums, libraries and archives: the London School of Economics and Political Science; Holborn Local Studies Library; Westminster Archives; Houses of Parliament Archives; the Friends' Library, London; Bristol City Museum; Manchester Central Library; Morrab Library in Penzance; The Royal Institution of Cornwall, Truro; and Cornwall Record Office, where Alison Campbell alerted me to an uncatalogued archive of Hobhouse family papers. Penzance Public Library made tireless efforts to track down obscure reference books without number.

My sincere thanks to Elria Wessels, senior historian at the Anglo-Boer War Museum at Bloemfontein, for sharing her knowledge of the Steyn Archive, to Etna Labuschagne for her searches amid the museum's magnificent photographic collections, and to Marise Bronkhorst at the Cape Town Archives. In Europe, I am indebted to Hans van der Kamp at The Hague and Professor Paulo Carloni of Bologna University.

I am grateful to Sir John Trelawny, Bt, for family recollections of Emily Hobhouse; to my much missed neighbour, the late Hon Piers St Aubyn, for the account of his family; to Elizabeth Crawford for suggesting avenues of enquiry into the "lost period" of Emily's life in Bloomsbury; to Frank Beer for his knowledge of St Ive; to Mrs Belinda Norman-Butler for family stories of Emily's connections the Potter sisters; to John Barham for making available unpublished letters of his great aunt Alice Greene; to Dr Robert Fyson for his insight into the "agitations" of the 19th Century; to Oliver Colman, present owner of Emily's last home; and to Peter Tummons, managing director of Methuen, Emily's publishers. My understanding of Emily's controversial medical treatment was much advanced by Dr Sue Williams and Dr David Gibbons. I am grateful to Mark Penrose for drawing my attention to the letter of Marcel Proust referring to Lord Kitchener. Paul Hitchens was tireless in solving my computer crises.

Clergy in Cornwall and elsewhere kindly answered queries and suggested lines of research: the Rt Rev William Ind, Bishop of Truro; Canon Dr Stephen Dawes; Canon Michael Adams; Canon Michael Fisher; Rev Andrew Wade. Thanks are also due to Antony Carr-Gomm, archivist of St Mary Abbots Church, Kensington, and to Robert Cook, treasurer of the Friends of St Mary Abbots, for unearthing records of Emily's funeral service; to Mr Cook I am further indebted for his research into corners of Kensington with Hobhouse associations. Golders Green Crematorium obligingly located the records of Emily's ashes.

Whatever the merits of this book, they would have been far fewer but for the wise suggestions of Christopher Rowe, its first reader, and the support and enthusiasm of Ivan and Heather Corbett of Truran. Finally, I must record thanks to friends and relations who bore the brunt of my fixation with Emily Hobhouse over so many years, above all to my wife Lilian, who endured three in a marriage with saintly patience.

PHOTOGRAPHIC CREDITS

Jennifer Hobhouse Balme: Frontispiece, pp4, 7, 8, 10, 13, 16, 21, 24, 35, 37, 68, 70, 83, 92, 149, 152, 160, 207, 223, 277, 280, 285.
Getty Images: pp218, 237.
Mary Evans Picture Library: 43, 110.
Cape Town Archive: pp33, 59, 74, 122, 157.
Anglo-Boer Museum, Bloemfontein: pp34, 58, 60, 65, 72, 76, 81, 164, 167, 193, 293, 294, 295.
John Hall: pp33, 59, 74, 122, 157.
Troubadour: p134
Truran: p276.

INDEX

A

Abbas Hilmi, Khevide 221
Addams, Jane 238
Albert Hall 201
Alexandra, Queen 246
Amiens, battle of 265
Anderson, Elizabeth Garrett 26, 109, 303
Annesley, Lady Clare 273
Armistice 1, 31, 265–269, 283, 284
Arthur, Sir George 136, 221, 244, 286, 297, 313
Asquith, Herbert 66, 201, 220
Asquith, Margot 227, 240
Astor, Viscountess 269
Avondale Castle, SS 123, 125–127, 129, 130, 131, 135, 136, 145

B

Baden-Powell, Col Robert 50, 67, 86
Badenhorst, Alida 170, 276
Baker, Hermione 48, 286
Baker, Valentine 48
Baldwin, Stanley 284
Balfour, Arthur 196
Barrett, John 14
Batchelor, Annie 23, 24
Bell, C.F. Moberly 73
Bell, Gertrude 251
Benson, Archbishop Edward White 9, 14, 18, 238
Beyers, Gen Christian 232
Birkenhead, Earl of: see Smith, F.E.
Birmingham, public meeting 54, 97, 105
Birmingham Daily Mail 170
"Black Week" 39, 49
Bloemfontein, failed conference 34, British enter 50, EH's arrival 72
Bloemfontein Post 85
Blood, Gen Bindon 119
Blunt, Wilfrid Scawen 97
Boer War, First 29, 31
Boer War, Second, origins of
Boshoff, Widow 189

Botha, Gen Louis 57, 59, 76, 78, 101–103, 119, 124, 148, 156, 158, 159, 169, 178, 196, 198, 209, 218, 219, 232, 240, 262, 270, 272, 285, 301n, 311n
Botha, Annie 101–103, 145, 301n
Botticelli's *Minerva* 206, 207, 311n
Bright, John 188
Bristol, public meeting 97, 106,
Bristol Mercury 106
British Expeditionary Force 48, 231
Brittain, Vera 177
Brodrick, St John 77, 93, 101, 103, 107, 111, 118, 141, 145, 168, 222, 301nBroome Park 220, 281, 310n
Brown, Captain 124, 126, 133, 134
Brunt of the War, The 68, 106, 147, 153, 154, 162, 163, 177, 277, 295
Buchan, John 121
Bude 13, 228, 229, 233, 239, 261, 265, 274, 275, 280
Buller, General Sir Redvers 39, 50, 124
Burger, Schalk 148
Burns, John 54, 201, 223, 269
Butcher, John 257
Byron, Lord 5, 309n

C

Campbell-Bannerman, Sir Henry 50, 56, 93, 95, 96, 103, 142, 185, 196, 197, 220, 301n
Canterbury, Archbishops of: see Benson, Davidson
Cape Times 83, 113
Cape Town, Kitchener's arrival 49, EH's arrival 64
Carisbrooke Castle, SS 126, 160, 161, 162
Carnegie, Andrew 160
Carloni, Dr 206, 208, 227, 285, 311n
Caradon copper mine 17
Caro, EH's dog 198, 199
Casement, Sir Roger 254, 256, 257, 262, 283, 311n
Cavell, Edith 259, 297
Caxton Hall, public meeting 185
Cecil, Lady Edward, later Lady Milner 67, 92, 197, 252, 259, 266, 270, 284, 301n
Cecil, Lord Edward 47, 48, 49, 78, 221, 246, 301n
Cecil, George 239
Cecil, Lord Hugh 95, 302n
Cecil, Lord Robert 236, 237, 250, 251, 252,

255, 256, 258, 259, 269.270, 301n

Cetshwayo 30, 202

Cezanne, Paul 147

Chamberlain, Joseph 32, 33, 34, 50, 52, 53, 54, 56, 58, 60, 61, 66, 78, 91, 98, 99, 118, 119, 120, 121, 125, 145, 146, 149, 155, 156, 157, 159, 169, 172, 196, 302n, 311n

Channon, Sir Henry "Chips" 238

Chenies Street Chambers 26, 108, 177, 224

Chester, Bishop of 172

Chicago 22, 23, 220

Childs, Gen Sir Wyndham 53, 137, 242, 243, 295

Chinese labour controversy 196

Christian Victor, Prince 71

Churchill, Winston 36, 39, 46, 197, 225, 232, 238, 244, 247, 259, 283, 299

Clark, Alice 265, 311n

Clark, Hilda 272, 311n

Clark, Margaret 188, 189, 192, 194, 195, 196, 197, 198, 200, 203, 210, 232, 261, 262, 271, 273, 287, 288, 302n

Clarkson, Thomas 41, 309n

Clemenceau, Georges 252, 270

Cleveland, Ohio 21

Cohen, Arthur 146

Colenso, Harriette 146

Colenso, Bishop John 30

Concentration camps, 57, 60, 68, 72, 309n; peak population 310n; final death toll 153, 311n; black camps 86, 153, 171, 215, 299, 310n; 311n; EH visits 78, 80, 86, 95

Conan Doyle, Arthur 145

Connaught, Duke of 246

Conscription 225, 226, 239, 240, 241, 242

Cooper, Col 126–131, 138, 143, 144

Cornish Magazine 25

Cornish Times 52, 53

Courtney, Kate 38, 51, 54, 63, 98, 141, 143, 157, 160, 174, 199, 223, 234, 236, 238, 240, 246, 264, 266, 268, 269, 282, 289, 302n

Courtney, Leonard 36, 37, 38, 50, 51, 52, 54, 61, 63, 91, 94, 110, 112, 140, 142, 159, 185, 196, 197, 203, 220, 237, 239, 242, 254, 257, 264, 269, 278, 285, 289, 298, 302n

Craigen, Jessie 13

Cranborne, Viscount 48

Cranborne, Viscountess 61, 104, 149, 271, 302n

Cray, Major 73, 75

Cripps, Theresa 269

Cronje, Ellie 67

Cronje, Gen Piet 50, 309n

Cronwright-Schreiner, Samuel 177, 199, 216, 217, 274, 279, 298

Curzon, Lady 48, 220

Curzon, Lord 47, 48, 66, 119, 220, 268

"Cyanide Jones" 31

Cyprus 44, 309n

D

Daily Express 234

Daily Mail 97, 239

Daily News 141, 310n

Darlington, public meeting 106

Darwin, Charles 8

Davidson, Archbishop Randall 231, 256

De la Rey, Gen Koos 148–159, 233, 285, 303n

Deane, Lucy 108, 129

De Villers, Jaap 193, 194

De Villers, Sir John and family 163, 164, 196

De Vos, Professor 59

De Wet, Gen Christian 56, 57, 72, 73, 77, 103, 119, 150, 153, 156, 158, 159, 169, 232, 233, 285, 293, 303n

Diaz, Porfirio 22

Dickinson, Lowes 201

Dillon, John 146

Disraeli, Benjamin 31, 35

Dongola, battle 45

Douglas, Lord Alfred 283

Duncan, Patrick 171

E

East Wittering, EH at 287

Edgar, Tom 32

Edward VII 153, 158

Ellis, Edith 279, 289

Ellis, Henry Havelock 42, 175, 216, 228, 229, 278, 279, 312n

F

Fabian Society 56

Falkenhausen von Friedensthal, Baron 248, 249

Fawcett, Henry 110

Fawcett, Millicent Garrett 2, 26, 108–117, 120, 121, 123, 125, 146, 155, 201, 224, 232, 234, 235, 236, 241, 252, 266, 268, 269, 270, 284, 286, 299, 303n, 310n, 311n, 312n

Fawcett, Philippa 115
Fawcett Report 117
Fashoda Crisis 46, 239
Fichardt, Caroline 72, 73, 87, 166, 169, 303n
Fichardt, Charlie 213, 215, 303n
Fichardt, Ella 75, 303n
Fichardt, Maude 75, 303n
Fisher, Admiral Lord 226, 270
Fox-Davies, A.C. 291
Franco-Prussian War 43, 270
Franz-Joseph, Emperor 44
French, Gen Sir John 231, 297
Freud, Sigmund 170, 278
Fry, Sir Edward 36
Fry, Ruth 7, 14, 15, 35, 36, 106, 114, 117, 136, 137, 172, 195, 199, 200, 204, 205, 249, 257, 272, 277, 283, 287, 288, 289, 298, 303n

G

Gandhi, Mohandas 1, 202, 217, 218, 219, 229, 230, 283, 290, 304n
Gallipoli 244
Garrett, Agnes 27
Garrett, Edmund 113
Garth Castle, SS 221
General Strike 217, 287
George V (see also Princes of Wales) 158, 221, 246
Gerard, Lord 36, 39, 250, 255
Gillett, Arthur 197
Gillett, Margaret: see Clark
Gladstone, W.E. 6, 30, 31, 35, 45, 110
Glyn, Elinor 66
Gold , discovery of
Golders Green Crematorium 1, 289, 290
Gonne, Maud 125, 126, 129
Goold-Adams, Sir Hamilton 75, 82, 87, 118
Gordon, Gen Charles 14, 43, 45, 46, 112
Gore-Booth, Constance 269
Gosse, Sir Edmund 172
Great Trek 30, 88
Grant Duff, Sir Evelyn 236, 247–253, 283
Green, Alice Stopford 262, 311n
Greene, Alice 130, 131, 137, 141, 144, 160, 205, 304n
Grenfell, Julian 239
Grey, Sir Edward 39, 224, 226, 236, 253, 254, 255, 258, 269

H

Hague Convention 59, 154
Hague Peace Conference 233, 234, 250, 252
Haig, Gen Sir Douglas 247, 260, 264, 275, 297
Haldane, Lord 247
Hamilton, Gen Sir Ian 120, 121
Hampshire, HMS, sinking and controversy 245–249, 286, 291, 292
Hancock, Sir Keith 2, 201, 202, 213
Harmsworth, Alfred, Lord Northcliffe 97
Harris, Frank 32
Hebblethwaite, Rev Ernest 13
Heckford, Sarah 97
Heidelberg, Boer rally 169
Hely-Hutchinson, Lady 127
Hely-Hutchinson, Sir Walter 126
Hereford, Bishop of 98
Hertzog, Gen Barry 284, 295
Hicks-Beech, Sir Michael 91
Hill, Octavia 27, 38
Hitler, Adolf 283
Hobart, Rev Vere 289
Hobhouse ancestry 5–6
Hobhouse, Alfred 6, 9, 304n
Hobhouse, Blanche 6, 9, 304n
Hobhouse, Caroline 5–7, 9, 193, 304n
Hobhouse, Carrie, later Mrs Thornton 6, 9, 212, 260, 288, 304n
Hobhouse, Sir Charles 298, 305n
Hobhouse, Bishop Edmund 9, 18, 185, 193, 283, 305n
Hobhouse, Eleanor 205, 305n
Hobhouse, Emily: birth and family 5–6; appearance when young 12; lack of education 12; early suitors 14; leaves St Ive 16; mission in America 17; engagement to Jackson 20; leaves for Mexico 21; break with Jackson 25; at Chenies Street 26–7, 224–5; moves to Rossetti Mansions 27; outbreak of Boer War and anti-war campaigning 36; parallels with Kitchener 41–2; with Lloyd George at Liskeard 52–3; determines to go to South Africa 61; arrives at Cape Town 64; first camp visit 74; returns to England 90; interview with Brodrick 93; publishes report and sees Campbell-Bannerman 94–5; nationwide speaking tour 97; enmity of Mrs Fawcett 111; last appeal to Brodrick 123; arrest and deportation 126–139; brings legal action

143; completes *Brunt of the War* 147; greets "Glorious Trio" 156; returns to South Africa 162; helps blacks 171, 299; meets Smuts and Olive Schreiner 175; death of Uncle Arthur 186; sets up cottage industries 188; death of Aunt Mary 191; acquires dog 198; resigns from home industries board 199; moves to Italy 204; controversial cure 206; invited to unveil Women's Monument 209; critical of treatment of blacks 215, 284; intervenes for Gandhi 217; at outbreak of Great War 222; rents villa at Bude 228; returns to Continent 234; works for Peace Congress 235; travels to Germany 248; hears of Kitchener's death 248–9; passport confiscated 251; called to Scotland Yard 254; attacked in Parliament 256–7; at end of Great War 266; organises German charities 272; subscription fund for St Ives house 274; completes Tant' Alie 276–7; moves to London 282; last work abroad 282–3; final illness 287; death and cremation 288–290; state funeral in South Africa 293–6; legacy 297–9

Hobhouse, Henry V of Hadspen 9, 37, 64, 203, 305n, 310n, 311n

Hobhouse, Hugh 128, 304n

Hobhouse, John Cam, Lord Broughton 5, 41, 305n, 308n,310n

Hobhouse, Leonard 6-7, 10, 12, 15, 17, 24, 28–9, 38, 62, 85–6, 92–3, 98,102, 106, 123, 126, 141–2, 145, 153–5, 162, 168, 17–-3, 196, 203, 223–-4, 229, 235, 23–8, 290, 298, 304n, 309n

Hobhouse, Lady (Aunt Mary) 20, 35--, 59, 61–2, 64–5, 68-9, 71, 74, 76, 80, 91, 93, 123, 141–3, 159, 165–6, 305n

Hobhouse, Lord (Uncle Arthur) 5, 9, 35–6, 39, 61–2, 91, 141–6, 153, 173, 181, 185–7, 191, 289, 305n

Hobhouse of Woodborough, Lord 310n

Hobhouse, Margaret ("Maggie") 37, 242, 256, 263–4, 267, 269, 285–6, 289, 305n

Hobhouse, Maud, later Mrs Hebblethwaite 6, 10–13, 23, 142, 205, 228, 278, 287–8, 304n

Hobhouse, Nora 24, 28, 142, 162–3, 173, 288, 304n

Hobhouse, Oliver 142, 194, 203, 205–6, 242, 223–4, 256, 274, 287–8, 304n

Hobhouse, Paul 264, 267, 285–6, 305n

Hobhouse, Archdeacon Reginald 5–9, 13–15, 107, 110, 288, 304n

Hobhouse, Rosa 242, 246

Hobhouse, Stephen 6, 241–3, 263-4, 267, 305n

Hobhouse, Ursula 283, 305n

Hofmeyr, Rev Adriaan 91, 96, 172

Hofmeyr, Jan 107

Hull, public meeting 105

Hume, Captain Albert 76, 80, 82

Hunter, Gen Sir Archie 46

I

International Committee of Women for Permanent Peace 235

International Woman Suffrage Alliance 233

Iron Duke, HMS 245

Isaacs, Rufus 143

Isandhlwana, battle of 30

Isle of Wight, EH at 287, 291

J

Jackson, John Carr 20–26, 38, 42, 187, 198

Jacobs, Dr Aletta 252

Jagow, Gottlieb von 249, 250, 252, 254, 255, 258

Jameson, Dr Leander Starr 31, 32

Jellicoe, Admiral Sir John 244, 245

Joubert, Gen Piet 166

Jutland, battle of 244, 265

K

Kemp, Gen Jan 232

Kestell, Rev John 153, 178, 295, 305n

Khalifa, el- 45

"Khaki Election" 52, 54, 56, 91, 201, 223, 278

Khartoum, siege of 14, 40, 43, 45, 46

Kiel Mutiny 265

Kilvert, Rev Francis 10, 275

Kimberley, relief of 50

Kingsley, Mary 62, 309n

Kingsway Hall 233

Kipling, Rudyard 1, 17, 32, 39, 153, 221, 263, 266, 312n

Kitchener, Caroline 119, 120, 138, 305n

Kitchener, Herbert, Field Marshal Lord: birth and parallels with EH 41–2; early military career 43; peerage 46; supposed homosexuality 47; depressions 48, 221; lands in South Africa 49; assumes supreme

command 56; opposes farm burnings 57; allows EH into camps 68; parleys with Botha 77; sole master of South Africa 91; pressured on the camps 98; meets Mrs Fawcett 116; working habits 120; forbids EH to land 125; justifies deportation 141; warned of EH's legal action 146; nervous collapse 148; wins over Smuts 150; signs peace treaty 151; raised to viscoun 152; welcomes "Glorious Trio" 156; at outbreak of Great War 220; purchase of Broome and earldom 221; appointed secretary for war 222; first call to arms 227; resists conscription 240; last days and death 244–6; war predictions come true 268; dedication of memorial chapel 286; claim that body is discovered 291; likely postwar honours 297, 311n
Kitchener, Millie 42, 43, 44, 47, 306n
Kitchener, Gen Sir Walter 119, 120, 305n
Knox, Lady 108, 114, 116, 129
Kriel, Rev Abraham 190, 194, 195
Kruger, President Paul 31–34, 54, 56, 75, 88, 101–103, 118, 148, 159, 164, 178, 182, 210, 294, 306n

L
Ladysmith, relief of 50
Langlaagte 190, 192–195
Lansdowne, Marquis of 61, 62, 77, 263, 265
Le Matin 101
Leeds, public meeting 52, 97, 105, 106
Leipolt, L.S. 145
Leipzig, EH at 272, 274, 282
Lewis, Sir George 143, 145, 146
Lingham, Lieut 126, 128, 129, 130, 131, 138, 143, 144
Liskeard, riotous meeting at 52, 54
Lloyd George, David 52, 53, 54, 94, 95, 98, 112, 184, 225, 232, 239, 240, 241, 244, 246, 247, 259, 260, 261, 262, 265, 268, 270, 284, 297, 298, 306n
Louvain, library burning of 248
Loyal Ladies League 85
Ludendorff, General Erich von 265
Lyson, Paul

M
Macarty, concentration camp head 80
MacDonald, Ramsay 266, 268, 284, 310n
Mafeking, relief of 50, 67

Mahdi, el- 45, 46. 97
Majuba Hill, battle of 31
Manchester, public meeting 52, 97, 105, 106
Manchester Guardian 29, 39, 46, 60, 107, 123, 145, 155, 159, 190, 222, 238, 264, 286, 290
Markievicz, Countess: see Gore-Booth
Marling Roberts, Rev Ernest 289
Marne, battle of 231
Marsh, Canon Sidney 278
Mata Hari 254, 259
Maxwell, Frank, VC 121, 122, 148, 240
Maxwell, General John 104, 118
McGonicle, Rev James 18, 19, 172
Meintjes, Johannes 187
Merriman, John X 213
Methuen, Gen Lord 58, 84, 85, 148, 157, 169
Methuen, publishers 153, 154, 163, 310n
Mexico, EH in 22, 23, 24
Middleburg, abortive talks at
Mill, John Stuart 14
Milner, Sir Alfred, later Viscount 32–34, 48, 56, 57, 62, 64–69, 73, 75–77, 78, 79, 88–94, 99, 101, 103, 116, 118–121, 125, 126, 128–130, 136–138, 141, 143, 147, 149, 150–152, 156, 164, 165, 169, 175, 178, 180, 184, 185, 197, 202, 237, 239, 241, 247, 252, 259–264, 266, 270, 271, 284, 298, 306n
Mining in Cornwall 10, 17, 18
"Ministering Angels" 83
Minnesota Missionary and Church Record 17
Minto, Lord 220
Molteno, Betty 131–137, 156, 219, 273, 306n
Molteno, Percy 123, 138, 306n
Moltke, Count and Countess von 227
Moltke, Gen Helmuth von 47, 227, 231
Monkhouse, Mary 107, 169
Morant, "Breaker" 168
Morley, John 159, 220, 223, 238, 296
Morning Post 36
Mount Edgecumbe, Earl of 157
Murray, Caroline 64, 107, 115, 128, 129, 131, 138, 140, 144, 156, 162, 209, 293, 294, 306n
Mussolini, Benito 274, 283

N
Naude, Hugo 200, 310n
New York, EH at 17
New York Evening Post 159

New York Herald 104
Newman, Cardinal 8
Newton, Lord 255, 256, 283
Nicholas II, Czar 247, 261
Nicholson, Ben 275
Nicolson, Sir Harold
Nightingale, Florence 1, 2, 14, 84, 141, 290
Nineteenth Century 28, 111, 224
Northcliffe, Lord: see Harmsworth
Nursing Record 114

O

Oak, HMS 245
Omdurman, battle of 46, 48
Oratava, SS 115
Owl magazine 136
Oxford, cancelled public meeting 105
Oxford Times 105

P

Pall Mall Gazette 113
Pankhurst, Christabel 201
Pankhurst, Emmeline 2, 201, 202, 230, 241, 259, 284
Parry, Sir Hubert 268, 269
Pensilva 5, 8, 299
Peel, Sir Robert 5, 6
Penn-Symons, Gen Sir William 38, 39
Philippolis 186, 189, 190, 191, 192
Phillips, Elizabeth 123, 126, 128, 131–133, 135, 140
Picard, Miss 192
Pine-Coffin, Major John 58, 59, 309n
Portsmouth, public meeting 107
Potgieter, Mr and Mrs 90, 166
Potter, Georgina 311n
Poundstock 13, 304n
Power, Frank 291
Prinsloo, Commandant Gen Marthinus 101
Pretoria 31, 51, 56, 67, 71, 77, 90, 98, 99, 121, 125, 129, 147, 151, 168, 169, 178, 190, 191, 201, 210, 287, 310n
Pretyman, Gen George 72, 73, 75, 86, 104
Proust, Marcel 309n
Punch 97

Q

Queen's Hall 51, 52, 94, 98, 268, 269
Quiller-Couch, Sir Arthur 52, 53

R

Rand Daily Mail 171
Rasputin 247
Reitz, Deneys 148, 150
Rhodes, Cecil 31, 50, 91, 153, 164, 219
Richardson, Lawrence 170, 171, 195, 310n
Rimbaud, Arthur 44, 45
Ripon, Marchioness of 142
Ripon, Marquis of 107, 127
Roberts, Lieut Frederick 309n
Roberts of Kandahar, Field Marshal Lord 39, 47, 50, 52, 53, 56, 58, 60, 67, 73, 75, 90, 91, 98, 99, 101, 102, 103, 118, 119, 120, 121, 132, 156, 158, 231, 238, 309n
Rodd, Sir Rennell 235
Rogers, Rev Kenneth St Aubyn 7, 309n
Romberg, Baron von 247, 248, 249
Rome, EH moves to 204, 205
Rose Innes, Sir James 135, 136
Roslin Castle, HMT 130, 131, 137, 140, 141, 142, 143
Rostand, Edmond 145
Rowntree, Isabel, 142, 307n
Rowntree, Joshua 63, 105, 141, 307n
Rowntree, Marion, 192, 194, 203, 273, 307n
Ruhleben camp 250, 251, 254, 311n
Ruskin, John 28
Russian Babies Fund 272

S

St Aubyn family 278, 309n
St Germans, Earl of 9
St Ive 5–9, 13–15, 17, 24, 30, 41, 45, 53, 142, 248, 299, 304n
St Ives 5, 177, 275–279, 282, 283, 289, 299, 304, 308n, 312n
St Joan of Arc 2, 12, 61, 137
St Levan, Lord 278
St Mellion 9, 304n
St Quentin, battle of 264, 286
Salisbury, Marchioness of: see Cranborne, Viscountess
Salisbury, Marquis of 31, 45, 46, 47, 54, 71, 91, 120, 151, 301n
Save the Children Fund 272
Saxon, RM 89,–91, 99, 156, 157, 166
Scarborough, public meeting 105
Scarlett, Hon Ella 113
Scarlett, Gen James 113
Schreiner, Olive 2, 42, 175, 177, 178, 179, 199,

201, 206, 208, 216, 227, 228, 229, 233, 234, 261, 273, 274, 275, 277, 278, 285, 297, 304n, 307n
Schreiner, Will 177, 217, 289, 307n
Schwimmer, Rosika 250, 253
Scott, C.P. 145, 263
Scourey, Mary 18
Shaw, Flora 96, 298
Shaw, George Bernard 56
Simon, Sir John 236, 237, 252, 257, 259, 307n, 311n
Smith, F.E. 257
Smuts, Jan Christian 2, 32, 34, 57, 79, 81, 102, 103, 124, 148, 150, 153, 178, 179, 183, 184, 185, 187, 190, 191, 194, 195, 197, 199, 200–206, 209–213, 215, 218, 219, 223, 225, 230, 232, 233, 234, 240, 244, 261, 262, 263, 264, 265, 268, 270, 271, 272, 274, 275, 276, 279, 280, 284, 285, 286, 287, 288, 289, 295, 296, 301n, 302n, 306n, 307n, 308n, 310n, 311n
Smuts, Isie 180, 193, 197, 204, 213, 217, 307n, 308n, 310n
Somme, battle of 255, 256, 258, 261, 264
Sorabji, Alice 39
Sorabji, Cornelia 191
South Africa, white settlement of 17, 29, 30,
South African Conciliation Committee 36
South African Women and Children Distress Fund 62
Southampton 91, 101, 115, 123,
Speaker 238
Spectator 120
Spencer, Herbert 160, 289
Spilsbury, Sir Bernard 291
Spion Kop, battle of 50
Stanley, Venetia 232
Stead, W.T. 109, 112, 159
Steedman, Miss 124, 126
Steyn, Gladys 289, 308n
Steyn, Isabella 51, 63, 72, 103, 127, 137, 153, 159, 161, 181, 188, 191, 198, 210, 211, 212, 213, 214, 262, 263, 272, 274, 275, 276, 277, 278, 281, 282, 284, 287, 288, 294, 297, 308n, 312n
Steyn, President Marthinus 149, 150, 151, 152, 153, 156, 159, 160, 161, 178, 182, 187, 188, 189, 190, 198, 209, 211, 212, 214, 160, 185, 293, 294, 303n, 305n, 308n
Strachey, Ray (Rachel) 110, 111, 112, 116, 269, 270

T
Tant' Alie of Transvaal 170, 277
Tennant, Margot: see Asquith
The Times 14, 31, 45, 73, 95, 96, 97, 98, 101, 105, 143, 159, 170, 185, 204, 213, 219, 239, 257, 264, 268, 283, 290, 302, 308
Thomson, Sir Basil 254, 255, 256, 259, 283
Thornton, Rev Augustus 9, 13, 304n
Thornton, Dorothea 288
Thornton, Hugh 260
Tolstoy, Leo 241
Townshend, Anne 27, 224
Trelawny ancestry 5, 7, 10, 205
Trelawny, Bishop Jonathan 5, 128
Trelawny, Sir William Salusbury 5
Truro, Bishops of: see Benson, Wilkinson
Tschwangtwe, Alexander 171
Tweebosch, battle of 148

U
Uffizi Gallery 207

V
Van der Merwe, Dr Nico 295, 308n
Van Welie, Antoon 159, 200
Van Wouw, Anton 210, 211, 215, 216, 221, 311n
Vane-Tempest-Stewart, Lady Helen 48
Verdun, battle of 253, 258
Vereeniging, negotiations and peace terms 148, 149–151, 153, 155, 160, 178, 239, 270
Versailles, conference and treaty 270, 271, 280, 284, 290
Victoria, Queen 1, 3, 31, 32, 33, 44, 45, 46, 62, 70, 71, 83, 101, 109, 246, 301n, 302n
Virginia, Minnesota 17, 18, 20, 21, 24
The Virginia newspaper 22
Virginia Enterprise 19, 20, 21, 22

W
Wagner, Richard 112
Wales, Princes of: see George V and Windsor, Duke of
Wallis, Alfred 275
Walrond, Osmund 90, 91
War without Glamour 170, 308n
Waterston, Dr Jane 83, 108, 113, 116, 117, 129
Waterval, conference 103
Webb, Beatrice 14, 23, 37, 38, 56, 239, 240, 242, 264, 266, 291, 298, 302n, 305n, 307, 308n

Webb, Sidney 15, 28, 308n
Wesley, John 9, 13
Westminster Gazette 108
Wilberforce, Charles 309n
Wilhelm II, Kaiser 31, 56, 73, 159, 168, 188, 203, 224, 227, 231, 241, 244, 247, 258, 265, 311n
Wilkinson, Bishop Howard 14
William Cliff, SS 23, 24
Williamson, Lieut Col J.F. 132–139, 143
Wilson, President Woodrow 270, 271
Windsor, Duke of 232
Wingfield, Rev William Wriothersley 309n
Wood, Christopher 275
Women's International League 235, 236, 273, 299
Women's Monument 294, 305n, 308n
"Wonder Box" 277
Woolf, Virginia 275
Wynne, Maj Gen Arthur 126, 129, 141

Y
Yeats, W.B. 175
York, public meeting 97, 105
Yusupov, Prince Felix 247

Z
Zulu War 30, 44